Janice E. Stockard and George Spindler

STANFORD UNIVERSITY

# Yąnomamö

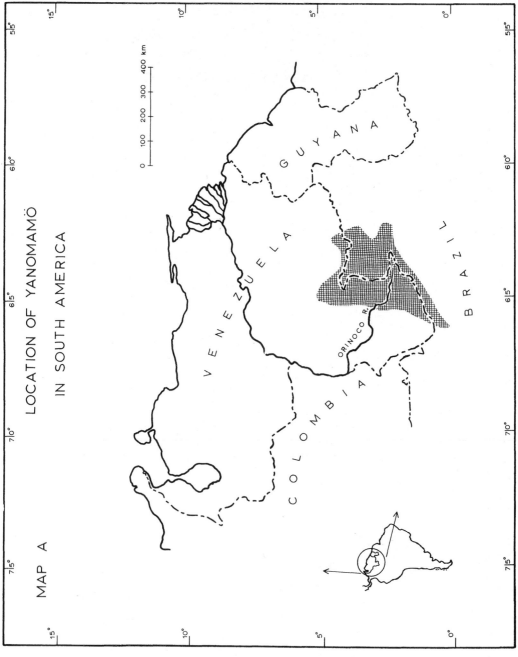

LOCATION OF YANOMAMÖ

IN SOUTH AMERICA

MAP A

WADSWORTH
CENGAGE Learning™

**Yąnomamö, Sixth Edition: The Legacy Edition**
Napoleon A. Chagnon

Publisher: Linda Schreiber-Ganster

Acquisitions Editor: Erin Mitchell

Editorial Assistant: Mallory Ortberg

Marketing Manager: Andrew Keay

Marketing Assistant: Jack Ward

Marketing Communications Manager: Laura Localio

Production Management, and Composition: PreMediaGlobal

Manufacturing Planner: Judy Inouye

Rights Acquisitions Specialist: Roberta Broyer

Series Editor: Janice E. Stockard

Cover Designer: Carole Lawson

Cover Image: Napoleon A. Chagnon

For product information and technology assistance, contact us at **Cengage Learning Customer & Sales Support, 1-800-354-9706.**

For permission to use material from this text or product, submit all requests online at **www.cengage.com/permissions**. Further permissions questions can be e-mailed to **permissionrequest@cengage.com.**

Library of Congress Control Number: 2011938965

ISBN-13: 978-1-111-82874-5

ISBN-10: 1-111-82874-1

**Wadsworth**
20 Davis Drive
Belmont, CA 94002-3098
USA

Cengage Learning is a leading provider of customized learning solutions with office locations around the globe, including Singapore, the United Kingdom, Australia, Mexico, Brazil, and Japan. Locate your local office at **www.cengage.com/global**.

Cengage Learning products are represented in Canada by Nelson Education, Ltd.

To learn more about Wadsworth visit **www.cengage.com/wadsworth.**

Purchase any of our products at your local college store or at our preferred online store **www.cengagebrain.com.**

Printed in the United States of America
1 2 3 4 5 6 7 15 14 13 12 11

# Yąnomamö

## SIXTH EDITION: THE LEGACY EDITION

**NAPOLEON A. CHAGNON**
University of California
Santa Barbara

Australia • Brazil • Japan • Korea • Mexico • Singapore • Spain • United Kingdom • United States

※

*I want to dedicate this, the Legacy Edition of* Yąnomamö, *to my lifelong friend and colleague, William G. Irons*

# Foreword

## ABOUT THIS SERIES

The *Case Studies in Cultural Anthropology* Series was founded in 1960 under the joint editorship of George and Louise Spindler, both anthropologists at Stanford University. Since that time, more than 200 case studies have been published, and the series has enjoyed wide readership in college and university classrooms around the country and abroad. With Louise Spindler's death in 1997, their series was left with one editor. In 2005, anthropologist Janice E. Stockard came on board as CSCA Series co-editor.

The case studies were originally conceived as descriptive studies of cultures intended for classroom use. By design they are accessible, short, and engaging. Their authors are anthropologists who have conducted extensive field research in diverse societies, experienced professionals who have "been there." They are also teachers. The goal of the series is to introduce a broad audience of students to cultural differences—as well as to demonstrate the commonalities of human lives everywhere.

In the early years of the series, many case studies focused on a single relatively bounded community—a group, tribe, or village—that could be distinguished by its own cultural practices, beliefs, and values. Today the case studies also reflect a world undergoing dramatic cultural change. One goal of the series is to continue to describe the distinctive features of the cultures of the world. Another goal is to analyze the sweeping changes underway as a result of accelerating trends in migration, urbanization, and the global "flows" of information, technologies, goods, and capital.

Thus for anthropologists today, the task remains to describe the distinctive features of the cultures of the world. In addition, the goal is also to document cultural transformations—and to decipher the ways in which the particular forms that change takes is influenced by the distinctive features of specific cultures and local cultural practices. A no less daunting task is to understand the meaning of these changes for the people who live with them.

Janice E. Stockard and George Splindler
CSCA Series Co-Editors, 2006

## ABOUT THE AUTHOR

Napoleon A. Chagnon was born the second of twelve children in Port Austin, Michigan, in 1938. He is married and has two children. He began his academic training at the Michigan College of Mining and Technology at Sault Ste. Marie, Michigan (now called Lake Superior State University), in the physics curriculum. After one year there, he transferred to the University of Michigan, changed his major to anthropology, and received his B.A. (1961), M.A. (1963), and Ph.D. (1966) degrees in anthropology at the University of Michigan. He then joined the faculty of the Department of Human Genetics at the University of Michigan Medical School from which position he participated in an extensive multi-disciplinary study of the Yąnomamö Indians of Venezuela and Brazil. During this time he also held a joint appointment in the Department of Anthropology at the University of Michigan, where he taught anthropology courses.

In 1972 he moved to the Pennsylvania State University to continue his data analysis and field research among the Yąnomamö, developing a long-term proj-ect funded by the U.S. National Science Foundation, the U.S. National Institute of Mental Health, and the Harry Frank Guggenheim Foundation. This project brought him and several of his graduate students into the field between 1974 and 1976 on several trips.

In 1968 and 1971 Chagnon was joined in the field by his film colleague, Timothy Asch, during which time they shot documentary film that has led to the production of 21 ethnographic films on the Yąnomamö. Many of these films have won prizes in national and international film competitions. They are listed on page 280.

In 1980 Chagnon was an invited participant in the King's College Research Centre, Cambridge University, and a Visiting Scholar in the Department of Social Anthropology, Cambridge University.

Chagnon then joined the faculty of Northwestern University in 1981 and was appointed Chairman of the Anthropology Department in 1983.

Chagnon moved to the University of California, Santa Barbara, in 1984 and initiated several new field research projects among the Yąnomamö from that campus, starting with a three-year project (1985–1987) funded by the U.S. National Science Foundation with his colleague, Raymond Hames. He is a Fellow of the American Association for the Advancement of Science and served as President of the Human Behavior and Evolution Society (1995–1997). He served as Editor of the Psychological Cinema Register, the Pennsylvania State University's film distribution unit. Chagnon has published numerous articles and book chapters on various aspects of his work among the Yąnomamö, and a methods study (1974) detailing the procedures he used in the field to collect the information on which most of his ethnographic publications are based. Some of his publications are mentioned in the text and listed in "References Cited." Over his 40-year career his interests shifted more toward the strategies used by individuals in their kinship and marriage behavior; some of this work can be found in his 1979 book, co-edited with William Irons. His recent views on anthropology as a discipline are contained in *Noble Savages,* his most recent book (2012).

## ABOUT THIS CASE STUDY

### PREFACE TO THE LEGACY SIXTH EDITION, 2012
### By Janice E. Stockard, CSCA Series Co-Editor

This Legacy Edition of Napoleon A. Chagnon's *Yąnomamö* is the sixth edition of an ethnographic case study first published in 1968—and which has now achieved historic levels of readership for ethnography in classrooms across this country. The case study presents the results of Chagnon's long-term field research and residence among the Yąnomamö, tropical forest Indians living along the Venezuelan and Brazilian border. At the time of his first research project, the Yąnomamö were a people living in then-remote villages. Chagnon's continuing field research among the Yąnomamö has now spanned more than forty years. Until now each new edition of the case study incorporated the author's developing perspectives on the increasingly dramatic and accelerating changes that have come to affect the Yąnomamö across the several decades of his research.

To mark the publication of this sixth edition we include a capstone interview with author Napoleon A. Chagnon, conducted by his anthropological colleague and friend of many years, William G. Irons. The Interview—"Reflections on the Yąnomamö: Fieldwork and Anthropology"—provides additional information and context for understanding the development of Chagnon's research and analytical perspectives, which also reflect changes within the field of anthropology itself. In addition, the interview presents Chagnon's views on the recent decade of controversies that his work has inspired among critics (including some anthropologists)—and his brief responses to it and references to three short (online) publications where the controversies are discussed in more detail.

With each new edition to the case study, Chagnon has provided readers with the opportunity to follow developments in the personal and public lives of individual Yąnomamö, along with updates on greater events and forces affecting the continuity of their lives and identities as Yąnomamö. Thus the case study chronicles both the dynamics of personal change as well as perspectives on larger cultural shifts. As Chagnon describes the case study, it is "not simply a single slice in time, a 'snapshot' of a society 'frozen' at a single point in time and in its history, nor in the life of the people discussed. It is a kind of continuing narrative of a people being changed *over* time and an account of the forces of that change—contact with the outside world; the transition in the larger political world around them from a federal territory to statehood; their incorporation at Mission posts into political entities with which they were unfamiliar—*alcaldes*; and the power of identity and the importance of names that outsiders assigned to them...." (Interview, page 269.)

By way of introducing this special Legacy Edition of Napoleon A. Chagnon's *Yąnomamö*, we include the preface written on the occasion of the publication of the fifth edition by its co-editors (and CSCA Series Founders), George and Louise Spindler.

## PREFACE TO THE FIFTH EDITION, 1997
### By George and Louise Spindler, CSCA Series Co-Editors

This fifth edition of *Yąnomamö*, in two entirely new chapters, brings new light into interrelationships among the people and the increasing perils to the survival of the Yąnomamö populations and culture. The role of the "Shamatari" referred to frequently in Chagnon's recent publications is clarified; the author has worked increasingly in more remote villages, especially among the Mishimishimaböwei-teri. Chagnon describes in moving detail the meeting of two men from two villages that have been estranged, in fact they had been at war, for more than twenty years, and their way of de-escalating hostile feelings.

The perils to Yąnomamö survival have increased as villages remote from navigable rivers were brought into greater contact with the outside world when they moved to the banks of the navigable rivers, and within relatively easy traveling distance of the Salesian missionaries. The spread of western diseases is a mounting threat as contact increases.

Equally perilous for the Yąnomamö is the deepening vortex of political forces surrounding them. Since the area they occupy is rich in gold and other mineral resources, Brazilian and Venezuelan economic and political forces are involved, and this in the midst of a struggle between Church and State for the supervisory role in Venezuela. A small cadre of acculturated Yąnomamö individuals have assumed roles of spokespersons for all Yąnomamö with additional political complications and intrigue.

Napoleon A. Chagnon is to be praised for continuing his field research with the Yąnomamö over a period of more than 30 years and making available to us the material and insights that only a long-term relationship with a people can produce.

Series Editors

George and Louise Spindler

# Author's Preface to the Sixth Edition

I was unable to take any new field trips to the Yąnomamö after the fifth edition appeared in 1997 because the three attempts I made were derailed by a small group of "activist" anthropologists once I reached either Venezuela or Brazil. Let me provide a little background to these extraordinary actions and I will take them up again in Chapter 9.

Things were changing in anthropology and these changes coincided with the mid-1990s—about the time the fifth edition of this ethnography appeared. Many of these changes were remarkable, complex, and far-reaching insofar as they potentially affected the field research of those of us whose work is ethnographic, that is, work intended to produce a meaningful, sympathetic, and repeatable description of another society/culture by living for long periods of time in that culture.

Anthropologists became more active politically and many turned away from standard ethnographic work in favor of advocacy of native tribesmen, their health problems, and their very survival. The world's tropical forests were disappearing and, in South America, this meant that the last remaining isolated Amazon basin tribesmen were likewise disappearing. It was the beginning of the end of a noble way of life and this made many of us sad. Many of the trends I described in the final chapter of the fifth edition continue, as my interview with William Irons in the final chapter of this edition discusses.

I would like to add a personal anecdote in this brief preface. It broke my heart to learn of the death of Kąobawä in 2001. He was a dear Yąnomamö friend, companion, and confidant. I learned of his death from a casual remark made by a young Yąnomamö man who was invited to George Washington University to discuss the changing situation for the Venezuelan Yąnomamö where I had spent so much time with Kąobawä and his people. What bothered me about the way I learned of his death was a simple aside made by this young man, almost as if Kąobawä were just another "old man" who died and who was, apart from being old, just another ordinary Yąnomamö.

The young man was invited to this conference essentially to tell an audience of anthropologists some of the negative things they wanted to hear about me. In this case, it was a story about how I had reneged on an alleged promise to give Kąobawä an outboard motor.

I don't know what was sadder—the fact that this young man seemed to be completely ignorant of how special Kąobawä was in the history of this village, or that he was invited there because he was willing to denounce me.

A preface goes at the beginning of a book. You will, in the pages that follow, learn more about Kąobawä and the reasons I thought he was a special person. The final chapter points you to additional readings that will introduce you more fully to the remarkable changes in the field of anthropology I refer to here.

✳

# Acknowledgments

The field research on which the original edition of this monograph is based was provided by the National Institute of Mental Health (1964–1966) when I was a graduate student in anthropology at the University of Michigan. While I was on the faculty of the Department of Human Genetics of the University of Michigan's Medical School (1966–1972) my salary and field research expenses came from a research grant to that department from the United States Atomic Energy Commission.[1] The Wenner-Gren Foundation supported one of my field trips in 1968 and another in 1992. Between 1974 and 1978 my field research was supported by the National Institute of Mental Health with additional support for data analysis provided by the National Science Foundation. Generous support was also provided by several grants between 1975 and 1989 from the Harry Frank Guggenheim Foundation. Between 1984 and 1986 the National Science Foundation's Anthropology Program provided support for three field trips and aspects of data analyses resulting from them. The Office of Research Development of the University of California, Santa Barbara, supported my research trips in 1990 and 1991, and two additional trips (1992, 1995) were supported by research grants from the Academic Senate of this university.

---

1. Because it is unusual for anthropological field research to be sponsored by an agency like the AEC, a brief explanation is in order. A very large fraction of research in human genetics in all universities was supported by the AEC after World War II. The Human Genetics department at the University of Michigan had a long-time contract with the AEC to monitor the possible genetic effects of atomic radiation on the survivors of Nagasaki and Hiroshima, an elaborate project that included the study of family composition and marriage practices. This was eventually extended to include comparative studies of marriage, demography, and reproduction patterns in other societies, including Amerindian societies like the Xavante and Yąnomamö. Funding for this was eventually assumed by the National Science Foundation as part of the U.S. Contribution to the International Biological Program.

I would like to thank the Trimble Navigation Corporation for loaning me GPS instruments and providing other support for my field studies from 1990 to 1995. The Patagonia Corporation generously provided items of field clothing during this same period, and Jandd Mountaineering Corporation contributed backpacks and related field equipment.

Charles Brewer-Carias, my long-time Venezuelan friend and co-researcher, deserves special thanks for the successful efforts he has made to secure helicopter support for several of our research trips between 1990 and 1996, and for his dip-lomatic efforts that made these trips possible at all. Needless to say, I am very grateful to the Venezuelan Air Force for this support and for the skills of the pilots who brought us into and out of places that were difficult to land in.

As this book has progressed through five editions many friends, colleagues, and associates have contributed advice and suggestions. Revisions sometimes lead to deletion of dated content, and this is true here as well. Nevertheless, I want to express my gratitude to those whose advice went into earlier editions whether or not it is retained and reflected in this edition. They include Bill Irons, Raymond Hames, Peter Matthiessen, Mary Ann Harrell, Verdun Chagnon, Greg and Kathy Gomez, Dante DeLuccia, Dirk Brandts, Melodie Knutson, Miguel Layrisse, and Marcel Roche.

As will be apparent in the text that follows, I owe a profound debt to indi-vidual Yąnomamö like Kąobawä and Rerebawä for their friendship, information, and comradeship during much of the time I worked among their people, and in more recent years, Dedeheiwä and Dararaiwä.

Finally, I owe the greatest debt to my wife, Carlene, who patiently and self-lessly encouraged me in my lifelong work that took me away from her and our two children for the months and years I spent in unnamed, unmapped, and unexplored regions of the Amazon basin. Few will be able to appreciate how difficult this can be for the family of the fieldworker and the worries and con-cerns that fieldwork of the kind described here causes.

I want to also thank my son, Darius, who spent three months with me among very remote Yąnomamö groups in 1991 as my companion, friend, co-worker, and especially as my son. This was the most enjoyable field experience I have ever had, despite the malaria and diarrhea we both got and the frustrating time we spent waiting, in a very remote place, for the helicopter to come back and get us—nearly a month after it was scheduled to do so.

# Contents

# Illustrations

**Photos**

## Diagrams and Genealogies

**Maps**

# Yąnomamö

✳

# Prologue

There is a large tribe of Tropical Forest Indians on the border between Venezuela and Brazil. They number approximately 20,000 people and are distributed in some 200 to 250 widely scattered villages. They are gardeners, and they have lived until very recent time in isolation from our kind of culture. The authorities in Venezuela and Brazil knew very little about their existence until anthropologists began going there. The remarkable thing about the tribe, known as the Yąnomamö, is the fact that they have managed, due to their isolation in a remote corner of Amazonia, to retain their native patterns of warfare and political integrity without interference from the outside world. They have remained sovereign and in complete control of their own destiny up until a few years ago. The remotest, uncontacted villages were living under those conditions during most of my fieldwork. Only a few villages are left that are still not directly contacted.

This case study is about the Yąnomamö and about their sovereignty. It is based on 60 months of residence in many of their villages, on fieldwork that began in 1964—before the major vectors of change began to impinge on some of their villages. My initial 15 months of field research, between 1964 and 1966, was conducted when very little accurate information existed about their culture, geographical distribution, tribal size, and cultural history. Government maps of this area were grossly in error, showing, for example, the headwaters of the Siapa River as the headwaters of the Mavaca River where much of my work was focused.

I want to begin with a description of an event that happened 15 years before I went to live with the Yąnomamö, an event I had to reconstruct from bits and pieces of information given to me by many Yąnomamö informants after I learned their language. They spoke no other language when I first went there. The event that I describe below led to the development of political relationships, alliances, and wars between many Yąnomamö villages that dominated their social

1

activities while I was there, but I had to proceed in ignorance because I knew nothing about the event.

The story contains a message about anthropological fieldwork on the one hand, and the nature of Yąnomamö political organization on the other. As to fieldwork, the lesson is that it is in some cases impossible to understand a society's 'social organization' by studying only one village or community of that society, for each community is bound up in and responds to the political ties to neighboring groups and the obligations and pressures these ties impose on them. Regarding Yąnomamö political organization, the lesson is that past events and history must be understood to comprehend the current observable patterns. As the Roman poet Lucretius mused, nothing yet from nothing ever came.

## The Killing of Ruwähiwä

The members of the village of Bisaasi-teri lived several days' walk from their southern neighbors, the Konabuma-teri. The Bisaasi-teri, about whom much of this monograph is written, were a splinter village of a much larger village: Patanowä-teri (see Figure 5.2 in Chapter 5). They were themselves at odds with the larger 'mother' village and beginning to fission away from them, forging their own new identity and seeking new allies. They saw in their southern neighbors, the Konabuma-teri, an opportunity to strengthen their political future by cultivating friendship with them.

The recent history of both groups (Patanowä-teri/Bisaasi-teri and Konabuma-teri) entailed a gradual, general migration from the northeast to the southwest as past wars and current alliances caused their villages to periodically relocate in new, virgin areas of the Tropical Forest. They spoke slightly different dialects of Yąnomamö, but no more different than what obtains between North Carolina English and Upstate New York English. Hunters from each group began running into each other in the lands between their villages, and eventually, in the late 1940s, they decided to begin visiting and trading with each other. Apparently the trading visits increased in regularity and frequency, and members of the two groups got to know each other well.

In Yąnomamö politics, members of allied villages often need each other's support, but often they cannot and do not trust each other much—especially if the allies are not historically and, therefore, genealogically related to each other, as was the case here.

Almost all deaths other than those obviously caused by human or animal intervention—killings with arrows or being attacked by jaguars, for example—are attributed to harmful magic. The Yąnomamö, and all tribal populations, suffer a high infant mortality rate. Babies do not have a good chance of survival, but die frequently for a host of reasons. With our technical medical knowledge, we can diagnose and describe sicknesses in precise, mechanical biomedical terms, but the Yąnomamö do not have such knowledge, and to them, babies die because someone sent harmful spirits—*hekura*—to steal their souls, or someone blew magical charms at them from a great distance, charms that caused them to sicken and die. Thus, in every village, the shamans spend many hours attempting to cure sick children and sick adults, driving out the malevolent forces that have caused their illnesses, and in turn, sending their own spirits and charms against the children in distant villages for revenge.

Several children died in the village of Bisaasi-teri as the alliance with the people of Konabuma-teri was developing and maturing. Shamans in Bisaasi-teri began suspecting that men in Konabuma-teri were secretly sending harmful charms and magic against them and their children and ultimately convinced themselves that their new allies were truly enemies. Unaware of this, one of the prominent men from Konabuma-teri arrived at Bisaasi-teri to visit and trade. His name was Ruwähiwä, and he came to their village with just a few people in his party. He entered the clearing in his pose of the visitor: erect, proud, motionless, and showing no fear. He was greeted by the host men, who came out with their weapons, cheering, hooting, and growling symbolic threats and intimidations as they inspected him. After a few minutes, he was invited to take up a hammock until food was prepared for him. Presently, a gourd of plantain soup was ready and he was invited out to drink of it before the house of the local headman. He squatted on his haunches, picked up the gourd, and began drinking, oblivious to his surroundings, happy to be welcomed in this customary way.

A man approached him silently from behind, Mamikininiwä, a mature man of 40 years whose decisions few would challenge. He carried the battered, worn remains of a steel ax, hafted clumsily to a short, stout handle. Ruwähiwä paid him no attention and kept drinking the plantain soup. Mamikininiwä raised his ax high above his head and then smashed it down violently, sharp edge forward, into Ruwähiwä's skull. Ruwähiwä lurched forward, trying to stand, but was mortally wounded. He fell to the ground and died in a pool of his own blood. Later that day, several old women carried his body out and off to his village.

Thus began the war between the villages of Bisaasi-teri and Konabuma-teri, a war that was going on 15 years later when I went to the Yąnomamö, but a war I was ignorant of when I went there.

Ruwähiwä's group then set about to avenge this killing. They enlisted the support of a third village that was on friendly terms with the Bisaasi-teri and managed to get them to host a feast at which the Bisaasi-teri would be the guests of honor. They invited men from a fourth village to join them in hiding outside the village. The unsuspecting Bisaasi-teri had come *en masse* for the occasion: men, women, and children. Shortly after the feast began, and while the Bisaasi-teri men were lying motionless and helpless in their hosts' hammocks, someone gave the signal. The hosts suddenly set upon them with clubs, bowstaves, and arrows, attacking them in their hammocks. Many died immediately, but some managed to escape outside. There, they ran into showers of arrows from the hidden archers. More died and more were wounded, some badly enough that they later died. Approximately a dozen men were killed that afternoon. A number of women and pubescent girls were taken captive, never to be seen by their families again. The survivors retreated deep into the jungle, to the north, and hid for many days while the wounded recovered enough to move on. The survivors, depressed and anguished, sought refuge in a village to the north, Mahekodo-teri. They arrived early in the year 1951, a date recorded by James P. Barker, the first missionary to make a sustained contact with the Yąnomamö a few months prior to this. He saw the Bisaasi-teri arrive at Mahekodo-teri, the village he had chosen for his mission station.

The Bisaasi-teri moved away from the Mahekodo-teri about a year later and settled further down the Orinoco River. They were the people I came to live with when I first went to the Yąnomamö. I knew nothing of this tragic event in their recent history when I joined them to begin my field research, but the significance of that event slowly unraveled over the months as I learned more of their language and set about to discover something about their history and recent settlement pattern. Only then did much of what I initially witnessed begin to make sense, and only then did their raids on and political dealings with neighbors become comprehensible.

Much of what follows in this book is about Bisaasi-teri and the people who live in that village.

# 1

✳

# Doing Fieldwork among the Yąnomamö[1]

## VIGNETTE

The Yąnomamö are thinly scattered over a vast and verdant tropical forest, living in small villages that are separated by many miles of unoccupied land. They have no writing, but they have a rich and complex language. Their clothing is more decorative than protective. Well-dressed men sport nothing more than a few cotton strings around their wrists, ankles, and waists. They tie the foreskins of their penises to the waiststring. Women dress about the same. Much of their daily life revolves around gardening, hunting, collecting wild foods and firewood, fetching water, visiting each other, gossiping, and making the few material possessions they own: baskets, hammocks, bows, arrows, and colorful pigments with which they paint their bodies. Life is relatively easy in the sense that they can "earn a living" with about three hours' work per day. Most of what they eat they cultivate in their gardens, and most of that is plantains—a kind of cooking banana that is usually eaten green, either roasted on the coals or boiled in pots (Figure 1.1). Their meat comes from a large variety of game animals, hunted daily by the men. It is usually roasted on coals or smoked, and is always well done. Their villages are round and open—and very public. One can hear, see, and smell almost everything that goes on anywhere in the village. Privacy is

---

1. The word Yąnomamö is nasalized through its entire length, indicated by the diacritical mark ",." When this mark appears on any Yąnomamö word, the whole word is nasalized. The vowel "ö" represents a sound that does not occur in the English language. It is similar to the umlaut "ö" in the German language or the "oe" equivalent, as in the poet Goethe's name. Unfortunately, many presses and typesetters simply eliminate diacritical marks, and this has led to multiple spellings of the word Yąnomamö—and multiple mispronunciations. Some anthropologists have chosen to introduce a slightly different spelling of the word Yąnomamö since I began writing about them, such as Yąnomami, leading to additional misspellings as their diacriticals are characteristically eliminated by presses, and to the incorrect pronunciation "Yanomameee." Vowels indicated as "ä" are pronounced as the "uh" sound in the word "duck." Thus, the name Kąobawä would be pronounced "cow-ba-wuh," but entirely nasalized.

**FIGURE 1.1** Bahimi, wife of Bisaasi-teri headman, harvesting plantains, a cooking banana that comprises a large fraction of Yąnomamö diet.

rare, but sexual discreetness is possible in the garden or at night when others sleep. The villages can be as small as 40 to 50 people or as large as 300 people, but in all cases there are many more children and babies than there are adults. This is true of most primitive populations and of our own demographic past. Life expectancy is short.

The Yąnomamö fall into the category of Tropical Forest Indians called "foot people." They avoid large rivers and live in interfluvial plains of the major rivers. They have neighbors to the north, Carib-speaking Ye'kwana, who are true "river people." Ye'kwana make elegant, large dugout canoes and travel extensively along the major waterways. For the Yᴀnomamö, a large stream is an obstacle and can be crossed only in the dry season. Thus, they have traditionally avoided larger rivers and, because of this, contact with outsiders who usually come by river.

They enjoy taking trips when the jungle abounds with seasonally ripe wild fruits and vegetables. Then, the large village—the *shabono*—is abandoned for a few weeks and everyone camps out for from one to several days away from the village and garden. On these trips, they make temporary huts from poles, vines, and leaves, each family making a separate hut.

Two major seasons dominate their annual cycle: the wet season, which inundates the low-lying jungle, making travel difficult, and the dry season—the time of visiting other villages to feast, trade, and politic with allies. The dry season is also the time when raiders can travel and strike silently at their unsuspecting enemies. The Yᴀnomamö continue to conduct intervillage warfare, a phenomenon that affects all aspects of their social organization, settlement pattern, and daily routines. It is not simply a "ritualistic" war: At least one-fourth of all adult males die violently in the area I lived in.

Social life is organized around those same principles utilized by all tribesmen: kinship relationships, descent from ancestors, marriage exchanges between kinship/ descent groups, and the transient charisma of distinguished headmen who attempt to keep order in the village and whose responsibility it is to determine the village's relationships with other villages. Their positions are largely the result of kinship and marriage patterns; they come from the largest kinship groups within the village. They can, by their personal wit, wisdom, and charisma, become autocrats, but most of them are largely "greaters" among equals. They, too, must clear gardens, plant crops, collect wild foods, and hunt. They are simultaneously peacemakers and valiant warriors. Peacemaking often requires the threat or actual use of force, and most headmen have an acquired reputation for being *waiteri*: fierce.

The social dynamics within villages are involved with giving and receiving marriageable girls. Marriages are arranged by older kin, usually men, such as brothers, uncles, and the father. It is a political process, for girls are promised in marriage while they are young, and the men who do this attempt to create alliances with other men via marriage exchanges. There is a shortage of women partly due to a sex-ratio imbalance in the younger age categories, but also complicated by the fact that some men have multiple wives. Most fighting within the village stems from sexual affairs or failure to deliver a promised woman—or out-and-out seizure of a married woman by some other man. This can lead to internal fighting and conflict of such an intensity that villages split up and fission, each group then becoming a new village and, often, enemies to each other.

But their conflicts are not blind, uncontrolled violence. They have a series of graded forms of violence that ranges from chest-pounding and club-fighting duels to out-and-out shooting to kill. This gives them a good deal of flexibility in settling disputes without immediate resort to lethal violence. In addition, they have developed patterns of alliance and friendship that serve to limit violence— trading and feasting with others in order to become friends (Figure 1.2). These alliances can, and often do, result in intervillage exchanges of marriageable women, which leads to additional amity between villages. No good thing lasts

**FIGURE 1.2**
Kạobawä, headman of
Upper Bisaasi-teri, trading
with his Shamatari allies
for arrows, baskets,
hammocks, and dogs.

forever, and most alliances crumble. Old friends become hostile and, occasionally, treacherous. Each village must therefore be keenly aware that its neighbors are fickle and must behave accordingly. The thin line between friendship and animosity must be traversed by the village leaders, whose political acumen and strategies are both admirable and complex.

Each village, then, is a replica of all others in a broad sense. But each village is part of a larger political, demographic, and ecological process, and it is difficult to attempt to understand the village without knowing something of the larger forces that affect it and its particular history with all its neighbors.

## COLLECTING THE DATA IN THE FIELD

I have now spent over 60 months with Yạnomamö, during which time I gradually learned their language and, up to a point, submerged myself in their culture and way of life.[2] As my research progressed, the thing that impressed me most

2. I spent a total of 64 months among the Yạnomamö between 1964 and 1995. The first
edition of this case study was based on the first 17 months I spent among them in
Venezuela.  I have, at the time of this writing, made 24 field trips to the Yạnomamö.

was the importance that aggression played in shaping their culture. I had the opportunity to witness a good many incidents that expressed individual vindictiveness on the one hand and collective bellicosity on the other hand. These ranged in seriousness from the ordinary incidents of wife beating and chest pounding to dueling and organized raids by parties that set out with the intention of ambushing and killing men from enemy villages. One of the villages discussed in the chapters that follow was raided approximately 25 times during my first 15 months of fieldwork—six times by the group among whom I was living. And, the history of every village I investigated, from 1964 to 1991, was intimately bound up in patterns of warfare with neighbors, which shaped the village's politics and determined where it was found at any point in time and how it dealt with its current neighbors.

The fact that the Yąnomamö have lived in a chronic state of warfare is reflected in their mythology, ceremonies, settlement pattern, political behavior, and marriage practices. Accordingly, I have organized this case study in such a way that students can appreciate the effects of warfare on Yąnomamö culture in general and on their social organization and political relationships in particular (Figure 1.3).

**FIGURE 1.3** Visitors dancing as a group around the *shabono* during a formal feast.

I collected the data under somewhat trying circumstances, some of which I will describe to give a rough idea of what is generally meant when anthropologists speak of "culture shock" and "fieldwork." It should be borne in mind, however, that each field situation is in many respects unique, so that the problems I encountered do not necessarily exhaust the range of possible problems other anthropologists have confronted in other areas. There are a few problems, however, that seem to be nearly universal among anthropological fieldworkers, particularly those having to do with eating, bathing, sleeping, lack of privacy, loneliness, or discovering that the people you are living with have a lower opinion of you than you have of them—or you yourself are not as culturally or emotionally "flexible" as you assumed.

The Yąnomamö can be difficult people to live with at times, but I have spoken to colleagues who have had difficulties living in the communities they studied. These things vary from society to society, and probably from one anthropologist to the next. I have also done limited fieldwork among the Yąnomamö's northern neighbors, the Carib-speaking Ye'kwana Indians. In contrast to many experiences I had among the Yąnomamö, the Ye'kwana were very pleasant and charming, all of them anxious to help me and honor bound to show any visitor the numerous courtesies of their system of etiquette. In short, they approached the image of "primitive man" that I had conjured up in my mind before doing fieldwork, a kind of "Rousseauian" view, and it was sheer pleasure to work with them. Other anthropologists have also noted sharp contrasts in the people they study from one field situation to another. One of the most startling examples of this is in the work of Colin Turnbull, who first studied the Ituri Pygmies (1965, 1983) and found them delightful to live with, but then studied the Ik (1972) of the desolate outcroppings of the Kenya/Uganda/Sudan border region, a people he had difficulty coping with intellectually, emotionally, and physically. While it is possible that the anthropologist's reactions to a particular people are personal and idiosyncratic, it nevertheless remains true that there are enormous differences between whole peoples, differences that affect the anthropologist in often dramatic ways.

Hence, what I say about some of my experiences is probably equally true of the experiences of many other fieldworkers. I describe some of them here for the benefit of future anthropologists—because I think I could have profited by reading about the pitfalls and field problems of my own teachers. At the very least I might have been able to avoid some of my more stupid errors. In this regard there is a growing body of excellent descriptive work on field research. Students who plan to make a career in anthropology should consult these works, which cover a wide range of field situations in the ethnographic present.[3]

---

3. See Spindler (1970) for a general discussion of field research by anthropologists who have worked in other cultures. Nancy Howell has recently written a very useful book (1990) on some of the medical, personal, and environmental hazards of doing field research, which includes a selected bibliography on other fieldwork problems.

## The Longest Day: The First One

My first day in the field illustrated to me what my teachers meant when they spoke of "culture shock." I had traveled in a small, aluminum rowboat propelled by a large outboard motor for two and a half days. This took me from the territorial capital, a small town on the Orinoco River, deep into the Yąnomamö country. On the morning of the third day we reached a small mission settlement, the field "headquarters" of a group of Americans who were working in two Yąnomamö villages. The missionaries had come out of these villages to hold their annual conference on the progress of their mission work and were conducting their meetings when I arrived. We picked up a passenger at the mission station, James P. Barker, the first non-Yąnomamö to make a sustained, permanent contact with the tribe (in 1950). He had just returned from a year's furlough in the United States, where I had earlier visited him before leaving for Venezuela. He agreed to accompany me to the village I had selected for my base of operations to introduce me to the Indians. This village was also his own home base, but he had not been there for over a year and did not plan to join me for another three months. Mr. Barker had been living with this particular group for about five years.

We arrived at the village, Bisaasi-teri, at about 2:00 P.M. and docked the boat along the muddy bank at the terminus of the path used by Yąnomamö to fetch their drinking water. It was hot and muggy, and my clothing was soaked with perspiration. It clung uncomfortably to my body, as it did thereafter for the remainder of the work. The small biting gnats *bareto* were out in astronomical numbers, for it was the beginning of the dry season. My face and hands were swollen from the venom of their numerous stings. In just a few moments I was to meet my first Yąnomamö, my first primitive man. What would he be like? I had visions of entering the village and seeing 125 social facts running about altruistically calling each other kinship terms and sharing food, each waiting and anxious to have me collect his genealogy. I would wear them out in turn. Would they like me? This was important to me; I wanted them to be so fond of me that they would adopt me into their kinship system and way of life. I had heard that successful anthropologists always get adopted by their people. I had learned during my seven years of anthropological training at the University of Michigan that kinship was equivalent to society in primitive tribes and that it was a moral way of life, "moral" being something "good" and "desirable." I was determined to work my way into their moral system of kinship and become a member of their society—to be "accepted" by them.

## How Did They Accept You?

My heart began to pound as we approached the village and heard the buzz of activity within the circular compound. Mr. Barker commented that he was anxious to see if any changes had taken place while he was away and wondered how many of them had died during his absence. I nervously felt my back pocket to make sure that my notebook was still there and felt personally more secure when I touched it.

The entrance to the village was covered over with brush and dry palm leaves. We pushed them aside to expose the low opening to the village.

The excitement of meeting my first Yąnomamö was almost unbearable as I duck-waddled through the low passage into the village clearing.

I looked up and gasped when I saw a dozen burly, naked, sweaty, hideous men staring at us down the shafts of their drawn arrows! Immense wads of green tobacco were stuck between their lower teeth and lips making them look even more hideous, and strands of dark-green slime dripped or hung from their nostrils—strands so long that they clung to their pectoral muscles or drizzled down their chins. We arrived at the village while the men were blowing a hallucinogenic drug up their noses. One of the side effects of the drug is a runny nose. The mucus is always saturated with the green powder and they usually let it run freely from their nostrils (Figure 1.4). My next discovery was that there were a dozen or so vicious, underfed dogs snapping at my legs, circling me as if I were to be their next meal. I just stood there holding my notebook, helpless and pathetic. Then the stench of the decaying vegetation and filth hit me and I almost got sick. I was horrified. What kind of welcome was this for the person who came here to live with you and learn your way of life, to become friends with you? They put their weapons down when they recognized Barker and returned to their chanting, keeping a nervous eye on the village entrances.

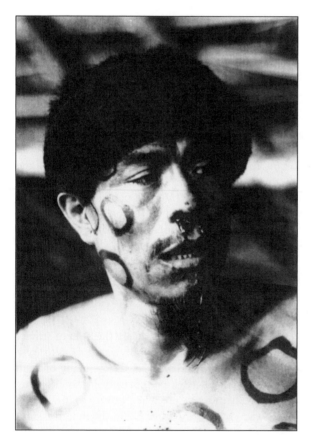

**FIGURE 1.4**
Yąnomamö man with a monkey-tail headband and with *ebene*, a hallucinogenic snuff, drizzling from his nostrils.

We had arrived just after a serious fight. Seven women had been abducted the day before by a neighboring group, and the local men and their guests had just that morning recovered five of them in a brutal club fight that nearly ended in a shooting war. The abductors, angry because they had lost five of their seven new captives, vowed to raid the Bisaasi-teri. When we arrived and entered the village unexpectedly, the Indians feared that we were the raiders. On several occasions during the next two hours the men in the village jumped to their feet, armed themselves, nocked their arrows and waited nervously for the noise outside the village to be identified. My enthusiasm for collecting ethnographic facts diminished in proportion to the number of times such an alarm was raised. In fact, I was relieved when Barker suggested that we sleep across the river for the evening. It would be safer over there.

As we walked down the path to the boat, I pondered the wisdom of having decided to spend a year and a half with these people before I had even seen what they were like. I am not ashamed to admit that had there been a diplomatic way out, I would have ended my fieldwork then and there. I did not look forward to the next day—and months—when I would be left alone with the Yanomamö; I did not speak a word of their language, and they were decidedly different from what I had imagined them to be. The whole situation was depressing, and I wondered why I ever decided to switch from physics and engineering in the first place. I had not eaten all day, I was soaking wet from perspiration, the *bareto* were biting me, and I was covered with red pigment, the result of a dozen or so complete examinations I had been given by as many very pushy Yanomamö men. These examinations capped an otherwise grim day. The men would blow their noses into their hands, flick as much of the mucus off that would separate in a snap of the wrist, wipe the residue into their hair, and then carefully examine my face, arms, legs, hair, and the contents of my pockets. I asked Barker how to say, "Your hands are dirty;" my comments were met by the Yanomamö in the following way: They would "clean" their hands by spitting a quantity of slimy tobacco juice into them, rub them together, grin, and then proceed with the examination.

Mr. Barker and I crossed the river and slung our hammocks. When he pulled his hammock out of a rubber bag, a heavy, disagreeable odor of mildewed cotton and stale wood smoke came with it. "Even the missionaries are filthy," I thought to myself. Within two weeks, everything I owned smelled the same way, and I lived with that odor for the remainder of the fieldwork. My own habits of personal cleanliness declined to such levels that I didn't even mind being examined by the Yanomamö, as I was not much cleaner than they were after I had adjusted to the circumstances. It is difficult to blow your nose gracefully when you are stark naked and the invention of handkerchiefs is millennia away.

## Life in the Jungle: Oatmeal, Peanut Butter, and Bugs

It isn't easy to plop down in the Amazon Basin for a year and get immediately into the anthropological swing of things. You have been told about horrible diseases, snakes, jaguars, electric eels, little spiny fish that will swim up your urine into your penis, quicksand, and getting lost. Some of the dangers are real, but your imagination makes them more real and threatening than many of them really are. What my teachers never bothered to advise me about, however, was the mundane, unexciting, and trivial stuff—like eating, defecating, sleeping, or keeping clean. These turned out to be the bane of my existence during the first several months of field research. I set up my household in Barker's abandoned mud hut, a few yards from the village of Bisaasi-teri, and immediately set to work building my own mud/thatch hut with the help of the Yąnomamö. Meanwhile, I had to eat and try to do my "field research." I soon discovered that it was an enormously time-consuming task to maintain my own body in the manner to which it had grown accustomed in the relatively antiseptic environment of the northern United States. Either I could be relatively well fed and relatively comfortable in a fresh change of clothes and do very little fieldwork, or I could do considerably more fieldwork and be less well fed and less comfortable.

It is appalling how complicated it can be to make oatmeal in the jungle. First, I had to make two trips to the river to haul the water, Next, I had to prime my kerosene stove with alcohol to get it burning, a tricky procedure when you are trying to mix powdered milk and fill a coffee pot at the same time. The alcohol prime always burned out before I could turn the kerosene on, and I would have to start all over. Or, I would turn the kerosene on, optimistically hoping that the Coleman element was still hot enough to vaporize the fuel, and start a small fire in my palm-thatched hut as the liquid kerosene squirted all over the table and walls and then ignited. Many amused Yąnomamö onlookers quickly learned the English phrase "Oh, shit!", and, once they discovered that the phrase offended and irritated the missionaries, they used it as often as they could in their presence. I usually had to start over with the alcohol. Then I had to boil the oatmeal and pick the bugs out of it. All my supplies, of course, were carefully stored in rat-proof, moisture-proof, and insect-proof containers, not one of which ever served its purpose adequately. Just taking things out of the multiplicity of containers and repacking them afterward was a minor project in itself. By the time I had hauled the water to cook with; unpacked my food; prepared the oatmeal, milk, and coffee; heated water for dishes; washed and dried the dishes; repacked the food in the containers; stored the containers in locked trunks; and cleaned up my mess, the ceremony of preparing breakfast had brought me almost up to lunch time!

Eating three meals a day was simply out of the question. I solved the problem by eating a single meal that could be prepared in a single container, or, at most, in two containers, washed my dishes only when there were no clean ones left, using cold river water, and wore each change of clothing at least a week to cut down on my laundry problem—a courageous undertaking in the tropics. I reeked like a jockstrap that had been left to mildew in the bottom of some dark gym locker. I also became less concerned about sharing my provisions with the rats, insects, Yąnomamö, and the elements, thereby eliminating the need for my complicated storage process. I was able to last most of the day on *café con leche*, heavily sugared espresso coffee diluted about five to one with hot milk. I would prepare this in the evening and store it in a large thermos. Frequently, my single meal was no more complicated than a can of sardines and a package of soggy crackers. But at least two or three times a week I would do something "special" and sophisticated, like make a batch of oatmeal or boil rice and add a can of tuna fish or tomato paste to it. I even saved time by devising a water system that obviated the trips to the river. I had a few sheets of tin roofing brought in and made a rain water trap; I caught the water on the tin surface, funneled it into an empty gasoline drum, and then ran a plastic hose from the drum to my hut. When the drum was exhausted in the dry season, I would get a few Yąnomamö boys to fill it with buckets of water from the river, "paying" them with crackers, of which they grew all too fond all too soon.

I ate much less when I traveled with the Yąnomamö to visit other villages. Most of the time my travel diet consisted of roasted or boiled green plantains (cooking bananas) that I obtained from the Yąnomamö, but I always carried a few cans of sardines with me in case I got lost or stayed away longer than I had planned. I found peanut butter and crackers a very nourishing "trail" meal, and a simple one to prepare. It was nutritious and portable, and only one tool was required to make the meal: a hunting knife that could be cleaned by wiping the blade on a convenient leaf. More importantly, it was one of the few foods the Yąnomamö would let me eat in relative peace. It looked suspiciously like animal feces to them, an impression I encouraged. I referred to the peanut butter as the feces of babies or "cattle." They found this disgusting and repugnant. They did not know what "cattle" were, but were increasingly aware that I ate several canned products of such an animal. Tin cans were thought of as containers made of "machete skins," but how the cows got inside was always a mystery to them. I went out of my way to describe my foods in such a way as to make them sound unpalatable to them, for it gave me some peace of mind while I ate: They wouldn't beg for a share of something that was too horrible to contemplate. Fieldworkers develop strange defense mechanisms and strategies, and this was one of my own forms of adaptation to the field work. On another occasion I was eating a can of frankfurters and growing very weary of the demands from one of the onlookers for a share in my meal. When he finally asked what I was eating, I replied: "Beef." He then asked: "Shąki!"[4] What part of the animal are you eating?" To which I replied, "Guess." He muttered a contemptuous epithet, but stopped asking for a share. He got back at me later, as we shall see.

Meals were a problem in a way that had nothing to do with the inconvenience of preparing them. Food sharing is important to the Yąnomamö in the context of displaying friendship. "I am hungry!" is almost a form of greeting with them. I could not possibly have brought enough food with me to feed the entire village, yet they seemed to overlook this logistic fact as they begged for my food. What became fixed in their minds was the fact that I did not share my food with

---

4. They could not pronounce "Chagnon." It sounded to them like their name for a pesky bee, shąki, and that is what they called me: pesky, noisome bee.

whomsoever was present—usually a small crowd—at each and every meal. Nor could I easily enter their system of reciprocity with respect to food. Every time one of them "gave" me something "freely," he would dog me for months to "pay him back," not necessarily with food but with knives, fishhooks, axes, and so on. Thus, if I accepted a plantain from someone in a different village while I was on a visit, he would most likely visit me in the future and demand a machete as payment for the time that he "fed" me. I usually reacted to these kinds of demands by giving a banana, the customary reciprocity in their culture—food for food—but this would be a disappointment for the individual who had nursed visions of that single plantain growing into a machete over time. Many years after beginning my fieldwork, I was approached by one of the prominent men who demanded a machete for a piece of meat he claimed he had given me five or six years earlier.

Despite the fact that most of them knew I would not share my food with them at their request, some of them always showed up at my hut during mealtime. I gradually resigned myself to this and learned to ignore their persistent demands while I ate. Some of them would get angry because I failed to give in, but most of them accepted it as just a peculiarity of the subhuman foreigner who had come to live among them. If or when I did accede to a request for a share of my food, my hut quickly filled with Yąnomamö, each demanding their share of the food that I had just given to one of them. Their begging for food was not provoked by hunger, but by a desire to try something new and to attempt to establish a coercive relationship in which I would accede to a demand. If one received something, all others would immediately have to test the system to see if they, too, could coerce me.

A few of them went out of their way to make my meals downright unpleasant—to spite me for not sharing, especially if it was a food that they had tried before and liked, or a food that was part of their own cuisine. For example, I was eating a cracker with peanut butter and honey one day. The Yąnomamö will do almost anything for honey, one of the most prized delicacies in their own diet. One of my cynical onlookers—the fellow who had earlier watched me eating frankfurters—immediately recognized the honey and knew that I would not share the tiny precious bottle. It would be futile to even ask. Instead, he glared at me and queried icily, "Shąki! What kind of animal semen are you pouring onto your food and eating?" His question had the desired effect and my meal ended.

Finally, there was the problem of being lonely and separated from your own kind, especially your family. I tried to overcome this by seeking personal friendships among the Yąnomamö. This usually complicated the matter because all my "friends" simply used my confidence to gain privileged access to my hut and my cache of steel tools and trade goods—and looted me when I wasn't looking. I would be bitterly disappointed that my erstwhile friend thought no more of me than to finesse our personal relationship exclusively with the intention of getting at my locked-up possessions, and my depression would hit new lows every time I discovered this. The loss of possessions bothered me much less than the shock that I was, as far as most of them were concerned, nothing more than a source of desirable items. No holds were barred in relieving me of these, since I was considered something subhuman, a non-Yąnomamö.

The hardest thing to learn to live with was the incessant, passioned, and often aggressive demands they would make. It would become so unbearable at times that I would have to lock myself in my hut periodically just to escape from it. Privacy is one of our culture's most satisfying achievements, one you never think about until you suddenly have none. It is like not appreciating how good your left thumb feels until someone hits it with a hammer. But I did not want privacy for its own sake; rather, I simply had to get away from the begging. Day and night for almost the entire time I lived with the Yąnomamö I was plagued by such demands as: "Give me a knife, I am poor!"; "If you don't take me with you on your next trip to Widokaiya-teri, I'll chop a hole in your canoe!"; "Take us hunting up the Mavaca River with your shotgun or we won't help you!"; "Give me some matches so I can trade with the Reyaboböwei-teri, and be quick about it or I'll hit you!"; "Share your food with me, or I'll burn your hut!"; "Give me a flashlight so I can hunt at night!"; "Give me all your medicine, I itch all over!"; "Give me an ax or I'll break into your hut when you are away and steal all of them!" And so I was bombarded by such demands day after day, month after month, until I could not bear to see a Yąnomamö at times.

It was not as difficult to become calloused to the incessant begging as it was to ignore the sense of urgency, the impassioned tone of voice and whining, or the intimidation and aggression with which many of the demands were made. It was likewise difficult to adjust to the fact that the Yąnomamö refused to accept "No" for an answer until or unless it seethed with passion and intimidation— which it did after a few months. So persistent and characteristic is the begging that the early "semi-official" maps made by the Venezuelan Malaria Control Service (*Malarialogia*) designated the site of their first permanent field station, next to the village of Bisaasi-teri, as *Yababuhii*: "Gimme." I had to become like the Yąnomamö to be able to get along with them on their terms: somewhat sly, aggressive, intimidating, and pushy.

It became indelibly clear to me shortly after I arrived there that had I failed to adjust in this fashion I would have lost six months of supplies to them in a single day or would have spent most of my time ferrying them around in my canoe or taking them on long hunting trips. As it was, I did spend a considerable amount of time doing these things and did succumb often to their outrageous demands for axes and machetes, at least at first, for things changed as I became more fluent in their language and learned how to defend myself socially as well as verbally. More importantly, had I failed to demonstrate that I could not be pushed around beyond a certain point, I would have been the subject of far more ridicule, theft, and practical jokes than was the actual case. In short, I had to acquire certain proficiency in their style of interpersonal politics and learn how to imply subtly that certain potentially undesirable, but unspecified, consequences might follow if they did such and such to me. They do this to each other incessantly in order to establish precisely the point at which they cannot goad or intimidate an individual any further without precipitating some kind of retaliation. As soon as I realized this and gradually acquired the self-confidence to adopt this strategy, it became clear that much of the intimidation was calculated to determine my flash point or my "last ditch" position—and I got along much better with them. Indeed, I even regained some lost ground. It was sort of like a political, interpersonal game that everyone had to play, but one in which each individual sooner or later had to give evidence that his bluffs and implied threats could be backed up with a sanction. I suspect that the frequency of wife beating is a component in this syndrome, since men can display their *waited* (ferocity) and "show" others that they are capable of great violence. Beating a wife with a club is one way of displaying ferocity, one that does not expose the man to much danger—unless the wife has concerned, aggressive brothers in the village who will come to her aid. Apparently an important thing in wife beating is that the man has displayed his presumed potential for violence and the intended message is that other men ought to treat him with circumspection, caution, and even deference.

After six months, the level of Yąnomamö demand was tolerable in Bisaasi-teri, the village I used for my base of operations. We had adjusted somewhat to each other and knew what to expect with regard to demands for food, trade goods, and favors. Had I elected to remain in just one Yąnomamö village for the entire duration of my first 15 months of fieldwork, the experience would have been far more enjoyable than it actually was. However, as I began to understand the social and political dynamics of this village, it became patently obvious that I would have to travel to many other villages to determine the demographic bases and political histories that lay behind what I could understand in the village of Bisaasi-teri. I began making regular trips to some dozen neighboring Yąnomamö villages as my language fluency improved. I collected local genealogies there, or rechecked and cross-checked those I had collected elsewhere. Hence, the intensity of begging was relatively constant and relatively high for the duration of my fieldwork, for I had to establish my personal position in each village I visited and revisited.

For the most part, my own "fierceness" took the form of shouting back at the Yąnomamö as loudly and as passionately as they shouted at me, especially at first, when I did not know much of the language. As I became more fluent and learned more about their political tactics, I became more sophisticated in the art of bluffing and brinksmanship. For example, I paid one young man a machete (then worth about $2.50) to cut a palm tree and help me make boards from the wood. I used these to fashion a flooring in the bottom of my dugout canoe to keep my possessions out of the water that always seeped into the canoe and sloshed around. That afternoon I was working with one of my informants in the village. The long-awaited mission supply boat arrived and most of the Yąnomamö ran out of the village to see the supplies and try to beg items from the crew. I continued to work in the village for another hour or so and then went down to the river to visit with the men on the supply boat. When I reached the river I noticed, with anger and frustration, that the Yąnomamö had chopped up all my new floor boards to use as crude paddles to get their own canoes across the river to the supply boat.[5] I knew that if I ignored this abuse I would have invited the Yąnomamö to take even greater liberties with my possessions in the future. I got into my canoe, crossed the river, and docked amidst their flimsy, leaky craft. I shouted loudly to them, attracting their attention. They were somewhat sheepish, but all had mischievous grins on their impish faces. A few of them came down to the canoe, where I proceeded with a spirited lecture that revealed my anger at their audacity and license. I explained that I had just that morning paid one of them a machete for bringing me the palm wood, how hard I had worked to shape each board and place it in the canoe, how carefully and painstakingly I had tied each one in with vines, how much I had perspired, how many *bareto* bites I had suffered, and so on. Then, with exaggerated drama and finality, I withdrew my hunting knife as their grins disappeared and cut each one of their canoes loose and set it into the strong current of the Orinoco River where it was immediately swept up and carried downstream. I left without looking back and huffed over to the other side of the river to resume my work.

They managed to borrow another canoe and, after some effort, recovered their dugouts. Later, the headman of the village told me, with an approving chuckle, that I had done the correct thing. Everyone in the village, except, of course, the culprits, supported and defended my actions—and my status increased as a consequence.

Whenever I defended myself in such ways, I got along much better with the Yąnomamö and gradually acquired the respect of many of them. A good deal of their demeanor toward me was directed with the forethought of establishing the point at which I would draw the line and react defensively. Many of them, years later, reminisced about the early days of my fieldwork when I was timid and *mohode* ("stupid") and a little afraid of them, those golden days when it was easy to bully me into giving my goods away for almost nothing.

Theft was the most persistent situation that required some sort of defensive action. I simply could not keep everything I owned locked in trunks, and the Yąnomamö came into my hut and left at will. I eventually developed a very effective strategy for recovering almost all the stolen items: I would simply ask a child who took the item and then I would confiscate that person's hammock when he was not around, giving a spirited lecture to all who could hear on the antisociality of thievery as I stalked off in a faked rage with the thief's hammock slung over my shoulder. Nobody ever attempted to stop me from doing this, and almost all of them told me that my technique for recovering my possessions was ingenious. By nightfall the thief would appear at my hut with the stolen item or send it over with someone else to make an exchange to recover his hammock. He would be heckled by his covillagers for having been caught and for being

---

5. The Yąnomamö in this region acquired canoes very recently. The missionaries would purchase them from the Ye'kwana Indians in the north for money, and then trade them to the Yąnomamö in exchange for labor, produce, or "informant" work in translating. It should be emphasized that those Yąnomamö who lived on navigable portions of the Upper Orinoco River moved there recently from the deep forest in order to have contact with the missionaries and acquire the trade goods the missionaries (and their supply system) brought.

embarrassed into returning my item for his hammock. The explanation was usually, "I just borrowed your ax! I wouldn't think of stealing it!"

## Collecting Yąnomamö Genealogies and Reproductive Histories

My purpose for living among the Yąnomamö was to systematically collect certain kinds of information on genealogy, reproduction, marriage practices, kinship, settlement patterns, migrations, and politics. Much of the fundamental data was genealogical—who was the parent of whom, tracing these connections as far back in time as the Yąnomamö knowledge and memory permitted. Since "primitive" society is organized largely by kinship relationships, figuring out the social organization of the Yąnomamö essentially meant collecting extensive data on genealogies, marriage, and reproduction. This turned out to be a staggering and very frustrating problem. I could not have deliberately picked a more difficult people to work with in this regard. They have very stringent name taboos and eschew mentioning the names of prominent living people was well as all deceased friends and relatives. They attempt to name people in such a way that when the person dies and they can no longer use his or her name, the loss of the word in their language is not inconvenient. Hence, they name people for specific and minute parts of things, such as "toenail of sloth," "whisker of howler monkey," and so on, thereby being able to retain the words "toenail" or "whisker" but somewhat handicapped in referring to these anatomical parts of sloths and monkeys, respectively. The taboo is maintained even for the living, for one mark of prestige is the courtesy others show you by not using your name publicly. This is particularly true for men, who are much more competitive for status than women in this culture, and it is fascinating to watch boys grow into young men, demanding to be called either by a kinship term in public, or by a teknonymous reference such as "brother of Himotoma" (see Glossary). The more effective they are at getting others to avoid using their names, the more public acknowledgment there is that they are of high esteem and social standing. Helena Valero, a Brazilian woman who was captured as a child by a Yąnomamö raiding party, was married for many years to a Yąnomamö headman before she discovered what his name was (Biocca, 1970; Valero, 1984). The sanctions behind the taboo are more complex than just this, for they involve a combination of fear, respect, admiration, political deference, and honor.

At first I tried to use kinship terms alone to collect genealogies, but Yąnomamö kinship terms, like the kinship terms in all systems, are ambiguous at some point because they include so many possible relatives (as the term "uncle" does in our own kinship system). Again, their system of kin classification merges many relatives that we "separate" by using different terms: They call both their actual father and their father's brother by a single term, whereas we call one "father" and the other "uncle." I was forced, therefore, to resort to personal names to collect unambiguous genealogies or "pedigrees." They quickly grasped what I was up to and that I was determined to learn everyone's "true name," which amounted to an invasion of their system of prestige and etiquette, if not a flagrant violation of it. They reacted to this in a brilliant but devastating

manner: They invented false names for everybody in the village and systematically learned them, freely revealing to me the "true" identities of everyone.
I smugly thought I had cracked the system and enthusiastically constructed
elaborate genealogies over a period of some five months. They enjoyed watching
me learn their names and kinship relationships. I naively assumed that I would
get the "truth" to each question and the best information by working in public.
This set the stage for converting my serious project into an amusing hoax of the
grandest proportions. Each "informant" would try to outdo his peers by invent-
ing a name even more preposterous or ridiculous than what I had been given by
someone earlier, the explanations for discrepancies being "Well, he has two
names and this is the other one." They even fabricated devilishly improbable
genealogical relationships, such as someone being married to his grandmother,
or worse yet, to his mother-in-law, a grotesque and horrifying prospect to the
Yąnomamö. I would collect the desired names and relationships by having my
informant whisper the name of the person softly into my ear, noting that he or
she was the parent of such and such or the child of such and such, and so on.
Everyone who was observing my work would then insist that I repeat the name
aloud, roaring in hysterical laughter as I clumsily pronounced the name, sometimes laughing until tears streamed down their faces. The "named" person would
usually react with annoyance and hiss some untranslatable epithet at me, which
served to reassure me that I had the "true" name. I conscientiously checked and
rechecked the names and relationships with multiple informants, pleased to see
the inconsistencies disappear as my genealogy sheets filled with those desirable
little triangles and circles, thousands of them.

My anthropological bubble was burst when I visited a village about 10
hours' walk to the southwest of Bisaasi-teri some five months after I had begun
collecting genealogies on the Bisaasi-teri. I was chatting with the local headman
of this village and happened to casually drop the name of the wife of the
Bisaasi-teri headman. A stunned silence followed, and then a villagewide roar
of uncontrollable laughter, choking, gasping, and howling followed. It seems that
I thought the Bisaasi-teri headman was married to a woman named "hairy cunt."
It also seems that the Bisaasi-teri headman was called "long dong" and his brother
"eagle shit." The Bisaasi-teri headman had a son called "asshole" and a daughter
called "fart breath."

And so on. Blood welled up to my temples as I realized that I had nothing
but nonsense to show for my five months of dedicated genealogical effort, and
I had to throw away almost all the information I had collected on this the most
basic set of data I had come there to get. I understood at that point why the
Bisaasi-teri laughed so hard when they made me repeat the names of their
covillagers, and why the "named" person would react with anger and annoyance
as I pronounced his "name" aloud.

I was forced to change research strategy—to make an understatement to
describe this serious situation. The first thing I did was to begin working in private with my informants to eliminate the horseplay and distraction that attended
public sessions. Once I did this, my informants, who did not know what others
were telling me, began to agree with each other and I managed to begin learning

the "real" names, starting first with children and gradually moving to adult women and then, cautiously, to adult men, a sequence that reflected the relative degree of intransigence at revealing names of people. As I built up a core of accurate genealogies and relationships—a core that all independent informants had verified repetitiously—I could "test" any new informant by soliciting his or her opinion and knowledge about these "core" people whose names and relationships I was confident were accurate. I was, in this fashion, able to immediately weed out the mischievous informants who persisted in trying to deceive me. Still, I had great difficulty getting the names of dead kinsmen, the only accurate way to extend genealogies back in time. Even my best informants continued to falsify names of the deceased, especially closely related deceased. The falsifications at this point were not serious and turned out to be readily corrected as my interviewing methods improved (see below). Most of the deceptions were of the sort where the informant would give me the name of a living man as the father of some child whose actual father was dead, a response that enabled the informant to avoid using the name of a deceased kinsman or friend.

The quality of a genealogy depends in part on the number of generations it embraces, and the name taboo prevented me from making any substantial progress in learning about the deceased ancestors of the present population. Without this information, I could not, for example, document marriage patterns and interfamilial alliances through time. I had to rely on older informants for this information, but these were the most reluctant informants of all for this data. As I became more proficient in the language and more skilled at detecting fabrications, my informants became better at deception. One old man was particularly cunning and persuasive, following a sort of Mark Twain policy that the most effective lie is a sincere lie. He specialized in making a ceremony out of false names for dead ancestors. He would look around nervously to make sure nobody was listening outside my hut, enjoin me never to mention the name again, become very anxious and spooky, and grab me by the head to whisper a secret name into my ear. I was always elated after a session with him because I managed to add several generations of ancestors for particular members of the village. Others steadfastly refused to give me such information. To show my gratitude, I paid him quadruple the rate that I had been paying the others. When word got around that I had increased the pay for genealogical and demographic information, volunteers began pouring into my hut to "work" for me, assuring me of their changed ways and keen desire to divest themselves of the "truth."

### Enter Rerebawä: Inmarried Tough Guy

I discovered that the old man was lying quite by accident. A club fight broke out in the village one day, the result of a dispute over the possession of a woman. She had been promised to a young man in the village, a man named Rerebawä, who was particularly aggressive. He had married into Bisaasi-teri and was doing his "bride service"—a period of several years during which he had to provide game for his wife's father and mother, provide them with wild foods he might collect, and help them in certain gardening and other tasks. Rerebawä had already been given one of the daughters in marriage and was promised her younger sister as his second wife. He was enraged when the younger sister, then about 16 years old, began having an affair with another young man in the village, Bäkotawä, and making no attempt to conceal it. Rerebawä challenged Bäkotawä to a club fight. He swaggered boisterously out to the duel with his 10-foot-long club, a roof-pole he had cut from the house on the spur of the moment, as is the usual procedure. He hurled insult after insult at both Bäkotawä and his father, trying to goad them into a fight. His insults were bitter and nasty. They tolerated them for a few moments, but Rerebawä's biting insults provoked them to rage. Finally, they stormed angrily out of their hammocks and ripped out roof-poles, now returning the insults verbally, and rushed to the village clearing. Rerebawä continued to insult them, goading them into striking him on the head with their equally long clubs. Had either of them struck his head—which he held out conspicuously for them to swing at—he would then have the right to take his turn on their heads with his club. His opponents were intimidated by his fury, and simply backed down, refusing to strike him, and the argument ended. He had intimidated them into submission. All three retired pompously to their respective hammocks, exchanging nasty insults as they departed. But Rerebawä had won the showdown and thereafter swaggered around the village, insulting the two men behind their backs at every opportunity. He was genuinely angry with them, to the point of calling the older man by the name of his long-deceased father. I quickly seized on this incident as an opportunity to collect an accurate genealogy and confidentially asked Rerebawä about his adversary's ancestors. Rerebawä had been particularly "pushy" with me up to this point, but we soon became warm friends and staunch allies: We were both "outsiders" in Bisaasi-teri and, although he was a Yąnomamö, he nevertheless had to put up with some considerable amount of pointed teasing and scorn from the locals, as all inmarried "sons-in-law" must (Figure 1.5). He gave me the information I requested of his adversary's deceased ancestors, almost with devilish glee. I asked about dead ancestors of other people in the village and got prompt, unequivocal answers: He was angry with everyone in the village. When I compared his answers to those of the old man, it was obvious that one of them was lying. I then challenged his answers. He explained, in a sort of "you damned fool, don't you know better?" tone of voice that everyone in the village knew the old man was lying to me and gloating over it when I was out of earshot. The names the old man had given to me were names of dead ancestors of the members of a village so far away that he thought I would never have occasion to check them out authoritatively. As it turned out, Rerebawä knew most of the people in that distant village and recognized the names given by the old man.

I then went over all my Bisaasi-teri genealogies with Rerebawä, genealogies I had presumed to be close to their final form. I had to revise them all because of the numerous lies and falsifications they contained, much of it provided by the sly old man. Once again, after months of work, I had to recheck everything with Rerebawä's aid. Only the living members of the nuclear families turned out to be accurate; the deceased ancestors were mostly fabrications.

**F I G U R E   1.5**   Rerebawä, one of the author's closest friends and a constant companion on long trips into remote villages.

Discouraging as it was to have to recheck everything all over again, it was a major turning point in my fieldwork. Thereafter, I began taking advantage of local arguments and animosities in selecting my informants, and used more extensively those informants who had married into the village in the recent past. I also began traveling more regularly to other villages at this time to check on genealogies, seeking out villages whose members were on strained terms with the people about whom I wanted information. I would then return to my base in the village of Bisaasi-teri and check with local informants the accuracy of the new information. I had to be careful in this work and scrupulously select my local informants in such a way that I would not be inquiring about *their* closely related kin. Thus, for each of my local informants, I had to make lists of names of certain deceased people that I dared not mention in their presence. But despite this precaution, I would occasionally hit a new name that would put some informants into a rage, or into a surly mood, such as that of a dead "brother" or "sister"[6] whose existence had

---

6. Rarely were these actual brothers or sisters. In Yąnomamö kinship classifications, certain kinds of cousins are classified as siblings. See Chapter 4.

not been indicated to me by other informants. This usually terminated my day's work with that informant, for he or she would be too touchy or upset to continue any further, and I would be reluctant to take a chance on accidentally discovering another dead close kinsman soon after discovering the first.

These were unpleasant experiences, and occasionally dangerous as well, depending on the temperament of my informant. On one occasion I was planning to visit a village that had been raided recently by one of their enemies. A woman, whose name I had on my census list for that village, had been killed by the raiders. Killing women is considered to be a bad form in Yąnomamö warfare, but this woman was deliberately killed for revenge. The raiders were unable to bushwhack some man who stepped out of the village at dawn to urinate, so they shot a volley of arrows over the roof into the village and beat a hasty retreat. Unfortunately, one of the arrows struck and killed a woman, an accident. For that reason, her village's raiders *deliberately* sought out and killed a woman in retaliation—whose name was on my list. My reason for going to the village was to update my census data on a name-by-name basis and estimate the ages of all the residents. I knew I had the name of the dead woman in my list, but nobody would dare to utter her name so I could remove it. I knew that I would be in very serious trouble if I got to the village and said her name aloud, and I desperately wanted to remove it from my list. I called on one of my regular and usually cooperative informants and asked him to tell me the woman's name. He refused adamantly, explaining that she was a close relative—and was angry that I even raised the topic with him. I then asked him if he would let me whisper the names of *all* the women of that village in his ear, and he would simply have to nod when I hit the right name. We had been "friends" for some time, and I thought I was able to predict his reaction, and thought that our friendship was good enough to use this procedure. He agreed to the procedure, and I began whispering the names of the women, one by one. We were alone in my hut so that nobody would know what we were doing and nobody could hear us. I read the names softly, continuing to the next when his response was a negative. When I ultimately hit the dead woman's name, he flew out of his chair, enraged and trembling violently, his arm raised to strike me: "You son-of-a-bitch!", he screamed, "If you say her name in my presence again, I'll kill you in an instant!" I sat there, bewildered, shocked, and confused. And frightened, as much because of his reaction as because I could imagine what might happen to me should I unknowingly visit a village to check genealogy accuracy without knowing that someone had just died there or had been shot by raiders since my last visit. I reflected on the several articles I had read as a graduate student that explained the "genealogical method," but could not recall anything about it being a potentially lethal undertaking. My furious informant left my hut, never again to be invited back to be an informant. I had other similar experiences in different villages, but I was always fortunate in that the dead person had been dead for some time, or was not very closely related to the individual into whose ear I whispered the forbidden name. I was usually cautioned by one of the men to desist from saying any more names lest I get people "angry."[7]

## Kạobawä: The Bisaasi-teri Headman Volunteers to Help Me

I had been working on the genealogies for nearly a year when another individual came to my aid. It was Kạobawä, the headman of Upper Bisaasi-teri. The village of Bisaasi-teri was split into two components, each with its own garden and own circular house. Both were in sight of each other. However, the intensity and frequency of internal bickering and argumentation was so high that they decided to split into two separate groups but remain close to each other for protection in case they were raided. One group was downstream from the other; I refer to that group as the "Lower" Bisaasi-teri and call Kạobawä's group "Upper" (upstream) Bisaasi-teri, a convenience they themselves adopted after separating from each other. I spent most of my time with the members of Kạobawä's group, some 200 people when I first arrived there. I did not have much contact with Kạobawä during the early months of my work. He was a somewhat retiring, quiet man, and among the Yạnomamö, the outsider has little time to notice the rare quiet ones when almost everyone else is in the front row, pushing and demanding attention. He showed up at my hut one day after all the others had left. He had come to volunteer to help me with the genealogies. He was "poor," he explained, and needed a machete. He would work only on the condition that I did not ask him about his own parents and other very close kinsmen who had died. He also added that he would not lie to me as the others had done in the past.

This was perhaps the single most important event in my first 15 months of field research, for out of this fortuitous circumstance evolved a very warm friendship, and among the many things following from it was a wealth of accurate information on the political history of Kạobawä's village and related villages, highly detailed genealogical information, sincere and useful advise to me, and hundreds of valuable insights into the Yạnomamö way of life. Kạobawä's familiarity with his group's history and his candidness were remarkable (Figure 1.6). His knowledge of details was almost encyclopedic, his memory almost photographic. More than that, he was enthusiastic about making sure I learned the truth, and he encouraged me, indeed, *demanded* that I learn all details I might otherwise have ignored. If there were subtle details he could not recite on the spot, he would advise me to wait until he could check things out with someone else in the village. He would often do this clandestinely, giving me a report the next day, telling me who revealed the new information and whether or not he thought they were in a position to know it. With the information provided by

---

7. Over time, as I became more and more "accepted" by the Yạnomamö, they became less and less concerned about my genealogical inquiries and, now, provide me with this information quite willingly because I have been very discrete with it. Now, when I revisit familiar villages I am called aside by someone who whispers to me things like, "Don't ask about so-and-so's father."

**FIGURE 1.6**
Kąobawä, the headman,
alert for any telltale sign
from the forest.

Kąobawä and Rerebawä, I made enormous gains in understanding village inter-relationships based on common ancestors and political histories and became life-long friends with both. And both men knew that I had to learn about his recently deceased kin from the other one. It was one of those quiet understandings we all had but none of us could mention.

Once again I went over the genealogies with Kąobawä to recheck them, a considerable task by this time. They included about 2,000 names, representing several generations of individuals from four different villages. Rerebawä's information was very accurate, and Kąobawä's contribution enabled me to trace the genealogies further back in time. Thus, after nearly a year of intensive effort on genealogies, Yąnomamö demographic patterns and social organization began to make a good deal of sense to me. Only at this point did the patterns through time begin to emerge in the data, and I could begin to understand how kinship groups took form, exchanged women in marriage over several generations, and only then did the fissioning of larger villages into smaller ones emerge as a chronic and important feature of Yąnomamö social, political, demographic, economic, and ecological adaptation. At this point I was able to begin formulating more sophisticated questions, for there was now a pattern to work from and one to flesh out.

Without the help of Rerebawä and Kąobawä it would have taken much longer to make sense of the plethora of details I had collected from not only them, but dozens of other informants as well.

I spent a good deal of time with these two men and their families, and got to know them much better than I knew most Yąnomamö. They frequently gave their information in a way which related them to the topic under discussion. We became warm friends as time passed, and the formal "informant/anthropologist" relationship faded into the background. Eventually, we simply stopped "keeping track" of work and pay. They would both spend hours talking with me, leaving without asking for anything. When they wanted something, they would ask for it no matter what the relative balance of reciprocity between us might have been at that point. I will speak of both of them—and their respective families—frequently in the following chapters, using them as "examples" of life in Yąnomamö culture. For many of the customary things that anthropologists try to communicate about another culture, these two men and their families might be considered to be "exemplary" or "typical." For other things, they are exceptional in many regards, but the reader will, even knowing some of the exceptions, understand Yąnomamö culture more intimately by being familiar with a few examples.

Kąobawä was about 40 years old when I first came to his village in 1964. I say "about 40" because the Yąnomamö numeration system has only three numbers: one, two, and more-than-two. It is hard to give accurate ages or dates for events when the informants have no means in their language to reveal such detail. Kąobawä is the headman of his village, meaning that he has some-what more responsibility in political dealings with other Yąnomamö groups, and very little control over those who live in his group except when the village is being raided by enemies. We will learn more about political leadership and war-fare in a later chapter, but most of the time men like Kąobawä are like the North American Indian "chief" whose authority was characterized in the following fashion: "One word from the chief, and each man does as he pleases." There are different "styles" of political leadership among the Yąnomamö. Some leaders are mild, quiet, inconspicuous most of the time, but intensely competent. They act parsimoniously, but when they do, people listen and conform. Other men are more tyrannical, despotic, pushy, flamboyant, and unpleasant to all around them. They shout orders frequently, are prone to wife-beating, or pick on weaker men. Some are very violent. I have met headmen who run the entire spectrum between these polar types, for I have visited some 60 Yąnomamö villages. Kąobawä stands at the mild, quietly competent end of the spectrum. He has had six wives thus far—and temporary affairs with as many more, at least one of which resulted in a child that is publicly acknowledged as his child. When I first met him he had just two wives: Bahimi and Koamashima. Bahimi (Figure 1.1) had two living children when I first met her; many others had died. She was the older and enduring wife, as much a friend to him as a mate. Their relationship was as close to what we think of as "love" in our culture as I have seen among the Yąnomamö (Figure 1.7). His second wife was a girl of about 20 years, Koamashima. She had a new baby boy when I first met her, her first child (Figure 1.8). There was speculation that Kąobawä was planning to give

**FIGURE 1.7** Kąobawä and his oldest and favorite wife, Bahimi. She is his mother's brother's daughter.

Koamashima to one of his younger brothers who had no wife; he occasionally allows his younger brother to have sex with Koamashima, but only if he asks in advance. Kąobawä gave another wife to one of his other brothers because she was *beshi* ("horny"). In fact, this earlier wife had been married to two other men, both of whom discarded her because of her infidelity. Kąobawä had one daughter by her. However, the girl is being raised by Kąobawä's brother, though acknowledged to be Kąobawä's child.

Bahimi, his oldest wife, is about five years younger than him. She is his cross-cousin (see Glossary)—his mother's brother's daughter. Ideally, all Yąnomamö men should marry a cross-cousin, as we shall discuss in a later chapter. Bahimi was pregnant when I began my fieldwork, but she destroyed the infant when it was born—a boy in this case—explaining tearfully that she had no choice. The new baby would have competed for milk with Ariwari, her youngest child, who was still nursing. Rather than expose Ariwari to the dangers and uncertainty of an early weaning, she chose to terminate the newborn instead. By Yąnomamö standards, this has been a very warm, enduring marriage. Kąobawä claims he beats Bahimi only "once in a while, and only lightly" and she, for her part, never has affairs with other men.

Kąobawä is a quiet, intense, wise, and unobtrusive man. It came as something of a surprise to me when I learned that he was the headman of his village,

**FIGURE 1.8**
Koamashima, one
of Kạobawä's younger
wives, with her first child.
Because of her youth,
she enjoys his favor
more regularly.

for he stayed at the sidelines while others would surround me and press their demands on me. He leads more by example than by coercion. He can afford to be this way at his age, for he established his reputation for being forthright and as fierce as the situation required when he was younger, and the other men respect him. He also has five mature brothers or half-brothers in his village, men he can count on for support. He also has several other mature "brothers" (parallel cousins, whom he must refer to as "brothers" in his kinship system) in the village who frequently come to his aid, but not as often as his "real" brothers do. Kạobawä has also given a number of his sisters to other men in the village and has promised his young (eight-year-old) daughter in marriage to a young man who, for that reason, is obliged to help him. In short, his "natural" or "kinship" following is large, and partially because of this support, he does not have to display his aggressiveness to remind his peers of his position.

Rerebawä is a very different kind of person. He is much younger—perhaps in his early twenties (Figure 1.5). He has just one wife, but they have already had three children. He is from a village called Karohi-teri, located about five hours' walk up the Orinoco, slightly inland off to the east of the river itself. Kạobawä's village enjoys amicable relationships with Rerebawä's, and it is for this reason that marriage alliances of the kind represented by Rerebawä's marriage into Kąobawä's village occur between the two groups. Rerebawä told me that he came to Bisaasi-teri because there were no eligible women for him to marry in his own village, a fact that I was later able to document when I did a census of his village and a preliminary analysis of its social organization. Rerebawä is perhaps more typical than Kąobawä in the sense that he is chronically concerned about his personal reputation for aggressiveness and goes out of his way to be noticed, even if he has to act tough. He gave me a hard time during my early months of fieldwork, intimidating, teasing, and insulting me frequently. He is, however, much braver than the other men his age and is quite prepared to back up his threats with immediate action—as in the club fight incident just described above. Moreover, he is fascinated with political relationships and knows the details of intervillage relationships over a large area of the tribe. In this respect he shows all the attributes of being a headman, although he has too many competent brothers in his own village to expect to move easily into the leadership position there.

He does not intend to stay in Kąobawä's group and refuses to make his own garden—a commitment that would reveal something of an intended long-term residence. He feels that he has adequately discharged his obligations to his wife's parents by providing them with fresh game, which he has done for several years. They should let him take his wife and return to his own village with her, but they refuse and try to entice him to remain permanently in Bisaasi-teri to continue to provide them with game when they are old. It is for this reason that they promised to give him their second daughter, their only other child, in marriage. Unfortunately, the girl was opposed to the marriage and ultimately married another man, a rare instance where the woman in the marriage had this much influence on the choice of her husband.

Although Rerebawä has displayed his ferocity in many ways, one incident in particular illustrates what his character can be like. Before he left his own village to take his new wife in Bisaasi-teri, he had an affair with the wife of an older brother. When it was discovered, his brother attacked him with a club. Rerebawä responded furiously: He grabbed an ax and drove his brother out of the village after soundly beating him with the blunt side of the single-bit ax. His brother was so intimidated by the thrashing and promise of more to come that he did not return to the village for several days. I visited this village with Kąobawä shortly after this event had taken place; Rerebawä was with me as my guide. He made it a point to introduce me to this man. He approached his hammock, grabbed him by the wrist, and dragged him out on the ground: "This is the brother whose wife I screwed when he wasn't around!" A deadly insult, one that would usually provoke a bloody club fight among a more valiant Yąnomamö. The man did nothing. He slunk sheepishly back into his hammock, shamed, but relieved to have Rerebawä release his grip.

Even though Rerebawä is fierce and capable of considerable nastiness, he has a charming, witty side as well. He has a biting sense of humor and can entertain the group for hours with jokes and clever manipulations of language. And, he is one of few Yąnomamö that I feel I can trust. I recall indelibly my return to Bisaasi-teri after being away a year—the occasion of my second field trip to the Yąnomamö. When I reached Bisaasi-teri, Rerebawä was in his own village visiting his kinsmen. Word reached him that I had returned, and he paddled downstream immediately to see me. He greeted me with an immense bear hug and exclaimed, with tears welling up in his eyes, "Shąki! Why did you stay away so long? Did you not know that my will was so cold while you were gone that I could not at times eat for want of seeing you again?" I, too, felt the same way about him—then, and now.

Of all the Yąnomamö I know, he is the most genuine and the most devoted to his culture's ways and values. I admire him for that, although I cannot say that I subscribe to or endorse some of these values. By contrast, Kąobawä is older and wiser, a polished diplomat. He sees his own culture in a slightly different light and seems even to question aspects of it. Thus, while many of his peers enthusiastically accept the "explanations" of things given in myths, he occasionally reflects on them—even laughing at some of the more preposterous of them (see, for example, the humor in his skepticism as he tells the myth of "Naro" in the film described in the film list at the end of this book). Probably more of the Yąnomamö are like Rerebawä than like Kąobawä, or at least try to be.

## BEYOND THE BISAASI-TERI AND INTO THE REMOTE VILLAGES

As my work progressed with Kąobawä, Rerebawä, and many other informants, a very important scientific problem began to emerge, one that could be solved only by going to visit many distant Yąnomamö villages to collect genealogies, demographic data, and local histories from the people there. But the fieldwork required to solve the scientific question led to some exciting and even dangerous adventures, for it meant contacting totally unknown Yąnomamö—people who had never before seen foreigners. The "first contact" with a primitive society is a phenomenon that is less and less likely to happen, for the world is shrinking and "unknown" tribes or villages are now very rare. In fact, our generation is probably the last that will have the opportunity to know what it is like to make first contact. For this reason, I include a description of what one such situation was like, put into the context of the scientific reasons for going into the unknown Yąnomamö area.

### The Scientific Problem That Emerged

It became increasingly clear that each Yąnomamö village was a "recent" colony or splinter group of some larger village, and a fascinating set of patterns—and problems—began to emerge. I could see that there were cause-effect relationships among a number of variables. These included village size, genealogical composition of villages, age and sex distributions, ecological and geographic variables, and marriage ties or "alliances" between "families." Moreover, it became abundantly clear that intervillage warfare was an indelible force that affected village size and village distribution—how large villages got to be before they would "fission" and divide into two groups, and where the newly created groups would move as they avoided their old enemies, attempted to get away from those they had just separated from, or sought new allies in distant places. I will discuss the details of this problem in a later chapter, but the simple discovery of the pattern had a marked influence on my fieldwork: It meant that I would have to travel to many villages in order to document the genealogical aspects of the pattern, take detailed censuses, collect local versions of "historical truth" from all parties concerned, and map as best I could the locations of existing villages and locations of sites that they had abandoned in the recent past, sometimes penetrating new, virgin, unknown forest as pioneers on the expanding front of their population. What was exciting about this was the formal and ecological similarity that it suggested during the early centuries of the discovery of agriculture, and how our own ancestors in Eurasia and Africa spread agriculture into new lands, lands formerly inhabited by hunters and gatherers, or lands that had never been occupied.

Getting to some of these new villages turned out to be a staggering problem for a number of reasons. First, I was living in Bisaasi-teri, and old wars and current animosities prevented me from easily recruiting trustworthy guides who were politically able to visit some of the distant villages, or if able, willing to. Second, I had to deal with the political pressures put on any of my guides by the older men in the village, who would have much preferred to have me dispense all my goods and gifts in *their* village and not take them inland to other Yąnomamö. Some of the older men went to great lengths to sabotage my plans to visit other villages, putting pressure on my guides to back out or to cause me to turn back once started. Third, some of the villages were at a great distance and their precise locations to my guides unknown: They were uncontacted villages many days by trail away, and usually bitter, mortal enemies of the Bisaasi-teri among whom I lived—and with whom I was somewhat identified by Yąnomamö in all surrounding villages. My first year's research, which unraveled many details of previous wars, killings and treachery, convinced me that the Bisaasi-teri were justified in holding very caustic, hostile attitudes toward some of their distant neighbors, particularly members of villages that they collectively referred to as "the Shamatari." The Shamatari, to the Bisaasi-teri, were a congeries of many interrelated villages to the south, some of which had a long history of bitter warfare with the Bisaasi-teri. All the Shamatari villages were related to each other and had come into existence as larger villages fissioned into smaller ones, grew, fissioned again, and occupied new lands, moving in a general direction from northeast to southwest (see maps in Chapter 2). Two of the closest "Shamatari" villages lay immediately to the south of the Bisaasi-teri, and I visited both of them on foot my first year in the field—a 10-hour walk to the closest one, a two-day walk to the more distant one. These two groups were on somewhat friendly terms with the Bisaasi-teri, and a number of intermarriages had recently taken place between them. They were Kąobawä's allies, but a good deal of mutual suspicion and occasional expressions of contempt also marked their relationships.

Far to the south and southeast of these two Shamatari villages lay other Shamatari villages, mortal enemies to the Bisaasi-teri. It became clear to me, as my genealogical, demographic, and settlement pattern histories accumulated, that I would have to visit them. They had never before seen outsiders and the Bisaasi-teri chronically advised me about their treachery and viciousness, particularly Kąobawä and Rerebawä, who genuinely had my personal safety at heart.

The group of Shamatari I wanted to reach on my initial foray into this region was known to the Bisaasi-teri as "Sibararíwä's" village, Sibararíwä being the headman of the village and a man who was hated by all of Bisaasi-teri for engineering a treachery that led to the deaths of many of Bisaasi-teri, including Kąobawä's father (see Prologue). Sibararíwä was *waiteri* and had a reputation for aggressiveness in many villages, even in villages whose members had never met him or members of his village.

The first attempt I made to contact Sibararíwä's village was in 1966, near the end of my first field trip. It was unsuccessful primarily because my young guides, three in number, forced me to turn back. Two were from Bisaasi-teri and the third was from one of the friendly Shamatari villages, Mǫmaribǫwei-teri, a 10-hour walk away. We ascended the Mavaca River for about two days, chopping our way through large trees and tons of brush that clogged the river and made canoe passage very difficult. The river had not been ascended that far up in many years, perhaps 75 years if the historical sources reveal any clues (Rice, 1921). The last adventurers ran into hostile Yąnomamö, and some died at their hands (Rice, 1921). Apparently my young guides banked on the assumption that the hardships would discourage me and I would give up. Much to their consternation, I refused to turn back and, on the third day's travel, we began running into fresh signs that Shamatari hunters or travelers had recently crossed the Mavaca. We found their flimsy foot bridges made of poles and vines. These signs began to worry my guides as we ran into more and more of them. By that night they were adamantly opposed to going any further and even refused to sleep at the place where I had pulled in the canoe: It turned out to be right on a recently traveled trail, a trail that my young guides concluded was used only by raiders. Angered, I had no choice but to go back downstream to a location more suitable to them. We left for home, Bisaasi-teri, the next morning, and on reaching it, I was pressed for the payment I originally promised to my guides. I was reluctant to pay them because they forced me to turn back, and when I asked them why they agreed to guide me in the first place, they responded: "For the machetes you promised to us! We *never* thought we would get to the Shamatari!"

It was too late that year to make another attempt. On my next field trip I tried again to reach Sibararíwä's village. This time I chose my guides more carefully, or at least that was my plan. I picked an older man whose name translates into "Piranha." He was from a village far to the north and had married into Kąobawä's village recently. Thus, he had no personal reasons to either fear the Shamatari or be despised by them, but he *was* from Kąobawä's village at this point and that might be taken with hostility by the Shamatari. The other guide

I picked was just a kid, a boy named Karina. I had met him briefly the year before, when he and his mother straggled into the village of Mömariböwei-teri, the Shamatari village 10 hours' walk south of Kąobawä's. He and his mother had been abducted by Sibariwä's group some 10 years earlier, so Karina had grown up, to the extent he was grown at all, in Sibariwä's village and knew all the current residents. He had been terrified at the sight of me—his first glimpse of a non-Yąnomamö—the year before (Figure 1.9), but several visits to Kąobawä's village exposed him to the missionaries there and he gradually lost his fear of foreigners. Still, he was only about 12 or 13 years old. This, actually, was an advantage in one respect: He was still innocent enough to give me the accurate names and shallow genealogies of all the residents of Sibariwä's village before I had even reached it.

The first attempt in 1968 ended when I discovered that all my "gasoline" had been stolen and replaced with water, a common problem in the Upper Orinoco where gasoline is scarce, has to be hauled in by an eight-day river trip, and filched by all who come in contact with it at every step of the way,

**FIGURE 1.9** Karina, my young guide when I first met him—a year before he led me into Shamatari country.

including the very people you paid to bring it to you. We had gotten far up the Mavaca when I switched to one of my reserve gasoline tanks and the motor died—the tanks were full of plain water. We thus had to return to Bisaasi-teri where my gasoline supplies were stored and where I could dismantle my motor and spend the night cleaning it.

We set off again the next morning with fresh gasoline supplies and again were high up the Mavaca when I switched to one of my reserve tanks. This time it wasn't water, but it wasn't gasoline either. It was kerosene. Back down the Mavaca again, clean the engine again, and set off again. By this time—four or five days after starting the first trip—my guides were growing impatient and weary. My older guide failed to show up at dawn as agreed, and Karina, the 12-year-old, was feeling ill and didn't want to go. I persuaded Karina that he would feel better in a day and he decided to come with me again.

He was my only guide at this point. I sat in my canoe, tired and depressed, wondering if I should try to make it with just a 12-year-old guide. It was a murky, dismal dawn. I hadn't slept more than a few hours each night, for I had to dismantle and reassemble my outboard motor each time we floated back home, a task I had to do at night to save time to assure my waning guides that we would make progress. As I sat there, half ready to throw in the towel, a young man, Bäkotawä, appeared at the river to take an early bath. He was the young man that Rerebawä had challenged to the club fight over the possession of Rerebawä's wife's younger sister. He knew that my other guide had backed out and that I was down to just one. I asked him if he would be willing to go with me to Sibarariwä's village. He thought about it for a moment. "I'm a Bisaasi-teri, and they might kill me," he said, adding "... but I could tell them that I'm really a Patanowä-teri and they wouldn't know the difference." I turned to Karina, who lay whimpering in the canoe in the most comfortable "bed" I could arrange, using my pack and gasoline tanks as props. "Would you vouch for him if he said he was a Patanowä-teri?" I asked. He grunted, unenthusiastically, that he'd go along with the deception and agreed that it was better than being a Bisaasi-teri. At that, we agreed that Bäkotawä would be my second guide. He rushed off to the *shabono* (village) to collect his hammock and a few items to trade, and returned a few minutes later, ready for the great adventure into unknown lands where his older kin feared to tread. I brought along a second shotgun that I said he could "use" (he didn't know which end to put the cartridges in), and this pleased him immensely, not to mention bolstering his confidence.

We thus set off for the headwaters of the Mavaca in my large wooden dugout canoe, on top of which I carried a smaller, lighter aluminum boat for negotiating the high Mavaca where the big boat could not get through. My plan was to go as far in the bigger, heavier boat as we could, dropping off gasoline and other stores along the way for the trip back.

The dry season was at its peak and the rivers were very low, so low that we only made it about a day and a half upstream in the larger canoe before reaching an insurmountable obstacle: two very large trees had fallen across the river and were half submerged. They were there before, but the water was high enough that I managed to get the canoe across them. But the river had dropped since then. They were too thick to chop through with axes, and too much of the trunks was above the water to permit the three of us to horse the heavy dugout over. We thus had to leave the big canoe at that point, transfer everything to the smaller aluminum boat, and set off, badly overloaded, for the headwaters of the Mavaca. Karina was feeling normal again. He began goading Bäkotawä, asking rhetorically, "What would they do if they knew you were really a Bisaasi-teri? Maybe I might slip and tell them that you are Bisaasi-teri." Bäkotawä grew silent, then moody, then visibly nervous. On the third day, Karina rose up to his knees, began looking intently at the river banks on both sides, and then exclaimed: "I know this place! We're getting close to Sibarariwä's village! Their trail to Iwähikoroba-teri is just a short way off the river, over there!" as he pointed to the east bank of the tangled, narrow river—a stream so small at this point that it would have been difficult to turn our boat around without lifting it most of the way. We proceeded a few hours further upstream, slowly, because the river was both shallow and narrow, but mostly because it was now choked with deadfalls and branches through which we had to constantly chop our way.

We pulled over at about midday and dragged the boat up a bank after unloading the supplies. We would walk inland from this point, for the river was now too narrow to proceed any further. We were in a hilly region and could catch glimpses of relatively high peaks, all covered with dense vegetation and punctuated with scraggy outcroppings of rocks. We were in the headwaters of the Mavaca, and beyond the stark ridge ahead of us lay the almost legendary Shukumöna kä u, the River of Parakeets and homeland of the Shamatari—and the lair of the legendary Sibarariwä and his warriors.[8]

I divided the supplies into those we would take inland with us and those we would leave behind for the return trip. As I did, I was alarmed at the relatively small amount of food we had at that point. In my concern over gasoline and sputtering motors, I had failed to restock the food after each aborted trip. There was enough for several days, but if we failed to contact the Shamatari, we would have to ration ourselves carefully.

Karina said the village was to the southeast, indicating the distance as Yąnomamö always do, by pointing to where the sun would be if we left now and where it would be when we reached the village. It was about a four- or five-hour walk by his description, and it meant that we would reach the village just before dark—not a good thing to do on a first contact. Even the Yąnomamö like to have as much daylight as they can get when they visit a strange village. That way, you have time to make friends and assess the situation. We set off with our back packs at about 2:00 P.M. and soon began running into fresh signs of human activity—footprints made a day before, husks of palm fruits,

---

8. At this time in my fieldwork the Shukumöna Kä u, that is, the Siapa River, was not even correctly shown on official maps of Venezuela. Its true location and course was not "officially" established until 1972 when aerial radar maps of the region were developed. Most maps, prior to that, incorrectly showed the headwaters of the Mavaca River as the Siapa River.

discarded items of no value, broken twigs where someone cleared the trail as he proceeded along it, and so on. My heart began to pound, for clearly we were close to Sibarariwä's village.

A ferocious rain, the onset of the rainy season, hit us about an hour after we began walking, and we had to huddle together under a small nylon tarp I always carried for such occasions. We lost about an hour because of the rain and decided that we should camp for the night: We would reach the village too late in the day to "make friends." We ate some boiled rice and strung our hammocks in an abandoned temporary hut made by some Shamatari hunter months earlier. As dusk settled, Karina began teasing Bäkotawä about the nastiness of Sibarariwä's group, reminding him mischievously that he was really a Bisaasi-teri, not a Patanowä-teri. Bäkotawä lay sullenly and unhappily in his hammock, and I had to scold Karina for his ill-natured humor. At dawn we got up and began packing. Bäkotawä quietly informed me that he was going no further and intended to return to the canoe; he honestly and frankly admitted, "*Ya kirii*" (I am frightened).

I gave him a share of the food and a quick lesson in how to load and fire the shotgun, providing him with a box of 25 cartridges. I told him we would be gone about "three days" (indicating the duration by three fingers) before we would rejoin him at the canoe. He assured me that whereas he was frightened here, he would be safe and confident at the canoe and he would make his camp there, waiting for our return. Karina and I set off to the southeast. Bäkotawä disappeared silently into the shadowy forest, heading north, back toward the canoe. Karina and I walked for several hours, continuing to run into fresh signs of Yąnomamö travelers. We found footprints that had been made just that morning, last night's rainwater still oozing into the depressions. A banana peeling here, a discarded bunch of palm fruits there. We were now very close. Karina grabbed my arm and whispered excitedly: "The village is just beyond the top of this hill!" We crept to the ridge and looked down into the valley below, where a gigantic, well-kept banana plantation surrounded an extremely large, circular *shabono*, the largest one I had ever seen up to then. We were there. Karina peered intently and then urged me to follow. In a few minutes we were in the garden, and shortly after we could see the back side of the *shabono* roof, the village structure, and the clearing. But something was wrong: no noise. No babies crying, no men chanting to the hekura spirits, no smoke, no dogs barking, and no buzzing of voices. The shabono was *broke*—empty.

Deserted, but only recently deserted. Karina went to investigate the garden, returning with a pile of ripe plantains a few minutes later and with the information that someone had been in the garden that very morning to harvest plantains. He guessed that Sibarariwä's group was camped out, but camped close enough to the garden so that they could return easily to harvest food. He guessed that they would be further upstream, at a place they often camped at this time of the year because certain wild fruits were in season there. We decided to leave our packs behind, in the abandoned village, and strike off to find them. The sun was high, and we would have all afternoon to look for them.

By this point I was down to my hammock, sneakers, shotgun, and a red loincloth I had borrowed from one of the Bisaasi-teri men—I had given all my new loincloths away. I wanted to look as inconspicuous as possible when I contacted these people, and wearing a loincloth instead of clothing would help. Karina brought only his bow, several arrows, and a large wad of now-aging tobacco tucked behind his lower lip—and his own loincloth. As we walked, we ran into fresher and more abundant signs of Sibarariwä's group, and I knew that we would soon run into them. As dusk began to settle we smelled smoke and, a few minutes later, saw a lazy cloud of bluish smoke drifting through the grey forest and rising slowly to the tree tops. Then we heard the chatter of many voices and babies crying. We had found their camp at last.

We approached quietly and cautiously, stopping at a small stream just short of the campsite to "beautify" ourselves. Karina scolded me and urged me to clean up—my legs were all muddy and my loincloth dangled haphazardly between my scratched knees. I made myself as "presentable" as I could, washing the mud and perspiration off, straightening my loincloth, and tying my sneakers. We had no feathers or red *nara* paint to add final touches. Karina handed me his bow and arrows and took up my shotgun, commenting, as he headed for the camp: "They might be frightened by your shotgun, so I'll take it. You carry my bow and arrows and wait for me to tell you to come in. They'll really be scared to see a *nabä* (non-Yąnomamö)!" He disappeared into the jungle, whistled a signal to alert people that a visitor was coming in. A chorus of cheers, whistles, and welcoming hoots rebounded through the darkening jungle as they welcomed him in.

I suddenly realized the absurdity of my situation and the magnitude of what I was doing. Here I stood, in the middle of an unexplored, unmapped jungle, a few hundred feet from a previously uncontacted group of Yąnomamö with a reputation for enormous ferocity and treachery, led there by a 12-year-old kid, and it was getting dark. My only marks of being human were my red loincloth, my muddy and torn sneakers, my hammock, and a bow with three skinny arrows.

An ominous hush fell over the forest ahead: Karina had obviously told them that I was waiting outside, and they were now pondering what to do. Uncomfortable recollections flashed through my head, and I recalled some of the tales that Kąobawä had recited to me about the Shamatari. I reflected on his intensely serious warnings that it would be hazardous to try to find them. They would pretend to be friendly, he explained, but when my guard was down they would fall on me with bow staves and clubs and kill me. Perhaps they would do it on the spot, but they might wait until I had taken up a hammock, as visitors are supposed to do, and lay there defenseless. Perhaps they would do it at night, as I slept, or just before dawn. Silence. Anxiety. My temples pounded. I wanted to run. I could hear the hushed buzzing of voices and people moving around in the jungle, spreading out: Some of them were leaving the camp. Were they surrounding me? Could I trust Karina? Was someone now staring at me down the long shaft of his war arrow?

Karina suddenly appeared on the trail and motioned for me to come—to present myself. I tried to give the expected visitor's announcement, but I had trouble puckering my dry lips and only a pathetic hiss of meaningless air came forth as I tried to whistle. I walked by Karina and noticed his curious look. I could not decide if it were the same look he had when he told Bäkotawä he would vouch that he was a Patanowä-teri, but it was too late now to consider weighty implications and too late to do anything about them.

I was greeted by a host of growling, screaming men, naked and undecorated, who pranced nervously around me, menacingly pointing their long, bamboo-tipped war arrows at my face, nocked in the strings of their powerful bows. I stood my ground, motionless and as poised as I could be, trying desperately to keep my legs from trembling, trying to look dignified, defiant, and fearless. After what seemed like an eternity, one of them gruffly told me to follow him to one of the temporary huts. As we walked toward it, I could see young men scrambling to clear off the ground and straighten a nara-stained cotton hammock—intended for my temporary use. They worked quickly and nervously, and scattered as I approached. Karina placed my shotgun at the backpost and I reclined in the hammock, striking the visitor's pose—one hand over my mouth, staring at the space above me and swaying gently, pretending I was on display in Macy's front window with a noontime crowd peering in.

Eventually a few of the bolder men came closer, hissing commands to the others to "get some food prepared, quickly!" They began whispering excitedly to each other, describing my most minute and most private visible parts. "Look at how hairy his legs are! Look at all that ugly hair on his chest! Look how pale he looks! Isn't he strange looking, and did you see how 'long' he was when he was standing there? I wonder if he has a regular penis? What are those skins he has tied to his feet?" Their curiosity gradually became overwhelming. The bolder ones came in closer, duck-waddling right at me. A hand came forward and cautiously and ever so delicately touched my leg. The hand retracted quickly with a hiss of amazement from its owner—"Aaahhh!" A chorus of admiring tongue clicks followed from the less bold, and then more touches and hisses, and soon many hands were touching me all over, pulling on my hairs, and they smelled my spoor repeatedly in their red-stained cupped hands, clicking their tongues and marveling that someone so different was so similar. Just a bit longer, hairier, and lighter than they were. Then I spoke to them, and again they marveled: I spoke a "crooked" version of Yąnomamö, like the Bisaasi-teri do, but they understood me.

Soon we were jabbering and visiting like long-lost friends. They scolded me for not having come sooner, for they had known about me for years and had wanted to meet me. The Reyaboböwei-teri had told them about me and had passed on what they themselves had known directly from meeting me personally, and what they had learned from the Mǫmariböwei-teri or the Bisaasi-teri second-hand. The Yąnomamö language is very precise about what is known firsthand and what has come from second, hearsay, sources. I was flabbergasted at the detail and accuracy of what they knew about me. They knew I had a wife and two children, and the sexes and approximate ages of my children. They could repeat with incredible accuracy conversations I had had with Yąnomamö in many different villages. One of them even wanted to see a scar on my left elbow. When I asked what he meant, he described in intimate detail a bad fall I had taken several years earlier on a trip to Reyaboböwei-teri when I slipped on a wet rock and landed on my elbow, which bled profusely. He even quite accurately repeated the string of Yąnomamö vulgarities I uttered at the time, and my complaint to my guides that their goddamned trails foolishly went up and down steep hills when they could more efficiently go around them! For people who had never before seen a non-Yąnomamö, they certainly knew a great deal about at least one of them![9]

I stayed with them for several days, but Karina had revealed that I had a small treasure of trade goods at my boat and they were anxious to go there to examine them. They were also disappointed that Bäkotawä did not come to the village, for "they wouldn't have harmed him but would have befriended him." After systematically checking the genealogical data that Karina had given me about the current families and visiting with them at length, I reluctantly decided to take them to my boat and the cache of gifts I had left there.

It had taken Karina and me at least six hours of walking to get from the boat to this place, but since they were anxious to see the boat and the trade goods, they made very rapid time guiding me back to where I had left the river. We ran most of the way. They carried only their weapons. No food and no hammocks. I didn't know what they planned to do for sleeping or eating, since we left for the boat near midday. I guess I assumed that they planned to spend the night in their abandoned *shabono*, which they could probably have reached by dark even if they spent an hour at the boat with me.

We came upon the spot where we had separated from Bäkotawä. Soon after that we came upon two expended shotgun shells, then soon after that, two more, then two more, and so on. It appeared as though Bäkotawä had fired the gun every few minutes as he retreated to the boat, and it was obvious that he was out of ammunition by the time he reached it.

We crossed the last rise before reaching the spot where I had left the boat and supplies and, much to my horror, I discovered that the boat, motor, gasoline, food, tarps, and trade goods were all gone. Bäkotawä had panicked and had taken off, leaving me stranded with people he was sure would kill all of us.

I was in a decidedly unenviable position at that point, for nobody except a few Yąnomamö knew where I was. I couldn't walk out, for that would have taken at least two weeks in the best of conditions, and it had been raining regularly since I arrived. The river was rising fast, and that meant that the land between me and Bisaasi-teri was beginning to flood. We spent a miserable wet

---

9. In 1972, several of my colleagues from the University of Michigan Medical School made a trip to the Brazilian Yąnomamö to continue the biomedical research we had jointly pursued between 1966 and 1972. One of them casually mentioned my Yąnomamö name, Shąki, in front of a Yąnomamö. The Yąnomamö immediately and excitedly demanded to know where I was and if I were going to visit them. This Yąnomamö village was many miles away from any Yąnomamö village I had ever visited.

night huddling under my small tarp thinking about the problem. I decided that the only feasible way to get out would be by river.

My first scheme was to build a raft, similar to the log palisades the Yąnomamö make around their villages. I had one machete with me and we set about cutting numerous trees and vines for the raft. At the end of the day we assembled it in the river, and when I stepped onto it, it promptly sank.

The next day we went into Plan II—building a "trough" of the sort that the Yąnomamö characteristically use when they have ceremonial feasts. They make a bark trough and fill it full of plantain soup, but the same trough is occasionally used by them, when reinforced with a few ribs, as a temporary canoe that is suitable only for floating downstream (Figure 1.10). It is a kind of "throw-away" canoe, useful in the kind of circumstance I was presently in. This plan was laid to rest when they told me that no suitable trees could be found in the immediate area to make such a trough. They suggested that since I was a foreigner and since foreigners make canoes, why didn't I just make myself a canoe? I explained that it wasn't quite that simple. Canoe-making is a complex enterprise, and I was from one of those foreign villages where we had to "trade" with others for our canoes—we had

**F I G U R E  1.10**  Woman in a bark canoe. These canoes are occasionally made by the Yąnomamö for a single trip downstream or for fording rivers. After a few days they sag, leak, and deteriorate beyond use.

"forgotten" how to make them, as they had "forgotten" how to make clay pots in some villages. They insisted that it was easy to remember lost arts. I said that it took axes to make canoes. They said they had axes at the village. They would not take "No" for an answer, and sent young men running off to the village to fetch the axes. They returned in record time, after dark, with two of the most miserable "axes" I have ever seen. They had been worn down by years, perhaps decades, of heavy use and were about one third the size they had been when they were first manufactured. But their confidence inspired me, so we set about looking for the largest, pithiest tree we could find—one that could be easily hollowed out for a single voyage. We found one, cut in, and began hollowing it out. It took all day. It looked like a long, fat cigar with a square notch cut into it. We dragged it to the river. I knew it would roll over as soon as any weight were put into it, so I designed an outrigger system that served also as a pair of seats where the two poles were lashed to the gunwales. I then lashed a pithy long pole parallel to the axis of the canoe (Figure 1.11). We spent much of another day whittling canoe paddles—three of them. One for Karina, one for me, and one for a spare. They had given me a large number of bows and arrows in exchange for the knives that I had carried in my pack. We loaded these into the outrigger and then climbed in, very gently. We sank. We unloaded the bows and arrows and all non-necessary items from my pack. I kept only my notes, hammock, food, camera, and a small

**F I G U R E  1.11**  The canoe I made to descend the Mavaca River—with Karina, who clutches one of our hand-hewn paddles.

transistor radio for monitoring Mission broadcasts. With our burden thus reduced, we climbed in again, and to my delight, the water rose only to about half an inch from the gunwales: We could float and stay afloat if we kept perfectly balanced. But the Yąnomamö are "foot" Indians, not "river" Indians, and Karina was perhaps the classic example of what that meant. If the Yąnomamö had decided to be river Indians, they might be extinct. We probably swamped and sank 30 or 40 times in the first two days, despite my passionate explanations that it was hazardous to lean too far to the right or the left when paddling. Karina ignored my heated injunctions and, as he leaned too far one way or the other, paralysis invariably seized him and he stoically maintained his posture as we inevitably went under and had to dogpaddle the "canoe" to the bank to bail it out and start over again.

It still amazes me that we managed to make it all the way back down to the spot where we had earlier left the large canoe, and amazes me even more that Bäkotawä had left the large canoe there as he passed by, for he had stopped at every place and collected my stores of gasoline in his voyage downstream.

Eventually, we made it back to Bisaasi-teri, much to the genuine relief of Kąobawä and Rerebawä, who had assumed the worst... that Sibarariwä's group had killed me. Bäkotawä had gotten back several days before we did, and his fears provoked much anxiety in the village. I knew it would have been "unprofessional" to hunt Bäkotawä down when I returned, for my mind was full of very hideous and vindictive plans for his future. In anthropological jargon, I wasn't in a very relativistic mood. We eventually had our predicted confrontation, the details of which I have discussed elsewhere (Chagnon, 1974). He is alive and well yet today, we greet each other pleasantly, but he doesn't go on trips with me anymore.

That is what it is sometimes like to meet an uncontacted tribe of South American Indians. Other experiences I have had were much more dangerous. On one occasion my hosts very nearly succeeded in killing me as I slept (Chagnon, 1974: Chapter V). More recently, in 1990 and 1991, I also contacted Yąnomamö villages that had never been visited before, but these experiences were much less dramatic because the people there had heard a great deal about "foreigners" and, in most cases, at least some men of these villages had walked out to places where there were missionaries and had seen what foreigners look like (Brooke, 1990; 1991). While excited that they finally got to see me, they knew in advance what I probably looked like. The results of these trips are discussed in several of the following chapters, results that have led to significant new insights into Yąnomamö culture and political history.

# 2

---

✳

# Cultural Ecology

People everywhere must come to grips with the physical environments within which they live in order to survive and produce offspring, who carry on their traditions. The physical environment, however, contains not only lands, forests, resources, and foods, it contains many other things as well. Perhaps one of the most compelling dimensions of the environment is the other people it includes. From the vantage of members of a particular community—a village, for example—the world beyond has both a physical and a sociopolitical dimension, and one must come to grips with both. Anthropologists usually discuss this process as cultural adaptation: the social, technical, and ideological means by which people adjust to the world that impinges on them. Much of that world is ontologically real in the sense that an outsider from a different culture can "see" and document it in a fashion that can be verified by other observers. But much of it lies hidden in the minds of the observed natives, whose cultural traditions, meanings, and assumptions infuse it with spirits, project into it meanings, and view it in a way that the outsider can discover only by learning the language and, through language, the intellectual dimensions of culture. This chapter explores Yąnomamö adaptations to the natural dimensions of the environment and how people make a living in that environment. More important, it explores the relationship between ecology, culture, and village dispersion over the landscape, describing how the Yąnomamö settlements fission and relocate in new areas. This process clearly must have been of enormous significance in our own culture's history when agriculture was developed and led to the rapid growth of populations, an event that we now call the "agricultural revolution." What we can learn from studying the Yąnomamö settlement pattern process can shed light on our own population's early history, a history we know now only through archaeology. The next chapter will consider the "intellectual" dimensions of how the Yąnomamö cope with their world through myths and ideology.

## THE PHYSICAL ENVIRONMENT

Kąobawä's village is located at the confluence of the Mavaca and Orinoco Rivers, the Mavaca being a relatively large tributary of the latter. His village lies at an elevation of about 450 feet above sea level on a generally flat, jungle-covered plain that is interrupted occasionally by low hills. None of the hills qualify as mountains, but in the nearby areas the terrain is very rugged and hilly and difficult to traverse on foot. I will discuss the importance of this kind of terrain in more detail below. Most of the rivers and streams begin in the hills as tiny trickles that are dry at some times of the year but dangerous torrents at other times. A sudden heavy rain can have a dramatic effect on even larger streams, and the Yąnomamö therefore avoid larger streams when they select garden and village sites. The Yąnomamö are "foot" Indians, as distinct from "river" Indians, a basic cultural division in the Amazon Basin.

While the hills do not qualify as mountains, they do reach heights of 3,500 feet in some places. Almost all of them are covered with jungle, but far to the east of Kąobawä's village, in the Parima mountains, relatively large natural savannas occur at higher elevations, and one finds Yąnomamö villages there as well. Much of the lowland area is inundated during the wet season, making it either impossible to travel there or unwise to locate a village and garden there.

The jungle is relatively dense and contains a large variety of palm and hardwood trees. The canopy keeps the sunlight from reaching the ground, and on overcast days it can be very dark and gloomy in the jungle. Scrub brush and vines grow in most areas, making travel by foot difficult. Along the rivers and streams where the sunlight can penetrate to the ground, luxuriant vegetation grows, a haven for many kinds of birds and animals.

### Trails and Travel

Yąnomamö villages are scattered irregularly, but usually thinly, over this vast tropical landscape. Distances between the villages can be as short as a few hours' walk to as much as a week or 10 days' walk, depending on the political relationships between the groups. Warfare between villages generally keeps the villages widely separated, while alliances of various sorts (see below) and descent from common ancestors tend to reduce the distance, but there are exceptions.

All villages have trails leading out into the jungle and to various villages beyond. Many trails simply go to the gardens that surround the village and terminate there. A Yąnomamö trail is not an easy thing to see, let alone follow, particularly a trail that is used only sporadically. Most of them wind through brush, swamps, rivers, and hills, but tend to be quite direct—annoyingly so at times, as when they go straight up a steep hill to the peak, and then straight down the other side, instead of following more convenient terrain that the anthropologist might have chosen.

It takes experience to recognize a Yąnomamö trail. The most certain spoors are the numerous broken twigs at about knee height, for the Yąnomamö constantly snap off twigs with their fingers as they walk along. Another frequent sign is a footworn log across a stream or ravine, usually so slippery that at first I had to shimmy across them on hands and knees while my traveling companions roared with laughter. Most Yąnomamö trails cross streams and rivers, often going for several hundred feet in the river itself. It is easy to get lost on these trails, for it is never obvious when the trail leaves the stream and continues across land. When I first began my field work, the Yąnomamö, for amusement, would tell me, "Kahä wa baröwo!" ("You take the lead on the trail, we'll follow.") Within minutes they would be laughing hysterically—I would soon wander off the trail and end up in a dense thicket.

Friendly neighbors visit regularly, and the most commonly used trail from Kąobawä's village went south, to the two friendly Shamatari villages: Reyabo-böwei-teri and Mǫmariböwei-teri. Hardly a week went by during the dry season without someone, usually small groups of young men, going from one of the Shamatari villages to Bisaasi-teri or vice versa. Young men can make the trip easily in one day, for they travel swiftly and carry nothing but their bows and arrows. A family might also make it in one day if it kept on the move, but it would be a dawn-to-dusk trip if the women had to carry their babies or items they or their men planned to trade. Should the whole village decide to visit, it might be a two- or three-day trip, depending on how anxious they were to reach the village. On one occasion, Kąobawä invited me to accompany his entire village on a trip to Mǫmariböwei-teri. I packed my supplies carefully and left with them. We walked about 20 minutes inland, to the south, and stopped to let the women and children rest. Much to my surprise and chagrin, that is where we made our first night's camp! We were barely outside their garden! It would have taken them at least a week to reach their destination at that pace, so I simply went on with a young man to guide me, spent a day and a night visiting, and returned home before the Bisaasi-teri even reached the village.

On this trail, and many others like it, there are numerous temporary "camping places" along the route, a collection of dilapidated pole huts in various stages of decay where earlier visitors spent a night. These huts can be put back into repair in a few minutes by simply replacing the dry, leaky roof leaves, but the whole structure can be built from scratch in about 15 minutes.

Walking entails certain kinds of risks. The Yąnomamö have no shoes or clothing, so thorns are always a problem. A party of 10 men can rarely go more than an hour without someone stopping suddenly, cursing, and sitting down to dig a thorn out of his foot with the tip of his arrow point. While their feet are hardened and thickly calloused, walking in streams and through muddy terrain softens the calluses so that thorns can get deeply imbedded.

Snakebite is another hazard. A surprisingly large number of Yąnomamö die from snakebites, and almost everyone, if he lives long enough, eventually gets bitten by a snake.[1] Most bites are not fatal, although all are painful. I treated several nonfatal bites with antivenom during my work, but no case was very serious. In my more recent fieldwork I used an electrical "stun gun," a hand-held, battery-operated, self-defence instrument that delivers a low-amperage, high-voltage charge that can disable a person for several minutes. I had an electrical engineer reduce the voltage from 40,000 V to about 15,000 V and would "shock" the area of the snakebite. In reported cases from other parts of the world, this technique has been known to dramatically reduce the severity of the snakebite and seems to neutralize the venom. A few snakebites can be severe enough to cause the loss of either the limb or its functionality. One of my Yąnomamö friends lost his leg some 15 years prior to the beginning of my fieldwork; it just rotted away and fell off. He hopped around rather effectively on his remaining leg. Snakebites are almost as frequent in the garden or near the village as they are on the remote trails, and one must always be careful when picking up firewood from the pile or wandering around in the garden. With this in mind, the Yąnomamö try to keep the garden and paths weeded. Abandoned gardens seem to attract snakes because they attract rodents, and, for this reason, one must use extreme caution in measuring and mapping old gardens.

In Kąobawä's area, most travel between villages is done from September through March, the dry season. During the wet season, substantial portions of the trail are under water and small "lakes" replace the swampy lowlands. Communication between villages nearly ceases at the peak of the rainy season and most villages are isolated from most outside visits during that time. Streams that were mere trickles in March become raging torrents in May and June. If the group must travel in the wet season, it will make simple pole-and-vine bridges over the smaller streams, but will have to avoid large streams altogether, making wide detours around them. These bridges are essentially a series of X frames linked together with long poles (where the legs of the X cross) and vine railings. Generally a gap of 10 to 15 feet separates each X until the stream is bridged. Bridges are usually washed out within a few weeks, but occasionally a few of the poles will last into the dry season.

## Technology

Much of Yąnomamö technology is like the pole-and-vine bridge just described: crude, easy to fashion from immediately available materials, effective enough to solve the current problem but not destined to last forever. Perhaps the only durable artifact that an archaeologist would readily find in ancient, abandoned sites is the crude, poorly fired clay pot traditionally used by the Yąnomamö (Figure 2.1). It is nearly an inch thick at the bottom and tapers to almost nothing at the rim. It is undecorated, very fragile, and pointed at the bottom. Women, who are considered clumsy by the men, are rarely allowed to use them. The pots

---

1. I eventually compiled statistics on causes of death of adult Yąnomamö (see Chagnon, 1974:160, for statistics).

**FIGURE 2.1** Clay pots were common when I began my fieldwork, but these have been almost completely replaced by aluminum ware that is traded from village to village.

are often used to prepare food for a feast—and men do all the food preparation for that. The pot is made by the "coil" technique and fired by simply stacking brush and wood around it. When it breaks, usually relatively soon after being manufactured, the pieces are used by the men as a grinding surface for preparing their hallucinogenic snuff powder. Clay pots were relatively common when I first began my field research, but almost completely disappeared by the late 1970s. As we shall see below, members of only a few villages made the pots and traded them to their neighbors.

Yąnomamö technology is very direct. No tool or technique is so complex that it requires specialized knowledge or raw materials, and each village, there-fore, can produce every item of material culture it requires from immediately available resources. Nevertheless, some "specialization" in manufacturing and trade does occur, but the establishment of political alliances has more to do with this, as we shall see, than the actual distribution of resources: People create "shortages" in order to have to trade with distant neighbors. Yąnomamö tech-nology could almost be classified as that which would be more characteristic of hunters and gatherers, but the Yąnomamö are in fact horticultural.

Bowstaves, some 5 to 6 feet long, are always made from palm wood. One species grows wild, and the other, the preferred kind, is cultivated for its fruits. The wood of both is very dense, brittle, and hard. One cannot, for example, drive a nail into it. Bowstrings are made from the fibers of the inner bark of a tree. The bark is twisted into thick cords by rolling the fibers vigorously between the thigh muscle and the palm of the hand; the cords are so strong that one can use them, in a pinch, as hammock ropes. The bowstave is painstakingly shaped by shaving the stock with the incisors of a wild pig. The lower projecting teeth of this pig are worn razor sharp from eating, and the entire mandible is kept as a wood plane for making bows. The completed bow is oval or round in cross-section and is very powerful—comparable in strength to our own hunting bows. With age and use, they become brittle and often shatter when drawn too hard.

A pencil-shaped splinter of palm wood is also used for one type of arrow point: the curare-poisoned *husu namo* point. The splinter is weakened at about 1-inch intervals along its length by cutting partially through the wood; this causes it to break off inside the target, allowing the curare to dissolve in the bloodstream. While it is primarily used to hunt monkeys, it is also used in warfare. A monkey can pull an ordinary arrow out, but it cannot pull out a point that is broken off deep in its body. The curare gradually relaxes the monkey, and it falls to the ground instead of dying high in the tree, clinging to a branch. The Yąnomamö carry several extra curare points in their bamboo quivers, for they break when they strike anything, and usually must be replaced after every shot. These arrow points are manufactured in large bundles of 50 or 60 in several villages near Kąobawä's and are prized trade items (Figure 2.2). The poison comes from a vine that is leached in hot water; other vegetable ingredients are added to make it sticky so that it adheres to the wood. Men often wrap a leaf around the poisoned point to keep the rain from dissolving the poison as they travel. In some areas, other vegetable poisons are used, one of them being an hallucinogen.

**FIGURE 2.2**
Man painting curare poison on palm-wood arrow points over glowing embers. The poison is leached with hot water and painted in many coats; the water evaporates, leaving a sticky coating of poison.

In a pinch, the men can scrape the poison off and get high by snuffing it deeply into their nostrils.

The arrow-point quivers—*tora*—which all men have dangling in the middle of their backs, are made from a section of bamboo, usually about 3 inches in diameter and about 15 to 18 inches long. A natural joint in the bamboo serves as the bottom; the open top is covered with the skin of some animal, usually a snake, monkey, or jaguar. The bamboo grows wild in large stands and some villages are known to "specialize" in trading bamboo quivers. The quiver usually contains several arrow points, fibers, resin, and strings for repairing arrows and, occasionally, a magical charm. A piece of old bowstring is used to hang the quiver around the neck, whence it dangles in the middle of the back. A pair of *tomö nakö* (agouti-tooth) "knives," used to trim the lance-shaped, broad, bamboo arrow point—*rahaka*—is attached to the outside of the quiver, as is, occasionally, a fire drill made from the wood of the cocoa tree. One piece of cocoa wood, about 10 inches long and lanceolate, contains several holes along the edges worn into the wood by the friction of the longer circular piece of wood that is rapidly spun between the palms of the hands. The lower piece is held secure by the foot, the other spun into it until the friction produces the glowing dust that is quickly fed tinder until a fire starts. Men work in pairs to generate fire with the drill, taking turns: As one finishes his downward spinning with his palms, the other starts at the top, and so on. The drill is wrapped in leaves to keep it dry. Today, matches in enormous quantities are provided as trade goods in those villages that have contact with outsiders, and these are traded far inland. Like the clay pot, fire drills are rapidly disappearing, even in the most remote villages.

Arrows are made from 6-foot-long shafts of cultivated cane. They are often assumed to be "spears" by people who see them for the first time, either in photographs or when they physically handle them.

Two long black feathers from the wing of the *paruri* (a wild turkey-like bird) are attached as fletching in such a way as to cause the arrow to spin when shot. A thin fiber from a cultivated plant was traditionally used to attach the fletching, but manufactured white cotton thread traded in from missionaries is now commonly used in most villages. A nock is carved from a piece of hardwood, using the small agouti-tooth knife. The nock looks like a golf tee when completed, except that it has a notch in it for the bowstring. It is stuck into the shaft behind the fletching and fastened with pitch and fine fibers wrapped tightly around the arrow shaft.

Three arrow points are commonly used and are interchangeable; "spares" are often carried in the arrow-point quiver. The most effective point for killing large game, such as tapir, is a lanceolate point made from a section of bamboo. These are often painted with red, black, or purple pigments, and some of them acquire a reputation and history if they have been used to take many animals or their former owner was a prominent man. These histories are recited in some detail when the point is traded to another owner, and much raising of eyebrows, clicking of tongues, and expressions of amazement accompany the transaction as the new owner praises his trading partner's generosity in divesting himself of a property so valuable and lucky. Bamboo points are fastened to the arrow shaft by simply pushing one of the sharp ends into the pith of the arrow cane as far as it will go, usually about one-eighth of the length of the point itself. The arrow shaft is prevented from splitting during this procedure by binding it tightly for about 2 inches or so with fine but strong cord. The second most useful and effective arrow point is the curare-smeared, pencil-like palm-wood point (Figure 2.2). These are weakened by cutting nearly through them every few inches or so along the axis, causing them to break off inside the animal, thus enabling the curare to dissolve and eventually kill the animal. The third kind of point is barbed and is used primarily for bird hunting. The barb is made from a sliver of bone, often a monkey bone. The barb prevents the arrow from coming out of the bird, and the weight of the shaft plus its unwieldiness keeps the bird from flying away. A fourth kind of arrow point is made from a twig with many branching stems. It is usually fashioned on the spot in a few seconds and discarded after one or two uses. Small birds, often sought only for their decorative feathers, are shot with such points.

The Yạnomamö do not rely extensively on fish, but during certain times of the year fish are abundant and easily taken. One method is to simply wait for the rainy season to end. Then, areas of the jungle that have been flooded by the overflowing rivers begin to dry out, leaving pools of fish stranded. As the pools get shallow, it is a simple matter to wade into them and catch dozens of fish by hand. Fish poisons made of wild lianas are used to poison small streams (Lizot, 1972). The men put the poison into the water upstream from where a small dam has been made from sticks and mud, and wait for the fish to become stupefied. They float or swim clumsily to the surface, stunned by the poison, where the women and girls scoop them up by hand or with large circular baskets (Figure 2.3), biting the larger ones behind the head to kill them. Sometimes the women get shocked by eels while fishing, and the eel must be found and killed before the work continues.

The Yạnomamö use a splinter of a kind of reed—*sunama*—to shave their heads bald on the top and to trim their "pudding bowl" bangs. A sliver of this reed is wrapped around the finger and scraped on the scalp, neatly cutting the hair off with no more discomfort than what would be associated with shaving with a dullish razor blade. Men with large deep scars on their heads acquired from club fights present a somewhat grotesque image, especially when they rub red pigment on their scarred bald scalps. This enhances and exaggerates the scars and draws attention to them.

The size of the tonsure varies markedly from area to area. The Shamatari, for example, sport relatively small tonsures, about 3 inches in diameter. The Yạnomamö north and east of Kạobawä's village shave so much of their head that they look like they have just a narrow fringe of hair, like a black strap, wrapped around their heads just above the temples. Women wear the same hair style as men. If head lice become extremely noisome, they shave their heads completely, for it takes a considerable amount of time to "groom" (delouse) someone. While grooming someone is also an expression of affection and friendship, it can become a tedious job. Children, in particular, are often shaved when lice become too much of a problem for parents to handle (Figure 2.4). Amusingly,

**FIGURE 2.3**
Women collecting
stunned fish with
baskets in a small
stream that has been
dammed with brush
and mud. The men
put barbasco poison
in the water upstream
to stun the fish so
the women can catch
them easily.

the Yąnomamö get "revenge" on the lice by either eating them or biting them to kill them. I recall the time when I was in elementary school, when the county nurse had to come to school to delouse all the students, whether or not all of us needed it. Head lice are not all that far behind in our own culture's sanitation problems—and continue to be a problem in some areas of the United States.

## Hallucinogenic Drugs

The jungle provides several highly prized plant products that are used in the manufacture of hallucinogenic snuff powders. The most widely distributed source of drugs is the *yakowana* tree, whose soft moist inner bark is dried and ground into a powder. To this are added snowy white ashes made from the bark of another tree. The mixture is moistened with saliva and kneaded by

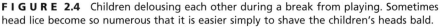

**FIGURE 2.4** Children delousing each other during a break from playing. Sometimes head lice become so numerous that it is easier simply to shave the children's heads bald.

hand into a somewhat gummy substance, which is then placed on a piece of heated pot sherd (or, now, in some villages, the top from a gasoline drum) and ground into a fine green powder. But the more desirable hallucinogen is from the *hisiomö* tree, whose tiny, lentil-sized seeds are painstakingly skinned and packed into 10- or 15-inch-long cylinder-shaped wads and traded over a wide area. The tree has a spotty distribution, and villages located near natural groves tend to specialize in trading *hisiomö*. It is more desirable than *yakowana*, and more powerful. Like *yakowana*, it is kneaded with ashes and saliva and then pulverized into a green powder on a piece of heated pot sherd. A smooth stone, often a stone ax, is used to grind it into a powder. Several other plants are used to make hallucinogens. The Yąnomamö cultivate a variety of small bushes of the genus *justicia* and snuff these, but they are less potent and less desirable than the other two. All the drugs are referred to by a generic name when they are in powdered form: *ebene* (Chagnon, LeQuesne, and Cook, 1971).

The men usually make a batch of *ebene* every day; sometimes several different groups of men in a village each make their own batch. It takes quite a bit of kneading and grinding to produce a half cupful, enough for several men, depending on appetites and whether it is *hisiomö* or *yakowana*. The men paint themselves elaborately with red pigment, put on their fine feathers, and then gather around the front of the house of the host. A long hollow tube, *mokohiro*, is used to blow the powder into the nostrils. A small amount, about a teaspoonful, is pushed by finger into one end of the tube to load it. The other end, to which a large, hollowed palm seed has been fashioned as a nostril piece, is put

**F I G U R E 2.5** The man on the left is blowing ebene powder in the other's nostrils. The initial pain is severe, but the effects are eventually pleasant.

into a companion's nose. The green powder is then blown into the nasal cavity with a powerful, long burst of breath that starts slowly and terminates with a vigorous blast (Figure 2.5). The recipient grimaces, chokes, groans, coughs, gasps, and usually rubs his head excitedly with both hands, or holds the sides of his head as he duck-waddles off to some convenient post where he leans against it waiting for the drug to take effect. He usually takes a blast of *ebene* in each nostril, sometimes two in each, and "freshens" it with more blasts later. The recipient immediately gets watery eyes and a profusely runny nose—long strands of green mucus begin to drip from each nostril. Dry heaves are also very common, as is out-and-out vomiting. Within a few minutes, one has difficulty focusing and begins to see spots and blips of light. Knees get rubbery. Profuse sweating is common, and pupils get large. Soon the *hekura* spirits can be seen dancing out of the sky and from the mountain tops, rhythmically prancing down their trails to enter the chest of their human beckoner, who by now is singing melodically to lure them into his body where he can control them— send them to harm enemies or help cure sick kinsmen. (See the film *Magical Death*, listed at the end of this book, for a dramatic documentary of drug-taking and shamanism.)

Trade in *hisiomö* seeds was unexpectedly interrupted by changing warfare patterns while I was conducting field research in Kąobawä's village. The response to this by some individuals was fascinating, for it illustrated the kind of ingenuity that must lie behind the whole process of plant domestication. Rerebawä, who had grown very fond of the drug, took it upon himself to make sure that the source could not be interrupted by wars. He made several trips to an area far to the northeast, where the tree abounded, and brought many seedlings back with him. Some of them he transplanted in his own village, and others he transplanted in Kąobawä's village. Yet others he traded inland, to men in the Shamatari villages. While many of the seedlings did not survive, some did—and later produced quantities of seeds. The Yąnomamö quickly disperse novel or more desirable varieties of other cultigens through trade, and when they discover such plants in distant villages, they generally try to get seedlings, cuttings, or seeds to bring home to their own gardens. For a while, the new variety of plant tends to be remembered as having come from a particular village, but over time people forget where it came from and tend to adopt the position that they have always had it. It should be recalled that the Yąnomamö are highly dependent on cultivated plantains, a domesticant that was introduced to the Americas after Columbus—yet they believe that they have always cultivated it, and have origin myths about it. Prior to plantains, the Yąnomamö were probably much more highly dependent on several other of their native Amazonian domestic foodstuffs (see below).

## Shelter

All house construction materials are collected from the jungle: poles, vines, and leaves. The Yąnomamö make a sharp distinction, as do many humans, between "domestic" and "natural," that is, between Culture and Nature. The focal point of this distinction is the village and its surrounding garden. Things found here are *yahi tä rimö*: of the village, culture. All else is *urihi tä rimö*: of the forest, nature.

The village may be constructed of natural things, but it becomes cultural through the intervention of human effort and the transformation such effort entails.

The permanent house and its central plaza is called the *shabono* and is probably one of the most labor-intensive products in the entire culture. A high degree of planning and cooperation is necessary to build a village, not to mention many days of work. Unfortunately, the *shabono* lasts only two years or so because the leaves begin to leak or the roofing becomes so infested with roaches, spiders, and other insects that it must be burned to the ground to get rid of them. The roaches can become so numerous that a constant buzzing noise can be heard, increasing in intensity when someone's head passes close to the roofing and alarms the bugs, or when someone places something—bows and arrows—into the roof thatch. Kąobawä's village was so infested at one point that every time someone would move, dozens of roaches would fall from the roof and scurry away. The roaches can get as large as small birds or be so tiny that they can manage to get between the elements in your camera lenses. For some reason, they just loved my Sony shortwave radio.

The *shabono* looks like a large round communal house to the untrained eye, but in fact it is a coordinated series of individual houses (Figure 2.6). Each family builds its own section of the common roof. The men usually do the heavy work of fetching the poles for the frame, placing them into the ground or overhead,

**FIGURE 2.6** A small Yąnomamö village from the air, located near the edge of the plantain garden and the Demini River.

and weaving the scores of thousands of leaves that go into the thatch. Women and older children also help in the thatching, as well as in gathering the necessary leaves and vines that constitute the major items in building the structure. If it is palisaded, the men do this heavy work.

The first step in building a new *shabono* is selecting the proper site. If the *shabono* is simply being reconstructed after burning the old one, the location might be either on that same spot or a few yards away—as long as it is not in a depression and likely to be flooded in the rainy season. If it is a new location entirely, the primary consideration is the location of enemies and allies, and then, secondarily, the suitability of the land for gardens.

The four main posts of each house are sunk into the ground by digging holes with a stick or machete and scooping the dirt out by hand. Two short poles, about 5 feet high on the back of the house, are set and then two long poles, about 10 feet high, are placed at the front. Front and back poles are about 8 to 10 feet apart to accommodate hammocks, which also determine how far apart the two front and two back posts are from each other.[2] Cross poles are then lashed to these, horizontal to the ground, near the tops of the upright posts. Long slender saplings—*hanto nahi*—are then placed diagonal to these, about a foot to 18 inches

------

2. See my 1974 publication, which gives exact dimensions of a large Yąnomamö *shabono* (Chagnon, 1974:257).

apart, and lashed to them with vines. These saplings are 20 to 30 feet long and run from near ground level at the rear of the house, arching up, bending under their own weight into a gentle arc, and are 20 to 25 feet off the ground at their tips. Vines are then strung between the long saplings, perpendicular to them, about every 12 inches. These hold the long-stemmed leaves most often used in roofing—*bisaasi kä hena*, whence comes the name of Kạobawä's village, Bisaasi-teri: roofing-leaf people. Thatching work begins at the bottom of the roof. A long-stemmed leaf is slid under the second vine and bent over until it reaches down and rests on the first vine (Figure 2.7). Another is placed a few inches away, bent over, then another, and so on. When one row that runs the entire length of the individual house is finished, a second, higher row is started. As the roof progresses, scaffolding made of poles and vines is erected to facilitate the work. The weight of the leaves bends the saplings even more, and support poles are added to hold up the overhang when the roofing is nearly completed. These support poles are often embedded in the ground and tied to the *hanto nahi* tips—to keep the roof from blowing off when strong winds occur. When club fights break out in the village, these support poles are often ripped out and used as clubs; and the roof sometimes sags and breaks when this happens.

When each house is finished, the effect is a circle of individual houses, each separated from the next one by a few feet of open space. These spaces are then thatched over, and the village looks like one continuous circular roof

**FIGURE 2.7**
Thatching the shabono roof with leaves from, the bisaasi kä hena plant.

surrounding the open plaza. Occasionally there will be an unroofed gap of a few feet to a few yards, and sometimes there will be a section of the village that is not connected to neighboring houses at either end. This makes the village appear to be composed of discrete sections, as it is, but the sections usually are not separated by open space in Kąobawä's area of the tribe. Elsewhere, to the north and east, Yąnomamö villages are seldom unified structures, such as the kind just described. There, the individual sections of the village might even be double-gabled, that is, have double-pitched roofs on each house. This feature could possibly be introduced from the outside, since the Yąnomamö on the north and northeast periphery of the tribe have had much more contact with either the Ye'kwana (Carib-speaking Indians who have had long-term contact with European culture) or missionaries.

The physical size of a village is a function of two important variables, at least in Kąobawä's area. First, and most obvious, the structure's size is a function of how many people there are in the group. Because warfare is common in this area of the tribe, villages tend to grow to a fairly large size before they can fission. They must contain at least 80 to 100 people in order to be able to fission, but they will sometimes grow much larger, as we will see in the next chapter. Obviously, a village with 400 people has to be larger than a village with 40 people. The second determinant of the physical size of a village is politics—the extent to which members of a village must enter into alliances and regular visiting with neighboring groups as part of their political strategy. This is a necessity in Kąobawä's area, and alliance obligations require that you invite all the members of your ally's village to visit you. To accommodate them, your village has to be physically larger than the space requirements of the permanent residents. Thus, the physical dimensions are such that accommodating an extra 100 or so visitors is not an impossibility. In a word, where alliances between villages are an inherent part of the political strategies of the Yąnomamö, a village that housed 80 people would be physically larger than a village that housed 80 Yąnomamö in a part of the tribe where alliances of this sort were less important.

Elevation and, therefore, temperature also affect village construction. Yąnomamö villages in the Parima highlands are located at an elevation of about 2,500 to 3,000 feet. I was initially puzzled by the fact that their *shabono* had large masses of banana leaves hanging down—almost to the ground—from the high point of the roof. I discovered why they did this on the first night I slept in such a village. The air temperature dropped to about 60 degrees Fahrenheit, and with the high humidity it felt like it was 40 degrees! The banana leaves kept the rising heat from the hearths from escaping too rapidly, but, unfortunately, also prevented the smoke from escaping. I felt like a smoked monkey each morning. But when you do not have clothing or blankets, you can learn to tolerate a good deal of smoke if it means keeping warm.

A new *shabono* is a pleasant place to be. It is clean, smells like fresh-cut leaves, and has a generally cozy, tidy appearance. It is like living in a new, very large wicker hamper.

The wind, however, can be a destructive problem: It blows the leaves off and, if very gusty, will literally rip the roof off and blow the whole thing into the jungle. To remedy this chronic problem, the Yąnomamö sometimes throw heavy branches and poles on the outside surface to help hold the leaves down, and use long poles tied to the roof with the butts buried in the ground as mentioned above. But the most common defense is magical. The shamans rush forth and chant incantations at *Wadoriwä*, spirit of the wind, pleading and enjoining him to stop blowing. He cooperates only occasionally. Very often a shaman in an enemy village is accused of causing the spirits to make the violent winds.

When the Yąnomamö travel to another village or go on extended collecting trips in the jungle, they make a simpler house, as mentioned above. It is essentially triangular in shape: two back poles and one front pole. They can erect one of these huts in a few minutes, and a whole group—all members of a village—can create a very homey camp of such huts in about half an hour. The roofing is usually made from the long broad leaf of the wild banana, *kediba*, a few of which suffice to make a waterproof roof that will last several days. Travelers run into such huts and simply string their hammocks up in them when it is time to camp, hoping that the roof will not leak. The roof always leaks, and if it rains, people spend most of the night in futile attempts to adjust and readjust the decayed leaves to keep the water out.

Permanent *shabonos* are often surrounded by 10-foot-high palisades if the residents have reason to believe they will be attacked by enemies. The palisade is made of logs, often palm trees, and is erected a few feet behind the lower part of the roof. The logs are sunk into the ground a foot or so and lashed together with vines. It is kept in good repair only if the threat of a raid is high; otherwise, people begin to pilfer the wood to cook with. Both the village entrances and the entrances through the palisade are covered with dry brush at night, the slightest movement of which makes enough noise to wake the dogs, and hence, the residents. Villages without palisades are more vulnerable, but people stack up their firewood under the low end of the roof in such a way that a nocturnal assassin could not easily take a shot at them from that vantage. In the darkness, all people look alike: The Yąnomamö made me stack my pack and any other containers, such as camera cases, against the back of the roof to add some personal safety, explicitly to thwart would-be raiders.

## HUNTING, GATHERING, AND GARDENING

### Wild Foods

The jungle provides numerous varieties of plant and animal food, some seasonal and others available at most times of the year, but access is often limited by rainfall. Groups of Yąnomamö could live entirely off the wild foods in their environment, but such groups would have to be relatively small and chronically migratory. Indeed, most of the villages in Kąobawä's area periodically go on *waiyumö*, "camping," for extended periods of time, usually breaking up into groups of about 30 or 40 people. During these times they depend very heavily on wild foods, especially palm fruits and game, and time their camping trips to coincide with the ripening of wild fruits. They remain relatively sedentary at their temporary camps, but they usually "hedge" their subsistence bets by bringing modest quantities of plantains with them from their gardens. Such camping trips are times of fun and relaxation for the Yąnomamö, for they can take a respite from gardening and delight in varying their diets by living off many kinds of wild produce when they are in season.

Generally, the most commonly taken game animals in Kąobawä's area are two varieties of large game birds that resemble our pheasant and turkey respectively (*mąrashi* and *parurî*), two species of wild pig, several varieties of monkeys, tapir, armadillos, anteaters, alligators (*caiman*), deer, rodents, and a host of small birds. Many varieties of insects, fish, larvae, tadpoles, and freshwater crabs are eaten with gusto and highly prized. In some areas, large snakes are also eaten but are not considered to be very desirable—anacondas and boa constrictors in particular. Large toads and frogs are also eaten in some regions. Certain species of caterpillars are prized foods, as are the fat white grubs of the insect that lays its eggs in the pith of palm trees, or the grubs that live in the seeds of many palm fruits. In the Parima area, some groups eat the flesh of jaguars, a habit that Kąobawä and his people consider to be peculiar. Likewise, unlike many tropical forest peoples, Kąobawä's people very rarely eat the flesh of the capybara, the world's largest rodent, which abounds in the lowlands and weighs up to 100 or 150 pounds. They look like giant beavers, but with no tails. Fish, as mentioned above, are taken in considerable abundance in certain seasons and, with introduced fishhooks and fishline more common, are becoming increasingly important in the diet of those Yąnomamö who have access to fishing tackle.[3]

The Yąnomamö, in short, exploit a wide variety of animal protein resources and enjoy a high standard of living by world health standards (Neel's narration to *Yąnomamö: A Multidisciplinary Study*, 1971. Neel, James V., T. Asch, and N. Chagnon). As more foreigners come into their area and take up permanent residence, this situation will change quickly—and already has along the major river ways, where permanent missions have been established, whose personnel hunt with guns, lights, and canoes both day and night and seine fish from the rivers with nets. The meat is often frozen in kerosene freezers and dispensed generously to the many visitors who are beginning to flock to the missions to "see wild Indians."

---

3. The introduction of canoes and flashlights makes night hunting possible in those villages with chronic contact with missionaries, and the introduction of shotguns (after 1965) in these villages makes both night hunting and day hunting very efficient. Alligators (caiman), amota (a rodent about the size of a small beaver), and tapir are relatively easily taken at night if canoes, flashlights, and shotguns are available. No shotguns were in the hands of any Yąnomamö in the Mavaca area, when I began my field research in 1964. By 1975, members of at least 8 or 10 villages in that area experienced increased contact with missionaries and other outsiders to the point that some 40 shotguns could be found in these same villages. By 1991, shotguns were finding their way into more remote Venezuelan villages as well. The situation in Brazil is even more dramatic, for used shotguns are so inexpensive in Brazil that they can be used extensively as trade goods, costing about as much as I had to pay in Venezuela for a steel ax head—about $5.00 or $6.00. Needless to say, the introduction of shotguns in some Yąnomamö villages has changed not only hunting patterns, but the warfare patterns as well, as we shall see later.

## Vegetable Foods

Vegetable foods most commonly exploited by the Yąnomamö consist of the fruits of several species of palm, fruits of several hardwoods, brazil nuts, tubers, seed pods of the feral banana, and a host of lesser items, including some very delicious mushrooms. Palm hearts can be eaten almost endlessly, and I have joined the Yąnomamö in orgies of palm heart eating, in which 40 or 50 pounds divided among a dozen or so people was not uncommon.

Two of the most commonly eaten palm fruits are called *kareshi* and *yei*. The latter is about the size of a hen's egg, the former about half as large. Both fruits have a leathery skin and a very large, hard seed on the inside. Between the skin and the seed is a thin layer of slimy, sticky, stringy flesh, somewhat sweet to the taste, that is sucked and chewed off the seed. The overall flavor of both, however, strongly resembles that of a grade of inexpensive soap, and my throat would often burn when I ate these fruits. The seeds of both are later roasted, broken open by smashing them with stones and the white flesh inside eaten. A third palm fruit, *ediweshi*, abounds in swampy areas. It is a tangerine color, about the size of a large hen's egg, and covered with hundreds of small scales, not unlike fish scales. *Ediweshi* fruits look like tiny red hand-grenades. When the dry fruit first falls from the tree, it is very leathery and difficult to peel. The Yąnomamö usually throw the fruits into a pond of water, where most of them usually fall in the first place, and wait for them to be softened by soaking. Then the scaly skin can be scraped off with the fingernails. Underneath is a thin layer of yellowish, soft, sometimes slimy flesh that has a pleasant similarity to the taste of cheese. It was great fun to go "hunting" for *ediweshi* fruits with the Yąnomamö. We would probe around the knee-deep muddy water to find the fruit. When we accumulated a half-bushel or so, we would then gather around the pile and eat them and gossip. My general reaction to all the palm fruits just described is that it takes a tremendous number of them to fill your belly, and the effort required is enormous.

Wild honey is one of the most highly prized foods of all, and the Yąnomamö will go to great extremes to get it. Should someone spot a bee's nest, all other plans are dropped and honey becomes the priority of the day. One can usually assume that when someone returns to the village later than expected, he has been detained because he ran into a cache of honey.

Most honey—and there are many kinds—is harvested by ripping the combs out of the nest, often a hollow tree, and soaking wads of leaves in the liquid that remains in the nest. The honey-soaked leaves are rinsed in water. If nobody has a container with him, a shallow pit is dug in the ground, lined with broad leaves, and filled with water. The Yąnomamö dip the combs into the watery pit and eat them, larvae and all. The watery liquid usually has large numbers of larvae and a few stunned bees floating on top, as well as much other debris. They dip the liquid out using cups fashioned from leaves, or, if they have a cooking pot, they pass it around, blowing the debris aside before drinking. Should the nest contain a large amount, they squeeze the honey-soaked leaves onto a pile of broad leaves and wrap it up to take home. Leaf-lined pits filled with water are also used to make other beverages from a variety of palm fruits. The fruits are skinned and kneaded by hand in the water until it is sweet enough, and the beverage is consumed by dipping cupfuls out of the pit.

One of the most ingenious gathering techniques is the process of collecting the large, fat palm-pith grubs. The Yąnomamö fell a large palm and eat the heart. Many days later, they return to the decaying tree and begin chopping it apart to get at the soft spongy pith inside. By then, a species of insect has laid its eggs in the pith and the eggs have developed into large grubs, some the size of mice! This grub looks like a housefly maggot, but a very large one. As they dig the pith out with sticks they run into the fat grubs, perhaps 50 or 60 of them in a good-sized tree. Each squirming grub is bitten behind its head and held tightly between the teeth. A strong pull leaves the head and entrails dangling from the teeth. These are spit out, and the remainder is tossed, still squirming, into a leaf bundle. Grubs damaged by the digging sticks are eaten on the spot, raw. Leaf bundles containing grubs are tossed onto the coals of the fire and roasted, rendering down into liquid fat and a shriveled white corpse. The corpse is eaten in a single gulp, the fat enthusiastically licked from the leaves and fingers. I ate a number of different kinds of insects with the Yąnomamö, some of them quite tasty, but I simply could not bring myself to eat the palm-pith grubs. An experienced missionary who tried them said they tasted to him like very fat bacon, but I suppose anything fat that is cooked in a smoky fire would taste like bacon. The fascinating thing about palm-grub collecting is that it comes very close to being an incipient form of animal domestication, for the Yąnomamö clearly fell the tree with the intention of providing fodder for the insect eggs, and with the intention of harvesting the grubs after they mature to a desirable size.

Another interesting hunting technique has to do with taking armadillos. Armadillos live in burrows several feet underground, burrows that can run for many yards and have several entries. When the Yąnomamö find an active burrow, determined by the presence of a cloud of insects around the entry, an insect that is found only there, they set about smoking out the armadillo. The most desirable fuel for smoking out armadillos is the crusty material in old termite nests, which burns very slowly, producing an intense heat and enormous amounts of heavy smoke. A pile of this is ignited at the entry of the burrow and the smoke is fanned into the burrow. Other entries are soon detected as smoke begins to rise from them, and are sealed off with dirt. The men then spread out on hands and knees, holding their ears to the ground to listen for armadillo digging or movement in the burrow. When they hear it, they dig down into the ground until they hit the burrow and, hopefully, the animal. They might have to make several attempts, which is hard work—they have to dig two or more feet down before hitting it. On one occasion they had dug several holes, all unsuccessful; they even missed the burrow. One of the men then ripped down a large vine, tied a knot in the end of it, and put the knotted end into the armadillo entrance. He twirled the vine between his hands, gradually pushing it into the hole. When it would go no further, he broke it off at the burrow entrance, pulled it out, and then laid it on the ground along the axis of the burrow. They dug down where the knot was and found the armadillo on the first attempt, asphyxiated from the smoke.

## Gardening

Although the Yąnomamö actually spend as much or more time hunting as they do gardening, the bulk of their food comes from cultivated plants in most areas (summarized in Hames, 1989, 1992). The Yąnomamö were persistently described by early visitors to the region as "hunters and gatherers," but that was a characterization based on misinformation or on the romantic assumption that a tribe so unknown and so remote simply had to exist in the "most primitive" conditions imaginable, and therefore had to be hunters and gatherers. Upwards of 80% to 90% of the food eaten by the Yąnomamö is from their gardens in most areas (Chagnon, 1966; Lizot, 1971c), and their political, economic, and military activities reflect this fact in an overwhelming manner. Of their domesticated foods, plantains are by far the most important item in their diet. To be sure, this horticultural emphasis must certainly be a post-Columbian phenomenon, but it would be reasonable to assume that prior to plantains they relied heavily on manioc, maize, and several indigenous varieties of cultivated tubers (see below).

The Yąnomamö are constantly aware of the potentials and suitability of the regions they hunt as future village and garden sites, for their warfare patterns dictate that they must eventually move their villages to such new areas. When I hunted with them, evening conversations around the campfire would frequently revolve around the merits of this particular area as a potential new garden site. Hunters are the ones who usually discover the regions that will be the future sites of their villages when a long move is required. Land for a new site should not be heavily covered with low, thorny brush, since it is difficult to clear and burn. The larger trees should not predominate in an area, for too much labor would be required to fell them. Ideally, the new site should have very light tree cover, should be well drained, and, most important, should not be inundated in the wet season. It should be near a reliable source of convenient drinking water. One conception they have about potential new garden sites is implied in their word for savanna: *börösö*. Savanna to them is not merely a stretch of land that is treeless, but a jungle that has widely spaced trees that would be relatively easy to clear for gardening. They occasionally also refer to a potentially useful tract of jungle by the very name they use for a cleared garden itself: *hikari täkä*, a "hole" in the jungle where a garden exists.

The first activity in making a new garden is to cut the smaller trees and low brush. The larger trees, *kayaba hii*, are left standing until the undergrowth is cleared. Then most of the larger trees are felled with steel axes and left lying on the ground for several weeks so the branches and leaves can dry out. Especially large trees are felled by chopping them down from scaffolds, which are built 10 or more feet above the ground: There the stump is not so thick and less chopping is required to fell the tree.

My older informants claimed that they did not have steel axes when they were younger and had to kill the big trees by cutting a ring of bark off the base of the stump with a crude stone or by piling brush and deadfall wood around the bases of the large trees. They burned the brush to kill the tree, which would then drop its leaves and allow enough light to reach the ground to permit their crops to grow. The dead trees were simply allowed to remain standing. Informants also claimed that making a garden was much more work in those days because a large area would have to be scoured in order to accumulate enough wood and brush to kill the larger trees with fire. Today steel axes are so common that even the uncontacted villages enjoy relatively new ax heads that get traded into them via the intermediate Yąnomamö villages that link theirs to the mission posts whence most steel tools now come. Still, I have contacted remote villages where steel axes were not only rare, but so badly worn from previous use that at least 50% of the blade was gone. The rate at which steel tools and other Western items are now entering the region is nothing short of incredible. One Catholic missionary I knew very well, Padre Luis Cocco, gave the members of his village—some 130 people—over 3,000 steel machetes in a 14-year period, plus hundreds of axes, aluminum cooking pots, knives, and hundreds of thousands of meters of nylon fishing line and an equivalent number of steel fishhooks. These items were quickly dispersed, through trade, to not only the villages immediately adjacent to his, but far inland to the most remote villages (Chagnon and Asch, 1974b). Other mission posts where permanent contact with the Yąnomamö now exists provide large quantities of these same items to the Yąnomamö on both the Venezuelan and Brazilian sides of the border. Before the arrival of missionaries, the Yąnomamö appear to have gotten steel tools from the Carib-speaking Ye'kwana Indians to their north, who have been known to be in contact with Westerners for 200 years. The Ye'kwana, a people who have carried the art of dugout canoe building to a high degree of sophistication, would take trips as far away as Georgetown, Guyana, to trade with the English colonists there—long before Westerners penetrated their area to establish permanent contacts. Whole villages of Yąnomamö would go to the Ye'kwana villages to work for them for several months to earn steel tools and other items, tools that would eventually be traded further and further inland to the remote Yąnomamö villages, whose members had never seen the Ye'kwana. A similar relationship between the northern Yąnomamö villages and the Ye'kwana still exists, a relationship that has occasionally and erroneously been called "slavery" (see Arvelo-Jimenez, 1971; Hames, 1978 for discussions of Ye'kwana/ Yąnomamö political relationships).

I draw attention to the trade in exogenous items for a number of reasons. First, to make it clear that the Yąnomamö have had access to some steel tools for as long as 100 years, perhaps in some areas near the Ye'kwana for longer than that. This might possibly be important in understanding the rapid population growth that I have documented among several large clusters of Yąnomamö villages for the past 125 years—a "population explosion" that might be related to both the introduction of an efficient, productive cultigen—plantains—on the one hand, and steel tools that make gardening much more efficient and productive on the other. Second, I want to emphasize that "uncontacted" as a description of some villages is a relative term: The residents of such villages might never have seen outsiders, but they and their ancestors might have had some benefits derived from exogenous items that were introduced into the New World by Europeans—such as steel tools and certain cultivated plants. Useful items often spread rapidly between cultures, a process that does not require direct contact, and such items often set about changes in the recipient cultures that transform them into new and different kinds of cultures. Classic examples of this process abound in the anthropological literature. For example, the nomadic equestrian buffalo-hunting cultures of the North American Great Plains region came into existence only after the introduction of firearms via the French and English traders in Canada and the introduction of horses via the Spaniards in Mexico (Secoy, 1953). Prior to this, the cultures of the Great Plains that we emphasize in both our anthropology textbooks and our theatrical films simply did not exist in any form resembling what we now have fixed in our impressions. Again, many of the dramatic cultural processes and situations that are found in Highland New Guinea and in much of Micronesia and Polynesia owe their form and content to economies based on the cultivation of the sweet potato, a plant that was brought to these areas from the New World after the discovery of the Americas in the 16th century. Finally, many traditions and technoeconomic realities affecting Western European culture took form because of borrowed plant crops from the Americas. Karl Marx, for example, once mused that the Industrial Revolution could not have succeeded without the white potato, a cheap and efficient food for a large labor force: The potato came to Europe from the Andes. And what would pizza be like without tomato sauce, the tomato being another New World plant introduced to Europe after Columbus?

Thus, the Yąnomamö clear their trees with steel tools today, often not knowing the provenance of the tools they use or paying much attention to the question in the first place—other than "we got this ax from the Monou-teri" or "that machete came from the Abruwä-teri." They then plant these sites primarily with a crop that was introduced to the New World after Columbus (Reynolds, 1927).

The larger trees are usually felled toward the end of the wet season, although I have seen them do this kind of work at other times of the year, especially when military relationships imposed compelling schedules on them. In general, clearing the jungle tends to be a wet season activity and burning the brush and smaller branches a dry season activity, but Yąnomamö gardening is far less systematic than the slash-and-burn schedules found in many other parts of the world (see Conklin, 1961, for a useful bibliography on swidden farming; and Carneiro, 1960, 1961, for an excellent analysis of swidden cultivation in the Amazon Basin). An adequate burning of the felled timber can be achieved even during the rainy season, provided that the fallen timber has had two or three days of sunshine in succession to dry it out. Only the smaller branches are burned, along with the brush and scrubby vegetation, and it is therefore not necessary to wait until the large trunks are dry. They are left lying helter-skelter on the ground and serve as "boundaries" between patches of foodcrops owned by different families and as firewood.

## Other Garden Products

Many kinds of additional foods and other nonfood cultigens can be found in most Yąnomamö gardens. Among the more important foods not yet discussed are several root crops. Manioc, a starchy root staple widely found throughout the Amazon Basin, is cultivated in small quantities by most Yąnomamö. They usually grow the sweet variety, that is, a variety that contains little or no cyanic acid, a lethal poison that must be leached from the manioc pulp before it can be eaten (see Cock, 1982). When the pulp of the poisonous manioc is exposed to air, as it is when it is uprooted and peeled, the toxin oxidizes into hydrocyanic acid, found in the substance used in those states that use the gas chamber in capital punishment. The Yąnomamö are beginning to use larger and larger amounts of bitter (poisonous) manioc in the north, where their villages are found near the villages of the Carib-speaking Ye'kwana, who have diffused both the plant and the proper refining techniques into the Yąnomamö area. In Kąobawä's area, the sweet manioc variety is dominant. It is refined into a pulp by grating the roots on rough rocks. The moist white pulp is made into thick patty cakes about 10 inches in diameter, and then cooked on both sides by placing the cakes on a hot piece of broken pottery (Figure 2.8). Ye'kwana cakes are much larger—up to 3 feet in diameter. In general, the Yąnomamö prefer foods that require little or no processing, a kind of "take it from the vine, throw it on the fire" attitude that applies to both vegetable and animal foods alike.

Three other root crops are also widely cultivated and provide relatively large amounts of calories in the Yąnomamö diet. One is called *ohina*, a South American variety of taro (*xanthosoma*). Sweet potatoes (*hukomo*) are also cultivated, as is another potato-like root known in Spanish as *mapuey* and in Yąnomamö as *kabiromö*, or a slightly different variety called *aha akö*. All these are usually roasted in the hot coals of the hearth, peeled by finger after cooking, and eaten with no condiments.[4]

Perhaps another dozen food items of less importance are grown by the Yąnomamö, but not all of them are found in every garden. Avocados, papaya trees, and hot peppers are among the more important of these.

Several very important nonedible cultigens are also found in all or most Yąnomamö gardens. Arrow cane is grown for its long, straight shafts, which are dried in the sun and made into hunting or war arrows, exceptionally long by our standards: 6 feet. They are light and springy, but can be shot completely through the body of an animal or a man.

Without a doubt, the most significant nonfood cultigen in any Yąnomamö garden is tobacco, to which men, women, and children are all addicted. Their word for "being poor" is literally "to be without tobacco": *hǫri*. They chew rather than smoke their tobacco, but the chewing is perhaps better described as sucking. Each family cultivates its own tobacco patch and jealously guards it from

---

4. The Yąnomamö make a salty-tasting liquid from the ashes of a particular tree on rare occasions, and dip their food into it. It is probably calcium chloride rather than sodium chloride. When the Yąnomamö first taste salt, they detest it and claim that it 'itches' their teeth and gums. They gradually become addicted to it, and beg for it frequently.

**FIGURE 2.8** Kạobawä's younger brothers preparing packs of food at the end of a feast. These will be given to the guests to eat on their way home. Each pack contains vegetable food—cassave bread in this case—and smoked meat. (Yạnomamö cassave bread is smaller and moister than that made by their Carib neighbors.)

the potential theft of neighbors—a common problem when someone in the village runs out of tobacco, either by giving too much away to visitors in trade or having his crop fail. It is the only crop I saw in a Yạnomamö garden that is sometimes fenced off to remind avaricious neighbors that the owner is overtly and conspicuously protecting his crop from theft. The fence, a flimsy corral of thin sticks stuck into the ground and laced together with vines, would not prevent theft; it is merely a proclamation that the owner is prepared to defend his tobacco plants with more than the usual vigor. I have even seen some Yạnomamö bury "booby traps" in their tobacco patches to cause any poacher severe discomfort; very sharp, long splinters of bone were buried, and an unsuspecting intruder would have a painful sliver in his foot for a long time. Addiction to tobacco is so complete that even relatively young children—10 years old or so—are hooked. They prepare their tobacco in a somewhat complex way. It is first harvested, selecting the individual leaves at the peak of maturity. The leaves are then tied together by the stems, 15 or 20 at a time, and hung over the hearth to cure in both the heat and the smoke of the fire. Once dried, the leaves are stored by making large balls, wrapped in other leaves to keep insects and moisture out. As needed, several leaves of the cured tobacco are removed from the ball, dipped in a calabash of water to moisten them, and then kneaded in the ashes of the campfire until the entire leaf is covered with a muddy layer of wood ashes. The ashes of particular kinds of wood are preferred for this. The ashy leaf is then rolled into a short, fat, cigar-like wad, which is often bound with fine fibers to keep it in that general shape. The large wad is then, with conspicuous pleasure, placed between the lower lip and teeth, and the preparer reclines in his or her hammock with a blissful sigh and sucks on the gritty, greenish, and very large wad. They are also very sociable about tobacco. When someone removes his wad and lays it down for a second, another might promptly snatch it up and suck on it until its owner wants it back. The borrower may be a child, a buddy, a wife, a stranger, or, if willing, the anthropologist. It should be clear that tobacco use among the Yąnomamö lends itself very effectively to the rapid spread of viruses and infectious diseases at both the village and regional levels.

Cotton is also an important cultigen. Cotton yarn is used for hammock manufacturing as well as for "clothing" (Figure 2.9). One must have a fairly generous interpretation of the last word, since Yąnomamö clothing is largely symbolic and decorative. Indeed, some well-dressed men sport nothing more than a string around their waists to which they tie the stretched-out foreskins of their penises. As a young boy begins growing and maturing, he starts to act masculine by tying his penis to his waist string. The Yąnomamö use this cultural/ontogenic phase to quite accurately describe the age of young boys: "My son is now tying his penis up." A certain amount of teasing takes place at this time, since it is difficult to control the penis when you are young and inexperienced. It takes time to stretch the foreskin to the length required to tie it adequately and securely, and until that happens, it keeps slipping out of the string, much to the embarrassment of its owner and much to the mirth of the older boys and men around. Sometimes older boys and men accidentally get "untied," causing great embarrassment—for it is like being completely naked.[5] A penis string is not comfortable. Take my word for it. Wherever possible, as at mission posts, the

---

5. So circumspect are the men about this that in the passion of a serious fight or duel they will cease hostilities momentarily should one of the contestants come untied. There is an amusing scene in our film *Yąnomama: A Multidisciplinary Study* (listed at the back of the book) in which two men are pounding each other violently in a chest-pounding duel. The penis string of one of them comes untied and both, without any discussion, temporarily cease the duel until he gets his penis tied up again, at which point they resume slugging it out. Women, too, are very careful and modest despite the fact that they are dressed no more adequately than the men. Thus, a girl or woman will be very careful when rising from a sitting position, crossing her legs to conceal as well as she can her otherwise naked pubis.

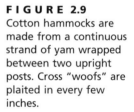

**FIGURE 2.9**
Cotton hammocks are made from a continuous strand of yam wrapped between two upright posts. Cross "woofs" are plaited in every few inches.

men become rapidly accustomed to wearing short pants or loincloths and these become popular trade items very quickly. Men who wear pants stop tying their penises. It should not be assumed that all customs are enjoyed or liked by the practitioners, a topic of anthropological research that deserves far more attention than it has thus far received.

Most cultivated cotton is used for making hammocks. A continuous strand of spun cotton yarn is wrapped around two upright posts until the proper width of the finished hammock is achieved, and then cross-seams are plaited vertically every few inches to hold the strands in place (Figure 2.9). When this is done, the posts are removed from the ground and the ends of the hammock are tied with stronger cotton yarn, giving a finished hammock about 5 to 6 feet long. Everyone wants to have a permanent cotton hammock, but since they are often given in trade, many people make do with a flimsier, less comfortable hammock made of vines. Women also use cotton yarn to make a small waistband that is quite pretty but covers nothing. Cotton yarn is also used to make armbands and a loose, multistring, halter-like garment that is worn by women that is crossed between the breasts and in the middle of the back. Some men often wear a fat cotton belt that looks like a giant sausage; they tie their penises to this. Men, women, and children wear single strands of cotton string around their wrists, ankles, knees, or chests. Apart from this, there is no other "clothing."

Finally, in some villages a variety of magical plants are cultivated. Most are associated with casting spells on others, spells that are often nonmalevolent as in the case of "female charms" called *suwä hqrö*. Tiny packets of dusty powder, wrapped in leaves, are used by men to "seduce" young women. The charm is forced against the woman's nose and mouth. When she breathes the charm, she swoons and has an insatiable desire for sex—so say both the men and the women. The women also cultivate magical plants in some villages that allegedly cause the men to become tranquil and sedate. It is thrown on the men especially when they are fighting, the intended effect being to make the men less violent.

In villages to the north of Kąobawä's, people allegedly cultivate an especially malevolent plant that can be "blown" on enemies at a great distance, or sprinkled on unwary male visitors while they sleep. A particularly feared class of these is called *oka* and is said to be blown through tubes at enemies, causing them to sicken and die. Kąobawä's group does not use *oka*, but they insist that their enemies do. Their enemies, in turn, disclaim its use but claim that Kąobawä's group uses it. It is one of those harmful practices that you are sure the enemy employs but one that you yourself do not engage in. All Yąnomamö groups are convinced that unaccountable deaths in their own village are the result of the use of harmful magic and charms directed at them by enemy groups.

## Slash-and-Burn Farming

Each man clears his own land for gardening, usually starting this life-time activity once he is married. Adult brothers will usually clear adjacent portions of land and, if their father is still living, his garden will be among theirs. Thus, connections between males that are important for other social relationships (to be discussed in a later chapter) are also significant in the distribution of garden plots and land use. The size of a plot is determined, in some measure, by one's family size and kinship obligations, but some men are poor planners and occasionally underestimate how much land they have to clear in order to plant sufficient food to take care of their family's needs. I once overheard a Yąnomamö headman, who was annoyed that one of the inmarried men in his village chronically had to borrow food from others, scold the man viciously as he inspected his garden: "This isn't big enough for your wife and children!" He warned, "You will have to beg plantains from others if you don't make it bigger! See that tree over there? Clear your garden out to there and you will have enough—and you won't have to beg from the rest of us later!" His tone of voice was such as to make it clear that future begging would be greeted with no small amount of reticence. One mistake might be overlooked, but persistent ones are not.

Headmen tend to make larger gardens than other men, for they assume a considerable responsibility for entertaining periodic groups of visitors that must be fed. They also contribute much more food to a feast when all the members of an allied village arrive to spend several days. Kąobawä's garden is much larger than those of other men. He is helped by younger brothers in some of the heavy work and by his wife's brother, a man who has no wife or dependent children— largely because he is something of a brute and a bit on the stupid and unattractive side. He is, however, an unflinching supporter of Kąobawä and will work indefatigably to help him garden. This man's son also helped Kąobawä in gardening, for he was eligible to marry any of Kąobawä's daughters, putting him into a relationship in which he "owed" Kąobawä favors and service. The young man is Bäkotawä, the guide who abandoned me in the headwaters of the Mavaca River when I made first contact with Sibarariwä's group.

When the garden plot is ready to burn, the brush and smaller branches are stacked into piles and ignited. Other brush is added as it is ripped from the fallen trees. A man might have several such fires going in his garden, and each man burns his garden at a time most convenient for him. Sometimes the fires are placed around the large, fallen timbers, which dries them out and makes them easier to split into firewood, the collection of which is almost entirely the woman's task and the quantities of which are staggering. I had not anticipated that firewood could be such a major concern of the Yąnomamö or any tropical forest society, but very large quantities of firewood are needed—for cooking, for keeping warm at night, and for cremating the remains of dead people. Women spend a large amount of daily effort collecting firewood, and try to do so with minimal inconvenience and effort. Thus, a fallen tree in the garden plot— especially a species that splits easily—is jealously regarded and becomes a useful resource. Over time, the more useful large trees are gradually split, broken, or chopped into firewood by the women and the garden gets "cleaner" as it matures. A woman should not take firewood from the garden plot of a neighbor unless invited to do so. Firewood is not only valuable and important to the Yąnomamö, but somewhat to my own surprise, is a strategic resource in many other parts of the world as well (*National Academy of Science*, 1980).

Planting the newly cleared and burned garden proceeds in one of two ways. If the site is at a considerable distance from the village, a great deal of strategic planning is involved as to crop mixture and maturity of the cuttings that will be transplanted. If the new garden is simply an extension of the old one, a different kind of strategy is involved, for the transport of seeds and cuttings is a small problem.

# THE CULTURAL ECOLOGY OF SETTLEMENT PATTERN

## Micro Movements of Villages and Gardens

Let us consider the first and simplest scenario of making new gardens. A Yąnomamö garden lasts about three years from the time of initial planting. As the garden becomes overrun with scrub vegetation and thorny brush and foodcrops nearly depleted, an extension is added to the garden by simply clearing the land around the periphery. At this point, the old garden is referred to as an old woman—unable to produce anymore. The new extension is called the "nose"' and is added onto the old woman part as the latter is allowed to fall into disuse. The old woman part is also called the "anus" of the garden.

Some anthropologists during the 1950s and 1960s, when the theory of cultural ecology first began having a major impact on studies of cultural adaptation, argued that slash-and-burn gardens in tropical forest regions such as the kind occupied by the Yąnomamö had to be abandoned simply because the crops exhausted the soil nutrients and new, fresh land had to be brought under cultivation because of this problem. As the argument went, local villages in the tropical forest could not exceed a certain size limit, and complex cultural developments were impossible because the generally poor quality of the soils demanded chronic movement and relocation. In the 1950s, an anthropologist named Robert L. Carneiro decided to put this argument to an empirical test, using his own meticulous field research, among the Kuikuru of the Brazilian Xingu area (Carneiro, 1960, 1961). His work literally overturned the "poverty of the soil" argument that purported to account for village relocations in this kind of environment. By measuring crop yields in Kuikuru gardens, testing soil samples for declining fertility, and noting several measurable variables, such as acreage required to support an average family or an individual, distance from the garden to the village that cultivators were willing to travel, and how long it took an old garden to regenerate new forest after being abandoned, he showed quite convincingly that tropical forest villages larger than 500 people were easily feasible, that villages did not have to move because of soil depletion, and that a high level of horticultural productivity could be maintained in the lands immediately surrounding a typical village. In short, he argued that whatever it was that lay behind the village relocations of tribes like the Kuikuru, exhaustion of soil nutrients was not a very persuasive explanation. Moreover, soil exhaustion could not be convincingly given as the explanation for why villages failed to exceed 500 people, or be used as an explanation of cultural inertia due to low productivity. Indeed, he was able to show that the Kuikuru produced more calories per acre than Inca farmers and did so with much less labor effort (Carneiro, 1961). Few people argue today that settlement relocation in the aboriginal societies of the tropical forest of Amazonia can be reduced simply to soil poverty. The issue is much more complex than that, and many variables are involved in the decisions that lie behind village movements.

The short movements of gardens by the Yąnomamö can be thought of as "micro" movements and entail either the extension of an existing garden or the clearing of a new garden a few hundred or so meters from the existing garden. In either case, the planting of new crops is relatively easily accomplished, for the seeds and cuttings do not have to be carried very far. The reasons given by the Yąnomamö for making new gardens in this way are similar to those found among the Kuikuru studied by Carneiro and are also documented for other Amazonian cultivators: The vegetation that begins to grow up in maturing gardens is dense and usually very thorny, and therefore very unpleasant and tedious to clear and burn. This must be done by people who wear no clothing, and if you ever have to make your way through such vegetation in the buff, you will immediately understand the wisdom of avoiding such brush. Another reason the Yąnomamö do not like to work in old gardens is the snake problem mentioned above.

Figure 2.10 illustrates micro movements of Yąnomamö gardening and how adjacent new land is brought under cultivation. Since, as I have described above, the *shabono* must be rethatched every two or three years, the movement of a garden a few hundred yards might be the occasion to move the *shabono* as well—to keep it located conveniently near the food crops.

The Yąnomamö prefer to remain in one general area a long time, especially one that has a reliable source of game within a reasonable walk from the village. My research has revealed many cases of the same village remaining in one area for 60 to 80 years, leaving it only when the military pressures on it are

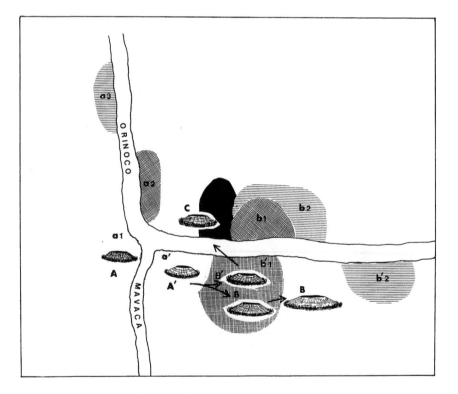

**FIGURE 2.10**  "Micro" movements of the Bisaasi-teri between 1960 and 1968, showing how new gardens were added as extensions of older ones. When the Bisaasi-teri moved here, there were two shabonos on opposite sides of the Mavaca River, just a few hundred feet from each other (A and A'). Kąobawä's group (A') decided to make two new shabonos (B and B') when they extended their gardens, the first sign of a fission. Eventually one group (B') moved across the Orinoco to begin a separate existence (C). Kąobawä's group remained behind (B) and just a few hundred feet from the two other shabonos. (From Chagnon, 1968c.)

overwhelming. A second attraction for remaining in the same general area has to do with the domesticated peach palm trees that produce very large crops of prized fruits every year. They continue to produce long after the garden is abandoned, so the Yąnomamö like to remain reasonably close to old, abandoned gardens to harvest these fruits. This palm is an exception to my earlier generalization that it takes a great many palm fruits to get a full belly. Peach palm fruits have a relatively small seed (some have no seed at all) and a very large amount of mealy flesh, about the texture of boiled potatoes, rich in oil, and very tasty. Families usually plant one or several of these trees every time a garden is cleared, and the trees produce very large crops of fruits for many years after the gardens have been abandoned (Figure 2.11). Thus, if the Yąnomamö remain in a general area, their peach palm crops can be easily and conveniently harvested and yield enormous quantities of tasty, nutritious fruit.

Plantains, bananas, and manioc are cultivated by the generative process, that is, cuttings are transplanted: No seeds are sown. As a plantain tree matures, it sends out underground suckers that sprout, each of which in turn can grow into a new productive tree. Each mature plantain tree produces one bunch of fruits, often very large (depending on variety), and when this is cut, the plant is

**FIGURE 2.11**
Rerebawä climbing a rasha tree to harvest the fruit. He rests on one "A-frame" and pushes the second one up higher, climbs onto that one, and then pulls the lower one up. In this fashion he painstakingly reaches the top of the 75-foot tree; he lowers the fruit with a vine.

then useless and it, too, is cut to the ground to make room for the growing young suckers. The suckers are the next generation of plantain, for each will produce a new bunch of fruits at maturity. These can be transplanted when they are very small—a few inches high—or when they are very large—several feet high. The larger they are, of course, the heavier they are. But the larger they are, the sooner they yield their fruit. Thus, a man who wants to have a new crop of plantains soon will transplant large suckers, each weighing 10 pounds or more. But one does not want all the plantains to mature at the same time, for most of them will be wasted. Thus, a good garden has plantains in various stages of growth and nearness to maturity to ensure that there will be reliable, abundant food all year long. Probably 80% of the calories from cultivated foods comes from plantains, and the gardens reflect that emphasis in terms of the proportion of land that is given to plantain cultivation. It takes about four months for a large sucker to yield a ripe bunch of plantains— perhaps six months for a small sucker to do the same.

## Macro Movements of Villages and Gardens

The warfare pattern waxes and wanes in all Yąnomamö areas. Years may go by in some regions, such as on the periphery of the tribe, where no intervillage conflicts occur. Where all villages are surrounded by neighbors on all sides, as in Kąobawä's area, the periodicity of active wars is as follows. First, it is rare for long periods of tranquility between villages to occur. Several years might pass without raids on or by some neighboring group, but anything beyond that is not common. Second, once hostilities between villages erupt and someone gets killed, the contestants are locked in mortal relationships for many years and do not have the option of migrating away into a new, totally unoccupied area, as do the villages on the periphery of the tribe. This essentially means that villages in Kąobawä's area have no choice but to develop political alliances with some neighbors, for it is impossible to move into distant land and escape from enemies, and it is unwise to "leapfrog" past distant neighbors, for there are other, less known Yąnomamö beyond them who may be more difficult to deal with than one's immediate neighbors. But the distance between Yąnomamö villages is very large in Kąobawä's area, so relatively long moves can sometimes be effected— four or five days' walk—in order to escape from enemies and start a new garden elsewhere. I have characterized this situation as *social circumscription* (Chagnon, 1968b), similar in effect to Carneiro's (1961) "geographic circumscription." Carneiro argued that the world's major civilizations—Egypt, Mesopotamia, the Incas, and so on—all developed in regions that were circumscribed by deserts, the sea, or other geographical features that restricted expansion and therefore encouraged increasing intensification of land use within the developing region (Carneiro, 1961). He argued that this leads to increased complexity in social organization. My argument about social circumscription is similar, for Yąnomamö villages, whose ability to move is restricted by the existence of neighbors on all fronts, seem to be somewhat more complex in organization and much larger in population than those on the tribal periphery, where migration to virgin unoccupied lands is not impeded. Carneiro (1970), in turn, adopted the notion of social circumscription into his general theory of the origin of the state. The long moves made by the Yạnomamö are not provoked by horticultural techniques or the demands made on gardening from crop type, soils, maturity of gardens, or deterioration of the *shabono*. I call these *macro movements*. They are motivated by politics and warfare and must be understood in this context. The most relevant "ecological" variables here are human neighbors, not so much technology, economic practices, or inherent features of the physical environment as such.

Figure 2.12 illustrates how a macro move is effected when a group of Yạnomamö must abandon its currently producing garden and begin a new one a long distance away. It will become increasingly clear why "alliances" with neighbors is a kind of cultural adaptation that permits the Yạnomamö to have some flexibility in dealing with—adapting to—intervillage warfare and conflict. Chapter 6 describes this pattern in considerable detail, in the context of a specific war and settlement relocation.

The first phase in some macro moves is the recognition that continued residence in the village or area will lead to violent fighting in which someone near and dear to you (or you yourself) will be badly injured or killed—with clubs, machetes, axes, or arrows. All the members of a village might be united and act collectively in a move, the threat or danger being the presence of hostile enemies in other villages, enemies who begin raiding your group chronically and take a small toll per raid but one that over time becomes significant. The constant fear

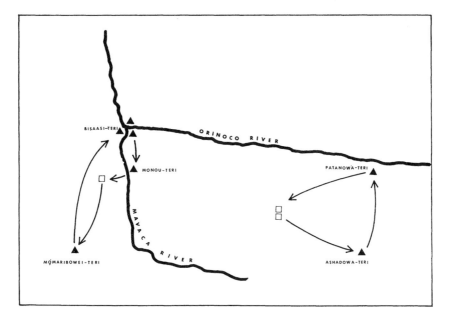

**FIGURE 2.12** How new gardens/villages are established at a long distance (short-term "macro" movements) from old garden/village. (From Chagnon, 1968b.)

and worry that raiders might be lurking outside is sufficient to increase the level of anxiety and tension in a village and disrupt the normal patterns of movement and social existence. When raiders are feared, nobody leaves the village alone. Even the women, who must collect firewood and water daily, have to be escorted the few yards to the garden or stream by armed men, who nervously keep their eyes peeled for telltale sounds and movements in the jungle, or the disturbance of birds in the distance, fidgeting with their nocked war arrows as the women collect the wood or water. During these times, people are even afraid to leave the village to defecate, and they are forced to do so on leaves, which are then thrown over the palisade. Several weeks or months of this is exhausting, and life could be more relaxed if one lived elsewhere, a greater distance from the known enemy. In other cases, there might be factions within the village that become increasingly hostile to each other and increasingly violent in their arguments and duels, usually over sexual trysts and infidelity, which are easily provoked by snide comments, thinly veiled insults, or any one of a host of trivialities that ruffles someone's feathers the wrong way. As villages grow larger, internal order and cooperation become difficult, and eventually factions develop: Certain kin take sides with each other, and social life becomes strained. There appears to be an upper limit to the size of a group that can be cooperatively organized by the principles of kinship, descent, and marriage, the "integrating" mechanisms characteristically at the disposal of primitive peoples, a fascinating question to which we will return later. Suffice it to say here, kinship-organized groups can only get so large before they begin falling apart—fissioning into smaller groups. This size limit appears to be as much a function of the inherent properties of kinship and marriage alliance as it is a function of "strategic resources"— the material things that sustain people and permit them to live in large social groups that are sedentary and fixed. One might, in this vein, view the long history of both our hunting and gathering ancestral past, as well as our more recent shorter history as cultivators, as a struggle to overcome the limitations on group size imposed by the traditional principles of organization that mark most of our history: transcending kinship and adding new kinds of organizational principles. Many general discussions of our social past as hunters and early cultivators allude to the "magic" numbers of 50 to 100 as the general community size within which our recent cultural and biosocial evolution occurred (see Lee & Devore, 1968), a maximal community size that was transcended only in the very recent past—within the last several thousand years.[6]

Thus, large villages eventually break up and subdivide into smaller villages, usually by a bifurcation of the large group into two similar-sized smaller villages, occasionally into three. One of the groups retains possession of the existing, productive garden—or that portion of it that belongs to them—and the other faction must move away to clear, burn, plant, and begin life elsewhere in a new garden.

---

6. See Briggs (1983) for a summary of the remarkable rate at which large cities have emerged. Carneiro (1970) draws attention to the tremendous significance of the first development of supra local political organization of a nonkinship sort.

The distances between the recently fissioned groups can be small or large, depending on the precise nature of the confrontation that causes the fission. Thus, they may simply build two separate *shabonos* located only a few yards away from each other and live *he borarawä*, side by side. This solution occurs when it would be hazardous for the larger group to fission and create two small, distantly located villages that would be easy prey to hostile neighbors who might otherwise avoid attacking the larger village or one of the two closely situated splinter villages. Such a solution or alternative is not possible, however, if the final confrontation that determines the split leads to the death of someone. Then, despite the number and determination of other enemies, the group must fission into two parts and one of the new groups must move far away and begin a new, separate garden.

Making a new garden from scratch and keeping yourself well fed can be a problem if you must abandon your existing productive garden without warning. If, for example, 100 people from a village of 200 must suddenly pull up roots and immediately leave the group after a fight that led to the death of someone, they have only two choices. Either they can flee to a neighboring village that has been "friendly" to them in past dealings and "mooch" off them for several months, or they can tough it out by a combination of living extensively off wild foods and periodic visits to friendly villages where they rest, gorge themselves on their host's cultivated foods, and eventually depart, bringing as much cultivated food with them as they can carry or their hosts are willing to give them. Meanwhile, they are busy clearing a new garden and attempting to get crops producing as soon as possible. Here is where a cost/benefit decision par excellence has to be made, for one must carry all the cuttings and seeds that will be transplanted in the new garden. The issue is essentially a question of an early return of desirable foods, in which case you carry few but large plantain cuttings (Figure 2.13), or a longer-term security of enduring desirable foodstuffs, in which case you carry larger numbers of smaller, lighter cuttings but have to wait longer for them to begin producing. A compromise of sorts occurs with maize. It is less desirable than plantains, but its seeds are light, easily transported in large quantities, and the maturity time is short—two to three months. Thus, one can quickly get an abundant, early, low-effort crop into the ground in a hurry, have a surfeit of food for a spell, and wait for the plantains to start maturing. I have visited Yąnomamö gardens that had been established under these circumstances, and they are totally different from "standard" gardens in the sense that the overwhelming fraction of the new garden is given over to maize cultivation. In time, plantains are gradually transplanted in large quantities and the garden composition shifts from mostly maize to mostly plantains.

The other important variable in such a move, also a function of the Yąnomamö dependence on garden produce, is the direction and precise location of the new site. Neighbors who are friendly are usually willing to provide plantain suckers for transplanting, and if it is impossible to return to the old garden to get such cuttings, the new garden must necessarily be located somewhere within a reasonable distance from a friendly neighbor who will provide the cuttings. But the combination of variables can be quite mixed and complex. For example, the

**FIGURE 2.13** Plantains are transplanted by cutting "suckers" from a larger plant, producing ivithin a few months if they are large. But the larger they are, the heavier, and transporting them a long distance is difficult and inefficient.

increase in village tensions might provoke some members of the group to begin clearing a new garden at a long distance away, anticipating the eruption of a fight that will inevitably cause a fission. One can, in short, predict the disaster and plan for it under some circumstances, and get a new garden under production prior to the final confrontation. If it never comes, the new garden is a convenient haven in which to "camp out," and may serve, ultimately, just that purpose. A more common combination of variables entails a pattern, of the sort schematically represented in Figure 2.12, in which a newly formed fission group (or any group) can sequentially exploit several human and natural resources. They can periodically return to their original productive garden to rest up, eat voraciously from their ripe crops, and leave, taking both food and cuttings with them, and camp out in their new garden where they work at felling or burning trees or planting crops, living off a combination of transported foods from their old garden and seasonally available wild foods and game. They might even send young men back to the old garden periodically to fetch more food, or to the village of a friendly neighbor, where supplies are begged. The entire group will follow a cyclical pattern of working in the garden, moving en masse to the village of an ally for a fortnight or so, thence to their producing garden, and back to the new garden.

However, this pattern involves several kinds of risks. The first one is the risk of being attacked at the old garden or getting into a fight with the members of the group from which yours is now separating. The second risk is the dependency that one enters into with the allies who provide food, refuge, or both. The

Yąnomamö are quick to take advantage of those who are vulnerable, and the "cost" of getting food or accepting refuge from allies is usually the expected sexual license with which your wives, sisters, and daughters are treated: Disadvantaged groups have to expect that the tendered friendship and support of an ally will invite some sexual advances from men of the allied village. This can be resisted only up to a point, and then one either is no longer welcome in the village or one must be prepared to overlook the chronic attempts of the hosts to seduce the women of the guests. The best solution is to visit allies for as short a time as possible, extract the maximum amount of economic and political aid in the available time, and then repair to either another ally or one of the gardens, as shown in Figure 2.12.

Once a new garden is established and is yielding crops in a chronic, reliable manner, labor follows a more regular pattern. There is no peak harvest period, for plantains, if planted in the proper fashion, are ripening all year long. Peach palm fruits do, however, ripen all at once and large quantities of them are eaten at this time—February and March. Some trees produce a smaller crop in June and July.

The dry season (September through March) is the time for feasting, visiting other villages, trading, and for many groups, the time for raiding enemies. Garden activities are at a minimum at this time of year, but ambitious families will spend an hour or two each day weeding their gardens, transplanting plantain suckers, and burning small piles of brush and debris. In general, the Yąnomamö—and many other tribal peoples who rely on either hunting and gathering or on swidden agriculture—achieve an adequate, if not abundant, subsistence level with very few hours of work per day (Lee, 1968, 1979; Hames, 1989, 1992). So notable is this aspect of primitive economies that one distinguished anthropologist referred to hunters and gatherers as the "original affluent society" (Sahlins, 1968a, b), stressing the fact that the difference between what they "need" and the "means" for achieving it is very small. In terms of absolute labor given to work this is equally true, for hunters and gatherers, like the Bushmen of the Kalahari Desert, make a living on only a few hours per day (Lee, 1979, 1984) and Yąnomamö productive efforts are about the same. By comparison, those of us in industrial society are condemned to a life of hard labor and overtime by the forces of the market!

## Population and Village Dispersal Over Time

The micro and macro movements of Yąnomamö villages distribute the population and the villages thinly over the landscape. Immediate concerns for warfare and alliances with neighbors fix the villages with respect to each other at any given point in time as their respective members attempt to "optimize" their garden and village locations. They want to be as far from active enemies as possible, but as close to current allies as they can be. With each village move, they also try to remain close to their ancient, abandoned gardens so they can continue to exploit their peach palm trees. And they do not want to make moves that entail severe deprivation caused by excessive labor (transporting cuttings a great distance) or catastrophic flight that leads to intense dependence on some erstwhile ally. Finally, some of the choices, as well as the timing of movements, are a function of the demographic properties of the village—especially the number of active, healthy adult males who will live in the new garden and village. These will be discussed in the next chapter.

The longer-term patterns that result from the immediate decisions can be determined only by interviewing scores of old people who can recall all the gardens they lived in during their lifetimes and the major events that transpired there. Two of the most important events are the enemy/ally patterns obtained at that site and the fissioning of larger groups into smaller ones. This information, when added to the genealogical information that links individual to individual by kinship and marriage ties, results in an overall settlement history of many villages, whose members are both historically and genealogically related to each other.

Figure 2.14 graphically represents the historical movements of several "blocs" of Yąnomamö, based on approximately 250 garden relocations over a period of about 150 years. This is only a fraction of the information on garden relocation in my data files to date, but it is sufficient to illustrate the point that there is a dynamic relationship between population growth in local villages and the dispersal of both populations and the villages into which they subdivide.

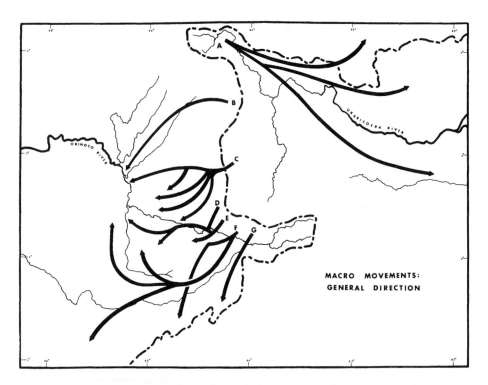

**FIGURE 2.14** Long-term effects of "macro" movements of seven groups of Yąnomamö over a 125-year period. Populations grow, fission, and spread into new areas. In time, a given region will have as many as a dozen interrelated villages that derived from the same "mother" village many years back. Kąobawä's population bloc is labeled "D"; his Shamatari neighbors are "F". (From Chagnon, 1968c.)

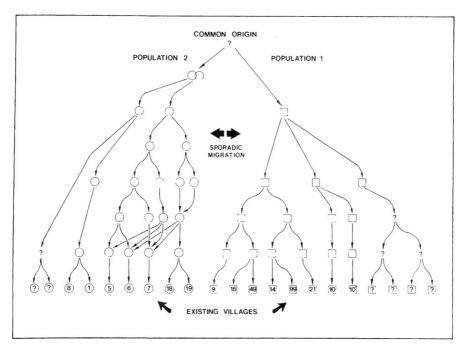

**FIGURE 2.15** Schematic showing how Namowei-teri villages (Population 2) and Shamatari villages (Population 1) are related to each other historically. (From Chagnon, 1979a.)

Figure 2.14 thus summarizes this in schematic terms, showing that it is possible to identify discrete "population blocs" and describe the long-term migration pattern each follows. Figure 2.14 in fact identifies seven such population blocs (A through G). It is possible that as many as 30 or 40 such blocs could be identified among the Yąnomamö if the field research were conducted along the lines described here and elsewhere (Chagnon, 1974).

Only two of the seven population blocs shown in Figure 2.14 are the focus of most of the discussion in this book—the bloc to which Kąobawä's group belongs and the bloc that I have called Shamatari. I have designated Kąobawä's bloc as "Namowei-teri," the name of an ancient site where the ancestors of his group and the villages related to his lived over 100 years ago (Chagnon, 1974). Figure 2.15 shows how the villages in these two population blocs are related to each other historically and how they fissioned from each other. Kąobawä's village is shown on this diagram as "Village 5."

## NEW DATA FROM 1990 AND 1991 FIELDWORK

In 1990 and 1991, I began new field research in several areas of Yąnomamöland I had not been able to visit up to then because they were extremely difficult to reach by river or by foot, the only means of travel I was able to use up to that

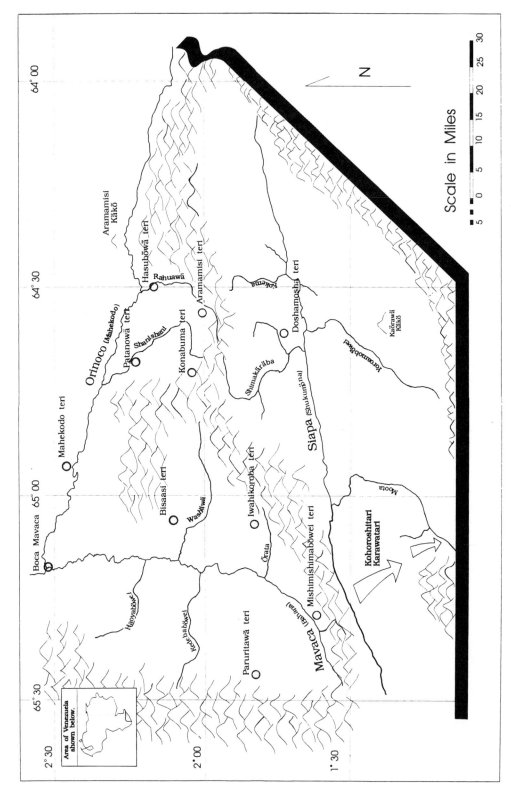

Scale in Miles

5 0 5 10 15 20 25 30

N

64° 00

64° 30

65° 00

65° 30

2° 30

2° 00

1° 30

Aramamisi Kākō

Hasubōwä teri

Rahuawä

Orinoco (Mahekodo)

Patanowä teri

Shanishani

Mahekodo teri

Konabuma teri

Aramamisi teri

Kokema

Doshamoshä teri

Shimakä ä ba

Siapa (Shukumïna)

Koramabōwei

Kaūrawä Kākō

Boca Mavaca

Bisaasi teri

Wänitoma

Iwahikoroba teri

Okrata

Mishimishimabōwei teri

Moota

Kohoroshitari
Karawatari

Haoyabōwei

Kōbebabīwei

Paruritawä teri

Mavaca (Bahasi)

Area of Venezuela
shown below.

84

**F I G U R E 2.16 (facing)** Map of the Mavaca, Orinoco, and Siapa basins showing relationships between mountainous regions and lowlands. The rivers are shown accurately, but the mountains are represented schematically. Villages are shown as they were distributed with respect to each other in the recent past.

time. I reached these remote areas via Venezuelan Air Force helicopters and made several trips into new villages in this area over the next several years.[7]

These trips enabled me to spend six months in villages whose names and residents I knew only from informants living in nearby groups. These trips helped me develop new perspectives on Yąnomamö settlement patterns and warfare that I will present here as preliminary findings that will be documented more extensively in my future publications. I believe these are exciting findings and will probably help explain why the known variations in warfare intensity and fighting over women are so extreme from one region of the Yąnomamö to another.

On the six trips I made in 1990 and 1991 into these areas I also used, for the first time, GPS instruments—very small, hand-held instruments that receive signals from a network of satellites launched by the U.S. Department of Defense in the past several years. GPS instruments allow you to identify your position (latitude and longitude) anywhere on the surface of the earth to within approximately 30 meters of accuracy, or to within inches if you use several of them in the appropriate (but more complex) manner. Such instruments are rapidly entering the commercial and scientific world and are now being regularly used, for example, as precise navigational aids by yachtsmen and by scientists whose research focuses on geographical locations in remote, poorly mapped areas of the world. For the first time in my 27 years of field research I was able to identify the actual locations of major rivers, mountains, and, most important, many of the some 500 ancient gardens that were established in the area where Kąobawä's people originated over 100 years ago.

Figure 2.16 shows a *schematic* representation of the large area whose current and former residents figure prominently in the history of Kąobawä's village. If the current estimates of the population of all Yąnomamö living in Brazil and Venezuela, 20,000 people, are accurate, then approximately 25% of all living Yąnomamö either live in or recently lived in the region shown in Figure 2.16.

In this map the major rivers—Orinoco, Mavaca, and Siapa[8]—are accurately represented, but the mountainous areas separating them are shown somewhat schematically or in an "idealized" fashion for the purpose of laying out the arguments or hypotheses that follow. In addition, the locations and identities of the Yąnomamö villages are schematic, in the sense that they are presented as

---

7. My research companion was Dr. Charles Brewer-Carias, a life-long friend, well-known in studies of many aspects of the Amazon Basin.

8. The Yąnomamö name for the Siapa River is Shukumöna kä u, "river of the Parakeets," as I often designated it in previous publications (e.g., Chagnon, 1974).

approximations to their locations and memberships in the recent past when the social, political, and military patterns that are found today took form. For example, Kąobawä's village is shown as being located in the Mavaca basin and identified as Bisaasi-teri. In fact, when he and his immediate ancestors lived in that region the group contained people who have subsequently fissioned away and are now known by other village names. Similarly, the group shown as "Iwahikoroba-teri" is today distributed among four different villages that live in other locations. This kind of argument applies to all the other groups shown in Figure 2.16.

Let me draw attention to several important geographical and ecological features of this area. First, there are large areas of relatively low-lying, flat plains that are traversed by the large rivers just mentioned, as well as major tributaries of these rivers. The Yąnomamö can easily cross most of these tributaries at most times of the year, but have considerable difficulty crossing the lower reaches of the Orinoco, Mavaca, and Siapa Rivers much of the year and have generally avoided settling in these areas until the advent of missionary activities and the introduction of canoes by missionaries after about 1965. These low, flat areas in regions where the rivers are small and easily crossed are the regions that Kąobawä's people—and many other groups—appear to have preferred as settlement locations for the past 150 or so years; and these areas are dotted with hundreds of long-since abandoned gardens—more than 500 of them.

These low-lying areas also appear to be richer in the kinds of natural resources the Yąnomamö traditionally utilize—game animals, plants for food, construction and manufactures, and well-drained, easily cultivated land for gardens.

By contrast, there are mountainous zones and rugged hills adjacent to these low-lying desirable lands and these, too, are occupied by Yąnomamö groups. My 1990 and 1991 field research focused in part on some of the groups living in this highly distinct highland ecological zone. These highland areas are characterized by very rugged terrain that is more difficult to cross, make gardens in, find game animals and other resources in, and generally more energetically costly to make a living in. Just collecting firewood and water each day is enormously more costly in simple energy terms than the same activities in the lowlands: Women have to walk up and down very steep slopes to get to the river sources of firewood. Or, men, to make gardens, have to climb up and down these steep slopes, fell trees on them, pile up the brush to burn it, and so forth, all much costlier in energy terms than doing the same work on a flat surface.

If a cross-section were drawn north to south on Figure 2.16—from about where the village of Patanowä-teri is shown southward through the village of Doshamoshateri—a schematic representation of the cross section would look something like the one shown in Figure 2.17. Five different ecological zones are represented in Figure 2.17: Zone A for the low-lying river bottoms immediately adjacent to the large rivers like the Orinoco or lower reaches of its affluents like the Mavaca and Ocamo; B for the slightly higher but relatively low-lying, relatively flat inland regions that are well drained and rather extensive in area;

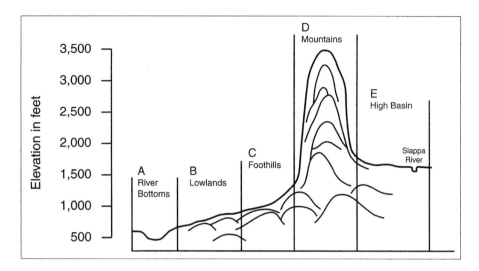

**FIGURE 2.17**   Schematic of Yąnomamö ecological zones.

C for rugged foothills that constitute the transition from the lowlands to the mountains; D for the very rugged mountainous terrain at elevations ranging from 2,500 to 3,500 feet; and E for the high, relatively flat basin of the Siapa River—known to the Yąnomamö as *Shukumöna kä u*, the river of the Parakeets.

Figure 2.17 is accurate insofar as elevation information is concerned, but schematic in its representation of the relative extent of the several ecological zones, which changes for each cross section one might slice through various portions of Figure 2.16. For example, the Orinoco River is at approximately an elevation of 500 to 600 feet near Patanowä-teri and the Siapa River basin is approximately at an elevation of 1,800 feet at Doshamosha-teri. Higher peaks of the narrow chain of mountains separating the Siapa basin from the Orinoco basin are about 3,500 feet above sea level.

As mentioned above, the Yąnomamö have traditionally avoided the lowest-lying terrain (Zone A) near the large rivers like the Orinoco, in part because they are difficult to cross most of the year and almost impossible to cross during the rainy season. But they also avoid them because the terrain adjacent to, and immediately inland from, these larger rivers periodically inundates and it is risky to clear gardens and settle too close to the big rivers. I was astonished on several trips I made up the Manaviche River, which flows into the Orinoco from the north between Boca Mavaca and Mahekodo-teri, and regularly visited several of the villages that had made gardens and *shabonos* along its banks. I made several visits during the rainy season in different years and was able to dock my dugout canoe right at the entrance to the *shabono* in some of these villages! The water had risen so high that the entire *shabono* was in danger of being flooded, and, of course, so were their gardens. Even at Boca Mavaca, where Kąobawä's village is located, the Orinoco sometimes rises high enough to flood the village for a few days in years when the rainfall is particularly heavy or concentrated.[9]

Zone B, as described above, appears to be the most desirable ecological niche because it is generally higher, better drained, gently sloping rather than steep, and characterized by larger amounts and more predictable quantities of a large variety of resources on which the Yąnomamö depend. Groups located here tend to "command" much larger areas than they need for purely subsistence purposes, most likely because they must periodically retreat into various distant regions within these areas when warfare pressure on them becomes particularly intense. They must, therefore, exclude others who try to occupy them. Safe havens are essentially a strategic geographical/ecological resource here.

Zone C marks the transition between the lowlands and the mountains and appears to be a refugee area—When groups are unable to hold their own militarily in the lowlands, they take refuge in the adjacent foothills where life is more secure, but making a living is more difficult. Their members usually attempt to return to the lowlands when military pressure wanes.

Zone D is very much a refugee niche—Many groups that have been thoroughly beaten and victimized by larger villages in the lowlands seem to retreat to the safety of the mountainous area to avoid further predation. Making a living in this region is much more difficult and is energetically more costly.

Finally, Zone E is the basin of the Siapa River, still basically unknown and largely unexplored. Most of my field research from 1990 to 1996 was in villages located here. The Siapa basin, while well drained and generally flat, is at an elevation some 300 meters (about 1,000 feet) higher than most of Zone B and possibly because of this has never been as densely settled as Zone B. As will be discussed in more detail below, Yąnomamö groups that have moved into this large region from Zones B, C, and D tend to be widely scattered and generally do not remain there very long; they either move back into Zones B, C, and D or migrate to the south, cross the border mountains separating Venezuela from Brazil, and thence into lower-lying terrain in Brazil that is similar to Zone B.

These ecological and geographical differences seem to lie behind social, political, demographic, and historical differences when villages from the two areas are compared. Some of the immediately noticeable differences are the sizes of the villages. Almost all the villages in the lowlands have been larger, occasionally reaching upwards of 300 to 400 residents. Mishimishimaböwei-teri, for example, had nearly 300 residents when I first contacted them in 1968 and, later, the Kedebaböwei-teri, who numbered well over 100 people, fissioned away from them. Yet their population was still some 250 people after this fission due mainly to new births (Chagnon, 1974). By contrast, villages in the rugged

---

9. In June 1996, extraordinarily heavy rainfall forced thousands of Yąnomamö and Ye'kwana from villages that were located along the lower reaches of the Ocamo, Padamo, Cunucunuma and the other rivers in this area and led to a major health and survival crisis. The gardens were all destroyed because of the flooding, resulting in severe privation for months afterwards. Most of the affected communities had recently moved to these otherwise avoided areas at the invitation of missionaries and the exotic and highly desirable material items they bring.

**FIGURE 2.18** Taking a GSP "fix" in a remote Yanomamö village with a Trimble Navigation GPS instrument. Two Yanomamö headmen look on as Charles Brewer, my Venezuelan collaborator, and I determine the latitude, longitude, and elevation of this village.

foothills or mountainous regions are much smaller—40 to 80 people, but occasionally some villages reach 100 people for reasons to be discussed in a moment.

The most startling difference is the degree to which violence and warfare—and the consequences of these—distinguish highland and lowland groups from each other. Warfare is much more highly developed and chronic in the lowlands. Men in the lowland villages seem pushy and aggressive, but men from the smaller, highland villages seem sedate and gentle. Not unexpectedly, alliance patterns are more elaborate in the lowlands and dramatic, large, regular feasts are characteristic, events in which large groups invite their current allies to feast and trade. Larger numbers of women in the lowland villages are either abducted from or coerced from weaker, smaller neighbors—including highland villages.

By contrast, highland villages have fewer abducted women, and when they do, they usually come from other small highland groups, not from the more bellicose, larger, and more powerful lowland villages. In addition, fewer of the adult men in the highland villages are *unokais*, that is, men who have participated in the killing of other men (see Chapter 6 for a discussion on *unokais*). My preliminary findings for eight of the "marginalized" highland villages are shown in Table 2.1. Three of these eight villages have only recently moved into the peripheral area from the lowlands and, for this reason, some of their statistical

**T A B L E  2.1    Selected sociodemographic features of recently studied "refugee" villages in the Siapa/Shanishani drainages.**
Villages pursuing a refugee strategy are generally smaller, have lower rates of polygynous marriage, fewer abducted women, and fewer *Unokais*.

| Village | Size | Number Men Polygynous | % Abducted Females | %Unokai Males |
|---|---|---|---|---|
| 69 | 53 | 1 | 14.3 | 7.7 |
| 71 | 43 | 1 | 33.3 | 36.4 |
| 64 | 99 | 2 | 14.5 | 27.6 |
| 72 | 28 | 1 | 0.0 | 57.1 |
| 59 | 81 | 2 | 0.0 | 21.4 |
| 57 | 81 | 1 | 15.0 | 15.4 |
| 68 | 54 | 1 | 14.3 | 0.0 |
| 67 | 40 | 0 | 0.0 | 12.5 |
| Totals: | 479 | 9 | — | — |
| Averages: | 59.9 | 1.1 | 11.7 | 21.2 |

attributes are possibly artifacts of conditions they lived in prior to seeking refuge in the highlands or the foothills near them. These three villages (numbers 64, 71, and 72 in Table 2.1) have only recently been pushed into this region. All three have relatively high percentages of *unokais* compared to their neighbors, and one of them has a very high proportion of abducted females. Projected studies of uncontacted highland groups that have been there for longer periods of time are likely to show a more dramatic contrast than I can offer at this early stage. Table 2.1 summarizes some of these preliminary findings.

Some comparative data for the larger villages found in the adjacent lowlands are instructive (drawn from Chagnon, 1988a, 1990). There, the average fraction of adult males who have participated in the killing of another person is over twice as high (44%) but the average number of victims killed per *unokai* is only slightly higher in the lowland villages—1.13 compared to 0.96. The percentage of females in the lowland villages who have been abducted is significantly higher: 17% compared to 11.7% in the highland villages.

## Bellicose and Refugee Strategies

My recent field studies have also begun to reveal patterns of settlement location and relocation for both the highland and the lowland villages that seem to add up to the following kind of picture. Groups that live in the lowlands have to be large and bellicose in order to control the large, desirable, and wide-open ecological niche they live in. They seem to keep their neighbors at a comfortable distance by adopting an extremely bellicose strategy that entails frequent raiding and chronic attempts to either abduct women from their neighbors or coerce weaker neighbors into ceding more women to them than they ultimately "repay" via marriage alliance agreements. To be effective at this, they must maximize village size, for in numbers there is military strength and credibility of threat. But, since Yąnomamö villages can only become so large before they fission—because kinship, descent, and marriage alliance principles seem to set limits on village size and the solidarity required to hold groups intact—all villages eventually subdivide into smaller and more vulnerable groups and their previous enemies turn the tables on them if or when they can. At this point several alternatives seem to have been followed historically.

1. The two newly formed groups simply live *he borarawä*, that is, locate their two new *shabonos* side by side while continuing to exploit their previous gardens. This enables them to act as a unit in military conflicts with their neighbors but separates the group into smaller units where within-*shabono* arguments, conflicts, and fights are greatly reduced. Over time the two groups grow in size and might move further and further apart, but this depends on how many larger neighbors they have, who has alliances with whom, and who is actively raiding whom. Some of them succeed in growing to be large enough to hold their own against other large villages in the lowlands.

2. One or both of the groups become "peripheralized" and have to move out of the more desirable lowlands into the foothills or the mountains for refuge. They may spend a generation or two in these less desirable areas until the political circumstances in the lowlands make it possible for them to return there. Their numbers grow during this time, making it increasingly difficult to make a living in the less bountiful highlands and more logical or necessary to return to the lowlands for economic reasons. Some of the highland groups I have recently begun studying, Narimöböwei-teri for example, is in this situation today (indicated on Figure 2.16 as the "Aramamisi-teri"). They live *he borarawä* because their total population (two groups) is approximately 200 people. They have attempted to move back into the more productive lowlands, the Siapa basin in this case, but once they did they entered into wars with stronger neighbors and were forced back into the highlands again.

3. They "pioneer" new, unoccupied areas of lowlands that are nearby and characterized by ecological features that are similar to the regions in which they originated (Chagnon, 1968b). An excellent example is the history of the Upper Mavaca River basin, shown in Figure 2.16 as being occupied by the Mishimishimaböwei-teri, Iwahikoroba-teri, and Paruitawä-teri. All these groups originated in the area shown as being occupied by the Patanowä-teri, Hasuböwä-teri, and Konabuma-teri, and all these groups can be traced back to a single, large village that fissioned into these now separate groups. Another example is Kąobawä's group itself. It was forced out of the Patanowä-teri region and crossed over the foothills separating the tributaries of the Mavaca River from tributaries of the Orinoco River, especially the branch of the Orinoco indicated as *Shanishani kä u*. They did not remain long in the area because of wars with the Iwahikoroba-teri, also refugees from the Shanishani drainage.

The Upper Mavaca River has been the route followed by the Yąnomamö groups who were forced out of the Shanishani drainage, groups that are only remotely related to the villages shown in Figure 2.16. Two previous waves of migrants—the Karawatari and Kohoroshitari populations (Chagnon, 1966, 1974) also did the same thing, probably about the turn of the century. Most of the Yąnomamö groups living in Brazil immediately south of the area shown in Figure 2.16 are the contemporary descendants of these two groups; the remainder are recent migrants related to the villages shown on Figure 2.16, indicating that this migration process from Venezuela to Brazil is still going on today.

In a sense, the Shanishani drainage appears to have been and continues to be some kind of "demographic pump" that spews rapidly growing, relatively warlike groups of Yąnomamö into the adjacent areas. Those groups who manage to remain there over long periods of time, such as the Patanowä-teri (represented in 1991 by several relatively large, yet-belligerent groups living close to each other), seem to be able to do so by adopting a decidedly antagonistic stance toward all their neighbors. Groups that are forced out seem to fall into two different kinds in terms of their military attributes. If they are forced into the highlands, they become rather docile, nonmilitant refugees. If they pioneer into lowlands, they continue the tradition that they knew in the past: They continue to be large, militant, and belligerent villages.

A few caveats must be discussed regarding this scenario or model. One is that the Siapa basin, essentially unexplored and anthropologically unknown at this point, has a number of cultural-ecological peculiarities not found in the Orinoco or Mavaca basins. The most prominent of these is the fact that it is approximately 300 to 350 meters *higher* than immediately adjacent areas of the Mavaca and Orinoco drainages. Thus, while it is very large, generally flat and low-lying, it might not be as ecologically rich as the adjacent drainages and therefore not as desirable as a place to live or make a living. These questions will be resolved during the projected research I have just initiated.

There are several different kinds of reasons to suspect that this is the case. One is that, in general, species abundance and diversity tend to diminish with altitude, and the Siapa basin is much higher than the Orinoco drainage. Game animals and other useful species might be less abundant here. Groups that migrate into the Siapa basin seem to remain there for relatively short periods of time, especially in the western portion of this drainage where only one village is found today—Yeisikorowä-teri with a population of approximately 220 people. Recall that two earlier populations fled from the Mavaca basin—Karawatari and Kohoroshitari—but moved far to the south, across this drainage, and settled in Brazil. A second possible reason that the Yąnomamö who have moved into or through the lower Siapa do not remain there might be that the rivers are too large for them to deal with. The Siapa itself, immediately south of the Mavaca headwaters, is a very large, fast and deep river and difficult for the Yąnomamö to cross for most of the year, and its major tributaries in this general region are also very large. However, the upper reaches of the Siapa (from the area starting at and east of the village shown as Doshamosha-teri) is occupied by a number of Yąnomamö villages that have not yet been directly contacted. These will be visited and studied during my projected field studies, and their political and ecological attributes documented in detail.

A third reason, also to be explored in the projected research, has to do with the history of "outsiders" moving close the Yąnomamö territory from the Brazilian side as distinct from the Venezuelan side. It is possible that outposts of modern Brazilian culture—missions, FUNAI[10] posts, criollo communities—were an attraction to the Yąnomamö who penetrated the Siapa from the north. These non-Yąnomamö were a source of desirable items like machetes, metal cooking pots, axes, and so forth. Since these attractions appeared slightly earlier in Brazil than they did in Venezuela, it is possible that, once these foreigners were "discovered" by the Yąnomamö in the Siapa basin, their settlement patterns and directions of movements were dramatically influenced by them. An example of how this occurred in at least one instance is documented in the gripping story of Helena Valero, a Brazilian girl who was captured by the Kohoroshitari Yąnomamö in approximately 1937 just south of the area shown on Figure 2.16 and who spent most of her adult life living as a captive among them, most of it in the Shanishani drainage (Biocca, 1970; Valero, 1984).

Thus, in the area shown in Figure 2.16 there are two broadly defined kinds of Yąnomamö villages. One kind comprises those traditionally large communities whose members are very bellicose and who have historically been heavily involved in warfare, coercing allies out of women or abducting them forcibly, and whose mortality patterns reflect high frequencies of death due to violence. Kąobawä's people come from this group. The other kind might be described as "refugees" who have fled from these larger groups and sought safety in the more rugged highland terrain where making a living is more difficult, but where political security is higher and predation lower. They are smaller, less bellicose, and gentler and have fewer militarily successful males, lower rates of polygyny, fewer abducted women, and lower rates of death due to violence.

Anthropologists who work in different regions of the same tribal population frequently report data that shows very different patterns or statistical frequencies in some variables than what their colleagues report. These are generally taken by responsible anthropologists to be genuine and valuable pieces of information that illustrate variability within the same tribal group, variability that must be explained. For reasons unclear to me, my well-documented statistical information on frequencies of death due to violence and high rates of abductions of females in the area I have been studying for 27 years has not been charitably taken this way by a number of French and Brazilian anthropologists who have subsequently done field research in other areas of the Yąnomamö distribution where these frequencies appear to be much lower. A number of them have publicly claimed that I have invented the data I have reported, I have "exaggerated" violence, or that I am unable to tell a symbolic death from a real one (Albert & Ramos, 1988; Carneiro da Cunha, 1989; Lizot, 1988; cf. Chagnon, 1995). Some of the motivation behind these unprofessional claims is intimately related to the tragic events surrounding the 1987 gold rush in Brazil that now threatens the cultural and biological survival of the Brazilian Yąnomamö, to be discussed in Chapter 7.

---

10. FUNA1 is Brazil's "Indian Protection Agency."

If the ecological differences discussed here have wider applicability in other areas of the Yąnomamö distribution, then many of the reported variations in degrees or levels of violence and warfare in different areas of the tribe might ultimately be explainable in these cultural-ecological terms.

## THE GREAT PROTEIN DEBATE: YĄNOMAMÖ DATA AND ANTHROPOLOGICAL THEORY

Let me conclude this chapter with a more general discussion of cultural-ecological theory and how the kinds of data I have been collecting and publishing on the Yąnomamö, often in collaboration with graduate students and colleagues, has led to major modifications and improvements in it.

The publication of the first edition of this case study in 1968 coincided with the rapidly developing emphasis in anthropology on what is generally known as cultural ecology theory. That theory explores the relationships between culture and environment in the broadest sense, attempting to demonstrate that the environment imposes limitations on the patterns that cultures can evolve and maintain and, in addition, seeks to identify the specific ways that cultures and human populations adapt to their physical environments. The general theory has two components or dimensions. The first has to do with how the various parts of culture—kinship rules, descent rules, residence rules, economic practices, and so on—articulate with each other and function to maintain the whole cultural system and how they influence each other as the system changes over time. The second is borrowed from the field of general biology and has to do with the relationships of animal populations to their resources and how certain critically important resources limit the growth and dispersal of populations and the densities that they might achieve given the fact that the resources might vary in abundance, predictability, desirability, and reliability. The addition of the concept culture to evolutionary ecology— that is, combining anthropological insights and understanding with general ecological principles—thus amounts to a kind of partial synthesis of anthropology and ecology and to an attempt to combine the best arguments of both.

The major emphasis in anthropology by many who are intrigued by this emerging synthesis is on the limitations or possible limitations that food and other critical resources impose on human population clusterings, the size to which they can grow, the densities they achieve, and the extent to which social and cultural institutions reflect the material (food/resources) substrate that all populations rest on. Most anthropologists would accept the general arguments, logic, and desirability of the cultural-ecological approach, and most of my own work is built on this general approach.

But this synthesis, coming primarily from anthropologists inspired by biology, is proceeding faster and with greater enthusiasm than the facts warrant. In addition, anthropological appropriation of biological theory has not been attendant to recent changes in biological theory. Portions of the argument that are borrowed from biology were borrowed at a time when biology itself was undergoing a major intellectual revolution that dramatically affected the whole field of

**FIGURE 2.19**
Chagnon and the headman of Doshamosha-teri, a remote village in the Siapa River basin. I had known about this legendary headman for 20 years before meeting him.

ecology. One fundamental change in biology was the shift away from the argument that whole populations or species adapted to their food and resource base to the argument that individuals within the population were the units of adaptation, and that the proper and theoretically most appropriate vantage in ecological studies was the individual and how the behavioral strategies (mating, foraging, social interactions) they adopted affected their personal chances of surviving and reproducing (Williams, 1966; Chagnon and Irons, 1979). In this view, the attributes of the population are the sum of the attributes of the individuals. There is, in short, a fundamental difference between a herd of fleet deer and a fleet herd of deer (Williams, 1966). The *group* is in a fundamental sense a sum of its *individual* parts. This is contrary to much of anthropological, if not philosophical, thinking. The *assumption* that human proclivities and behavior are the product of group selection can no longer be justified in any of the social sciences and this issue must now be reexamined in light of the important new discoveries in theoretical biology (see Williams, 1971, for a readable and comprehensive summary of these issues).

The debate that is emerging is between those anthropologists who have expended some effort to try to learn what the recent theoretical issues in biology are all about and why individual selection arguments have to now be considered in cultural ecology arguments that assume that group selection is still the name of the theoretical game. The group perspective has always been a traditional focus in anthropology. Anthropologists focus on cultures, villages, clans, institutions, and so forth, and then try to figure out what the role of the individual is in maintaining these groups, how individual goals are subordinated to the group's collective interests, and so forth. It should not surprise anyone why group selection arguments appeal to anthropologists, especially those who traditionally argue that culture is superorganic (beyond or above the individual) and is a process *sui generis* (having a life of its own; independent of the humans who bear it; causing itself). While in some contexts and for some purposes these assumptions are useful, the correct form of stating these arguments is often forgotten: These are "as if" statements. We can look at cultures and institutions as if people or individuals were not present and learn a great deal about these things in this way, that is, as if humans didn't exist. But some of us want to look at the same kinds of things and take into consideration the fact that people *are* involved in culture as organisms, and their evolved nature must then be taken into consideration. That evolved nature can be best understood by evolutionary biology, the only comprehensive theory about life on earth as we know it. We want to look at and try to understand human behavior, not just the collective representation of them in the form of "ideal" institutions.

One issue in the theoretical debate has to do with the extent to which protein is the limiting resource par excellence in human cultural adaptations and human social behavior. My work on the Yąnomamö has been caught up in this debate, since some of the variables the protein "argument" purports to explain are things and "cultural institutions" such as warfare, infanticide, aggression, and population parameters, on all of which I have published extensively.[11] Some of the most relevant data needed to resolve some of these issues is Yąnomamö data, and therefore, the protein advocates have worked especially

---

11. I have stopped publishing on Yąnomamö infanticide, although I have a good deal of information on it that I have not published. This is an ethical problem. In 1985 I was asked to file a notarized affidavit in Venezuelan Congressional records on my 'view' of Yąnomamö infanticide practices. The official who asked me to do this prefaced his request with the statement that a prominent member of that Congress had heard that there were native peoples in Venezuela who killed some of their newborn offspring and wanted to mount a formal investigation, arrest the people involved, and try them for murder. In my report I stated that I had never seen a Yąnomamö kill an infant, a factually correct statement. This apparently was enough to bring the investigative motions to a halt. Marvin Harris holds the position that I have elected to not discuss Yąnomamö infanticide after 1985 because the evidence I have would support his 'theory.' Without having to rest my case on empirical evidence, let me simply point out on theoretical grounds that it is inconceivable that human mothers would willfully destroy their newborn children in order to make the 'ecological niche' safe for monkeys, armadillos, and peccaries.

hard to make the Yąnomamö "fit" the theory. I have, unfortunately, been less enthusiastic than they have been about the goodness of fit, since I collected the data and do not believe that it fits. I have also been skeptical about the assumptions and logic of the protein hypothesis because of the monocausal demands it makes, the failure of the data to fit the protein argument, and the devastating contradictions it contains in terms of the recent refinements in biological theory. The "theory" of materialistic cultural ecology will now change radically to conform to its intellectual fount, biology, and Yąnomamö data will be one of the major reasons for this change.

The most prominent champion of the protein theory is an anthropologist named Marvin Harris. We disagree a good deal and have "debated" the protein issue publicly on a number of campuses. My data will not change. He refuses to change his protein "theory"—at least not in one dramatic step. If his protein theory cannot explain the Yąnomamö, one tribe on which precisely the right kind of data exists that is germane to the theory, his theory is in serious difficulty. The Yąnomamö seem to be a critically important test case, and thus, data on them will play an important role in the modifications that will occur in ecological theory.

Although case studies are not usually the forum for explaining theoretical issues in anthropology, the issues are widely known to the public at large through several popular books written by Harris that, in my estimation, carefully edit Yąnomamö data to make the fit look better than it is. For this reason, I am discussing the protein hypothesis in this case study. Students are often better judges of evidence and theory than the passionate advocates who produce both or either.

The argument began when I cautioned the protein-deficiency advocates that the Yąnomamö did not suffer from a protein shortage and that their warfare (and warfare in any group) was too complex to reduce to a single variable such as protein scarcity (Chagnon, 1974). Professor Harris argued that the Yąnomamö probably were suffering from a per capita shortage of animal protein (Harris, 1974; Divale and Harris, 1976), as did several of his students (Gross, 1975; Ross, 1978). Harris took serious issue with my caution in this individual case because it challenged his more general proposition that many of the practices among tribesmen were most likely responses to a scarcity of protein and should be interpreted as "adaptations." These included such things as the practice of female infanticide to regulate population size and thereby avoid overexploiting the game animals, or conducting warfare to keep out of your hunting areas or adjacent lands that would be "reserves" for future protein exploitation—or even why Hindus love cows but Jews and Arabs abhor pork (Divale and Harris, 1976; Harris, 1974). These arguments seem plausible, even fascinating, but they also ignore enormous amounts of contradictory data in all cases. Nevertheless, Harris, as well as several of his students, advocated it as if it were the *only* or the *most scientific* theory able to explain many cultural adaptations and the general evolution of culture from time immemorial (Harris, 1974, 1977). The theory began emerging as some of my first publications on the Yąnomamö appeared, and some of my observations were selectively perused to find "evidence" of a protein shortage among the Yąnomamö. My several cautions were not only not taken seriously, but I soon found that I was being dismissed as some sort of villain for refusing to be "scientific," to go along with the more scientific Columbia crowd and assert that it was all a question of protein shortage. Instead, I persisted in my insistence that the protein theory—any theory—had to be based on evidence, and none of my evidence on the Yąnomamö suggested that the Yąnomamö were suffering from a shortage of protein. My demographic research had clearly demonstrated in a meticulous way that the Yąnomamö population was growing at a moderately high rate, which can hardly be taken as evidence that they had bumped up against the "carrying capacity" of their environment. Indeed, that is the best evidence that the Yąnomamö have *not* yet reached carrying capacity (Chagnon & Hames, 1979, 1980; Chagnon, 1990a).

For most of my early research on the Yąnomamö, I collaborated with a large team of competent and distinguished medical researchers whose thousands of biomedical, epidemiological, and serological observations on several thousands of Yąnomamö led them to conclude that the Yąnomamö were one of the best nourished populations thus far described in the anthropological/biomedical literature (Neel, 1970). This does not easily lend itself to the interpretation that their diet is marginal or deficient, and such a finding would cause some caution among scholars who might propose a dietary deficiency as the major driving force behind Yąnomamö warfare and infanticide.

As the Yąnomamö gradually came to be a popular "textbook" culture and cited widely to exemplify specific aspects of tribal practices in general, the protein advocates found it more and more necessary to explain them away. Remarkably, their "theory" began with the flimsiest of evidence. "Evidence" in the 1960s and 1970s was, unfortunately, rather generously taken to include undocumented impressions; it rarely included statistical data. It often amounted to careful sifting of detailed ethnographic accounts to find suggestive statements about hunger, starvation, deprivation, or bad hunting luck that could, when stacked up in a pile, be used to make a circumstantial case for a "theoretical" argument. Very often the original ethnographer did not provide statistical facts to accompany his or her statements and did not intend them to be statistical statements, but even more remarkably, those who used the statements for "scientific" arguments themselves never collected such information either. The result was that an enormous amount of "science" was built on a nonempirical, anecdotal base. As one observer described their methods, it was "preemptive" theorizing (Neitschman, 1980). As far as Yąnomamö data go, the protein advocates insisted that the onus was on *me* to show that the Yąnomamö were *not* suffering from a protein shortage. The argument was that I had not actually weighed and measured the protein intake of the Yąnomamö, and until I had done so, they would refuse to accept my arguments to the contrary. I suppose that had they advocated yak fat, trace elements, heavy metals, saltpeter, or the absence of molybdenum in the diet as the cause of Yąnomamö warfare, it would presumably have been up to me to prove them wrong. That is what "preemptive" theorizing means.

Table 2.2 shows comparative data on animal protein consumption per capita for some Amazonian tribes. In general, the only quantitative data that exists for Amazonian tribes clearly indicates that they are consuming more than adequate quantities of animal protein. These should be taken as very conservative estimates, since vegetable protein is not counted nor is the protein that is inevitably consumed by the hunters while they are on hunting trips. The original sources for the data in this table report protein consumption in different forms: for example, as protein per

**T A B L E  2.2**    **Comparative Data on Animal Protein Consumption Per Capita for Some Amazonian Tribes**

| Society | Per Capita | Per Adult | Source |
|---|---|---|---|
| Jivaro | 79.3 | (103.0) | Berlin & Markell, 1977 |
| Jivaro | 84.4 | (116.2) | Ross, 1978 |
| Yąnomamö | 29.7 | 36 | Lizot, 1977 |
| Yąnomamö | 51.9 | 77 | Lizot, 1977 |
| Yąnomamö | 52 | 75 | Chagnon & Hames, 1979 |
| Wayana | (77.7) | 108 | Hurault, 1972 |
| Boni | (82) | 114 | Hurault, 1972 |
| Maimande | 26.3 | (36.2) | Aspelin, 1975 |
| Bari | 86.8 | (119.5) | Beckerman, 1978 |
| Ye'kwana | 77.3 | 95.5 | Hames, 1992 |
| Siona-Secoya | 64.3 | 96.7 | Vickers, 1978 |
| Averages | 64.6 | 88.8 | |

adult male, protein per all adults, or protein per family. Hames and I adjusted the figures to make them all comparable. All are presented here as both protein per adult and per capita. Data in parenthesis indicates that either per capita or per adult consumption figure was missing in the original source and was estimated by standard conversion factors from the original statistics (revised from Chagnon and Hames, 1979). Figures reported by Harris (1975:430) indicated that the highest per capita animal protein consumption among developed countries is about 70 grams per day, in Australia and New Zealand. The next highest level is for the United States and Canada, at about 66 grams per day. Amazonian Indians do better than the republics that constituted the former U.S.S.R., the United Kingdom, Germany, Portugal, and Japan among developed countries, all of whose per capita consumption of animal protein falls below the 64.6 figure given in the table below.

In a very serious scientific attempt to lay these concerns to rest forever, I agreed to meet with Professor Harris and his several supporters at Columbia University on the eve of my departure to the Yąnomamö in 1974 to continue my research. My expedition members, three graduate students, two senior anthropologists, and I would collect the data that Harris and his supporters thought would empirically settle the issue. We discussed the matter at length and agreed that if the Yąnomamö consumed the equivalent of one Big Mac per day, a suggestion made by Harris himself, Harris would eat his hat. A Big Mac contains about 30 grams of animal protein.

We left for the field the next day. The three students initiated their field research, one component of which was the determination of per capita protein intake per day. I will not go into some of the darker, unethical, and astonishing events that eventually transpired around this issue—at least not in this book—but simply report some of the results that eventually were published. Table 2.2

summarizes the per capita protein consumption of the Yąnomamö, several other South American Indian groups, and selected industrialized nations—the latter data taken from tables in one of Harris' own textbooks. What it indicates is that the Yąnomamö are consuming large quantities of protein by comparison to even citizens in very affluent industrialized nations. Indeed, if a correlation between protein consumption and frequency, intensity, or seriousness of warfare exists at all, it is that protein *abundance*, not protein *scarcity*, correlates with fighting and warfare. One might even argue that too much protein, not too little, causes war—if one wanted to reduce the "causes" of war to arguments of this order of simplicity.

I have, in many publications, drawn attention to the fact that much of Yąnomamö fighting and conflict arises over sex, infidelity, suspicion of infidelity, failure to deliver a promised wife to a suitor—in a word, women.[12] I explained Harris' theory of their warfare to the Yąnomamö: "He says you are fighting over game animals and meat, and insists that you are not fighting over women." They laughed at first, and then dismissed Harris' view in the following way: "Yąhi yamakö buhii makuwi, suwä käbä yamakö buhii baröwö!" ("Even though we do like meat, we like women a whole lot more!") Some protein advocates dismiss the suggestion that Yąnomamö—or any humans—will fight over sexual matters as "libidinal speculation" on the part of their observer. That suggests they think that much of the theory of evolution by natural selection is, simply, libidinal speculation. I strongly urge these critics to read the literature on what Darwin (1871) called "sexual" selection or try to make a plausible case that the long antlers on male deer and elk, the spectacular gaudy plumes on male peacocks, or the gigantic sizes of bull elephant seals developed as a consequence of their libidinal speculation.

The protein debate has now been pretty much laid to rest for two general reasons. One is that more people have taken time to explore and learn about the new theoretical ideas in biology and what these ideas mean for anthropological theory and assumptions about human behavior or human cultural institutions, for example, that human infanticide exists in order to maximize future protein resources for the good of the group. Students of human behavior are increasingly less willing to believe that a woman will kill her own newborn to make the jungle more productive in monkey protein for future members of the groups because one of the "functions" of culture is to "limit" population growth. The other is that very large amounts of highly detailed statistical data have been collected on the relevant economic, ecological, and demographic issues, particularly in South American tribal societies like the Yąnomamö (Hames and Vickers, 1983 is a convenient reference marking the shift in this empirical direction). The projected field work on the Yąnomamö discussed in this chapter will lead to empirical results that will contribute more to understanding these exciting and important theoretical issues.

---

12. Other important causes cited by the Yąnomamö include the powerful motive of revenge and accusations of sorcery or harmful magic that "causes" death (Chagnon, 1988b).

# 3



# Myth and Cosmos

## THE SPIRITUAL ENVIRONMENT

The comparative simplicity of Yąnomamö material culture contrasts sharply with the richness and ingenuity of their beliefs about the cosmos, the soul, the mythical world, and the plants and animals around them. One fascinating dimension of their intellectual world is the extent to which individuals can manipulate and elaborate on the ideas and themes, but within a set of limits demanded by orthodoxy and local versions of "Truth." Not only can individuals experiment as artists and creators, but there is room for poets and verbal essayists as well. Despite lacking a written language, the Yąnomamö have considerable freedom to turn a clever phrase or state something in a more sophisticated way than others are capable of doing. Some Yąnomamö play with their rich language and work at being what we might call literary or learned. The conception of primitive peoples having grunt-like languages, whose poor vocabularies require lots of sign signals, is not only ignorantly wide of the mark, but also ironic: the working vocabulary of most Yąnomamö individuals is probably much larger than the working vocabulary of most people in our own culture. While it is true that the absolute content of our language's vocabulary greatly exceeds the content of Yąnomamö vocabulary, it is also true that we know much less of ours than they do of theirs. When you do not have a written language you have to store more in your head. One might even suggest that the possession of a dictionary has made us lazy, for we can always "look it up" if we can't remember it, and we probably tend to "not remember" for that very reason. It is in this context that the often-heard Yąnomamö comment "I possess the Truth" makes a great deal of sense. To make the point as a Yąnomamö might, if we're so smart, why don't we have a word to describe that part of our body between the forearm and bicep? The best we can do is call it "inside elbow." The same for the "back knee." I can't imagine words more useful! The Yąnomamö have a rich vocabulary and a complex language, and they delight in making poetic use of them in their marvelous stories and sagas of the cosmos and of Man's place in it.

## The Cosmos

The Yąnomamö conceive of the cosmos as comprising at least four parallel layers, each lying horizontally and separated by a vague but relatively small space (Figure 3.1). The layers are like inverted dinner platters: gently curved, round, thin, rigid, and having a top and a bottom surface. The edges of at least some of the layers are considered to be "rotten" and somewhat fragile, as if to walk on them might be like walking on the roof of a badly deteriorated building. A good deal of magical stuff happens out in this region, a kind of netherland dominated by spirits, a place that is somewhat mysterious and dangerous. The most highly advised geographers and sailors in our own recent historical past had conceptions not markedly different, and Magellan was nothing short of relieved when his ships didn't fall off what was then thought to be the edge of a flat earth, a mere 475 or so years ago!

The uppermost layer of the four (there might be more according to some Yąnomamö) is thought to be "pristine" or "tender": *duku kä misi*. At present this layer is empty or void (*broke*), but many things had their origin there in the distant past. Things tend to move downward in the Yąnomamö cosmos, falling or descending to a lower layer. Sometimes the uppermost layer is described with the term "old woman," as are abandoned, nonproducing gardens. The tender layer does not play a prominent role in the everyday life or thoughts of the Yąnomamö, not even in their shamanism or myths. It is something that is just *there* and once had a vague function.

## THE COSMOS

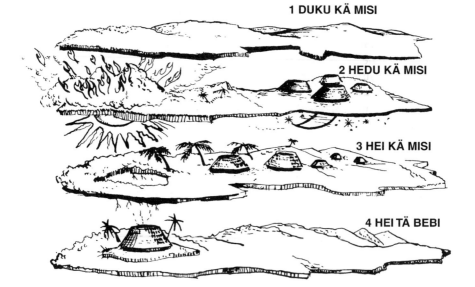

**FIGURE 3.1** The four parallel layers of the Yąnomamö cosmos.

The next layer down is called *hedu kä misi*: the "sky" layer. The upper surface of *hedu* is invisible to us, but is believed to be similar to what we know on earth—it has trees, gardens, villages, animals, plants, and, most important, the souls of deceased Yąnomamö who are in some sense similar to mortal men. They garden, hunt, make love, eat, and practice witchcraft on each other. Everything that exists on earth has its replica or counterpart in *hedu*, as if *hedu* were a mirror image of life as mortals know it.

The bottom surface of *hedu* is what we on earth can actually see with our eyes: the visible "sky." Stars and planets are somehow or other "stuck" onto this layer and move across it along their individual trails, east to west. Some Yąnomamö think the stars are fish, but they have a generally undeveloped set of astronomical ideas about the stars and planets and nothing that we would call named constellations. The bottom of *hedu* is conceived to be relatively close to earth, for I repeatedly was asked if I bumped into it when I took rides in airplanes.[1]

Man—Yąnomamö—dwells on "this layer": *hei kä misi*. "This layer" was created when a chunk of *hedu* broke off and fell downward. As all can plainly see, "this layer" is characterized by jungle, rivers, hills, animals, plants, gardens, and so on, and is covered with people who are essentially slightly different variants of Yąnomamö—speaking a dialect of Yąnomamö that is "wrong" or "crooked." Even foreigners (*nabä* or, in some dialects in Brazil, *krgiwä*) are thought to dwell in *shabonos*, for foreigners are simply degenerate copies of real humans—Yąnomamö. In fact, the Yąnomamö thought I was a "reincarnated" version of them and would ask me frequently if I had "drowned" and had come back to life. The reason for this question was that in one of their myths, a great flood occurred and some Yąnomamö escaped death by grabbing onto logs. They floated downstream and were not seen again and presumably most of them drowned. Some now return, floating on logs (canoes), and look different and speak "crooked"—foreigners. A spirit named Omawä fished them out of the water downstream, wrung them out, made them come to life again, and sent them back "home."

Finally, the surface below "this layer", *hei tä bebi*, is almost barren. A peculiar variant of Yąnomamö live there, a people called Amąhiri-teri. They originated a long time ago when a piece of *hedu* broke off and crashed to "this layer," knocking a hole in it and continuing downward. It hit "this layer" at a place where the Amąhiri-teri lived, carrying them and their village downward to the new layer. Unfortunately, just the garden and *shabono* of the Amąhiri-teri was carried downward and not their jungle where they hunted. Thus, they have no game animals and have changed into cannibals: They sent their spirits upward, to "this layer,"

---

1. Airplanes were only rarely seen in 1964 when I began my fieldwork, for there were no airstrips in the Upper Orinoco region at that time. Shortly after this, some missions began clearing airstrips for small, light planes, a process that rapidly accelerated in the following years—leading to an almost uncontrolled influx of curious visitors and tourists at some mission stations. Today, airplanes and helicopters are commonly seen, even by the most remotely located Yąnomamö populations.

to capture the souls of children, which are carried down to their village and eaten. In some Yąnomamö villages the shamans contest regularly with the Amąhiri-teri, attempting to thwart their cannibalistic incursions. The Yąnomamö have an almost morbid fear of becoming cannibals, almost as though humans are precariously close to an inherent predisposition to devour members of their own species, an act they find not merely repugnant, but a possibility that seems to them very real and must therefore be constantly opposed. Whenever I hunted with them and we shot a tapir, I would always cut off a thick juicy slice of tenderloin and fry it lightly on both sides—a rare steak that dripped juicy delicious blood as I cut it and ate it. This so disgusted and alarmed them that they could not bear to watch me eat it, and invariably accused me of wanting to become a cannibal like a jaguar, a disgusting eater of raw human flesh. For their part, they cook their meat so much that you could almost drive nails with it.

The Amąhiri-teri people lived at the time of the *no badabö*: the original humans. These original humans were distinct from the living Man in that they were part spirit and part human, and most were also part animal—and the myths frequently explain how this transformation occurred. When the original humans died, they turned into spirits: *hekura*. The term *no badabö* means "those who are now dead." In the context of myth and stories of the cosmos, it means "the original humans" or "those who were here in the beginning of time."

## Myths: The Beginning of Time and the No Badabö

It is difficult, if not impossible, to get the Yąnomamö to explain how the first beings were created. They seem to assume that the cosmos began with these people present. Most of the *no badabö* had specific functions or roles in creative events that transpired after they themselves existed, events that, for example, explain the origin of certain animals or plants. The *no badabö* figure prominently in myths, and many bear the names of plants and animals useful or sometimes trivial to the Yąnomamö. The *no badabö* are the spirits of these living things, there being relatively little correlation between the mythical importance of some of them and the usefulness of the plant or animal whose name they bear.

Some of the characters in Yąnomamö myths are downright hilarious, and some of the things they did are funny, ribald, and extremely entertaining to the Yąnomamö, who listen to men telling mythical stories or chanting episodes of mythical sagas as they prance around the village, tripping out on hallucinogens, and adding comical twists and nuances to the side-splitting delight of their audiences. Everybody knows what Iwariwä (Caiman Ancestor) did, and that part cannot be changed. But how he did it, what minor gestures and comments he made, or how much it hurt or pleased him as he did it is subject to some considerable poetic license, and it is this that is entertaining and amusing to the listener. Occasionally the inspired narrator will go a bit beyond what is acceptable, a violation for which his own peers might good-naturedly forgive him, but a violation that people in other villages might object to, as they did when I taped the narrative and had people in other villages comment on it. "He's got it wrong! He's lying! It wasn't that way at all!" they would complain, adding that if I wanted the "Truth," I would be well advised to consult with them. Usually the degree of objection to someone's narrative was a function of the degree of contempt they had for the members of that person's village—war and the orthodoxy of myth parallel each other. Most of the time it was a function of simple ethnocentrism and chauvinism: Nobody does things quite as properly and faithfully as "my people," a conviction and sentiment almost all peoples exhibit to some degree.

With my filmmaking colleague, Timothy Asch, I have produced a number of films that record specific myths and specific variants of some of the myths. These are easily and readily available through two major nonprofit distribution agencies (see the list of Ethnographic Films at the end of this book) and are widely used as supplements to this monograph. They capture something of the humor and wit of the storyteller, not to mention the humorous content of some of the myths themselves. They also reveal the high degree of dramaturgical skill of storytellers like Kąobawä and illustrate the qualitatively different impact that documentary film makes on people compared to the written word. It would be very difficult to capture the humor, subtlety, and wittiness of Yąnomamö myths without using motion picture films, a distortion of reality no more severe than writing it down with a pencil on a piece of paper. (Advocates of the latter are occasionally quick to criticize the use of film for recording myths.) While we filmed quite a large number of the myths, only a few have been produced as final films to date. I should like, given this situation, to illustrate some of the other dimensions of Yąnomamö myth by focusing here on themes and stories that are not available through the currently distributed films.

Sex is a big thing in Yąnomamö myths—the general relationships between men and women at the level of comparative status on the one hand and their relative biological attributes on the other. Sex is also a big thing in everyday life among the Yąnomamö, as it is elsewhere, and much of their humor, insulting, fighting, storytelling, and conceptions about humans revolves around sexual themes. If I were to illustrate the dictionary I have been patiently collecting on my field trips, it would be, as one of my puckish graduate students once commented, very good pornography! The proverbial Eskimos are proverbially alleged to have thousands of words for snow, the point being that vocabulary often reflects what is important in a particular culture. You would expect Eskimos to have a lot of words for snow. The Yąnomamö, by contrast, have no words for snow, but on the kind of argument posed here, one certainly would have no difficulty concluding that sex is their equivalent of snow if one had a representative dictionary of Yąnomamö language!

A few examples from their stories of the *no badabö* will suffice to illustrate the wit, humor, and themes in Yąnomamö intellectual life. Some seem to have morals or lessons in them while others purport to explain or justify why things are the way they are in the mortal world today. Yet others seem to have no obvious point, such as the simple story of the exchange that Armadillo Ancestor and Jaguar Ancestor made with their teeth, each giving the other his own teeth, reversing their original roles and natures.

One of the themes that periodically crops up has to do with the relationships between men and women. Men are considered to be not only different from women, but superior in some regards to them. In this the Yąnomamö are not unique. And, as is sometimes found in the myths of other people, a peculiar intellectual struggle is implicit in the myths about male and female relationships. Levi-Strauss, the famous French anthropologist who devoted much of his brilliant efforts to creating a discipline dealing with the mythical themes of Man, drew attention to this problem and has dealt repeatedly with it in his many publications. The problem is more general than just the relationships between the sexes and has broadly to do with "working out" via myths certain irreconcilable human beliefs and concerns. Thus, as the distinguished British anthropologist Edmund Leach (1970) succinctly put it in his scholarly but brief assessment of Levi-Strauss' view of the anthropology of myths, it is a problem of the following order of magnitude. Humans often phrase, in ideological terms, the general proposition that men and women are more or less equal, no matter what other additional beliefs and attitudes they might have about the relative importance of males and females. But humans also explicitly condemn the practice of incest within the nuclear family. We have in these two statements the making of a contradiction that is hard to avoid and difficult to reconcile. If men and women are in fact equal, then they must have parents who are equal. Most creation stories begin with two individuals who people the earth with humans, but the only way that the first two people could be absolutely equal would be if they are siblings, brother and sister. If they are brother and sister, then all humans are the consequence of an original act of blatant incest, of brothers copulating with sisters. That's pretty distasteful in most cultures, but only some solve the problem by having a separate creation myth for women and men. It avoids the incest problem, but runs smack into a different one. If they are created separately, they are not therefore absolutely equal. That is how the Yąnomamö solve the problem. They have separate origin myths for women. The Christian Bible opts for a more incestuous solution: Eve was created from a portion of Adam's body, his rib, and therefore, they somewhat incestuously go about creating the rest of us. A pre-Biblical account might have been adopted by the Bible, but wasn't: Adam set about his procreative work with a mate named Lilith, part human and part fabulous animal (Leach, 1970). The choice of the founders was probably a tough one, but we got the incest version. One of the Yąnomamö myths on the creation of Man is itself apparently ambiguous, for some Yąnomamö claim that only men were created in this story, the story of Moonblood (see the 16-mm film listed at the end of the book, Chagnon and Asch, 1975), while other Yąnomamö argue that both men and women were created from Moon's blood. In the Moonblood story, one of the ancestors shot the Moon in the belly. His blood fell to earth and changed into Men, but Men who were inherently *waiteri*: fierce. Where the blood was thickest, the men who were created there were very ferocious and they nearly exterminated each other in their wars. Where the droplets fell or where the blood thinned out by mixing with water, they fought less and did not exterminate each other, that is, they seemed to have a more controllable amount of inherent violence. Because of this, humans are *waiteri*: fierce. The time of "Moonblood" is also a phrase frequently used by the Yąnomamö to indicate something like "the beginning of time." While collecting genealogies I would eventually get to the last ancestor known to my informant and further questioning about his parents would usually be met with the answer: "Whaa! Those people lived at the time of Moonblood!", that is, too far in the past for anyone to know today.

Those Yąnomamö who maintain that only males came from the blood of Moon also argue that females came from a kind of fruit called *wabu* in the following way.

> *Those created by Moon's blood were all males, and they had no women with whom to copulate. They went out collecting vines one day, and began pulling them from the trees. The headman of the group noticed that one of the vines had a newly opened wabu fruit attached to it, and the fruit had "eyes" on it. He thought to himself: "Ummm. I'll bet that's what women look like!" and he tossed it on the ground. It changed immediately into a woman and immediately developed a large vagina. They continued to collect vines, not aware that the fruit had turned into a woman. As they dragged the vines home, the woman kept at a distance and would step on the ends of the vines, jerking the men off guard as she did, hiding behind trees when they turned back to look. She finally just stood on one of the vines, causing the men to screech to a halt. They turned and looked, and saw her. They were startled that she had a vagina—a very long and very hairy one. They stared at it and were overcome with lust. They rushed at her and all took a turn copulating frantically with her. They brought her back to the village and let all the men there have a turn copulating with her. Eventually she had a baby—a daughter, another, and another. As each daughter came out, everyone copulated with her and eventually there was an abundance of females, all descended from the wabu fruit, and that is why there are so many Yąnomamö today.*

## Jaguar Myths

A theme that repetitiously appears in Yąnomamö myths is about Man's relationship with Jaguar. In mortal form, the jaguar is an awesome and much-feared beast, for he can and does kill and eat men. He is as good a hunter as the Yąnomamö are and is one of the few animals in the forest that hunts and kills men—as the Yąnomamö themselves do. He is in that sense like Man, but unlike Man, he is part of Nature, not of Culture. This distinction is fundamental in Yąnomamö conceptions, for the Yąnomamö separate themselves invidiously from the animals, and point out, as proudly as we do, that humans have Culture and the animals do not. Thus, they bifurcate the world into *urihi tä rimö* (things of the forest) and *yahi tä rimö* (things of the village). The former is Nature; the latter is Culture. It is tempting to speculate about the nearly universal distribution of this opposition and whence it comes and what it means. It seems to be an idea that is somewhat "fixed" in human conceptions, a polarity that we can only with difficulty learn to view as a *continuous* scale of "more natural" or "more cultural." There is probably not a single reader of this who has not been confronted with the kind of argument that pits "learning" against "instinct," or "cultural" against "biological." It is "in our heads" and it takes considerable effort to translate it into something more sophisticated than simply a Culture/Nature dichotomy, and there is some considerable evidence that "cultures" must be very special and work very hard to break down this particular dichotomy—to the extent that one can say that cultures "work" at anything. Be that as it may, the Yąnomamö pit Culture against Nature, as we often do, and see the cosmos in many contexts as an "either/or" moiety. Thus, an animal, captured in the wild, is "of the forest," but once brought into the village, it is "of the village" and somehow different, for it is then part of Culture. For this reason, they do not eat their otherwise edible pets—such as monkeys, birds, and rodents—for to them, it is similar to cannibalism: eating something "cultural" and therefore "humanlike." Nothing disgusted the Yąnomamö more than my matter-of-fact comments that we ate our domestic animals, such as cattle and sheep, and many a missionary gave up in frustration after having attempted to introduce chickens at mission posts. The Yąnomamö liked the roosters because they crowed at dawn, and kept them essentially for this aesthetic reason if they kept them at all, but would refuse to kill and eat them. They believed that the roosters and chickens were "of the village" and part of Culture. They did, however, have a different attitude toward eggs and ate them with gusto, for they were not quite the same thing as the chicken they produced, an attitude we also have when we discuss the moral and legal implications of abortion: We allow for the fetus as being different from the "human" being it eventually becomes, and are prepared, in some circles, to treat it differently in law and in medical practice.

Jaguar is an ambiguous creature to them, for he combines several human capacities while at the same time he is "natural." It is almost as if they both respect and fear jaguars, and the "dual" nature of Jaguar might be viewed as a kind of contradiction of the sort that Levi-Strauss had in mind when he viewed myths as the intellectual vehicle through which such contradictions are reconciled. The many stories that the Yąnomamö have about jaguars seem to all make the point, in one way or another, that Man is ultimately the master over Jaguar and can outwit him. Jaguar is usually portrayed as a large, clumsy, stupid, and bungling beast—whatever he might be in real life. Indeed, the Yąnomamö are terrified at the prospect of having to spend the night in the jungle without fire, for they know that Jaguar hunts at night and they know that they are no match for him in this realm. I was awakened many times while I worked with the Yąnomamö and begged to go looking for some villager who failed to return by dark. They knew the villager had no fire drill or matches and were worried that jaguars might kill and eat him at night. I had to take them with my canoe and flashlights to help them find the wayward traveler, and the traveler was always very grateful that we found him before the jaguars did. I know how they feel, for I myself was stalked a number of times by jaguars, and on one occasion was nearly a meal for one of them. He walked into our camp at about 3:00 A.M. after our fire had gone out, and was sniffing me. Fortunately, I had given my flashlight to one of my guides, who awoke, shined the light on him, and he retreated quickly into the jungle as my guides hissed frantically into my ear: "Jaguar! Jaguar! Jaguar!" It is a word in Yąnomanö that I'll never forget, for the hot breath and the fearsome size of this animal has forever fixed in my mind his name: *öra*. Jaguars are also occasional daylight hunters. In August 1990, a large male attacked a party of armed Yąnomamö men in the village I was then studying and killed three of them without a single arrow being fired at him. The jaguar dragged one of them off and ate most of him before the others found his body and cremated what was left. Several years earlier, a crazed jaguar walked into a large Yąnomamö village and began attacking residents in broad daylight. The men managed to spear him to death with bowstaves before he killed anyone, but he left a lot of ugly claw scars on many of them.

Jaguar, then, is an ambiguous character to the Yąnomamö. He is like Man in that he hunts and is cunning and is so effective that one might say that the Yąnomamö are somewhat jealous of him. But in their stories about him, he is consistently portrayed as a stupid brute, constantly being outwitted by Man, and constantly subjected to the most scathing, ridiculous, and offensive treatments at the hands of Man.

Some stories are more oblique than others in this regard. In the story of the Jaguar named Kashahewä, or Hǫo, he is simply destroyed by men who use a palm-wood club called *himo*. These clubs are long, heavy, and sharpened at the upper edges, and made from a very dense, black, and heavy palm wood called *shidibasi*. They are slightly thicker than broom handles for most of their circular shaft, but widen out into a kind of skinny canoe paddle whose edges are very sharp.

The Yąnomamö sometimes have duels with these clubs, which deal a severe and often fatal blow due to their heavy weight and sharpness. They are for hitting people on the head, with the sharp edge forward.

*Jaguar, in a story in which he is known as Hǫo, has exterminated most of mankind. An old man in one of the villages is sleeping, snoring very loudly. Jaguar enters the village and carries his son off, who screams and protests that Jaguar is treating him like some common game animal. The members of the village—Shidibasi-teri (from which the name of the wood used in the club is derived)—decide to take a himo club to their neighbors, the Beribosihi-teri village, knowing that Jaguar has been devouring them. But when they reach the village, they find that it has already been wiped out by Jaguar, and enormous buzzards are finishing off the human remains that Jaguar didn't eat. It is growing dark, and they become frightened. They flee to a nearby tree and climb it, for they hear Jaguar roaring and whining in the nearby jungle. They climb an arausi tree and, once at the top, begin to scrape and peel the bark off the trunk. They get out their fire drill and make a fire from the bark, fasten it to the tree, and sit in the highest branches, waiting for Jaguar. The brother-in-law of the snoring man has the himo club. He has a vine hammock, slung between the branches, and stands (sic) in it, watching for Jaguar. Eventually Jaguar arrives, sniffing around, and climbs the tree after them. When he gets near the top, the man with the club wallops him soundly on the head, knocking him off the tree, and knocking him unconscious. Jaguar falls to the ground, eventually regains consciousness and climbs up again, and again gets clouted on the head by the himo club. Up and down, up and down, all night long. Meanwhile, they huddle closely around the fire and blow on it to keep it burning. Jaguar cannot make them out, and climbs close, peering at them, perhaps blinded by the fire. They smack him again with the club, and he falls to the ground again. Near dawn, Jaguar again climbs the tree. He gets almost up to them, stretches his arms out to catch them, and they hit him on the bridge of his nose with the sharp edge of the himo club. He falls again and lies motionless. One of them climbs down cautiously, and examines Jaguar, to see if he is breathing. Blood is oozing from his nostrils and the bees have begun to come for the blood. "Whaaa! He is dead! We got him!" they exclaim, and with that, depart. That is how the people of Palm-Wood Village got him with a palm-wood club.*

In another story, Jaguar is not at first given over to eating humans—he acquires the taste gradually. This story is interesting in the sense that it specifically discusses the use of red peppers as a form of "chemical warfare," a tactic described by early Spaniards who observed Tropical Forest peoples "smoking out" their enemies by burning red peppers upwind from them, the drifting smoke and toxic vapors driving the residents from their village coughing and gagging. The present Yąnomamö do not use red peppers in this fashion, but the myth clearly indicates that they are aware of its potential for producing a very disagreeable and toxic smoke, a potentially fatal poison.

Jaguar has the name Käyäkäyä or Kräyäkräyä in this story—his name keeps changing. In this story, Jaguar's son-in-law (or nephew) actually begins the dastardly act of eating humans. Note that Jaguar is somehow mysteriously human, so eating humans is in fact an act of cannibalism.

*Jaguar's son-in-law, Siroroma, saw some humans one day when they were hunting. He caught some game and then approached the wife of one of the humans, and gave her the meat. He copulated with her and got her pregnant. Her husband later began to suspect that he did not cause the pregnancy and grew very suspicious. His wife told him that a bird named Kawamari gave her the meat, for she wanted to conceal the fact that she was pregnant by a jaguar. He went hunting, and when he returned, he discovered that his wife had more meat—another turkey. "What the hell is going on here?" he thought to himself. He began watching her more carefully, and eventually he heard a noise in the forest. It was Jaguar's son-in-law, Siroroma. The husband immediately concluded: "Haaa! He's the one who has gotten her pregnant!" He decided to get rid of Siroroma and set about all day long collecting firewood. He made a huge bonfire in the village, and then approached Siroroma, grabbing him in a tight bear-hug, and threw him into the fire to roast. But Siroroma turned into a liquid and quenched the fire, and then attacked the husband, squirting a stinging liquid into his eyes in the form of spit. He blinded him, and the husband fled in agony, rubbing his hands into his blind eyes. Siroroma, scorched by the fire, then decided to peel his own skin off, using his fingernails. He skinned himself on the spot and took his own pelt home, where he hung it up in his roof—where it still hangs to this day.*

*Siroroma looked very different with no skin. He went home, where he joined his father-in-law (uncle), Jaguar. On seeing the skinned nephew, Jaguar thought: "Hooo! My nephew has sent a wild pig home for me to eat!" Not knowing he was eating his own son-in-law, Jaguar devoured him voraciously and developed a craving for the flesh. He decided at that point to hunt this kind of game, and from that time on, Jaguar has hunted humans. But soon humans began to catch on to his designs and appetites. They began avoiding him. Jaguar took to living in caves, where he reared his family and fed them on human flesh.*

*He went to a human village called Wayorewä-teri, in the mountains. He sang his hunting song as he approached the village—"Käyäkäyä, Käyäkäyä, Käyäkäyä...." He entered the village and found that all the adults were gone. They were away, hunting for naö fruits far from the village. Only an old woman, a large number of children, and a pubescent girl going through her first menses confinement were there. He entered and asked the old woman for water, and complained when he got it: It was stagnant. The old woman was the mother of the pubescent girl, and was mourning sorrowfully for the girl, for she knew the girl was hungry, but could not eat because of the menstrual taboos. Jaguar set his pack basket down, and the children grew apprehensive. He asked the old woman why there were no adults around, and he was told that they were out foraging for wild foods.*

The story becomes very funny here, but there is no way to convey the sophistication of the humor in literal English translation. I'll change the names of the fruits and animals to try to get the humor across—at the expense of the accuracy of the proper identification of the actual species mentioned. I will also change a few body parts, for Yąnomamö and we have different views of what parts are more important. (The liver is more important to them than the heart, and "liverthrob" doesn't come out as well as "heartthrob" in, for example, a romantic passage; "my liver and shadow" doesn't grab us as much as "my heart and soul," but it would be a reasonable translation.) Jaguar's motive was to insult as viciously as possible and he tried to be as obnoxious as he could with his caustic retorts to the old woman.

*"What kinds of food are they seeking?" he asked. "They went collecting peaches," said the old woman. "Hrumph! That will cause them to have fuzz all over their asses if they do that!" said Jaguar. "Well, they also mentioned that they wanted hardshell crabs," said the old woman. "Hrumpf! Their tits will turn into armour plating if they eat them!" said Jaguar. "Well, they also were after crayfish, too," added the old woman. "Hrumpf! Their peckers will turn pink and curl up if they eat any of them!" said Jaguar. "And they wanted to catch a few bullhead fish as well," said the old woman. "Hrumpf! That will cause them to have stringy tentacles growing from their snouts!" mused Jaguar.[2] "Moreover,*

---

2. There is no way to easily render allusions to the forehead and the complexion of skin in Yąnomamö insults. These include the foulest of insults in their language, like telling someone to "fuck off!"

they plan to catch some striped fish," added the old woman "Hrumpf! They'll look like zebras when they eat them!" quipped Jaguar. "Some said they wanted a few eggplants," said the old woman. "Hrumpf! They'll break their assholes trying to pass an eggplant!" said Jaguar.

She went to the river to get him some fresher water, leaving the pubescent girl and the children unattended. When the old woman had gone, Jaguar immediately entered the girl's puberty hut and killed her. The old woman heard a noise, and hastily returned to the village, asking what the noise was about. "I was just fanning the fire!" lied Jaguar. The woman left, satisfied, and Jaguar immediately set upon the children, killing them as quickly as he could catch them, stacking up their tiny corpses in his pack basket. He thought he had gotten them all, and was about to leave when he noticed two rather strange things. They were children, but their heads were shaved clean because they had lice. Jaguar thought they were dogs and decided to bring them along, as pets, to his lair. He grabbed them and stuck them on top of his basket full of dead children, and left for his cave.

As he got close to the cave, he passed under a vine. The older of the two children grabbed the vine and swung off the basket into the trees. Jaguar noticed the sudden change in the weight of his load, and investigated. He tried to entice the child down, but the child would not comply, so Jaguar left him there and went on to his cave. Jaguar's cave was actually an armadillo den. (Recall that Jaguar and Armadillo exchanged teeth with each other.) He entered it with his basket of human flesh and began distributing it among his kinsmen. The child who had escaped into the trees fled home and told the adults what had happened. The adults decided to go after him and kill him. They set about collecting a large pile of red peppers and a large quantity of termite nest material. They mixed them together and set off for Jaguar's den. They found all the entrances to the den and covered them with dirt and brush. They put the mixture of peppers and termite nest material in the entrances and lit it. Inside the den, Jaguar was distributing the meat: "Ahhh! Father has brought us some wild pigs!" exclaimed Jaguar's children.[3] They then cooked and ate the dead children. As they were eating, the parents of the victims were busily building fires in the red peppers and termite nests at the entrances to the den. The jaguars ate, sucking the marrow from the bones, passing bits and morsels back and forth as in a feast: "This is for your sister!" "This is for your brother-in-law!" "This is for your mother!" Outside, the adults were blowing the acrid smoke into the cave. As it seeped in, the jaguars inside began choking and coughing. There was smoke everywhere, and the jaguars began getting delirious and screamed from the pain of the pepper smoke. They began dying in large numbers. Flashes of lightning came from the entrances to the den. There is a giant basket at that mountain now, and many red peppers grow there. The basket makes noises like the spirits do: "Dei! Dei! Dei! Dei!" That is how Kräyäkräyä began to eat humans. When Yąnomamö chant to the spirits today, only the spirits of the Kräyäkräyä come, for the original ones were all exterminated by the poison gas.

---

3. The Mundurucu Indians of Brazil also equate hunting of pigs with killing of enemies (Murphy, 1960).

The story that most poignantly captures the cynicism and ambiguity the Yąnomamö have for Jaguar is the story of *Misi*, the tortoise. Tortoises and turtles are slow moving and virtually helpless when their feet are not touching the ground. Indeed, some South American Indian groups store turtle meat by capturing large numbers of them and just turning them upside down, where they squirm helplessly until it is time to cook them.

> *The Original Beings from the village of Manakae-teri were traveling through the forest, hunting and collecting. They came upon a tortoise and were delighted. It would be their "pet," their "dog." Little did they know that Jaguar was systematically exterminating everyone and that they would soon become his victims. Jaguar eventually came and began preying on them. They fled their village to escape his depredations, but before they did, they tied their tortoise by a vine and suspended him from the roof, as they always do with special possessions—to keep them dry and clean. He was thus helpless, dangling from the cord, unable to do anything but move his legs and head randomly and ineffectually. Jaguar approached the deserted village and entered it, looking for people to eat. He slowly wandered around the periphery, but the houses were empty. He eventually came to the house where Misi was dangling from the rafters. Misi's head waved from side to side, and he made a helpless noise like "beek, beek, beek...." Jaguar approached him to sniff, and Misi grabbed his snout with his beak. He held on tightly as Jaguar struggled to free himself, tightening his bite the longer and more violently the Jaguar struggled. He hung on to Jaguar's snout until Jaguar weakened and collapsed. He released his grip and Jaguar gasped his final breath. Jaguar's eyes gradually dulled and he died. Misi then packed his belongings (sic) and set off on a camping trip. On the way he came to the big river where his owners had made a palm-wood bridge and crossed. He caught up to the Manakae-teri, who were overjoyed to see their "dog." They examined him and discovered that he had been in a fight, for there was blood on his beak. They all went back to the village where they found the dead Jaguar and exclaimed: "Whaaa! Just look how big he is!" On hearing that, Misi dropped dead. His owners were so grateful that he had killed Jaguar that they began mourning him. They decided to cremate his body and eat his ashes, reciting his exploits and achievements as they wept for him. Word reached other people that Misi had died, and all requested gourds of his ashes so they, too, could honor him by drinking his ashes. The spirit of the Jaguar that Misi killed now roams the forest and is meat hungry. He eats only agouti rodents today.*

The irony of this story is that a simple, helpless turtle overcame and destroyed Jaguar, King of Amazonian Beasts. A stupid King of Beasts in myth alone.

## The Twins Omawä and Yoawä

Several stories the Yąnomamö tell involve paired male ancestors, Omawä and Yoawä (Yoasiwä). They do many things and are involved in the creation events that led to the distribution of many plants, animals, and customs the Yąnomamö are now familiar with. The two characters are somewhat complementary opposites—one is smart, beautiful, competent, and admirable while the other is stupid, ugly, a boob, and contemptuous. Sometimes there is a change of identities in the stories and the dumb one is the smart one and vice versa. Of all the fabulous events and situations that describe the activities of these two Original Beings, the story of the "Origin of Copulation" is the most humorous. In this story, in the versions told by the Shamatari, Omawä is the attractive one of the two, and Yoawä the stupid one.

> *Yoawä went fishing one day. He tied bait to his fishing line and cast it into the river.[4] As he fished, he came upon a beautiful maiden. She was Raharaiyoma, daughter of the giant river monster, Raharariwä. There were no women at that time and Yoawä wanted to capture her so he could copulate with her. She was in the river, spinning cotton into yarn—and very sexy. "Wow! A real female! She has a beautiful vagina! I'd like to try it!" he said to himself. He knew she would not cooperate, so he decided to change into a small bird and lure her up to the surface where he could catch her. He decided to change into a bird that had a long beak and a combed head, in which form he fluttered above her trying to be seductive. She noticed him, and dismissed him with insults, saying he looked ugly with such a long snout and ridiculous apparatus growing out of his head. He then changed into a spotted, flecked bird and hovered above her, trying to be sexy. She again insulted him, for his skin was blemished with spots all over it. He tried several other bird guises, but failed each time and was dismissed with her biting insults. He was frustrated and angry, and went home in a huff. He threw his catch of fish onto the smoke rack and retired in disgust. His beautiful brother asked him in the morning why he let his fish cook to a black, charred inedible mess and why he was so moody. He explained that he was horny because he saw his first woman and could not seduce her. Omawä had compassion and explained a plan to catch the woman, for Omawä also grew horny. He insisted that Yoawä show him where she was, and the two of them set off to find her. She was still in the river, this time casually delousing herself. Again, Yoawä transformed himself into a small bird, but the woman dismissed him because he had ugly blemishes all over his body. He changed into another bird and was dismissed because his skin was too dark. He changed into a hummingbird, and she again dismissed him with insults, saying that his eyes were beady and he squinted. Yoawä then asked Omawä to help him. Omawä advised him to change into a small, minnowlike fish, which he did, and he hid in the water near her. Omawä then changed himself into a beautiful small bird with scarlet feathers and hovered above the woman. She was attracted and told her father that she wanted to catch this beautiful crimson bird and keep it as her pet. As she surfaced to reach for the bird, the two of them grabbed her, one on each arm, and dragged her from the water out onto the land. She screamed and struggled, but they got her out of the water. Her father, the water monster, came to her aid, but they fled, dragging the woman with them until they escaped. They brought their sexy little trophy back home with them, and were anxious to copulate with her.*

---

4. The Yąnomamö claim that they used to fish with lines made of native fibers. They would tie a piece of bait to the string and wait for a fish—usually a small one—to swallow it. They would then pull the fish out of the water. I never saw them fish this way.

*Their nephew lived with them—Howashi, the white (Cappuchin) monkey.*
*He saw her vagina and the provocative pubic hair and was immediately overcome*
*with lust. "Let me have her first! Let me have her! I'm horny as hell, and just*
*look at that fantastic vagina!" They let him have the first turn. He passionately*
*mounted her and stuck his penis into her vagina with a mighty pelvic thrust—*
*and immediately screamed in agony, withdrawing his bloody stump. She had*
*piranha fish inside her vagina and they bit the end of his penis off. He screamed*
*and howled and fled into the forest, holding what was left of his bloody penis.*[5]

*Yoawä removed the fish from her vagina with a barbed arrow and then*
*mounted her. He was consumed with lust, and made long, passionate pelvic*
*thrusts. His penis went in deep, and came back out rhythmically, and made a*
*foul, disgusting noise: "Soka! Soka! Soka! Soka!" Omawä threw up his arms in*
*dispair, for such clumsy copulating, such foul noise, would anger people who*
*might overhear it. He demanded that Yoawä cease and dismount so he could*
*show him how to copulate in the proper manner. He then mounted as Yoawä*
*observed. He copulated with slow, discreet pelvic thrusts and made no noise as he*
*proceeded. "See? That is how to copulate properly, so nobody can hear your*
*penis going in and out!" From that time on, people have been able to copulate*
*discreetly.*

## The Soul

Yąnomamö concepts of the soul are elaborate and sophisticated. The "true" or "central" part of the soul is the will, or *buhii*. At death, this turns into a *no borebö*, escapes up the hammock ropes, and travels to the layer above. When it reaches the upper layer, it travels down a trail that has a fork in it. There, the son of *Yarn* (Thunder), a spirit named Wadawadariwä, asks the soul if it has been generous or stingy during mortal life. If the person has been stingy and niggardly, Wadawadariwä directs the soul along one path—leading to a place of fire: *Shobari Waka*. If the person was generous with his possessions and food, he is directed along the other path—to *hedu* proper, where a tranquil semi-mortal existence continues.

The Yąnomamö do not take this very seriously, that is, do not fear the possibility of being sent to the place of fire. When I asked why, I got the following kind of answer: "Well, Wadawadariwä is kind of stupid. We'll just all lie and tell him we were generous, and he'll send us to *hedu.*"

Another portion of the soul, the *no uhudi* or *bore*, is said to be released during cremation. It wanders around on earth and lives in the jungle. Some Yąnomamö claim that children always change into *no uhudi* and do not have a *no borebö* because their "wills" (*buhii*) are *mohode*: innocent, unaware. It would appear that one's soul experiences an ontogeny that parallels human development and that a certain amount of living has to occur before parts of the soul develop.

---

5. Howashi monkeys have penises that look like ten-penny nails: straight with a flattened head. This story explains how Howashi monkeys got penises like that.

Some of the wandering *bores* are malevolent and attack travelers in the jungle at night. They have bright glowing eyes and beat the mortal travelers with clubs and sticks. In 1968, I brought Rerebawä to Caracas for a few days—a hilarious but informative experience for him—where he saw automobiles for the first time. As we drove along at night, the oncoming cars with their bright pairs of headlights terrified him. It was a constant stream of *bore* spirits rushing at him at incredible speed and whizzing by.

The most critical component of the soul is known as the *möamo* and lies inside the thoracic cavity, near (perhaps even inside of) the liver. This portion can be "lured" out and stolen, and is very vulnerable to supernatural attack if removed from the body. The person who has lost his *möamo* sickens and eventually dies, and the daily shamanistic attacks are usually directed at the *möamo* portions of the souls of enemies, or directed to recover this soul and return it to its owner. (See the 16-mm film *Magical Death*, listed among the Ethnographic Films at the end of this book.)

In addition to multifaceted souls, all individuals have an animal counterpart, an "alter ego," known as the *noreshi*. It is a dual concept, for the *noreshi* is not only an animal that lives in the forest but is likewise an aspect or component of the human body or psyche. People can "lose" their *noreshis*.

A male inherits his *noreshi* from his father, but a girl inherits hers from her mother. Male *noreshis* are said to "go above" and female *noreshis* "go below." Thus, certain monkeys and hawks are male *noreshi* animals and are found in high places, whereas snakes and ground-dwelling animals are female *noreshi* animals and travel low, a sexual superior/inferior equation. Kạobawä, for example, has the black spider monkey, *basho*, as his alter ego, which he and all his brothers inherited from their father: "We are of the *basho mashi!*" they would say, the "lineage" of the spider monkey. Kạobawä's wife, Bahimi, has the *hiima* (dog) as her *mashi*, which she and her sisters inherited from their mother. This Up/Down = Superior/Inferior = Male/Female duality occurs in other contexts, including very mundane ones. Men tie their hammocks up high and women sleep in hammocks below them. When the campfire gets low, the men just dangle a foot over the edge of their hammocks, nudge their wives who unhappily grunt and sleepily throw another piece of wood onto the fire.

*Noreshi* animals duplicate the lives of their human counterparts. When Kạobawä or Rerebawä go hunting, so too do their *noreshi* animals go hunting. When they sleep, so do their *noreshis*. If one gets sick, so also does the *noreshi*. A two-day trip for one is a two-day trip for the other.

While the human and his *noreshi* theoretically live far apart and never come into contact, it is said that misfortunes occasionally occur, as when a hunter accidentally shoots and kills his own *noreshi*—and thus dies himself. Moreover, if another hunter kills your *noreshi*, you, too, die. In a sense, hunting game animals is like hunting and killing humans, for some of the animals are the *noreshi* of humans.

The close association the Yąnomamö make between "soul loss" and sickness is best exemplified in the shamanistic practices of the men. They spend several hours each day, if they are shamans, chanting to their tiny *hekura* spirits, enjoining them to either attack the souls of enemies or help them recover souls lost by people in their own village. This is a constant battle, and the men take hallucinogenic snuff—*ebene*—daily to contest with their enemies through the agency of their personal *hekura*. (This is illustrated in the film *Magical Death*, listed at the end of this book.)

But not all aspects of the soul are equally vulnerable. When I showed them pictures of themselves or other people, they called the photographs *noreshi*. They called tape recordings, in contrast, *no uhudi*. They seemed, at first, to be more anxious about photographs and cameras and, indeed, were very annoyed with my photographic attempts in the beginning. They initially threw dirt and stones at me and, on one occasion, threatened to club me with red-hot fire-brands grabbed from the hearth. After about a year, they pretty much ignored my cameras, but a few would grumble from time to time. But they never objected to hearing tape recordings of their own voices and actually liked it—to the point that they would insist that I play back what I had recorded over and over again.

## Endocannibalism

Anthropologists distinguish between two general kinds of cannibalism: that which entails the eating of other people, or exocannibalism, and that which entails the eating of your own people, or endocannibalism. Neither form requires that the whole body be consumed and, in fact, most cannibalism entails the consumption of only selected parts. Most documented cases of cannibalism, except in extreme circumstances, are highly ritualistic and occur for religious or mystical reasons, although some of the advocates of the "protein theory" have since the early 1970s attempted to argue that the widespread consumption of humans by some peoples, such as the Aztecs, was a response to acute protein shortage (Harner, 1977; Harris, 1977; cf. Ortiz de Montellano, 1978). The issue has to do with the ultimate explanation of a hypothetical event. For example, a valiant warrior overcomes his equally valiant enemy in a mortal hand-to-hand contest. In celebration of his victory, he rips his enemy's heart out and ritually devours a portion of it to both honor his enemy and perhaps acquire some of his enemy's valor to add to his own. Is the valiant warrior short of protein, or is this more sensibly interpreted as a symbolic gesture? Perhaps the best way to drive home the argument is to ask whether the taking of Holy Communion is evidence of a calorie shortage or a symbolic, mystical—and ritually cannibalistic—act of eating the "body and blood" of a man called Jesus Christ. Holy Communion falls into a special category of cannibalism called theophagy, the Eating of Gods, and would make little sense if explained in terms of calorie or protein shortages. Most anthropophagy—the eating of men—is also like this.

The Yąnomamö are endocannibalistic anthropophagers—and that's a real mouthful! They eat portions of *their own* deceased: the ashes and ground bones that are left after a body is cremated. When someone dies, say an adult, his or her body is carried to the clearing in the village and placed on a pile of firewood. More wood is stacked up around and on top of the body and ignited. The children and those who might be sick are asked to leave the village, for the smoke from the burning corpse can contaminate the vulnerable and ill. They often wash their bows and arrows after a cremation, for the smoke of the burning corpse can contaminate such possessions. On one occasion, I saw them also wash all the smoked meat the hunters had brought back for a feast, for it, too, had been contaminated by the smoke of a cremated corpse.

Someone attends the fire, making sure the body is entirely burned. When the ashes have grown cool, they are carefully and solemnly sifted. Unburned bones and teeth are picked out and placed into a hollowed-out log, prepared for the occasion. A close kinsman or dear friend of the deceased pulverizes the bones by grinding them with a short stout pole about 5-feet long. When the bones are all pulverized, they are carefully poured onto a leaf and then transferred to several small gourds, each with a small opening in it. The dust and ash that remain in the hollow log are rinsed out with boiled ripe plantain soup and solemnly drunk as the assembled, squatting relatives and friends mourn loudly and frantically, rending their hair with their hands and weeping profusely. The log is then burned. The ash remains of a deceased person are often referred to as *madohe*, a word meaning "possessions," but in this context, "human remains." The gourds are carefully and tenderly stored in the roof of the kin's house, plugged shut with white down, and kept for a future and more elaborate ash-drinking ceremony that might be attended by kin who live in distant villages. At that time, a more elaborate ritual takes place. Large quantities of boiled ripe plantain soup are made and the ashes are poured into gourds full of the soup. The mixture in the gourds is passed around among close kin and friends and solemnly drunk while onlookers weep and mourn.

Children's corpses produce much less ash and bone, of course, and their remains are usually consumed by just the parents. More important adults who have many kin and many friends call forth a more elaborate ceremony, and many people partake of their ashes. In normal cases, all the remains are consumed in a single event. However, men who have been killed by enemy raiders are treated in a special fashion. Only women drink their ashes, and they do so on the eve of a revenge raid. Thus, the ashes of men who have been killed by enemies may remain in a village for several years—until their kin feel that their death has been avenged. One prominent man I knew, the headman of his village, was killed by raiders (see Chapter 6) in 1965. Ten years later gourds of his ashes were still in the rafters of his brother's house, and his group continued to raid the village that killed him—despite the fact that they had managed to kill several men in revenge.

Should many people die at one time, as during an epidemic, the bodies of the deceased are taken into the jungle and placed in trees, wrapped with bark and wood. After they decompose, the remaining flesh is scraped from the bones and the bones are burned, stored in gourds, and later drunk.

Finally, as one of the myths above suggests, some prized pets are cremated, especially good hunting dogs. The bones are buried afterward, not eaten. The bodies of ordinary dogs are discarded a short distance from the *shabono*, sometimes before the dog is dead.

## Shamans and Hekura

The word *shaman* is a word from the Arctic tribe, the Siberian Chuckchee, and has been widely used to describe men and women in any tribal society who manipulate the spirit world; cure the sick with magic, sucking, singing, or massaging; diagnose illness and prescribe a magical remedy; and generally intercede between humans and spirits in the context of health versus sickness (Figure 3.2).

Among the Yąnomamö, only men become shamans. It is a status or role to which any man can aspire if he so chooses, and in some villages a large fraction of the men are shamans. They are called *shabori* or *hekura* in Yąnomamö, the latter word being used also for the myriad tiny, humanoid spirits they manipulate.

One must, however, train to be a shaman. This entails a long period of fasting, a year or more, during which the novice loses an enormous amount of weight. He literally looks like skin and bones at the end. An older man or older men instruct the novice in the attributes, habits, songs, mysteries, and fancies of the *hekura* spirits. During the period of fasting, the novice must also be

**FIGURE 3.2**
Three shamans chanting to the hekura spirits while curing sick people.

sexually continent, for the *hekura* are said to dislike sex and regard it as *shami*: filthy. Novices attempt to attract particular *hekura* into their chests, a process that takes a long time and much patience, for the *hekura* are somewhat coy and fickle, apt to leave and abandon their human host. The interior of a shaman's body is a veritable cosmos of rivers, streams, mountains, and forests, where the *hekura* can dwell in comfort and happiness. Only the more accomplished shamans have many *hekura* inside their bodies, and even then they must strive to keep them happy and contented. Once you are on good terms with your *hekura*, you can engage in sex without having your spirits abandon you. I sometimes suspect that the older men have put one over on the younger men by insisting that it is good to be a shaman and that all of them should try it—and then insisting that they have to forsake women for extended periods of time. It is an effective way to reduce sexual jealousy in the village, one of the chronic sources of social disruption, and to allow for more mating opportunities among the older men. I have been confidentially told by young men that they didn't want to go through the shamanism training because it required sexual continence.

There are hundreds—perhaps thousands—of *hekura*. They are all small, but vary in size from a few millimeters to an inch or two for the really large ones. Male *hekura* have glowing halos around their heads called *wadoshe*, a kind of palm-frond visor that the Yąnomamö sometimes make and wear. Female *hekura* have glowing wands sticking out from their vaginas. All *hekura* are exceptionally beautiful, and each has his or her own habits and attributes. Most are named after animals, and most came into existence during some mythical episode that transformed some Original Beings—one of the *no badabö*—into both an animal and its *hekura* counterpart. The *hekura* are often found in the hills, or high in trees, often suspended there, but they can also live under rocks or even in the chest of a human. Many of them have special weapons used to strike or pierce souls (Taylor, 1974). Some are "hot" and some are *naiiki*: meat hungry and cannibalistic. Some are both hot and meat hungry, and these are often the ones sent to devour the souls of enemies. All of them have individual trails they follow when their human hosts call to them. The trails lead from the sky or the mountains, or even from the "edge of the universe," to the human host's body. There, the trails enter the feet of the human and traverse the body until they terminate in the thoracic cavity where villages, forests, and mountains can be found. The *hekura* come out of their mountains and lairs, reeling and dancing, glowing as they come, fluttering around in ecstasy, like a swarm of butterflies hovering over a food patch. Once they are there, they are subject to the designs of their human host, who sends them to devour enemy souls—especially children's souls—or to help their hosts cure sickness in the village.

The shamans have to take hallucinogenic snuff, *ebene*, to contact the spirits, but adept shamans with great experience need very little. Just a pinch is enough to get them going, get them singing the soft, melodic, and beautiful songs that attract the spirits. The *hekura* require beauty, and most shamans decorate their chests and stomachs with *nara* pigment, don their best feathers, and make themselves beautiful before calling to the spirits. The *hekura* have their own intoxicant, a magical beverage called *braki aiamo uku*, which they take when their human counterparts are snorting *ebene*.

As the *ebene* takes effect, the shamans begin singing louder and louder, often screaming, but always melodically and expertly. They recite the deeds of the *hekura*, the time of creation, the songs, and habits of the *hekura*, and explain many marvelous and fabulous events. Since this happens almost every day, most people in the village appear to be ignoring what is going on, but most of them are consciously or unconsciously listening to the songs and stories. Someone might even interrupt to add a correction to a slurred or inaccurate statement of "mystical truth" or to remind the shaman that he forgot to make a specific and characteristic gesture when he got to a certain spot in his mythical account. This is generally how the mythical times are revealed publicly, and often just snippets of the story are told, but all know what the whole story is. Sometimes the inept younger men take too much hallucinogen and "freak out," as if they had overdosed.

The men take *ebene* almost every day in the villages I lived in during most of my field work (Figure 2.5), but more recently I have lived in villages where the use of *ebene* is much less common. Taking *ebene* is noisy, exciting, and dramatic. It is sometimes unpleasant and nauseating as well, for the blast of *ebene* powder each man takes into his nostrils produces vomiting and profuse discharges of nasal mucus laden with green powder. In their stupor the men simply ignore this, and the long strands of green mucus drip down their chins onto their chests, or dangle and sway from their noses until they smear it all over their faces or it falls with a plop to the ground.

It is sometimes dangerous as well, for the trances are often the occasion for men to relieve the frustrations that have been building up. The Yąnomamö attitude seems to be that one is not quite responsible for his acts if he is in communion with the *hekura* and high on *ebene*. Thus one occasionally sees timid men use the opportunity to become boisterous and at times violent—running around the village in a stupor, wild eyed and armed, threatening to shoot someone with an arrow or hack someone with a machete. The same men would be unlikely to do this when sober, and I have always suspected that one of the primary functions of the daily hallucinogenic bouts is to give otherwise frustrated men a quasi-acceptable means through which they can work off their pent-up antagonisms and have, if only briefly and artificially, a moment of passion they might not otherwise be able to enjoy. When they become *waiteri* on drugs, people pay attention to them, chase them, disarm them, attempt to calm their tempers, and entreat them to calm down and stop being "fierce." Most of them allow their concerned peers to disarm them and calm them down, for they appear to be aware that carrying the event too far will strain credulity and invite less compassionate responses. Thus, the timid can, for a moment, be fierce and feared and can have their moment of ferocious passion, whether or not they would be able to meaningfully hold that status when sober. Even some of the stringent avoidance taboos are overlooked if people are intoxicated on *ebene*. Thus, sons-in-law can touch, talk to, and caress their fathers-in-law, something that would be unthinkable if both were sober. It is almost as if the psychological dimension of socially tripping out is a release valve for pent-up emotions and strains that the workday life imposes and generates.

But it can also get out of hand and be antisocial. In a village to the north of Kạobawä's, one of the men decapitated another with a single blow of his machete, provoking a violent fission in the village and a long war between the two related groups. It is not, in my estimation, irrelevant that the decapitated man was a chronic opponent of his killer and that there had been a long history of argumentation between them. I myself was nearly shot by a wild-eyed young man who was high on *ebene*, a man with whom I had had a disagreement earlier that day (Chagnon, 1974).

The Yạnomamö cosmos parallels and reflects the mortal world that men know, understand, and dwell in. When they die, they repeat life again elsewhere, in the layer above, hunting, collecting, gardening, making love, and making war. In *hedu* as it is on earth.

# 4

✳

# Social Organization and Demography

In this chapter I will discuss the daily social life and social organization of the Yąnomamö from several vantages, for there are, indeed, a number of acceptable and widely used approaches to the understanding of social organization in primitive societies. I will focus primarily on the fascinating problem of village fissioning among the Yąnomamö and how this reflects the "failure of solidarity;" the inability of villages to be held together by kinship, marriage, and descent from common ancestors; and the ephemeral authority of headmen such as Kąobawä. It would appear that primitive societies can only grow so large at the local level—the village in this case—if internal order is provided by just these commonly found integrating mechanisms: kinship, marriage, and descent.

I will also counterpose two points of view that are widely found in the field of anthropology. One of the approaches is the "structural" approach, which focuses on "ideal models" of societies, models that are constructed from the general rules of kinship, descent, and marriage. These are highly simplified but very elegant models, but they do not address the actual behavior of individuals in their day-to-day kinship roles, their actual marriage practices, their life histories, and why individuals simply cannot "follow" the ideal rules. The second approach is the "statistical models" approach, which is usually based on large numbers of actual behavioral and genealogical facts, but yields less elegant, less simplified models. However, such models conform more to reality. I prefer the latter, for they lead to a more satisfactory way to understand individual variation and therefore the ability to predict social behavior. To be able to engage in this approach, one must, of course, know what the "ideal" patterns are that people's behavioral choices deviate from.

A poignant way of illustrating the difference in these approaches is an anecdote I once heard the famous French anthropologist Claude Levi-Strauss use to justify his interest in ideal models and "structures." He likened social and cultural anthropology to a kind of science that studies crustaceans. It is legitimate, and even meritorious, he said, to concern oneself with the shell of the organism itself. Levi-Strauss preferred to consider the shells: They are attractive, symmetrical, pleasant to handle, and pleasant to think about. But he acknowledged that there were other ways of studying this life form. One could focus on the slimy, amorphous, rather unpleasant animal that lives in the shell—such as an oyster or snail. That, too, was a legitimate and meritorious endeavor, and he had no objection if others pursued that kind of approach. The issue, of course, has to do with the extent to which the shell and the amorphous animal inside it make much sense when considered alone and separately. My own view is that the animal inside the symmetrical shell is not as amorphous as it appears and itself has some structured integrity. I also believe that there has to be some kind of causal relationship between the animal and the type of structure it generates in the form of an elegant shell. The shell in this analogy is "social structure." The amorphous animal inside it is "social behavior." Once the question is posed, "What causes the animal to produce the elegant, symmetrical, shell?" then a great variety of possible answers—and theoretical issues—comes into play. These are questions about causes of human behavior and, in turn, how that behavior—acts, thoughts, sentiments found among individuals in particular cultures—is shaped by and reflects realities such as demographic facts, physiological differences between males and females, and the evolved nature of the organism itself.

## DAILY SOCIAL LIFE

### Male–Female Division

A number of distinctions based on status and physiology are important in daily life. Perhaps the most conspicuous and most important is the distinction between males and females and what each has to do as he or she becomes an adult.

Yąnomamö society is decidedly masculine—male chauvinistic if you will. Many Yąnomamö make statements like "Men are more valuable than women … boys more valuable than girls…." Female children assume duties and responsibilities in the household long before their brothers are obliged to participate in comparable useful domestic tasks. Little girls are obliged to tend to their younger brothers and sisters, and expected to help their mothers in other chores such as cooking, hauling water, and collecting firewood (Figure 4.1). By the time girls have reached puberty they have already learned that their world is decidedly less attractive than that of their brothers. Most have been promised in marriage by that time.

Girls, and to a lesser extent boys, have almost no voice in the decisions reached by their elder kin in deciding whom they should marry. They are largely pawns to be disposed of by their kinsmen, and their wishes are given very little consideration. In many cases, the girl has been promised to a man long before she reaches puberty, and in some cases her husband-elect actually raises her for part of her childhood. Boys seem to be more able to "initiate" the process and have their older kin make the first marital inquiries, but since males marry later in

**F I G U R E  4.1**  Woman and her young daughter returning with loads of firewood. Girls become economically useful sooner than boys and contribute significantly to household labor.

life than females, these "boys" are actually young men and the girls they are interested in are much, much younger, often just children. In a real sense, girls do not participate as equals in the political affairs of the corporate kinship group and seem to inherit most of the duties without enjoying many of the privileges, largely because of age differences at first marriage and the increase in status that being slightly older entails.

Marriage does not automatically enhance the status of the girl or change her life much. There is no "marriage ceremony," and the public awareness of her marriage begins with hardly more than comments like "her father has promised her to so-and-so." She usually does not begin living with her husband until after she has had her first menstrual period, although she may be "married" for several years before then. Her duties as wife require her to continue the difficult and laborious tasks she has already begun doing, such as collecting firewood and fetching water every day. Firewood collecting is particularly difficult, and women spend several hours each day scouring the neighborhood for suitable wood. There is usually an abundant supply in the garden within a year of clearing the land, but this disappears rapidly. Thereafter, the women must forage further afield to collect the daily supply of firewood, sometimes traveling several miles each day to obtain it. It is a lucky woman who owns an ax, for collecting wood is a tedious job without a steel tool. The women can always be seen leaving the village at about 3:00 or 4:00 P.M. and returning at dusk, usually in a procession, bearing enormous loads of wood in their pack baskets (Figure 4.2). If a woman locates a good supply of wood near the village, she will haul as much as she can and store it rather than let it be taken by her covillagers.

Women must respond quickly to the demands of their husbands and even anticipate their needs. It is interesting to watch the behavior of women when their husbands return from a hunting trip or a visit. The men march dramatically

**F I G U R E  4.2** Women returning from the garden at dusk with loads of firewood.

and proudly across the village and retire silently into their hammocks, especially when they bring home desirable food items. The women, no matter what they are doing, hurry home and quietly but rapidly prepare a meal. Should the wife be slow at doing this, some irate husbands scold them or even beat them.

Most physical reprimands meted out take the form of blows with the hand or with a piece of firewood, but a good many husbands are more severe. Some of them chop their wives with the sharp edge of a machete or ax or shoot them with a barbed arrow in some nonvital area, such as the buttocks or leg. Some men are given to punishing their wives by holding the glowing end of a piece of firewood against them, producing painful and serious burns. The punishment is usually, however, more consistent with the perceived seriousness of the wife's shortcomings, more drastic measures being reserved for infidelity or suspicion of infidelity. It is not uncommon for a man to injure his sexually errant wife seriously and some men have even killed wives for infidelity by shooting them with an arrow.

Women who are not too severely treated might even measure their husband's concern in terms of the frequency of minor physical reprimands they sustain. I overheard two young women discussing each other's scalp scars. One of them commented that the other's husband must really care for her since he has beaten her on the head so frequently!

A woman can usually depend on her brothers for protection. They will defend her against a cruel husband. If a man is too severe to a wife, her brothers may take the woman away from him and give her to another man. It is largely for this reason that women usually abhor the possibility of being married off to men in distant villages; they know that their brothers cannot protect them under these circumstances. Women who have married a male cross-cousin have an easier life, for they are related to their husbands by cognatic ties of kinship as well as by marriage. Bahimi is, for example, Kạobawä's Mother's Brother's Daughter (MBD), and their marital relationship is very tranquil. He does punish Bahimi occasionally, but never cruelly. Some men, however, seem to think that it is reasonable to beat their wife once in a while as if the objective is "just to keep her on her toes."

People sometimes ask me about what the Yạnomamö think about "love." They have a concept, *buhi yabraö,* that I thought, at first, could be translated into our notion of love. I remember being very excited when I learned this. I asked lots of questions, using concrete examples. "Do you 'love' so-and-so?" naming their brother or sister. "Yes!" "Do you 'love' so-and-so?" naming their child. "Yes!" "Do you 'love' so-and-so?" naming their wife. A stunned silence followed, then peals of laughter. "You don't 'love' your wife, you idiot!" One could plausibly argue that, if love in their culture is restricted to the kind of feelings you have toward close blood relatives, then one is more likely to have some of these feelings about spouses if, as in Kạobawä's case, one marries a blood relative—a close cousin—as he did.

A young man in Monou-teri shot and killed his wife a few years before I conducted my fieldwork. Even while I was there, a man in one of the villages shot his wife in the stomach with a barbed arrow. Considerable internal injury resulted when the arrow was removed. The missionaries had her sent out by airplane to the Territorial capital for surgery. Her wound had gotten infected, and the girl was near death by the time the incident came to their attention. Another man chopped his wife on the arm with a machete; the missionaries in that village feared that the woman would lose the use of her hand because some of the tendons to her fingers were severed. A fight involving a case of infidelity took place in one of the villages just before I left the field. The male culprit was killed in the club fight, and the recalcitrant wife had both her ears cut off by her enraged husband. A number of other women had their ears badly mutilated by angry husbands. The women wear short pieces of arrowcane in their pierced ear lobes; these are easily grabbed by the husband. A few men jerked these so hard that they tore their wife's ear lobes open.

There is a somewhat rare way a woman can escape the tragedy of marriage to an especially cruel or undesirable husband. They have a word for this: *shuwahimou*. This is applied to women who, on their own initiative, have fled from their village to live in another village and find a new husband there. It is rare because it is dangerous. If her own village is stronger than the one she flees to, they will pursue her and forcibly take her back—and mete out very severe punishment to her for having run away. They may even kill her. Most women who have done this have done it to escape the savage treatment they have received at the hands of a cruel husband.

By the time most women are 30 years old they have "lost their shape" because of the children they have borne, the children they have nursed for up to three years each, and the years of hard labor; and they seem to be much more often in "bad moods" than men. They seem, in these moods, to have developed a rather unpleasant attitude toward life in general and toward men in particular. To the outsider, the older women seem to chronically speak in what sounds like a "whine," frequently punctuated with contemptuous statements and complaints. When they are happy and excited, this whining character in their voices disappears, and they laugh gleefully, make wisecracks, and even taunt the men, or each other, with biting insults and clever jokes.

A woman gains increasing respect as she ages, especially when she is old enough to have adult children who care for her and treat her kindly. Old women also have a unique position in the world of intervillage warfare and politics. They are immune from the incursions of raiders and can go from one village to another with complete disregard for personal danger. In this connection they are sometimes employed as messengers and, on some occasions, as the recoverers of bodies. If a man is killed near the village of an enemy, old women from the slain man's village are permitted to recover his body.

All women fear being abducted by raiders and always leave the village with this anxiety at the back of their minds when their village is at war. They take their children with them, particularly younger children, so that if they are abducted, the child's future will not be put in jeopardy because of the separation of the mother. They are therefore concerned with the political behavior of their men and occasionally goad them into taking action against some possible enemy by caustically accusing the men of cowardice. The men cannot stand being belittled by the women in this fashion, and are badgered to take action by the biting insults of the women. This is clearly the case in the film *The Ax Fight* listed at the end of this book.

## Child–Adult Division

Despite the fact that children of both sexes spend much more of their time with their mothers, the boys are taught a number of sex-specific roles and attitudes by their fathers and are encouraged to learn "masculine" things by watching them. The distinction between male and female status develops early in the socialization process. Boys are encouraged to be "fierce" and are rarely punished by their parents for inflicting blows on them or on the hapless girls in the village. This can be seen in one of the scenes in the film A *Man Called Bee*, in which the five-year-old boys are not only beating each other on the head with toy clubs but are also beating the little girls as well (Chagnon and Asch, 1974a). Kąobawä, for example, lets Ariwari beat him on the face and head to express his anger and temper, laughing and commenting on his "ferocity." Although Ariwari is only about four years old, he has already learned that the appropriate response to a flash of anger is to strike someone with his hand or with an object, and it is not uncommon for him to give his father a healthy smack in the face whenever something displeases him. He is frequently goaded into hitting his father by teasing, being rewarded by gleeful cheers of assent from his mother and from the other adults in the household.

When Kąobawä's group travels, Ariwari emulates his father by copying his activities on a child's scale. For example, he erects a temporary hut from small sticks and discarded leaves and plays happily in his own camp. His sisters, however, are pressed into more practical labor and help their mother do useful tasks. Still, the young girls are given some freedom to play at being adults and have their moments of fun with their mothers or other children.

But a girl's childhood ends sooner than a boy's. The game of playing house fades imperceptibly into a constant responsibility to help mother. By the time a girl is 10 years old or so, she has become an economic asset to the mother and spends a great deal of time working. Little boys, by contrast, spend hours playing among themselves and are able to prolong their childhood into their late teens if they so wish. By that time a girl has married, and many even have a child or two. *Huyas* (young men, usually unmarried) are a social problem in almost all Yąnomamö villages and are often the source of much of the sexual jealousy since they try to seduce young women, almost all of whom are married.

A girl's transition to womanhood is obvious because of its physiological manifestations. At first menses (*yöbömou*), Yąnomamö girls are confined to their houses and hidden behind a screen of leaves. Their old cotton garments are discarded and replaced by new ones manufactured by their mothers or by older female friends. During this week of confinement, the girl is sparingly fed by her relatives; her food must be eaten by means of a stick, as she is not allowed to come into contact with it in any other fashion. She speaks in whispers, and then only to close kin. She must also scratch herself with another set of sticks.

After her puberty confinement, a girl usually takes up residence with her promised husband and begins life as a married woman.

Female students often ask me, "What do the women do when they have their menstrual periods? What do they 'wear' for sanitary napkins?" The Yąnomamö word for menstruation translates literally as "squatting" *(roo),* and that fairly accurately describes what pubescent females (and adult women) do during menstruation. They simply remain inactive during menstruation, squatting on their haunches and allowing the menstrual blood to drip on the ground. Yąnomamö women do not use the equivalents of tampons or sanitary napkins. And here lies an important difference between the "environment" we live in versus the one they live in. Sanitary napkins might be a useful invention if and when they are regularly and repeatedly needed, but Yąnomamö women menstruate relatively infrequently, for they are either pregnant or nursing infants much of their lives.

Males do not have their transition into manhood marked by a ceremony. Nevertheless, one can usually tell when a boy is attempting to enter the world of men. The most conspicuous sign is his resentment when others call him by his name. When the adults in the village cease using his personal name, the young man has achieved some sort of masculine adult status. Young men are usually very touchy about their names and they, more than anyone else, take quick offense when hearing their names mentioned. The Yąnomamö constantly employ teknonymy when a kinship usage is ambiguous. Thus, someone may wish to refer to Kąobawä in a conversation, but the kinship term appropriate to the occasion might not distinguish him from his several brothers. Then, Kąobawä will be referred to as "father of Ariwari." However, when Ariwari gets older he will attempt to put a stop to this in an effort to establish his status as an adult. A young man has been recognized as an adult when people no longer use his name in teknonymous references. Still, the transition is not abrupt, and it is not marked by a recognizable point in time.

Finally, the children differ from adults in their susceptibility to supernatural hazards. A great deal of Yąnomamö sorcery and mythological references to harmful magic focuses on children as the target of malevolence. Yąnomamö shamans are constantly sending their *hekura* to enemy villages. There, they secretly attack and devour the vulnerable portion of the children's souls, bringing about sickness and death. These same shamans spend an equal amount of time warding off the dangerous spirits sent by their enemies. Children are vulnerable because their souls are not firmly established within their physical beings and can wander out of the body almost at will. The most common way for a child's soul to escape is to leave by way of the mouth when the child cries. Thus, mothers are quick to hush a bawling baby in order to prevent its soul from escaping. The child's soul can be recovered by sweeping the ground in the vicinity where it most probably escaped, calling for it while sweeping the area with a particular kind of branch. I once helped gather up the soul of a sick child in this fashion, luring it back into the sick baby. One of the contributions I made, in addition to helping with the calling and sweeping, was a dose of medicine for the child's diarrhea.

## Daily Activities

Kąobawä's village is oval shaped. His house is located among those of his agnatic kinsmen, that is, men related through male ties. They occupy a continuous arc along one side of the village. Each built his own section of the village, but in such a way that the roofs coincided and could be attached by simply extending the thatching. When completed, the village looked like a continuous, oval-shaped lean-to because of the way in which the roofs of the discrete houses were attached. Each house, however, is owned by the family that built it. Shararaiwä, Kąobawä's youngest brother, helped build Kąobawä's house and shares it with him. He also shares Koamashima, Kąobawä's younger wife. Kąobawä's older wife, Bahimi, hangs her hammock adjacent to Kąobawä's most of the time, but when there are visitors and the village is crowded, she ties her hammock under his in order to be able to tend the fire during the night. Ariwari still sleeps with his mother, but will get his own hammock soon: he is nearly four years old. His parents are afraid he will fall into the fire at night and get burned, since he is still a little too young to sleep alone. This happened to one of the babies in Kąobawä's village—it slipped from his mother's arms while she slept and fell into the glowing embers. The infant died from the severe burns. The mother, shown in Figure 1.10, also died tragically from a snake bite not long after.

Daily activities begin early in a Yąnomamö village. One can hear people chatting lazily and children crying long before it is light enough to see. Most people are awakened by the cold and build up the fire just before daybreak. They usually go back to sleep, but many of them visit and talk about their plans for the day.

The entrances are all covered with dry brush so that any attempt to get through them is heard all over the village. There is always a procession of people leaving the village at dawn to relieve themselves in the nearby garden, and the noise they make going in and out of the village usually awakens the others. Covering the entrances with brush and poles also helps keep out unwanted malevolent spirits that roam near the village at night.

The village is very smoky at this time of day, since the newly stoked camp-fires smolder before they leap into flames. The air is usually very still and chilly, and the ground is damp from the dew. The smoke is pleasant and seems to drive away the coolness.

Clandestine sexual liaisons often take place at this time of day, having been arranged on the previous evening. The lovers leave the village on the pretext of "going to the toilet" and meet at some predetermined location. They return to the village, separately, by opposite routes.

This is also the time of day when raiders strike, so people must be cautious when they leave the village at dawn. If there is some reason to suspect raiders, they do not leave the confines of the upright log palisade that surrounds the village. They wait instead until full light and leave the village in armed groups. I have seen villages whose members cleared every blade of grass and shrub for a radius of 25 or 30 meters from the village to make sure raiders could not sneak

up close for an easy shot, and when people left the village they did so accompanied by groups of nervous men, often with one of their arrows already nocked in
their bows.

By the time it is light enough to see, everybody has started preparing breakfast. This consists largely of green plantains, easily prepared by placing them,
peeled, on the glowing coals of the family fire. Leftover meat is taken down
and shared, the men usually getting the tastiest portions. The meat is hung over
the fire by a vine to keep the vermin off it and to preserve it.

If any of the men have made plans to hunt that day, they leave the village
before it is light. Wild "turkey" (*paruri*) can be easily taken at this time of day
because they roost in conspicuous places. During the dry season the *hashimo* (a
kind of grouse) sing before dark and can be readily located. If any were heard the
night before, the men note these exact locations and leave at dawn to stalk them,
because they sing again at dawn and can be shot relatively easily.

Tobacco chewing starts as soon as people begin stirring. Those who have
fresh supplies soak the new leaves in water and add ashes from the hearth to
the wad. Men, women, and children chew tobacco, and all are addicted to it.
Normally, if anyone is short of tobacco, he can request a share of someone
else's already chewed wad, or simply borrow the entire wad when its owner
puts it down somewhere. Tobacco is so important to them that their word for
"poverty," *hori*, literally translates as "being without tobacco." I frequently justified my reluctance to give away possessions on the basis of my "poverty," using
their word *hori*. Many of them responded by spitting their wads out and handing
them to me contemptuously, for they knew I usually had many of the items they
wanted, an act that implied something like "If you are *that* poor, then take my
tobacco from me! At least one of us is willing to be generous and share in times
of poverty!"

Work begins as soon as breakfast is completed; the Yąnomamö like to take
advantage of the morning coolness. Within an hour after it is light the men are
in their gardens clearing brush, felling large trees, transplanting plantain cuttings,
burning off dead timber, or planting new crops of cotton, maize, sweet potatoes,
yuca, or the like, depending on the season. They work until 10:30 A.M., retiring
because it is too humid and hot by that time to continue with their strenuous
work. Most of them bathe in the stream before returning to their hammocks for
a rest and a snack.

The women usually accompany their husbands to the garden and occupy
themselves by helping with planting and weeding. In this way the men are sure
the women are not having affairs with other men. I have seen young men oblige
their newly acquired wives to keep within their eyesight almost all day long for
this reason. They assume, not without justification, that an unguarded mate will
eventually be approached by other men for sexual favors and might succumb to
the temptation, a concern that is equally well-grounded.

The children spend a great deal of time exploring the wonders of the plant
and animal life around them and are accomplished "naturalists" at an early age.
Most 12-year-old boys can, for example, name 20 species of bees and give the
anatomical or behavioral reasons for their distinctions, and they know which

ones produce the best honey. An eight-year-old girl brought me a tiny, uniden-tifiable egg on one occasion and asked me to watch it with her. Presently, it cracked open and numerous baby cockroaches poured out, while she described the intimate details of the reproductive process to me.

The younger children stay close to their mothers, but the older ones have considerable freedom to wander about the garden at play. Young boys hunt for lizards with miniature bows and featherless arrows. If they can capture one alive, they bring it back to the village and tie a string around it. The string is anchored to a stick in the village clearing and the little boys chase it gleefully, shooting scores of tiny arrows at it (Figure 4.3). Since lizards are very quick and little boys are poor shots, the target practice can last for hours. Usually, however, the fun terminates when an older boy decides to make an end to the unhappy lizard

**F I G U R E 4.3** Little boys practicing archery with a lizard that is tied by a string, using sticks, trying to knock them down. Sometimes the children will be organized by older men, who teach them how to go on raids. They usually sneak up on an effigy made of leaves and shoot it full of arrows on the command of the older men, and then "flee" from the scene.

and kills it with his adult-sized arrows, showing off his archery skills to the disgruntled small fry. The game that I found most ingenious and clever was the "get the bee" game. The children catch live bees and tie light cotton threads to their bodies, allowing them to try to fly off dragging the string behind them. The bees have difficulty flying and move very slowly, with the string sticking straight out behind them as the draft from their frantically beating wings holds it straight. The children then chase the bees.

The village is often almost completely empty for the midday hours, since people are out collecting, hunting, or doing other tasks. Those who remain in the village rest in their hammocks during the heat of midday.

If the men return to their gardening, they do so at about 4:00 P.M., working until sundown. Prior to, or often instead of, that they usually gather in small groups around the village and take hallucinogenic snuff, chanting to the *hekura* spirits as the drugs take effect. Most of the men enjoy doing it, despite the associated unpleasantries of vomiting and the pain that follows the blast of air as the powder is blown deeply into the nasal passages. This usually lasts for an hour or two, after which the men bathe to wash the vomit or nasal mucus off their bodies.

Whatever the men do for the afternoon, however, the women invariably search for firewood and haul immense, heavy loads of it to their houses just before dark.

The biggest meal of the day is prepared in the evening. The staple is plantains, but frequently other kinds of foods are available after the day's activities, usually some form of protein, such as small game animals or birds, a monkey, crabs, fish, or even insect larvae. It is a happy occasion, however, if someone should kill a bigger animal, such as a tapir, for then a large number of people will get a share, depending on their kinship ties. Hunters who kill tapirs are supposed to give all the meat away and eat none of it themselves. They usually give it to their brothers-in-law or father-in-law, and the sharing is done by them.

Both sexes participate in the cooking, although the women do the greater share of it. Men do all the cooking at feasts, a ceremonial occasion (see Chapter 5). Food preparation is not elaborate and rarely requires much labor, time, or paraphernalia. Spices are never used, although the salty ashes of a particular kind of tree are sometimes mixed with water to form a condiment of sorts. The food is dunked into the salty liquid and eaten (see Chapter 2).

Everyone eats in his hammock with his fingers. Some meals cannot be eaten from a reclining position, so the members of the family squat in a circle around the common dish. For example, large quantities of tiny fish are cooked by wrapping them in leaves and cooking them in the hot coals. When the fish are done, the package is spread open, and everyone squats around it and shares its contents. They gather around, and amidst much finger licking, spitting out of bones, tossing of inedible portions, and sighs of content, rapidly devour the contents of the package with alternate bites of plantain.

Animals are never skinned before cooking. They are merely put over the fire after their entrails have been removed, and roasted—head, fur, claws, and all.

Most of the fur is singed off in the process of cooking, or in some cases, a fire is made outside the village to singe the fur off the animal. Most small animals are cooked whole. Larger animals are cut up with knives or machetes before smoking or roasting. The head of a monkey is highly prized because the brain is considered a delicacy. Monkey is one of the more common meats, so that this delicacy is enjoyed rather frequently by the Yąnomamö. Certain parts of some animals are considered to be the prerogative of women, such as the heads of wild turkeys. Old women often eat some kinds of animals that younger people would refuse to touch, reflecting the fact that they tend to be very far down the list of who shares the better portions with whom.

By the time supper is over, it is nearly dark. The fires are prepared for the evening; if someone has allowed his own fire to go out during the day, he simply borrows two glowing sticks from a neighbor and rekindles his own hearth. The entrances to the village are sealed off with dry brush so that prowlers cannot enter without raising an alarm and so that harmful spirits will stay outside. Before retiring to their hammocks, the Yąnomamö first sit on them and wipe the bottoms of their bare feet by rubbing them together. This rubs off most of the debris that has accumulated on them during the course of the day. Everyone sleeps naked and as close to the fire as possible. Despite the inevitable last-minute visiting, things are usually quiet in the village by the time it is dark.

Things are not always quiet after dark. If anyone in the village is sick, a shaman will chant to his spirits most of the night to exorcise the sickness. Or, should anyone be mourning a dead kinsman, he or she will sob and wail long after the others have fallen asleep. Occasionally, a fight will break out between a husband and wife, and soon everybody in the village will be screaming, expressing opinions on the dispute. The shouting may continue sporadically for hours, dying down only to break out anew as someone gets a fresh insight into the problem. Once in a while someone, usually a prominent man, gives a long, loud speech voicing his opinion of the world in general. This is called *patamou* or *kąwa amou* by the Yąnomamö—to "act big." Those who are interested may add their own comments, but the audience usually grumbles about the noise and falls asleep. The more proficient I became in their language, the more I emulated them. I now frequently make nocturnal "speeches" myself, to the village at large, telling everyone what I plan to do the next day, going into elaborate detail and explaining what gifts I will present after I am done. I receive many complements on my *kąwa amou* speeches. This also helps them plan their own activities, since if I plan to work with women informants the next day the men know they don't have to hang around the village in case I start giving presents away to the men, and so forth.

## Status Differences and Activities

Daily activities, except those concerning gardening, collecting, and visiting, do not vary much from season to season. Much of the variation that does occur is a function of one's age or sex.

Other status differences do exist and account for some variation in the activities of particular individuals. Rerebawä, for example, is an outsider to Kąobawä's group and had no intention of joining the village as a permanent resident. Consequently, he did not participate in the gardening activities and had considerably more spare time than other married men. He spent this time hunting for his wife and her parents, one of his obligations as a son-in-law. He was quite dependent on them for the bulk of this diet because they provided him with all his plantains. He is quick to make reference to his hunting skills and generosity with meat, perhaps to draw attention away from the fact that he did not cultivate food for his wife and children. He was able to avoid making a garden because of his status as a *sioha*—an in-married son-in-law. He intended to return to his own village as soon as his bride service was over. But his in-laws wanted him to stay permanently so that he would be able to provide them with meat and garden produce when they are old. They have no sons to do this for them and even promised Rerebawä their second daughter on the condition that he remain permanently in the village. They prevented Rerebawä from taking Shihotama, his wife, and children home by keeping at least one of the children with them when Rerebawä went to visit his own family. They knew that Shihotama could not bear to be separated permanently from her child, and Rerebawä invariably brought her back home so that she could be with the child.

By Yąnomamö standards he has done enough bride service and deserves to be given his wife. Also, by their standards he has lived in the village so long that he should be obliged to make his own garden. But he was in a position to legitimately refuse to do this because he discharged his son-in-law obligations well beyond what was expected of him.

Kąobawä, on the other hand, has the special status of being his group's headman. Apart from this, he is also some 20 years senior to Rerebawä and has many more obligations and responsibilities to his larger number of kin. Rerebawä, in addition to initially refusing to make a garden, thought nothing of taking a week-long trip to visit friends, leaving his wife and children with her parents. His attitude toward the children, compared to Kąobawä's, was rather indifferent. For example, Kąobawä had planned to accompany me to Caracas to see how foreigners live until Ariwari began crying and appealed to his father's paternal sensitivities. Kąobawä stepped out of the canoe, took off the clothing I had loaned him, and picked up Ariwari. "I can't go with you," he explained. "Ariwari will miss me and be sad."

Kąobawä seems to "think" for the others in the village, many of whom are not able to perceive some of the less obvious implications of situations. In political matters he is the most astute man in the group, but he so diplomatically exercises his influence that the others are not offended. Should someone be planning to do something that is potentially dangerous, he simply points out the danger and adds parenthetically, "Go ahead and do it if you want to, but don't expect sympathy from me if you get hurt." Shararaiwä, his youngest brother, planned to take a trip to a distant village with me. I knew that the two villages were not on particularly good terms with each other, but they were not actively at war.

Kąobawä arrived at my canoe just as we were about to depart and asked me not to take Shararaiwä along, explaining that the Iyąwei-teri might possibly molest him and precipitate hostilities between the two groups. Shararaiwä was willing to take a chance that my presence would be sufficient to deter any potential trouble, but Kąobawä would not risk it.

On another occasion a group of men from Patanowä-teri arrived to explore with Kąobawä the possibility of peace between their two villages. They were brothers-in-law to him and were fairly certain that he would protect them from the village hotheads. One of the ambitious men in Kąobawä's group saw in this an opportunity to enhance his prestige and made plans to murder the three visitors. This man, Hontonawä, was a very cunning, treacherous fellow and quite jealous of Kąobawä's position as headman. He wanted to be the village leader and privately told me to address *him* as the headman. On this occasion Kąobawä let it be known that he intended to protect the visitors. For the better part of the day the village was in a state of suspense. Hontonawä and his followers were not to be found anywhere; a rumor spread that they had painted themselves black, were boasting of their fierceness, and were well armed. Kąobawä and his supporters, mostly his own brothers and brothers-in-law, remained in the village all day, their weapons close at hand. Late in the afternoon Hontonawä and his men appeared in their black paint and took up strategic posts around the village. He himself held an ax. He strutted arrogantly and with determination up to the visitors holding his ax over his head as if he were ready to strike. The village became very quiet, and most of the women and children fled nervously. Neither Kąobawä nor the Patanowä-teri visitors batted an eyelash as Hontonawä stood there, menacing the visitors, although the others were visibly anxious and sat up abruptly in their hammocks. It was a showdown.

But instead of striking the visitors with the ax as he seemed to be preparing to do, he brought the ax back down to his side and aggressively invited one of the visitors out to chant with him. Within seconds all three of the visitors had paired off with members of Hontonawä's group and were chanting passionately with them, explaining the reasons for their visit and giving their justification for the state of hostilities.

The crisis had been averted because of Kąobawä's implied threat that he would defend the visitors with force. A number of men in Hontonawä's group were visitors from Monou-teri; their headman had been killed a few months earlier by the Patanowä-teri. When Hontonawä failed to go through with his plan, they left the village in a rage, hoping to recruit a raiding party in their own village and ambush the visitors when they left.

Kąobawä realized that the visitors would not be safe until they got back home, since the Monou-teri would attempt to intercept them. He visited me that night and asked me to take the visitors back to their village at dawn in my canoe, knowing that I had already planned a trip there in a day or so. After I agreed to accelerate my own plans, he proceeded to give me instructions about the trip: I should not stop to visit at any of the villages along the Upper Orinoco River, for all of them were at war with the Patanowä-teri and would shoot my companions on sight. During that trip the Patanowä-teri men lay on the floor of my canoe and covered themselves with a tarp when we passed these villages. The men on the bank shouted curses at me for not stopping to visit and give them trade goods. At this time the Patanowä-teri were being raided by about a dozen different villages. We had to cover part of the distance to their village on foot, proceeding very cautiously because of the danger of raiders. At one point the men showed me the spot where a Hasuböwä-teri raiding party had killed a Patanowä-teri woman a week earlier. Thus, Kạobawä not only protected the visitors while they were in his village but he also arranged a "safe-conduct" for their return.

Kạobawä keeps order in the village when people get out of hand. Hontonawä, for example, is particularly cruel to his four wives and beats them severely for even slight provocations. None of his wives have brothers in the village, and few people are courageous enough to interfere with him when he is angry. On one occasion Kạobawä was holding a feast for the members of an allied village. His preparations were being duplicated by an equal effort on the part of Hontonawä, an obvious attempt by the latter to show that he was also a leader. Some of the visitors arrived early and were visiting in Hontonawä's house. He commanded one of his wives to prepare food for them, but the woman moved a little too slowly to suit him. Hontonawä went into a rage, grabbed an ax, and swung it wildly at her. She ducked and ran screaming from the house. He recovered his balance and threw the ax at her as she fled, but missed. By this time, Kạobawä had seen the ax go whizzing over the woman's head; he raced across the village in time to take a machete from Hontonawä before he could inflict much damage with it. He did manage, however, to hit her twice before Kạobawä disarmed him, splitting her hand wide open between two of her fingers with one of the blows. On another occasion one of Kạobawä's brothers took too much *ebene* and became violent. He staggered to the center of the village with his bow and arrows, while people ran frantically out of their houses to avoid being shot. Kạobawä managed to disarm him and hide his weapons.

During the several club fights that took place while I was in the field on my first trip, Kạobawä stood by with his bow and arrows to make sure that the fighting was kept relatively innocuous (Figure 6.1). In one of the chest-pounding duels, he managed to keep the fight from escalating into shooting with arrows by making sure that everybody in his group took a turn in the fighting. (See Chapter 5 for a description of the fight.) On this occasion his group was being trounced by their opponents, largely because only a few of the men were doing all the fighting for Kạobawä's group. These men were forced to take several turns in rapid succession, while a large number of men stood by and watched. The fighters wanted to escalate the battle into a duel with axes, hoping to intimidate their opponents into conceding. Kạobawä quickly forced the idle men to participate in the chest pounding, thereby distributing the punishment a little more evenly and reducing the possibility of a bloodier confrontation.

After the duel was over, Kạobawä cooly discussed the fight with the leaders in the opponents' group, explaining that he did not intend to raid them unless they raided first. A number of men in the village, notably Hontonawä and some of his followers, shouted threats at the departing opponents that they would shoot them on sight should they meet again. Hontonawä frequently boasted like this, but rarely put himself in a position that was potentially dangerous. He later ran into a party of hunters from the above-mentioned group while he was leading a raid against the Patanowä-teri. Instead of shooting them on sight as he threatened to do (they could have shot back, as they were armed), he traded arrows with them and rapidly retreated. He boasted in the village how he had terrified these men. I later visited their village and learned that Hontonawä was the one who was terrified. They themselves continued to hunt, while Hontonawä fled for home.

Kạobawä's personality differs considerably from Hontonawä's. Where the former is unobtrusive, calm, modest, and perceptive, the latter is belligerent, aggressive, ostentatious, and rash. Kạobawä has an established status in the village and numerous supporters, whose loyalties are in part determined by their kinship ties and in part because he is a wise leader. Hontonawä is attempting to share in the leadership and does not have a well-established position in this respect. It is obvious who the real leader is: When visitors come to Upper Bisaasi-teri, they seek out Kạobawä and deal with him, no matter how ambitiously Hontonawä attempts to emulate his position. Hontonawä does not have as many living brothers in his group as Kạobawä has, so his "natural following" is somewhat limited. In addition, two of his brothers are married to actual sisters of Kạobawä and have some loyalty to him. Hontonawä, therefore, has very little means with which to establish his position, so he is given over to using bluff, threat, chicanery, and treachery. This he does well, and many of the young men in the village seem to admire him for it. He has gained the support of some of these men by promising them his wives' yet *unborn* daughters. Remarkably enough, some of them cling to these promises and do his bidding. He is, in short, a manipulator.

Finally, one of Kạobawä's most unpleasant tasks is to scout the village neighborhood when signs of raiders have been found. This he does alone, since it is a dangerous task and is avoided by the other men. Not even Hontonawä participates in this. It is for this reason that a surprisingly large number of headmen are killed by raiders: They are exposed to more risks than most men.

Kạobawä has definite responsibilities as the headman and is occasionally called upon by the nature of the situation to exercise his authority. He is usually distinguishable in the village as a man of some authority only for the duration of the incident that calls for his leadership capacity. After the incident is over, he goes about his own business like the other men in the group. But even then, he sets an example for the others, particularly in his ambitions to produce large quantities of food for his family and for the guests he must entertain. Most of the time he leads only by example and the others follow if it pleases them to do so. They can ignore his example if they wish, but they turn to him when a difficult situation arises (Figure 4.4).

**FIGURE 4.4**
Kạobawä, the quiet,
unpretentious headman of
the Upper Basaasi-teri.

## SOCIAL STRUCTURE

One learns, after many months of living with people such as the Yạnomamö, that there are "abstract" rules and principles they can invoke to explain or justify the social interactions in which they participate. It is difficult to explain precisely how a fieldworker acquires this knowledge, for it is a gradual process. It is very much as we learn the "rules" in our own culture. Most of us cannot, for example, explain precisely how it is that we came to "know" that having sex with a sister or brother is "bad", but almost all of us know that it is. But anthropologists are aware, when they go into the field to study tribal societies, that there are usually rules about proper behavior and that these rules are often phrased in the contexts of (a) kinship, (b) descent, and (c) marriage. We therefore at least know where to begin looking for the rules and principles, even if we cannot always say precisely how it is we "learned" what they were. One such rule, for example, is about "who you should marry." It was difficult for me to get the Yạnomamö to state this in some sort of abstract way as a general principle or rule. I had to establish the rule in a more indirect way, such as asking individual men, "Can you marry so-and-so?" The answers, when pieced together, allowed me to formulate a general rule that they themselves take to be so self-evident that they can't imagine that others do not "know" whom to marry. Answers to that question would take the form, for example, of, "What? No! I can't marry so-and-so! She is my *yuhaya* (daughter of my child or sister; granddaughter)!" Or, "No! She is my *tääya* (daughter; brother's daughter)!" Eventually, I learned all the kinship terms that both men and women used for their kin and who among them was a prohibited spouse. I also learned, in this fashion, that men could marry only those women they put into the kinship category *suaböya*. By collecting genealogies that showed who was related to whom in specific ways, it was then possible to specify any man's "nonmarriageable" and "marriageable" female kin. As it turned out, men could marry only those women who fell into the category of kin we would call "cross-cousins." These are, from a man's point of view, the daughters of his mother's brother or the daughters of his father's sister. Figure 4.5 shows the difference between "cross-cousins and parallel cousins." The rule, therefore, is that the Yąnomamö marry bilateral cross-cousins. Bilateral means "both sides," that is, father's *and* mother's side of the family. From their vantage, therefore, one of their marriage rules is, "Men should marry their *suaböya*." In a very real sense, this is like saying "We marry our wives," for men call their wives and their female cross-cousins *suaböya*. Thus, to ask, "Whom do you marry?" seems somewhat peculiar to them. They marry their wives, as real people are supposed to do.

The interesting fact here is that this "marriage rule" is embedded in the kinship terminology itself as well as existing as a "principle": Men marry women they call *suaböya*. Their kinship system literally defines who is and who is not marriageable, and there are *no* terms for what we would call "in-laws." In a word, everyone in Yąnomamö society is called by some kinship term that can be translated into what we would call "blood" relatives. To be sure, they "extend" kinship terms to strangers who are nonkin. Kąobawä calls Rerebawä by a kinship term, but they are not related. The fascinating aspect of their society is that all neighbors are some sort of kin and therefore social life takes place in a kinship matrix. Nobody can escape it, not even the anthropologist. Kąobawä, for example, calls me *hekamaya*—nephew (sister's son). Rerebawä calls me *aíwä*— older brother. Everyone gets placed into some sort of kinship matrix which, to a large degree, specifies "in principle" how one is expected to behave vis-a-vis his or her kin of specific categories. Both Kąobawä and Rerebawä *know* I am not

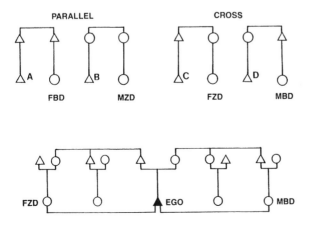

**FIGURE 4.5**

In Yąnomamö society, men may marry their FZD or their MBD—their cross-cousins. They may not marry their FBD or the MZD, who are parallel cousins and classified as "sisters." The upper half of the diagram shows parallel and cross-cousins and the relationship of men (A, B, C, and D) to the female cousins. The bottom half shows an "egocentric" kinship and how the four female cousins are traditionally diagrammed.

their sister's son or older brother respectively, but I must necessarily be put into *some* kinship category so that a general basis of proper and expected social behavior exists. To be outside of the kinship system is, in a very real sense, to be inhuman or nonhuman: real humans are some sort of kin. It is in this sense that anthropologists say that primitive society is, to a large degree, organized and regulated by kinship. Let me illustrate how kinship dictates the expected forms of behavior in which you should engage by giving two somewhat humorous examples. The Yąnomamö consider it very inappropriate to be familiar with the mother of the woman you may marry or have married. Indeed, they describe it as *yawaremou*: incest. Men should not look into the faces of their mothers-in-law, say their names, go near them, touch them, or speak to them. On one occasion I was mapping a deserted village with two young men who had remained behind to help me. As we proceeded around the village in our work, we came to a hearth. One of the young men walked out to the middle of the village, took three or four steps in the direction we were headed, and returned and stood on the other side of the abandoned hearth. When I asked why he did such a strange thing, the other whispered embarrassedly into my ear: "His mother-in-law lives there!" They both then blushed. I decided, some time later, to have some "fun" with this taboo. Their word for "mother-in-law" is *yaya,* but the same kinship term also means "father's sister" or "grandmother," women you need not avoid to the same degree. While visiting my wife's family in northern Michigan one year I deliberately took a photograph of me hugging my wife's mother, kissing her on the cheek. On my next field trip I brought this photo, along with many others of my family and wife's family, to the field. I showed them to Kąobawä's people. They were fascinated with them. Eventually I got to the photo of me hugging my mother-in-law. They recognized me and asked: "Who are you hugging?" I responded: "My yaya." Some chuckles and giggles followed. Then one of them asked: "Is she your father's mother?" "No." I casually replied. (It is alright to be somewhat familiar with a grandmother.) "Ahh! She must be your mother's mother!" I again nonchalantly said "No." Murmurs and whispers followed, and their amused smiles changed to intense looks of apprehension. There was only one legitimate choice left: "Ahh. She is your father's sister!" I paused before I answered, extending the suspense and, again, nonchalantly said "No, she's my wife's mother." Howls of embarrassed laughter and protests exploded from the group. They were incredulous at my audacity and flagrant violation of the incest avoidance prohibition … and even more so at carrying around photographic evidence of my misdeed. For several years after, visitors from distant villages would come to my hut and beg to see the photograph of me "committing incest" with my wife's mother … as if it were something intensely pornographic.

The "discovery" of one principle often helps you to identify and understand other principles. I knew, for example, that they had warm affectionate attitudes about men that they called by the term *shoriwä*. These men, it turns out, are brothers of the women you have married, will marry, or could marry—they are also your male cross-cousins. Similarly, the easily detected warm relationship of a man to his mother's brother (Figure 4.6) is also comprehensible in terms of the marriage rule: You can marry his daughter.

**FIGURE 4.6** Ariwari being fondled by his mother's brother, a very special kinship relationship among the Yąnomamö.

These general rules or principles also exist for notions of descent from remote, long-deceased ancestors—and are discovered by the anthropologist in essentially the way just described for "discovering" kinship rules. For the Yąnomamö, descent through the male line is more important than descent through the female line, especially as regards general principles of marriage. Patrilineal descent defines as members of one group—called a patrilineal lineage

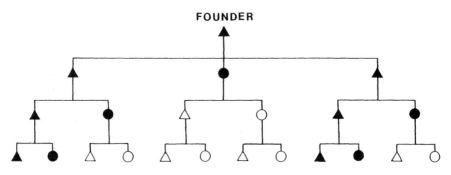

**FIGURE 4.7** A patrilineage: Members are indicated by solid coloring and belong to the patrilineal descent group of their fathers.

(or, simply, patrilineage)—all those individuals who can trace descent through genealogical connections back to some male ancestor *using only the male genealogical connections*. Figure 4.7 shows a patrilineage and who "belongs" to it. The general Yąnomamö rule about marriage, insofar as it can be phrased in terms of a descent rule, is simply that everyone *must* marry outside of his or her own patrilineal group. The Yąnomamö patrilineage is, therefore, an *exogamic* group: All members must marry outside of it into a different patrilineage. Kąobawä is in a different patrilineage than Bahimi, who is his cross-cousin. In Yąnomamö society, one's cross-cousins will always belong to a different lineage but parallel cousins will belong to your own lineage.

### An "Ideal" Model of Yąnomamö Society

Structural anthropologists, such as Levi-Strauss, are fascinated with the "models" that can be drawn to represent, in shorthand fashion, the social structure of individual societies. They use as the basis of the models or structures abstract rules or principles of the sort just described: rules about kinship, descent, and marriage. One can use such models as beginning points to make more detailed observations about other social phenomena, or one can compare the ideal models themselves. These models, in the analogy given at the beginning of this chapter, are the "symmetrical shells" that are pleasant or even pleasurable to manipulate and consider.

Figure 4.8 gives the ideal model of Yąnomamö society, based on their "general principles" of patrilineal descent, bilateral cross-cousin marriage, and the classification of bilateral cross-cousins as "wives." The model is at once elegant and incorporates all of the important "rules." It shows, in effect, that Yąnomamö society can be ideally represented as being bifurcated into two inter-marrying "halves" or "moieties." One half, the Xs, gives women to the other half, the Ys, and receives in return the women that they will marry. Each person belongs to the patrilineage of his or her father, and all men marry women who are *simultaneously* their Father's Sister's Daughters (hereafter FZD) *and* their Mother's Brother's Daughters (hereafter MBD). Such models are heuristic and

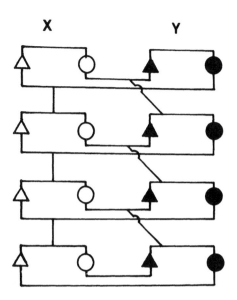

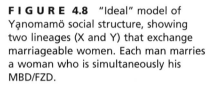

**FIGURE 4.8** "Ideal" model of Yąnomamö social structure, showing two lineages (X and Y) that exchange marriageable women. Each man marries a woman who is simultaneously his MBD/FZD.

useful, suggesting additional lines of inquiry for field research, and stating simple principles that let the observer take a "holistic" view of the social organization.

Such models can be used, in turn, to phrase other general questions and summarize other social processes, such as village fissioning. Consider how this kind of model can elegantly represent the fissioning of a larger Yąnomamö village into two smaller ones, as shown in Figure 4.9. Village A contains two patrilineages, X and Y, each subdivided into four "cadet" sublineages, 1, 2, 3, and 4. For purposes of simplicity, Figure 4.9 shows only the male members. You might want to assume that for each "triangle" representing a male there is also an unwritten "circle" to represent a female—the sisters. In Village A, the cadet lines of both lineages that are drawn opposite to each other exchange marriageable females: X-l gives its females to Y-l and gets females in return from them. In fact, the marriages are arranged by these cadet segments for the younger males and females in them: Older brothers and the father are *said to* make arrangements to give their sisters and daughters to men in the cadet segment of the opposite lineage (see below). Theoretically, any male of lineage X can marry any female of lineage Y, but past marriage exchanges tend to keep particular cadet lines "bound" to each other in a long-term obligation to exchange only their own females with each other. Notice also that the cadet lines 1 and 2 are genealogically "closer" to each other than either is to cadet line 3 or 4. Patrilineal descent, plus the Yąnomamö kinship classification system, would require all men of the same generation in the same lineage to call each other by "brother" terms. But the men in cadet line 1 of lineage X are "actual" brothers (they have the same father) to each other, whereas the men in cadet line 4 of lineage X are their distant (parallel) cousins but men they would have to classify as brothers in their kinship system. They are, as the diagram is drawn, second cousins. They are, in a very real sense, *competitors* with them for all the marriageable women in the opposite lineage.

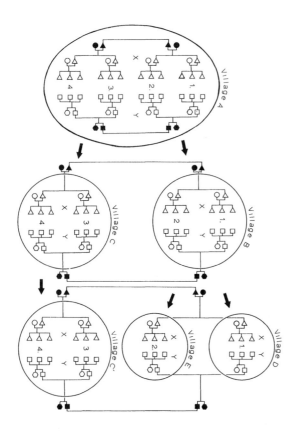

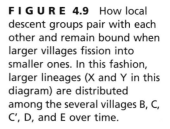

**FIGURE 4.9** How local descent groups pair with each other and remain bound when larger villages fission into smaller ones. In this fashion, larger lineages (X and Y in this diagram) are distributed among the several villages B, C, C', D, and E over time.

Whereas actual brothers are cooperative, distant brothers (parallel cousins) are competitive. A good deal of the competition can be nullified by faithfully giving your sisters and daughters to the men in the cadet lineage with whom your immediate group members have traditionally exchanged women.

As Village A grows in size, internal conflicts will increase among its members and it will eventually fission into two groups: Villages B and C. Notice how, in the diagram, the cadet lines 1 and 2 of lineages X and Y remain together in Village B and separate from their distant cousins, who go into Village C. Each new village contains members of both lineage X and lineage Y, and the cadet lines are still "bound" to each other by marriage ties. In this fashion, the members of a lineage are distributed in several villages. Kąobawä, for example, has "brothers" in Lower Bisaasi-teri, Monou-teri, and Patanowä-teri; but they are, in fact, his parallel cousins. His actual brothers are in his own village; the model shown in Figure 4.9 helps clarify, in "ideal" terms, how this comes about. Over time, Village B fissions, producing two new villages, D and E, as shown in Figure 4.9. Village C continues and does not undergo fission.

Figure 4.9 summarizes, in ideal terms, some of the important rules and processes that can be documented in Yąnomamö culture. It does this clearly and efficiently and enables us to get a good overall picture of how their social system "works" in ideal terms. Like Figure 4.8 above, it simplifies a great deal of otherwise confusing information by ignoring what *particular* individuals did in their marriages or what the actual lineage composition of *specific* villages is. The particulars of what individuals do in marriage or how actual villages are comprised in terms of descent group membership is, in the oyster analogy, the basis of the *statistical* representations that can be drawn.

It is to these kinds of "statistical" data that we will now turn. It is important to point out beforehand that very different kinds of field research *could* be entailed in the two different approaches. It is, for example, quite possible for a field researcher to do a "structural" analysis of information provided by a few key informants or even a single informant. In fact, this situation is often unavoidable, particularly when a formerly large tribe has been reduced to a small population by epidemics and where the demographic underpinnings of social organization have all but disappeared or have been destroyed. This would be similar to the problem faced by an archaeologist who finds the "parts" of a broken clay pot, but most of the parts are missing. His task is to try to "estimate" or reconstruct the nature of the larger, whole, original pot but has only a few fragments to work with.

But where there are large numbers of people and where the ravages of epidemics and acculturation have not yet had a marked effect on tribal social organization, a statistical approach is not only possible but highly desirable and can be conducted simultaneously with a structural study. This usually entails a more thorough and exhaustive collection of genealogical data, actual marriages and marriage dissolutions, and the reproductive histories of both males and females. The first chapter of this case study described some of this kind of field research, and the material that follows shows why I collected these details in the first place.

## THE DEMOGRAPHIC BASIS OF SOCIAL BEHAVIOR

I will illustrate the statistical approach by focusing on the question of *solidarity* as it relates to the process of village fissioning. Anthropologists have long been concerned with the problem of "social solidarity." The famous French anthropologist Claude Levi-Strauss dealt with this issue at great length in this now classic 1949 work, translated from French to English as *Elementary Structures of Kinship*, taking up themes on solidarity and reciprocal exchanges developed by his predecessors Marcel Mauss (1925) and Emile Durkheim (1938 [1895], 1933 [1893]) and applying them to kinship and marriage patterns that were commonly found in the primitive world. The arguments can be thought of as essentially what provides the "binding force" or "cohesion" in primitive societies, the "attraction" between both individuals and groups of individuals that permits them to live together amicably in large groups. One might think of "solidarity" as the "social glue" that holds groups together.

Yąnomamö village fissioning can be viewed in this context, for they grow to a certain size and then fission into smaller, more cohesive villages—they come "unglued." One might even think of the process of village growth and fissioning as the "failure" of solidarity in a certain sense, for the forces or principles that keep its members together in cooperative wholes fail to do so beyond a certain size limit. While there are many variables that affect village size—ecological, demographic, military, and social—much of the internal cohesion in Yąnomamö villages is generated through kinship relationships, marriage ties, and the charisma that particular individuals, such as Kąobawä, contribute to social amity and organization (Chagnon, 1975b).

Let us look at actual marriage patterns in a statistical way and try to relate this evidence to the problem of explaining why particular Yąnomamö villages are able to grow to a large size—300 or more people—while others seem unable to grow beyond a size of 125 or so people. The overall pattern of village size is as follows. The cluster of villages to which Kąobawä belongs differs from the cluster of Shamatari villages to the south in several important ways. In Kąobawä's area, his village and those to which his village is related historically and genealogically (the Namowei-teri villages; see Figure 2.16 of Chapter 2 and discussion) seem to fission at a lower size limit than the Shamatari villages. Could it be that there is something about the patterns of marriages in the two groups of villages that helps explain this difference? If so, what do you look for in marriages?

This question is actually an extension of one of the major questions posed by Levi-Strauss, who argued that *whole systems* of marriage were, as systems, capable of greater or lesser ability to promote solidarity (1949). The Yąnomamö "system" described in the previous section of this chapter was one of the three major systems discussed by Levi-Strauss, but the one that he dismissed as being as "inherently" capable as some other systems of marriage of promoting social cohesion and solidarity.

Let us convert Levi-Strauss' remarkable and heuristic argument to a different form: Instead of considering the *whole* system, let us examine the specific types of marriages *within the specific system*. This, more or less, is arguing something like that each individual marriage adds some "glue" and contributes something to holding the village together. Thus, Kąobawä married his first cross-cousin, Bahimi, and this marriage can be thought of as providing a little glue to the cohesion of Upper Bisaasi-teri. Rerebawä married Shjhotama, totally unrelated to him, and probably added less glue to the cohesion of the village because it didn't "tie" already present families closer together. Other men in the village had other marriages, each of which can be examined in genealogical detail, and so on. Such an approach allows us to see if there is a different kind of marriage pattern within Shamatari villages than within Namowei-teri villages. Both groups have the same *overall* system or set of rules, but individuals within them may either use them differently or are better able to marry specific kinds of cousins simply because they have more of them to begin with.

Such an exhaustive statistical examination requires the use of a computer. I did this. I coded all of the genealogical, marital, and reproductive data that I collected in the field in all the villages I studied. Each individual is an "Ego" about which some 20 different pieces of quantitative information are known, such as approximate year of birth (hence, age), birthplace (garden where born), mother's name, father's name, names of all spouses, order in which spouses were married, how many children Ego had by each spouse, village of residence of every Ego if alive, or place of death for each Ego if dead, and so on (Chagnon, 1974). The computer searches each Ego's

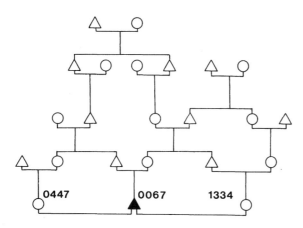

**FIGURE 4.10**
Genealogy of a
man's relationship to two
wives. See Table 4.1 for the
genealogical specifications.

**TABLE 4.1**    **Genealogical Specifications of EGO 0067 to his two wives, egos 0447 and 1334.**

Ego 0067 is genealogically related to wife 0047 in four different ways and to wife 1334 in six different ways. By Yąnomamö classification rules, each of these genealogical specifications would require that Ego 0067 call both women by the term meaning "wife," that is, "female cross-cousin."

| Spouse | Genealogical Relationship to Ego 0067 |
|--------|----------------------------------------|
| 0447 | FFDD |
|  | FMDD |
|  | MMFMSSDD |
|  | MMFMSSD |
| 1334 | MFSD |
|  | MMSD |
|  | MFFDDD |
|  | MFMDDD |
|  | FFFFSDSD |
|  | FFFMSDSD |

relationships and builds up an exhaustive genealogy or pedigree from the field data provided to it. It compares Ego to his or her spouse and spells out precisely all genealogical connections if any exist, that is, tells precisely how each person is genealogically connected to his or her spouse. The reciprocal marriage exchanges described above in elucidating the "ideal" model usually result in spouses being related to each other in many complex ways, as is the case in Figure 4.10, which shows the marriage of one man to two women. Table 4.1 describes the genealogical connections for these two marriages. This example immediately reveals a problem that has to do with classifying particular consanguineous marriages, for each "relationship loop" in the example specifies a kind of cross-cousin relationship between the man and his wives. Thus, it is difficult to characterize this man's marriages as examples of FZD or MBD types, for each marriage is both. Each relationship loop might, in the phraseology I am using here, contribute some glue to the system, and a marriage with four or five consanguineal loops between the spouses might represent more glue than a marriage in which only one loop can be shown, since the former kinds of marriages result from systematic exchanges between families" over several generations and the latter imply fewer such exchanges and obligations.

Most Yąnomamö marriages raise the same general problem, a methodological question that is real and important, but one that is beyond the scope of this case study. Here, we will simply focus on the numbers and kinds of connections between related spouses to get the general picture of patterns in the Namoweiteri and Shamatari villages.

The "ideal" model presented above (Figure 4.8) represents each man as marrying a woman who is simultaneously his MBD and FZD. In actual practice, this rarely happens, largely because of physiological and demographic reasons to be raised in the next section. What *does* happen is that men marry women who are sometimes FZDs or sometimes MBDs. However, there are many different types of both if you consider the precise genealogical connections between spouses: "Ideal" models show only "ideal" genealogical relationships in most cases. Figure 4.11 gives some illustrations, showing how *half-relationships* between

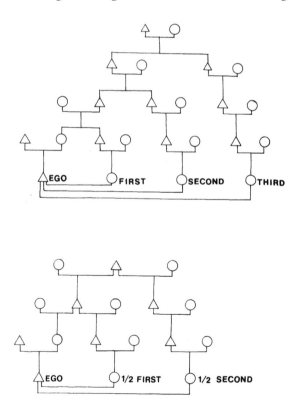

**F I G U R E  4.11**  Degrees of cousinship and half cousinship. The upper portion shows how first, second, and third cousins are genealogically related to ego; the lower half shows how half-first and half-second cousins are related to Ego. In Yąnomamö marriage, all these relationships would be classified simply as "cousins" and marriages with them would be legitimate. The main point is that the term "cousin" does not mean only full first cousin but includes larger numbers of more remote cousins.

siblings and degrees of remoteness of cross-cousins can combine and yield a variety of cross-cousins that are FZD and/or MBD to the male Ego (only matrilateral cross-cousins are illustrated in Figure 4.11).

It is these possible permutations and combinations that I have in mind when I speak of "patterns" or "types" of marriage within the general Yąnomamö system of marriage with bilateral cross-cousins. Does a marriage between a man and his FFDD contribute more "glue" to the cohesion of the village than a marriage between a man and his MMMFMSSDD? Both are "cross-cousins" to the men in question, but one of them is a "closer" cross-cousin than the other. The question, then, is about the relative frequency and distribution of some of these types in actual Yąnomamö villages and whether or not Shamatari villages have more or fewer of certain of the types compared to Namowei-teri villages.

I had the computer look at all the genealogical connections between spouses in the villages of interest. Figure 4.12 presents one of the results, the comparison of marriage types for both the Shamatari villages (pooled together) and the Namowei-teri villages (pooled together), giving the distributions of *all* of the "genealogical loops" between men and all of their spouses. In other words, it is not the distribution of individual marriages, but the distribution of the total number of relationship types for *all marriages*. Let me explain what this means. The marriage of Ego 0067 to his two wives discussed above is represented in

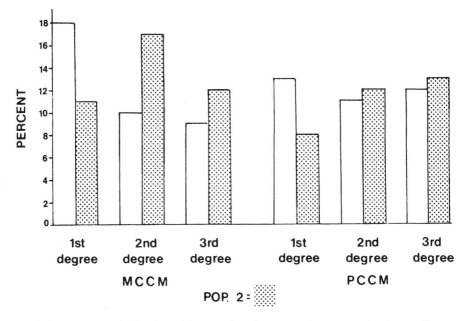

**FIGURE 4.12** Distribution of frequencies of cross-cousin marriage by degree (first, second, and third cousins) and laterality (matrilateral and patrilateral) for all marriages among living adults in the Shamatari (Population 1) and Namowei-teri (Population 2) villages. Shamatari men marry their full first cross-cousins more often than Namowei-teri men do—on both sides of the family (patrilateral and matrilateral).

this distribution as 10 different types, not as just two individual marriages, that is, all 10 are included in Figure 4.12. It is the *overall* pattern that is of interest here, simply to get a broad view of differences between the two populations in the types of connections men have to their wives.

What emerges in Figure 4.12 is that marriages in the two populations follow markedly different patterns. In the Shamatari villages, men tend to be more often related to their wives as first cross-cousins of both the FZD and the MBD types than are men in the Namowei-teri villages. The Shamatari men are marrying *closer* cross-cousins. This logically means, of course, that they marry proportionately fewer second or third cross-cousins. What is suggested by these data is that the maximum size to which a village might grow could somehow be related to the fact that men in those villages tend to marry "close" cousins more often than do men in Namowei-teri villages. A whole series of reasons why this might be true can be raised, but most of them are demographic in genre. One reason, not demographic, is that men might be "trying harder" to marry close cross-cousins in the Shamatari village, but this essentially means that their *parents*, who arrange the marriages, are actually the ones who are trying harder. This, in turn, comes to a question of how and to what extent the members of local descent groups enter into and continue reciprocal marriage exchanges over several generations. Thus, the question of "trying harder" to "follow the rules" is actually a much more complex question. In fact, all men "try hard" to find a wife and most men are delighted if they get any at all, and in this sense, they cannot be plausibly viewed as "trying to follow the marriage rules". If anything, as we shall see in a moment, they can more properly be thought of as trying to break the marriage rules when the rules get in the way—as they do. The frequency distributions seem most plausibly to be a major consequence of the demographic attributes with which each village begins its career, the role that a polygynous marriage plays in generating a "genealogical" pattern that is conducive to high frequencies of cross-cousin marriage of various types, and the strategies individuals use to give women to men in particular other groups as a means of making sure that they will get at least some women back for their brothers and sons.

## Polygyny, Genealogical Structures, and Close Kinship

The main point I wish to make in this section is that it is easy to marry a cross-cousin if you have a lot of them to choose from, and the more polygyny there is, the more cross-cousins there will be. More precisely, if some men are particularly successful in obtaining many wives, their male grandchildren will have large numbers of cross-cousins who will be potential marriage partners.

Polygyny in a society with patrilineal descent has very different consequences for social organization than polyandry in a society with matrilineal descent: One man with 10 wives can have many more children than one woman with 10 husbands. These physiological differences have profound implications for understanding lineage size and interlineage marriage exchange practices in societies like the Yąnomamö.

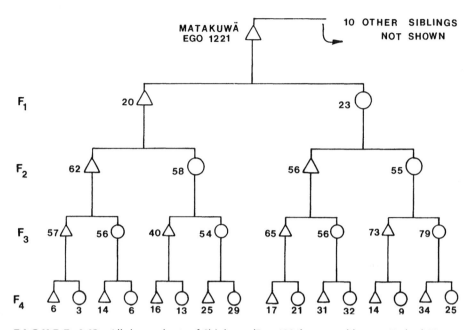

**FIGURE 4.13** All descendents of Shinbone (Ego 1221) grouped by sex. He had 20 sons and 23 daughters (F1 generation). The 20 sons in turn had 62 sons and 58 daughters, and so on. (Overlap in the F3 and F4 generations is not removed; descendants in generations F5 and F6 are not shown.)

There was a particularly accomplished man in the Shamatari population several generations back named Shinbone (Matakuwä). Some of his children are still alive today, so he is still remembered by many people who knew him personally. Shinbone had 11 wives, by whom he had 43 children who survived long enough for people to be able to recollect them. His children, of course, were all siblings or half-siblings to each other and therefore the males among them had many sisters to give away in marriage—in exchange for women they (or their sons) could marry. There were two or three other men like Shinbone around at the time, men with many wives and many children, but none rivaled Shinbone in reproductive performance. By entering into marriage alliances with these men and their sons, members of Shinbone's descent group became "bound" to them in long-term marriage exchanges. If you consider how Shinbone's grandchildren are related to each other, it is clear that they are all siblings, half-siblings, or full or half-cousins of either the parallel or cross varieties. Thus, his grandchildren had many cross-cousins to "choose" among as potential spouses and it was relatively easy for them to "follow" the rules of cross-cousin marriage (Figure 4.13).

While there were some men in the Namowei-teri population who did very well at getting extra wives and, as a consequence, producing large numbers of children, none did nearly as well as Shinbone or some of his Shamatari peers. In effect, the Shamatari population had fewer male founders, but these "founders" produced more children than was the case in the Namowei-teri population. Another way of saying this is that there are more lineages in the Namowei-teri population because there are more male founders. This, ultimately, is reflected in the lineal composition of villages and, therefore, the machinations of men who arrange marriages for their children. They can choose females from among a larger number of other lineages for future wives, but this results in the creation of more conflict and opportunism. In a hypothetical sense, if you belong to lineage Y and got a girl from lineage X several years ago for your son, you should continue to give your females to men in lineage X. But if you have a son who needs a wife right now and lineage X does not have one, there is a temptation to start "trading" with some other lineage, like Z if they have an eligible female. This means you have to then give a female back to the members of Z in exchange. This gets the men in lineage X angry. The more lineages there are, the more this is likely to happen. The long-term promises are often subverted by short-term opportunities that lead to conflict. In a formal and statistical sense, the best long-term game to play is to be faithful to your partners and remain bound to them, even if it means giving away more girls *to them* at any specific point in time than you get back at that point. An occasional alliance with another group can be "sneaked in" from time to time, depending on specific situations and the charisma of the individuals involved. Some are better than others at pulling this off.

One consequence of the marriage-arranging relationships between members of the larger lineages such as Shinbone's is that villages become characterized by higher levels of what we would call "inbreeding." Marrying close cousins raises amounts of kinship relatedness between *all* individuals over time, increasing the level of inbreeding each generation. The computer procedures described above to show how spouses are related can be used to show how *any pair of individuals* is related. As might be expected, the Shamatari villages also differ from the Namowei-teri villages in patterns of relatedness: Individuals have more relatives and are more closely related to their relatives than is the case in Namowei-teri villages. This is of great interest to anthropologists, particularly in the context of theories of solidarity. Some anthropologists argue that kinship, rather than marriage alliance, provides the solidarity and amity that keeps societies organized by lineal descent cohesive whereas others insist that it is the marriage bonds between the lineages—the so-called "alliance versus descent" argument between Edmund R. Leach (1957) and Meyer Fortes (1959; see Keesing, 1975, for an overview of some of the arguments) and other prominent anthropologists.

When you examine how every individual in the village is related to all others, using the computer procedure described above, the results clearly show that members of the Shamatari villages are, on average, more closely related to each other than are members of Namowei-teri villages, i.e., Shamatari villages are more "inbred." Translating this into the kinds of arguments made by anthropologists about solidarity, if solidarity is promoted by kinship *closeness*, then more "inbred" villages should have more solidarity. They achieve this by marrying cross-cousins.

This makes it difficult to decide which theory is more correct regarding the source of solidarity. Does it come from close cousin marriages that bind descent groups to each other or from the close kinship ties that cousin marriage produces via the offspring who are related to members of both groups? While these are fascinating issues in cultural anthropology, they go somewhat beyond what introductory courses—and monographs like this—traditionally focus on. I have, however, discussed some of these issues in more technical publications (Chagnon, 1974; 1975b; 1979a; 1979b; 1980; 1981; 1982; 1988b; Chagnon & Bugos, 1979).

In summary, villages that get large seem to be able to do so, in part, because of the kinds and frequencies of particular consanguineous marriages. These set into motion increasing levels of "inbreeding," i.e., average degrees of relatedness between all individuals gets higher. Using statistical procedures borrowed from the field of population genetics and computers makes it possible to discuss these issues in very precise metric terms and make statistical statements about "closeness" of kinship. But, kinship relatedness, patterns of marriage, and obligations based on descent seem to break down as solidarity-promoting mechanisms and villages seem to be unable to get larger than about 300 people before they fission into smaller ones. There is enough intermarriage between villages and abductions of women from different groups to "swamp" the effects of close inbreeding, so the process is not strictly cumulative over time.

## Kinship Rules, Reproduction, and Rule Breaking

I mentioned above that many Yąnomamö break their rules, especially kinship and marriage rules. Ideal models are often criticized for seeming to imply a "static" system, one that doesn't change or have much flexibility. Statistical models build in this possibility. The arena in which rule-breaking—the dynamics of marriage—is most conspicuous is incestuous marriage. Recall that Yąnomamö men define only one category of women as marriageable. All others are prohibited, and sex or marriage with people in these categories is considered to be incestuous (*yawäremou*). Their definition of incest is broader than ours but includes our prohibitions as well. Let me give an example of how this comes about.

Figure 4.14 is an example of a case of incest that led to a fight in Kąobawä's village and, ultimately, to the fission of his group from the Lower Bisaasi-teri. The man marked "A" is in Kąobawä's father's generation and, indeed, is called "father" by Kąobawä—they are in the same lineage. "A" is the headman of Lower Bisaasi-teri. This man had several sons and he wanted to find them wives. He cleverly redefined the woman labeled "B" in the diagram as his "sister," thereby moving her up one whole generation. (He was supposed to call her by a "niece" term, and did so most of his life.) Since she was now his "sister," his sons were eligible to marry her daughters—they were their FZDs—but in "classification" only. One of them did marry one of her daughters as shown, thus leading to a big fight and fission. The issue had to do with taking marriageable females out of the mate pool that other men were eligible to marry into, and

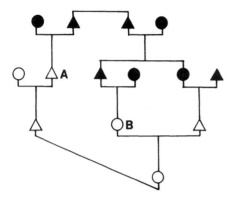

**FIGURE 4.14** An example of an "incestuous" marriage and manipulating kinship classification with matrimonial gain in mind. Ego A originally called B by the correct term meaning "niece" but arbitrarily changed his classification of her to a term that meant "sister." This enabled A's son to marry B's daughter as shown since she was terminologically his father's sister's daughter. A good deal of fighting and conflict resulted, for it removed A's daughter from the legitimate mate pool of other men.

they, of course, objected strenuously. Some people went along with the new kinship fabrication—those who had something to gain; others did not—those who had something to lose. The manipulator's son was the right age to marry his forbidden wife, who was also of marriageable age.

This example illustrates a problem of much larger proportions in Yąnomamö society. Incestuous marriages, by the Yąnomamö definition, are very common and are accompanied by manipulations of the kinship classifications of the kind just described. While the genealogical facts of who begot who cannot be changed, kinship classifications can, and a lot of Yąnomamö do it. Much of it appears to be done in order to increase someone's chances of finding a wife in a situation where it is difficult for men to find wives (Chagnon, 1972; 1974; 1979a; 1982; 1988a; Fredlund, 1982; Saffirio, 1985).

The source of this problem lies, in large part, in the reproductive attributes and life histories of individuals. Women marry young and therefore begin producing children while young. But their reproductive lifespan is relatively short—20 years or so. Men marry later, begin producing later, but their potential reproductive lifespans are very long. Men such as Shinbone had children that differed in age by at least 50 years: one of my best Shamatari informants and closest friends was an old man named Dedeheiwä, about 65 years old at the time the following incident occurred in his village. A young girl of about 10 years passed by and called him by a term meaning "older brother." I asked him why she did so, and he said that they were, in fact, half-siblings. His father had many wives and early in life sired Dedeheiwä. Fifty or so years later he sired this little girl by a different wife (Chagnon, 1974).

One consequence of these facts is that generation length through females is relatively short compared to generation length through males. This can be seen in the reproductive statistics summarized in Figure 4.13 by looking at the number of Shinbone's current descendents in the F4 generation. There are only nine (six males plus three females) descendants through the direct line of males (extreme bottom left side of Figure 4.13) but 59 (34 males plus 25 females) through the direct line of females (extreme bottom right of Figure 4.13). The net result is that the absolute ages of individuals gets out of synchrony with their generational identities. People will have brothers or sisters that are younger than their grandchildren. Since Yąnomamö kinship classifications utilize generational position, something must give. Girls are ready for marriage at puberty and boys when they are in their early 20s. No right-thinking Yąnomamö would sit patiently for 50 years until his sister's daughter is old enough to marry one of his sons. What "gives" is the kinship classification, which means that people *must* chronically reclassify some relatives in order to keep kinship classification more or less in harmony with ages and generational identities. They *must* break the kinship rules to make the actual marriage practices work (Chagnon, 1982; 1988a).

## The Decay of the Nuclear Family

The more I thought about the necessity of rule breaking, the more it fascinated me and caused me to investigate it further. These investigations led me to think about another set of problems, demographic problems, and I will end this chapter with a brief discussion of these and what they mean for understanding not only Yąnomamö social organization and social behavior but probably what might be found in many other tribal societies and what probably has characterized *our entire history* as humans.

Yąnomamö mortality patterns and birth rates lead to a characteristic distribution of the population into age and sex categories represented in the "age/sex" pyramid shown in Figure 4.15. Basically, there are many children because of a relatively high birth rate, but because of a relatively high death rate many children die before age 10, causing the step-like narrowing of the pyramid as each age-category is plotted. The biggest "step" is the reduction in numbers of children, i.e., the step between the first (bottom) age category and the second one. Note, however, that the mortality rates are high enough at all ages to cause the "steps" to be rather obvious and quite large. This means that many young adults are dying as well, albeit at a lower rate.

This distribution is characteristic for tribal populations all over the world where introduced diseases and other exogenous forces have not radically altered the demographic characteristics of the population—and this distribution has probably been characteristic of human populations throughout our history (Swedlund & Armelagos, 1976). One of the things that is *predictable* from this is that many children will be orphans at an early age because one or the other of their parents died prematurely (Chagnon, 1982). Many Yąnomamö children are "orphans" for this reason.

Divorce also occurs among the Yąnomamö—at a rate of approximately 20% (Chagnon, 1988b), a low rate by world standards. This also contributes to the fact that children will be raised in households where one, or both, of the parents is not a biological parent.

What does this mean for understanding the Yąnomamö "nuclear family"? Or, for understanding the nuclear family throughout our long history as hunters/gatherers and tribesmen?

I examined the composition of households for a large number of villages that had approximately 1,400 people living in them and basically asked the following

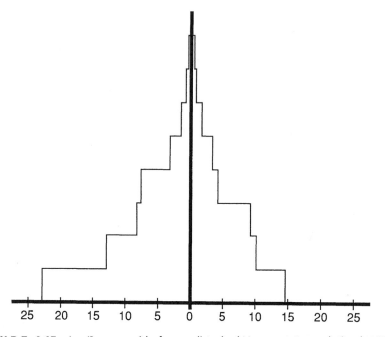

**FIGURE 4.15** Age/Sex pyramid of an undisturbed Yąnomamö population by 10-year age categories. Males are on the left half and females on the right half of the diagram. Note the excess of males in the first age category: Approximately 23% of the population consists of male children aged 0 to 10 years, but only about 15% are female children in this age category. The general "shape" of this distrubution—very wide at the bottom and rapidly narrowing—is the result of relatively high birth rates coupled with relatively high death rates in younger age categories. This is the characteristic shape of the population pyramid for undisturbed native peoples and probably of all human populations until recent times. (Redrawn from Chagnon, 1974, Figure 4.6, *N*=1466.)

kinds of questions for each individual, that is, had my computer "ask" the questions: Is the mother alive and in the same village? Is the father alive in the same village? Are the biological mother and father both alive and living in the same village? The statistical answers to these and similar questions are summarized in Figure 4.16, which shows the "decay" of the Yąnomamö nuclear family by age categories, i.e., what fraction of people have a living mother, father, and so forth, at each stage in their lives.

The results surprised even me. Most textbooks in anthropology refer to the nuclear family as the "fundamental building block" of all human societies, emphasize how important it is in understanding social ties, and how universal it is—dutifully noting that one or two societies like the Nyar seem to be unusual in not having a "nuclear family" by most definitions. What Figure 4.16 indicates is that by the time a Yąnomamö reaches the ripe ironic age of about 10 years, only about one out of three live in a family containing his yet-married mother and father, and by the age of 20 years, only about one in ten comes from such a family! There are good reasons to believe that this

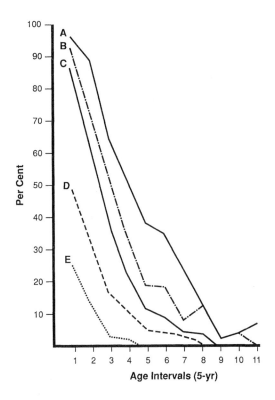

**FIGURE 4.16** The "decay" of the Yąnomamö nuclear family over time. Percentage of individuals of both sexes, arranged by 5-year age intervals, where (A) the mother is alive and coresident, (B) the father is alive and coresident, (C) both parents are alive, coresident, and married either monogamously or polygynously, (D) both parents are alive, coresident, and married monogamously, and have at least one grandparent alive and coresident. $N = 1327$. By whatever definition of "nuclear family" (C, D, or E), most Yąnomamö individuals do not live in such a family by the time they reach age 20 (age category 4). For example, only about 50% of Yąnomamö in age category 1 (birth to 5 years) live in a family of type D. By the time they are 15 years old (age category 3), only about 18% live in such a family. (Redrawn from Chagnon, 1982, Figure 4.6.)

has been true for most of our history. The so-called "fundamental building block" of human society appears to have a very short half-life when it is viewed statistically.

The issues become more intriguing when we begin thinking about what this means for understanding marriage practices or marriage systems in many societies, especially those where it is said that the parents, particularly the father, of the young people arrange their marriages. Most Yąnomamö men, when they reach marriageable age (early twenties) do not have a living father. Who arranges their marriages? This raises yet other questions and, sometimes, acrimonious debate at fundamental levels of theory. For example, I would predict that if a man had a biological son and a son he adopted when he married a woman who had children from a previous marriage and it came time for him to arrange marriages for both, he would most likely be more interested in the reproductive future of his biological son over that of his adopted son, especially if marriageable girls were scarce. Other anthropologists would argue that this is an unacceptable form of "biological reductionism" and, as a matter of principle, suggest he would be equally interested in doing a good job in both cases. There is no meaningful evidence whatsoever to support the latter position and a considerable amount of evidence to support the prediction I just made.

This scenario, perhaps laid bare for the first time by my research on the Yąnomamö, has implications for other aspects of tribal social organization and behavior, including kinship classification. For the reasons discussed above, the Yąnomamö must chronically "adjust" their kinship classifications to keep age and generation in synchrony. The statistical information on their "nuclear family" organization suggests that most males, when they reach marriageable age, will not have their father around to help them find and secure a wife ... and that they will have to rely on assistance from other adult males.

Given these two general and important facts, I was prompted to make some predictions about kinship and genealogical knowledge by sex and how the kinship reclassifications, i.e., "rule-breaking," might be patterned. The logic is as follows:

1.  Men have difficulty finding wives because women are in short supply. If they cannot rely on having a living father, they must pay attention to who might be the males who will do this—and this means learning genealogies and kinship classifications thoroughly because this information is useful to their reproductive future. Yąnomamö men should, in short, know more about genealogies and kinship than women, something that is probably counterintuitive to even anthropologists.

2.  Women never have trouble finding husbands and are always (or almost always) married throughout their lives. No amount of additional effort to learn genealogies or kinship classifications will alter this.

3.  If the kinship classifications have to be altered to keep age and generation in synchrony so the marriage systems "work" and men can only marry women they classify as *suaböya*, then men should show a bias in their reclassifications: they should tend to move women from reproductively useless categories into the "wife" category if they are going to reclassify them.

In 1985, I did a very elaborate test of these ideas (most of the results are published in Chagnon (1988b) and briefly summarized here). In three different villages I had informants of both sexes and all ages tell me what kinship term they used for everyone in the village. To make sure we both knew who I was talking about, I simultaneously showed each informant a Polaroid picture of each person as I whispered the name of that person into his/her ear and asked "What do you call so-and-so?" I timed all their responses.

I also knew from many previous years of fieldwork in these villages how everyone was genealogically related four or five generations before, and knew what they should have called the kinsmen that were related to them in the specifiable genealogical ways if they were following their "rules" of classification.

I did this with 100 informants of both sexes and all ages and got nearly 12,000 "kinship classification" responses, as well as a measure of the time it took each informant to classify all members of the village.

The results were as I predicted they would be. Males were faster than females at classifying their kin, suggesting that they knew more about genealogy and kinship than the females. They had the information "at the tip of the tongue," but women and girls frequently had to do some genealogical algebra of the sort, "Well, I call his father so and so and his sister such and such, so I suppose I'd call him "husband." This information also demonstrated that significant numbers of females in the village actually did not use specific terms for many co-residents, but used "vague" terms that did not require genealogical knowledge of any depth.

When the kinship classifications of "adult" males (17 years and older) were examined, it was clear that they showed a statistically significant pattern of reclassifying women into the "wife" category more than into any other category for female relatives: The bias was to move females from reproductively useless categories and put them into the only reproductively useful category, "wife." A detailed analysis of the women they moved into this category showed that most of these females were young and had high reproductive value, that is, they were not old women past their reproductive prime.

I learned a number of anthropological lessons by this rather elaborate exercise. One of them was that the "kinship system" was very dynamic, not a crystallized set of terms each person learns for others and faithfully recites for the remainder of his or her life. People simply *had to* change their kinship usage to keep the marriage system working, since marriageability was defined in large measure by what kinship term you called people around you. The second lesson was that the frequent accusations that others in the village were or had "committed incest" made more sense—marrying someone that, genealogically, was in an inappropriate category was, by definition, "incestuous." The third thing was that the initial manipulations were made by men who had great confidence that they could successfully "break" the rules and find support among their friends and kinsmen, many of whom benefited from these acts and manipulations. Incest was, in a very real sense, a kind of political act that reflected the status and authority of the initiator. The intriguing question is whether or not this "political" act was provoked, consciously or unconsciously, with reproductive gain in mind. The general result of many of these kinds of manipulations, however, seems to point to the fact that they generally have positive reproductive consequences.

Rerebawä once said to me, proudly predicting the future of Breakosi, his firstborn son. "He is a real fierce little guy! So fierce that when he grows up he will probably commit incest!" What he was saying was that he would know the kinship rules and genealogies so well that if these got in his way he would break them and put someone into a marriageable category that didn't belong there ... commit incest. You can only do this successfully and predictably in Yąnomamö culture if you are prepared to defend your rule violations, and your ability to do so depends largely on how much credibility of threat you can demonstrate, i.e., how "fierce" you are. The most flagrant cases of incest I have in my records—men marrying parallel cousins or, in one case, a half-sister—are cases of men who are not only headmen but headmen with reputations of "ferocity." Breaking the rules to gain some personal advantage is always easier in any culture if you have power—acquired or inherited. In Yąnomamö culture it is partly acquired, via demonstrations of individual prowess, and partly inherited, by having lots of kin who will endorse your manipulations and rule-breaking.

Finally, something else made sense to me after realizing all of this. When I showed them the picture of me hugging my wife's mother, i.e., "committing incest," some would blurt out: "Wow! You are really fierce!" I didn't understand, at first, why they equated incest with personal prowess and tended to predict one from knowing the other. They probably invented all sorts of fabulous activities I must have engaged in to be in a position to get away with hugging my mother-in-law.

# 5

✳

# Political Alliances, Trading, and Feasting

Yąnomamö feasts take place when one sovereign group entertains the members of another allied group. Feasts are *political* events. To be sure, economic and ceremonial implications are also significant, but these are relatively minor when compared to the functions of the feast in the context of forming or maintaining alliances. The chief purpose of entertaining allies is to reaffirm and cultivate intervillage amity in the intimate, sociable context of food presentations, thereby putting the ally under obligation to reciprocate the feast in his own village at a later date, bringing about another feast and even more intervillage amity. They also serve to reduce the possibility of warfare between groups.

I will describe in this chapter some of the relationships among trade, economic specialization, historical ties between groups, warfare, and intervillage marriage exchanges, all of which are intimately connected and interact with each other in the developmental process of political alliance formation.

I described in Chapter 2 how the members of independent villages cultivated friendships with each other in the process of establishing themselves in a loose network of allied villages. I then showed in Chapter 4 how Kąobawä's followers were related to him and how he, in turn, was related to the members of several other villages. Here I will take up some of the political consequences of the historical ties and how they shape and mold the nature of specific contemporary relationships between Kąobawä's group and groups that have political dealings with it. To illustrate this, I will describe the details of a particular feast in the context of the political ties, both historical and contemporary, existing between Kąobawä's group and the guests at the feast. First, however, I will comment on Yąnomamö alliances in general.

## GENERAL FEATURES OF ALLIANCES

One of the expectations and implications of alliance is that the partners are under obligation to provide shelter and sustenance to each other whenever one of them is driven from his village and garden by a powerful enemy. In some situations, the beleaguered partner may be obliged to remain in the village of his host for a year or longer, approximately the length of time required to establish a new garden and productive base from which an independent existence is possible. Twice in the recent history of Kąobawä's group they were driven from their gardens by more powerful enemies and were forced to take refuge in the village of an ally. In each case the group remained with the ally for a year or so, moving away only after their new garden began producing. In both cases, the hosts demanded and received a number of women from Kąobawä's group without reciprocating in kind, a prerogative they exercised from their temporary position of strength. The longer the group takes advantage of a host's protection, the higher is the cost in terms of women, so visitors always make an attempt to establish their gardens as quickly as possible and move into them as soon as they begin producing. Without allies, therefore, the members of a village would either have to remain at their single garden and sustain the attacks of their enemies or disband into several smaller groups and join larger villages on a permanent basis, losing many of their women to their protectors. The jungle simply does not produce enough wild foods to permit large groups to remain sedentary, and the threat of warfare is such that smaller groups would soon be discovered by their enemies and victimized.

Because of the ever-present risk of being driven from one's garden, no Yąnomamö village in Kąobawä's area can continue to exist as a sovereign entity without establishing alliances with other groups. Warfare is attended by a bellicose ideology which asserts that strong villages should take advantage of weaker ones and coerce them out of women; to prevent this, the members of all villages should therefore behave as if they were strong. Thus, the military threat creates a situation in which intervillage alliance is desirable, but at the same time it spawns an ideology that inhibits the formation of such alliances. Allies *need* but cannot really *trust* each other.

Alliances between villages are usually the consequence of a developmental sequence that involves casual trading, mutual feasting, and finally, exchanging of women. The most intimate allies are those who, in addition to trading and feasting, exchange women in marriage. Any developing alliance may stabilize at the trading or feasting stage without proceeding to the woman-exchange phase. The former are weak alliances but serve to limit the degree of war that might possibly obtain between the villages so related. The Yąnomamö tend to avoid attacking those villages with which they trade and feast, unless some specific incident, such as the abduction of a woman, provokes them. Allies that are linked by trade and feasting ties, for example, rarely accuse each other of practicing harmful magic. Allies bound to each other by "affinal" kinship ties, however, are more interdependent because they are under obligation to each other to continue to exchange women. It is, in fact, by the exchange of women that independent villages extend kinship ties to each other.

Members of allied villages are usually reluctant to take the final step in alliance formation and cede women to their partners, for they are always worried that the latter might not reciprocate as promised. This attitude is especially conspicuous in smaller villages, for their larger partners in defense pressure them into demonstrating their friendship by ceding women; the strong can and do coerce the weak in Yąnomamö politics. The weak, therefore, are compelled to advertize their alleged strength by bluff and intimidation and by attempting in general to appear to be stronger, militarily, than they really are, thereby hoping to convince their partners that they are equals, capable of an independent existence. By so doing, they also inform their partners that any attempt to coerce them out of women will be met with the appropriate reaction, such as a chest-pounding duel or a club fight. Nevertheless, each ally expects to gain women in the alliance and enters it with this in mind; and each hopes to gain more women than he cedes in return.

Hence, in order for an occasional nervous meeting of groups of men from different villages to evolve into a stable intervillage alliance based on the reciprocal exchange of women, the long and difficult road of feasting and trading usually must be traversed. Suspicion must give way to relative confidence, and this must develop into reciprocal feasting. Only then has the intervillage relationship reached a point where the partners begin ceding women to each other; and even then, the ceding is done cautiously, if not reluctantly.

This is, however, only the "ideal" pattern in the development of an alliance. Rarely does it develop far enough to reach the stage where women are exchanged between groups, particularly if the two villages concerned are of approximately the same military strength. Fights and arguments over women, food, etiquette, generosity, and so on develop, and the principals withdraw temporarily on semihostile terms, perhaps attempting a rapprochement sometime in the future. Or, if the principals are of obviously different military potential, the stronger of the two will try to coerce its weaker partner into ceding women early in the alliance's development, taking advantage of its own military strength and thus altering the course of alliance development in the opposite direction.

Whatever the specific developmental sequence leading to the woman-exchange phase, the milieu within which such developments take place is not conducive to the establishment of warm ties of friendship. Each principal's attempts to demonstrate his own sovereignty in order to convince the other that he does not really require the political alliance to keep his enemies in check. This is accomplished by bragging about past military victories and fierceness in past club fights and chest-pounding duels and by insinuating that one's group is always on the verge of exploding into a force so great that no combination of allies could overcome its terrible might. The smaller the village and more obvious its vulnerability, the greater is the pressure to insinuate this potential, especially if it's members are trying to maintain occupation in a desirable ecological niche as explained in Chapter 2.

Political maneuvering in this milieu is both tricky and potentially hazardous undertaking. Each principal in the negotiation must establish the credibility of his own threats, while discovering the point at which his partner's bluff will dissolve abruptly into action; he must discover the point beyond which he must not goad his ally, unless he himself is prepared to suffer the possibly violent outcome. It is a politics of brinkmanship, a form of political behavior in which each negotiator is compelled to expose his opposite's threats as bluffs at the risk of inciting him to violence—a club fight, immediately and honorably, or later and treacherously, a feast in which the hosts descend on their guests to kill their men and abduct their women.

## TRADING AND FEASTING IN ALLIANCE
## FORMATION

Because an ally is not beyond taking advantage of his weaker partner, especially when the alliance is just developing, there is very little in the way of natural attraction to encourage the two groups to visit each other. Considerations of pride and self-conceptions of status preclude obvious attempts to develop stable and predictable alliances and military interdependency. The Yąnomamö cannot simply arrive at the village of a potential ally and declare that they need military assistance because of the raids of a superior enemy. Doing so would admit vulnerability and perhaps invite predation from the potential ally. Instead, they conceal and subsume the true motive for the alliance in the vehicles of *trading* and *feasting*, developing these institutions over months and even years. In this manner they retain an apparent modicum of sovereignty and pride, while simultaneously attaining the ultimate objectives: intervillage solidarity and military interdependence.

Three distinct features of Yąnomamö trading practices are important in the context of alliance formation. First, each item must be repaid with a different kind of item; the recipient is under an obligation to repay his partner in a type of exchange called *no mraiha*. To the inexperienced observer, somebody who gives something *no mraiha* might appear to be giving it "freely," as a "gift," but long afterward the gift is remembered and used as a lever to ask for a reciprocal gift. Second, the payment is delayed, a temporal factor in the trading techniques that is likewise implied by the *no mraiha*. The consequence of these two trading features is that one trade always calls forth another and gives the members of different villages both the excuse and the opportunity to visit each other; and once the trading starts, it tends to continue, for the members of one village in an alliance always owe the members of the other village trade goods from their last confrontation. The third significant trade feature is the peculiar specialization in the production of trade items. Each village has one or more special products that it provides to its allies. These include such items as dogs, hallucinogenic drugs (both cultivated and collected), arrow points, arrow shafts, bows, cotton yarn, cotton and vine hammocks, baskets of several varieties, clay pots, and, in the case of the villages with direct or indirect contact with outsiders, steel tools, fishhooks, fishline, and aluminum pots.

This specialization in production cannot be explained in terms of the distribution of natural resources. Each village is, economically speaking, capable of self-sufficiency. (The steel tools and other products from civilization constitute the major exceptions.) The explanation for the specialization must be sought, rather, in the sociological aspects of alliance formation. Trade functions as a social catalyst, the "starting mechanism," through which mutually suspicious allies are repeatedly brought together in direct but amiable meetings. Without these frequent contacts with neighbors, alliances would be much slower in formation and would be even more unstable once formed. A prerequisite to stable alliance is repetitive visiting and feasting, and the trading mechanism serves to bring about these visits.

Clay pots are a good example of the specialization in labor that characterizes Yąnomamö production and trade. The Mǫmariböwei-teri (see map, Figure 5.2, below) are allied to both Kąobawä's group and the people of a distant Shamatari village, the latter being mortal enemies of Kąobawä. When I first began my field-work, I visited the Mǫmariböwei-teri, specifically asking them if they knew how to make clay pots. They all vigorously denied knowledge of pot making, explaining that they once knew how to make them but had long since forgotten. They explained that their allies, the Möwaraoba-teri (Sibarariwä's village), made them in quantities and provided all they needed, and therefore, they did not have to make them any more. They also added that the clay in the area of their village was not of the proper type for making pots. Later in the year their alliance with the pot makers grew cool because of a war, and their source of pots was shut off. At the same time, Kąobawä's group began asking them for clay pots. The Mǫmariböwei-teri promptly responded by "remembering" how pots were made and "discovering" that the clay in their neighborhood was indeed suitable for pot manufacturing. They had merely *created* a local shortage of the item in order to have to rely on an ally for it, giving sufficient cause to visit them.

Often the specialization is less individualized than in the case of clay-pot manufacture. Kąobawä's group, for example, exports cotton yarn to one ally, but imports it from another. Moreover, the exported cotton is frequently brought back in the form of manufactured hammocks, the importer merely contributing labor to the process. In some cases, the shortages are simply seasonal; Kąobawä's group may import cotton from a particular ally at one time of the year, but export it at another. Most of the trade, however, involves items that are readily manufactured or raised by any group, underscoring the fact that trade is the stimulus to visit. Food does not enter the trading system, although hospitality dictates that it must be given to friendly groups. Occasionally, a village will run short of plantains because of a particularly long hot spell that damaged their crop, and its members may visit an ally to borrow food to last a week or so. This hospitality is usually reciprocated, but it is not properly a part of the trading network.

Alliances between villages may stabilize at any one of three points: sporadic reciprocal trading, mutual feasting, or reciprocal women exchange. These are cumulative levels in the sense that the third phase implies the first two: Allies that exchange women also feast and trade with each other. Likewise, allies that merely feast together also trade, but do not exchange women. At the lower end of this scale of solidarity lie those villages with which one fights to kill, while at the upper end are those villages from whom one's group has recently separated. Frequently, the scale is circular rather than linear: a village's mortal enemy could be the group from which it has recently split. By way of example, Kąobawä's group trades sporadically with the Makorima-teri, Daiyari-teri, Widokaiya-teri, Mahekodo-teri, and Iyäwei-teri. These are fairly weak alliances and even permit limited fighting. Kąobawä's group has more intimate ties with the Reyaboböwei-teri and Mǫmariböwei-teri, with whom it feasts regularly. The alliance with the

Reyaboböwei-teri has even reached the point at which they are exchanging women with each other. Finally, at the other end of the scale, Kąobawä's group is at war with the Iwähikor-oba-teri, Möwaraoba-teri, and a segment of the Patanowä-teri. The first two of these groups are historically unrelated to Kąobawä's group, although they have a common history with two of his staunchest allies, the Reyaboböwei-teri and Mömariböwei-teri, from whom they fissioned in the recent past. The Patanowä-teri is related to Kąobawä and his followers, as was shown in Chapter 2 (Figure 2.15).

Nevertheless, they are bitter enemies with one faction of them and are at present raiding each other.

Although there is no rigid geographical correlation of the village settlement pattern to the degree of alliance solidarity, neighboring villages usually are at least on trading terms and are not actively conducting war on each other as discussed in Chapter 2. Should war develop between neighbors, one of the two principals will abandon its site and move to a new location. Whether the ties between the neighboring villages will be one of blood, marriage exchange, reciprocal feasting, or casual trading depends on a large number of factors, particularly on the village size, current warfare situation with respect to more distant groups, and the precise historical ties between the neighboring villages. Whatever the nature of the ties between neighbors, each strives to maintain its sovereignty and independence from the others.

The Yąnomamö do not openly regard trade as a mechanism, the ulterior function of which is to bring people repeatedly together in order to establish an amicable basis from which more stable types of alliance can develop. Nor do they overtly acknowledge the relationships between trading and feasting cycles to village interdependency. In this regard they are like the Trobriand Islanders of Melanesia. They have a "functional ignorance" of the more significant adaptive aspects of their trading institutions (Malinowski, 1922). To both the Yąnomamö and the Trobriand-ers, the mechanisms by which peoples from different groups are compelled to visit each other are ends in themselves and are not conceived to be related to the establishment of either economic or political interdependency. For the Yąnomamö participant in a feast, the feast itself has its significance in the marvelous quantities of food, the excitement of the dance, and the satisfaction of having others admire and covet the fine decorations he wears—and hopefully an opportunity to have a clandestine sexual affair with one of the host women. The enchantment of the dance issues from the dancer's awareness that, for a brief moment, he is a glorious peacock that commands the admiration of his fellows, and it is his responsibility and desire to present a spectacular display of his dance steps and gaudy accoutrements. In this brief, ego-building moment, each man has an opportunity to display himself, spinning and prancing about the village periphery, chest puffed out, while all watch, admire, and cheer wildly, as shown in the film *The Feast* (listed at the end of this book).

The hosts, too, have an opportunity to display themselves and strut before their guests. Moreover, the very fact that they have given the feast is in itself a display of affluence and surfeit apparently calculated to challenge the guests to

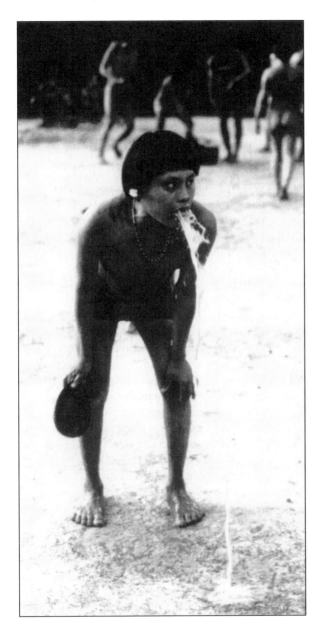

**FIGURE 5.1**
Visiting man vomiting
peach palm gruel at a ceremonial drinking bout in
the hosts' village.

reciprocate with an equally grandiose feast at a later date.[1] Indeed, in some areas
so much food is provided that the participants competitively drink enormous
quantities of banana soup or peach palm gruel, vomit it up, and return for
more (Figure 5.1). The plaza rapidly becomes dotted with large pools of slippery

---

1. The competitive aspects of feasting in many primitive societies have been dealt with at
length by Marcel Mauss, whose essay *The Gift* (1925) is now an anthropological classic.

vomit and one must be careful where he walks ... and avoid walking right in front of a celebrant who is about to regurgitate! Each good feast deserves and calls forth another, and in this way allies become better acquainted with each other as they reciprocate feasts during the dry season and over the years.

## HISTORICAL BACKGROUND TO A
## PARTICULAR FEAST

One of the feasts I witnessed exhibited all the features of intervillage politics. Before describing this feast, I will give the historical antecedents to the event, recapitulating a number of points discussed in Chapter 2 in the context of the history of Kąobawä's village. The significance of these events will then become clear, for Kąobawä's group's prior relationships to the guests at the feast had a great deal to do with the outcome.

In 1950 Kąobawä's group, then living at their site called Kręibȫwei-taka, almost friendless, beleaguered by enemies, and somewhat isolated, began cultivating an alliance with the Iwähikoroba-teri (Figure 5.2), a Shamatari village some two days' traveling distance south of their own village at Krgibȫwei. The Iwähikoroba-teri group members were on friendly terms with another Shamatari group, the Mȫwaraoba-teri, from whom they had separated some years before. Kąobawä's group, on the other hand, was at war with this village because members of his own group murdered a friendly Mȫwaraoba-teri visitor in the 1940s, touching off a series of raids between them (see Prologue). Anxious to develop an alliance, Kąobawä's group accepted a feast invitation from the Iwähikoroba-teri and visited that village at their garden called Amiana-täka to participate in the feast. Up to that point they were only on trading terms with them.

The Iwähikoroba-teri group, however, had made a prior arrangement with their friends, the Mȫwaraoba-teri group, to help them massacre Kąobawä's men and abduct his group's women.[2] Members of the Mȫwaraoba-teri group were hidden in the jungle outside the village when Kąobawä's group arrived. The men of Kąobawä's group danced both singly and then en masse and were invited into the homes of their hosts. At this point their hosts fell upon them with axes and staves, killing about a dozen men before the visitors could break through the palisade and escape (see Prologue). Kąobawä's father was among the victims. Once outside, they were shot from ambush by the Mȫwaraoba-teri group, who managed to kill a few more and wound many others with arrows. A number of women and girls were captured by the hosts, though some were later recaptured by Kąobawä's group in revenge raids. It was probably their hosts' greed for the women that permitted any adult male survivors at all, as my

---

2. A group of men from the village of Hasubȫwä-teri also participated as allies of the Iwähikoroba-teri in the treachery.

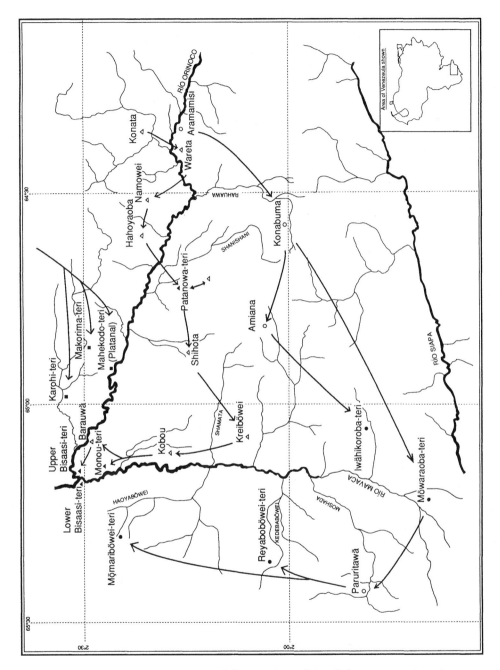

**FIGURE 5.2** Historical movements of the Bisaasi-teri (triangles) over approximately 135 years, beginning at the ancient site of Konata (upper right). Some neighboring villages of other population blocs are also shown in the north (squares) and south (circles). Solid symbols indicate contemporary villages.

informants asserted that the Iwähikoroba-teri began chasing the women while the men were still vulnerable. A few of the Iwähikoroba-teri and Möwaraoba-teri group members refused to participate in the slaughter and even helped some of Kąobawä's group escape.

Kąobawä and the survivors fled to Kobou, a site they had begun clearing for a new garden. Here they removed the arrow points and nursed their wounds before reluctantly returning to Krgiböwei, their only producing garden. Kobou was still too new to support the group, and hunger forced them to return to Krgiböwei. As this location was well known to their treacherous allies, they wished to abandon it as soon as possible, knowing that their enemies could easily inflict more casualties on their now badly weakened group and abduct more women.

Within a week or so of the treacherous feast, the Mahekodo-teri, a visiting ally of Kąobawä's group, learned of the massacre and offered aid. The Mahekodo-teri headman himself visited Kąobawä's village and invited the entire group to his village to take refuge. They accepted the offer, and in January of 1951, after conducting one revenge raid on the enemies, moved to Mahekodo-teri.[3]

The Mahekodo-teri had been allied to Kąobawä's group a generation earlier, but after Kąobawä's group moved away from the Orinoco River, the alliance activity had dwindled to just sporadic trading. True to Yąnomamö political behavior, the Mahekodo-teri, being in an obviously stronger bargaining position, offered their protection and aid with gain in mind: They demanded and received a number of their guests' women. Again, the members of Kąobawä's group suspected further treachery from their new protectors and assiduously worked at establishing a new garden. They were forced to stay with the Mahekodo-teri until their new garden could totally support them—for about a year. Even during this time, however, they spent weeks on end away from their hosts' village, carrying their food with them and working on their new plantations. They would return to obtain new food supplies, rest for a few weeks, and leave again. When Mahekodo-teri later split into three factions, Kąobawä and his group learned from one of them the details of a plot in which one of the Mahekodo-teri fractions was planning to kill the rest of the men and abduct the women. The only thing that prevented them from doing so was the development of a new war between Mahekodo-teri and another village, one that required the assistance of Kąobawä and his group.

For a few years after the separation from Mahekodo-teri, Kąobawä's group was invited to feast there. Because they suspected that the Mahekodo-teri group was plotting against them, however, usually the men alone would attend the feast, thereby reducing the probability of another massacre. The women and children were concealed in the jungle during the time the men were away at the feast. Gradually, the alliance cooled off again and the two groups remained relatively indifferent toward each other, but at peace.

---

3. This date is accurately known, since James P. Barker, the Protestant missionary discussed in Chapter 1, began living with the Mahekodo-teri just a few months earlier and witnessed the influx of the beleaguered Bisaasi-teri refugees.

By 1960, Kąobawä's group had regained some of its military strength and had begun cultivating an alliance with a third Shamatari group, one that was related to the two that conducted the massacre of 1950. The new Shamatari group, Parurita-wä-teri (see Figure 5.2), was at war with the Iwähikoroba-teri, but on feasting terms with the Möwaraoba-teri. Kąobawä's group persuaded their new Shamatari allies to invite the Möwaraoba-teri to a feast and planned a massacre similar to that of 1950, but with the tables reversed. Kąobawä's group would lie in ambush while the Paruritawä-teri attacked the guests within the village. The Möwaraoba-teri (then uncontacted) were being ravished by a malaria epidemic at this time, and only a handful of them actually came to the feast; the others were too sick to travel. With the aid of their newly found allies, Kąobawä's group managed to kill three of the five men and abducted four of their women. The other two visitors escaped to tell of the treachery. This revenge feast was only considered to be partially successful, and Kąobawä's group was not satisfied with the outcome. Their Shamatari allies, the Paruritawä-teri, were obliged to abandon their site to avoid the revenge raids, splitting into two groups in the process: Mǫmaribȍwei-teri and Reyabobȍwei-teri, both continuing to remain friendly to Kąobawä's group.

In early 1965, just a few months after I began my fieldwork, Kąobawä and his supporters left to visit Reyabobȍwei-teri, one of the two Shamatari allies, hoping to conduct another treacherous feast for the Möwaraoba-teri. They left a few men behind to protect the women and children. The men were gone almost two weeks. All during this time, those who remained behind flocked to my mud hut at dawn and remained in it the whole day, not permitting me to leave. Every hour or so they asked to see my shotgun. I soon discovered that they were frightened and suspected that the Widokaiya-teri (a village to the north, not on Figure 5.2) was going to raid them to abduct women, for they knew of the plot. My hut lay on the path most likely to be taken by Widokaiya-teri raiders, and the few remaining men stood guard next to my door, hoping to intercept the raiders should they attack at night.

I, unknowingly, guarded the women and children by day with my shotgun, while the men did the same at night with their own weapons. This incident indelibly underscores the almost complete lack of trust between allies; the members of Kąobawä's group expected a raid from their friends and allies rather than from their enemies!

About 10 days after the men had left, six visitors from another allied village passed through Upper Bisaasi-teri hoping to trade. It was obvious to them that the men were away and that the women were largely defenseless. They carried word of the situation up the Orinoco River to their own allies, one of which was the Mahekodo-teri.

The evening before the men returned from the trip, one of the Salesian missionaries, Padre Luis Cocco, visited me from his Ocamo mission, having traveled up the Orinoco River by dark—a dangerous undertaking at that time of the year. Padre Cocco had just received word by shortwave radio from the Salesian mission at Mahekodo-teri that a large party of men had left for Bisaasi-teri with an intention of capturing women. They had learned of the poorly guarded women from the six visitors and were determined to take advantage of the situation. My house was again full of women and children at dawn the following day, and the raiders were probably en route. I was in a difficult situation. On the one hand, if I told the Yąnomamö of the rumor, it would have been sufficient cause to start a war between Kąobawä's group and the Mahekodo-teri group. This would have been most unfortunate if the story proved to be false. On the other hand, I dared not remain silent. If raiders were indeed coming, they would probably kill the defenders to capture the women. Fortunately, I did not have to make a decision—Kąobawä and the men returned early in the afternoon, and I was able to remain neutral. The treacherous feast for their Shamatari enemies proved to be unsuccessful. The intended victims had accepted the invitation but were informed of the plot just before they arrived. One of the Reyaboböwei-teri who had close kinsmen among them had misgivings about the matter and warned them.

Late in the afternoon it was learned that the Mahekodo-teri were, in fact, in the vicinity of the village, allegedly on a "camping trip." Kąobawä, of course, suspected their story, but to demonstrate his friendship he invited them to be his guests at a feast. As he and his men had been away for nearly two weeks, there was an abundance of food in their gardens and they could easily afford to entertain the Mahekodo-teri and their traveling companions, the Boreta-teri. Together, the guests numbered about 100—after they fetched their women and children.

This sets the stage for the feast in the kind of context that makes it more intelligible: The specific historical relationships between the participants and the nature of their mutual mistrust. Now I will give the details of the events that followed.

## THE FEAST

Perhaps because he suspected the Mahekodo-teri and Boreta-teri of malintent, Kąobawä also invited the Karohi-teri to attend the feast. They are a small but dependable ally and had separated from the Mahekodo-teri many years ago. This is the village from which Rerebawä comes. This established more of a balance of power at the intended feast should any trouble arise, for the combination of both Boreta-teri and Mahekodo-teri was of sufficient strength to worry any host. With the aid of the Karohi-teri, Kąobawä's group was more equally matched to the visitors.

The feast started out on a sour note. It is the custom of the Yąnomamö visitors to arrive only after an invitation from their hosts, sent by messenger on the day of the feast. The Mahekodo-teri and Boreta-teri, however, arrogantly arrived nearly a week before Kąobawä's group was prepared to receive them and set up a large, temporary camp a short distance from the village. They were guests and could legitimately demand to be fed. Because of this, Kąobawä and his covillagers were under obligation to feed them, some 100 or so people, and took them to the gardens to supply them with enough plantains to last a week. Kạobawä was a little disturbed that they would be so impolite as to arrive uninvited, but he took the situation quite philosophically. After all, they had fed his group for the better part of a year.

He and several other men cut a large quantity of plantains, which were hung in his house and allowed to ripen for a week, to be boiled into *date*, a thick sweet soup resembling banana pudding, on the day of the feast. That afternoon Kạobawä and a few of the older men commissioned a hunting party composed of young men, several of whom were Kạobawä's brothers, whose responsibility would be to obtain a large quantity of meat to give to the visitors on the day after the feast. Most of them were reluctant to go, as their feet were still sore from the trip to the Shamatari village. A few of them claimed to be sick and managed to escape recruitment into the hunting party in this way. This hunt—the *heniyomou*—with the hanging of the plantains in the headman's house, initiated the feast. The excitement that usually attends a feast began at this time.

That evening the young men and women danced and sang in the village, an event called *amoamo*, to assure the hunters luck on the hunt. (The Yạnomamö *amoamo* on other occasions, but invariably do so on the day the plantains are hung in the village in anticipation of a feast.) Every evening the men were away on their *heniyomou*, which would last a week, the young women and girls sang and danced in the village to assure the men's success.

The hunters left at dawn the following morning, carrying a large supply of roasted and green plantains with them to eat while they hunted. They had picked a site some 15 miles up the Mavaca River for their hunt, as game was known to abound there—they had canoes to reach this distant area. Their task was to obtain monkeys, armadillos, wild turkeys, wild pig, caiman, tapir, or paruri birds, the only meat deemed worthy to give to guests. They would not be permitted to eat any of this game but could consume any other game they captured, such as amotas, agoutis, small birds, a small species of wild turkey, insects, or fish. The feast meat, however, was earmarked for the guests and could not be eaten by the hunters. On this particular hunting trip the men miscalculated the amount of food they would need to sustain them during the hunt, and one of them returned after four days to fetch more plantains. He also gave Kạobawä a report on the hunt's success, creating a small sensation in the village: they had already killed a large number of *basho*, a particularly large and very desirable monkey. They had also come upon a quantity of turtle eggs at a sand bar and were eating as many as they could. When they returned later, they cached the remaining eggs in my hut so as not to have to share them with the visitors.

Meanwhile, the visitors were making gluttons of themselves, and the hosts started to grumble about the large number of plantains they had already eaten. The week's supply they originally provided had been consumed in half that time, and the guests had been given permission a second time to harvest more from their hosts' gardens. This was no way for guests to behave, and it soon became apparent that they were, through their gluttony, deliberately intimidating Kąobawä's group. Still, he and his followers continued to supply them with all the food they needed, keeping their complaints to themselves. They did not want it to be known that they were worried about running short of food. Instead, they planned to conduct the feast on a scale that would be difficult to reciprocate.

The hunters returned and presented their catch to Kąobawä. It was brought to his house, smoked, and placed on the ground, wrapped up in leaf bundles. Kąobawä ignored it for a while and then slowly began to unpack one package of it (Figure 5.3) while everybody watched—especially the hunters, who were quite proud of the quantity of meat they had obtained: 17 *basho* monkeys, seven wild turkeys, and three large armadillos.

**FIGURE 5.3** Kąobawä unpacking a load of smoked meat that his hunters have brought home for the feast.

Kạobawä and his group were anxious to conduct the feast for their visitors and present them with the food because by so doing the visitors would be obliged to leave for home, thereby ending the drain on the gardens.[4]

The feast was scheduled for the day following the return of the hunters, even though the Karohi-teri allies had not yet arrived. Kạobawä and his group were so anxious to rid themselves of their ravenous guests by this time that they decided to hold a separate feast for the Karohi-teri after the departure of the Mahekodo-teri. This would involve a considerable amount of extra work, but they were more than willing to undertake it if it meant getting rid of their first group of visitors, who, by this time, had spent nearly a week eating Kạobawä's produce.

On the morning of the feast three large pieces of bark from the *masiri* tree were cut and brought to the village. These were made into troughs to contain the boiled, ripe plantain soup. All day long Kạobawä's younger brothers, who had returned from the hunt the day before, labored at cooking the enormous quantity of ripe plantains, pouring each boiling container full into the trough as it was prepared.[5]

The plantains that Kạobawä had hung from his house rafters a week before were now ripe. The young men who were preparing the soup would cut the bunches of plantains from the roof, split each fruit with a thumb, throw the two halves of the flesh into a cooking pot, and toss the skins onto a pile. They worked at this task from early morning until late afternoon, in addition to boiling a nearly equal quantity of green plantains, which provided the boiled vegetable food that customarily accompanies the presentation of smoked meat. Yạnomamö etiquette requires that meat must be accompanied by vegetable food and vice versa.[6] It is an insult, for example, to offer someone meat without simultaneously offering a vegetable food with it.

Peeling green plantains is a little more difficult than peeling ripe ones; they are very tough and brittle. The Yạnomamö solve this problem, as they solve so

---

4. I have seen several instances of Yạnomamö groups getting rid of visitors who have joined them semipermanently by holding a feast in their honor; when the ceremonial food is presented, the visitors are obliged to leave.

5. Kạobawä's group has access to aluminum pots now and uses them extensively in food preparations. Most Yạnomamö groups used crude clay pots in 1965, although these were being rapidly replaced by aluminum ware that is traded inland to even the remote villages.

6. The three vegetable foods most commonly considered to be suitable accompaniments for the meat presentation are boiled green plantains, boiled rasha fruit, and cassava bread. A number of missionaries and a few early scientific observers identified the Yạnomamö feast strongly with the *rasha* fruit (Zerries, 1955; de Barandiaran, 1966). If it is to be identified with any food, it should be called the "plantain feast," but to identify the feast with a food that sometimes (*rasha*) or invariably (plantains) accompanies it is to overlook the sociopolitical causes of the feast. Rasha is so unnecessary to the feast that it was served at only two of six feasts I attended between 1964 and 1966. In short, the Yạnomamö feast is a social and political event, not a harvest ceremony, and occurs independent of the abundance or availability of *rasha* fruit. *Rasha* fruit ripens in February, the peak of the dry season. It is primarily in the dry season that feasts are held, because travel is difficult or impossible at other times of the year. The correlation of the ripening of *rasha* and feasting is rather more fortuitous than causal.

many others, by using their teeth. Each plantain is bitten along its length several times, cracking the peel, which in turn is removed with the fingernails and further application of the dentition. On this particular occasion, two young men peeled, with their thumbs, enough ripe plantains to make approximately 95 gallons of soup, and, with their teeth, a sufficiently large quantity of green plantains to fill a dozen large pack baskets.

On the morning of the day of the feast, Kạobawä went to the center of the village clearing where all could see him and proceeded to pull weeds. The clearing has to look presentable to visitors, as it functions as the dancing plaza. As noted before, since Yạnomamö headmen cannot directly order their followers to execute tasks such as these, they usually initiate them and hope that others will follow (see the film *The Feast*). By and by, a number of older men joined him, as well as a few women, and when a sufficient number of workers were pulling weeds and hauling them out, Kạobawä quietly retired to his hammock, from which he oversaw the food preparations and calculated the distribution of meat.

Excitement in the village grew conspicuously as the hours passed, and by noon there was a constant din of laughter and chatter, punctuated now and then with a shrill scream from some young man overcome with the thrill of the feast. Occasionally, the visitors would reply to the shouts, setting off a brief contest of screaming between hosts and guests that gradually died off as each group busied itself in preparation for the dance.

Shortly after noon a rumor circulated through the village that the visitors had been raiding the gardens at night and stealing additional plantains. A number of people, particularly older men, were visibly upset by this new information, giving rise to another rumor that there would be a chest-pounding duel to set the matter straight. The guests had already worn their welcome thin by arriving uninvited a week in advance and by eating excessively. Their hosts were becoming angry with them, as it was all too obvious that they were deliberately taxing their hosts' patience: They were intimidating them.

The men of the host group had finished their preparations for the feast; they were all painted in red and black, bearing colorful feathers. They had cleaned the debris from their houses, had finished hauling out the weeds they had picked from the village clearing, and had brought in quantities of food to give their guests. Now, it was time for them to take *ebene*, the hallucinogenic drug. They separated into several groups and began blowing the brownish-green powder up each other's nostrils with 3-foot-long hollow tubes.

While the men were taking drugs, the women were busy painting and decorating themselves with feathers and red pigment. The visitors, also, were busy at the same tasks, and the excitement of the feast reached fever proportions by midafternoon.

A few women were still busy finishing trade baskets, while Kạobawä's younger brothers continued with the monotonous cooking of what seemed to them an endless number of plantains.

Finally, an old man from the visiting group entered the village and marched unceremoniously across the clearing while the members of Kạobawä's group cheered him. He was too old to join the dancing but too respected to wait behind with the women and children while the younger men put on their display. This was evidence that the visitors were about to send in their delegate to accept the feast invitation at Kąobawä's house.

The members of Lower Bisaasi-teri had joined Kąobawä's group for the feast, as they, too, were on friendly terms with the Mahekodo-teri and had benefited from the latter's hospitality after the treacherous feast in 1950. Besides, here was an opportunity for them to eat prodigiously someone else's food. Before Kąobawä's group had separated from the Lower Bisaasi-teri, there had been one headman over the entire composite village, an old man named Kumamawä. He was a brother to Kąobawä's father; when the groups split, the older man led the faction of Lower Bisaasi-teri, leaving Kąobawä to lead the Upper group. On this particular day, when the two groups had temporarily coalesced for the feast, Kumamawä was conceded the honor of chanting with the visitor's delegate, Ąsiawä, the son of the Mahekodo-teri headman.

Ten minutes after the old visitor entered the village, Ąsiawä entered the clearing, touching off an explosion of wild cheering that marked the opening of the dance. He was spectacular in his bright new loincloth, long red parrot feathers streaming from his armbands, and black monkey-tail headband covered with white buzzard down. He marched dramatically to the center of the village clearing, while all of Kąobawä's followers cheered, and struck the visitor's pose: motionless, head upward, and weapons held vertically next to his face. He stood there two or three minutes so his hosts could admire him. This gesture signified that he had come in peace and was announcing his benevolent intentions by standing where all could see him. If they bore him malice, they had to shoot him then or not at all.[7] He then marched to Kąobawä's house and was met by Kumamawä, the temporary leader of the combined host group, and the two men immediately began to chant. This was the formal acceptance of the feast invitation by Ąsiawä on behalf of his entire group. They chanted for five minutes or so, bouncing up and down from the knees, now face to face, now side to side, but always lively and loud. Suddenly, they stopped, and Ąsiawä squatted, his back to the sun, while old Kumamawä retired to his hammock. The cheering died down. Ąsiawä squatted for several minutes before one of Kąobawä's younger brothers brought a half gourdful of plantain soup to him and set it on the ground. He ignored it politely for several minutes, staring into the distance, holding his weapons horizontally next to his mouth. Presently, he put his weapons down, picked up the container of soup, and drained it in one draft before setting it back down. As soon as he had set it down, one of Kąobawä's younger brothers brought him a large pack basket filled with boiled green plantains and smoked armadillo meat. Ąsiawä stood while the strap of the basket was placed over his head and adjusted across his shoulders so as not to crumple his headdress. Trying to look dramatic, he staggered rapidly out of the village under his burden

---

7. I have a number of informants' accounts of visitors being shot down while standing in the clearing to announce their visit. Whenever I accompanied visitors to strange villages for the first time, I, too, was obliged to participate in this rite and always had an uneasy feeling about it. One instance of this is shown in the film *A Man Called Bee*.

of food, while the hosts again cheered wildly. This food was eaten by the visitors while they finished their decorating, each receiving a small portion.[8]

Within half an hour of Ạsiawä's departure the visitors had completed their decorating and had assembled just outside the entrance to the village. The men, all finely decorated, stood at the front of the gathering, while the women, girls, and young boys, also decorated, but each carrying a load of family possessions, remained at the rear. At the signal of Ạsiawä's father, Mahekodo-teri's true head-man, the first two dancers burst into the village, separated, and danced around the periphery of the clearing in opposite directions, while Kạobawä's group wel-comed them enthusiastically with shouts and shrill screams. The visiting dancers entered two at a time, pranced around the village periphery in opposite directions wildly showing off their decorations and weapons, and then returned to the group outside the *shabono*. Each dancer had unique decorations and a unique dance step, something personal that he could exhibit. He would burst into the village screaming a memorized phrase, wheel and spin, stop in his tracks, dance in place, throw his weapons down, pick them up again, aim them at the line of hosts with a wild, aggressive expression on his face, prance ahead a few steps, repeat his performance, and continue on around the village in this manner, while the hosts cheered wildly. When everyone had had an individual turn, the entire group entered, danced in a single file around the periphery several times clacking their arrows against their bows, and gathered at the center of the clearing, where they formed a tightly knit group (Figure 5.4). They stood motionless, except for the heaving of their chests, holding their weapons vertically. After a few moments—in a final display of decorations—Kạobawä's followers emerged from their houses and approached the center of the village, each man inviting one or more of the visitors into his house, leading him away from the village center by the arm. As each visitor was led away, his family, watching from the village entrances, unceremoniously joined him at the host's house, bringing the family possessions along. Within a few minutes, the dance plaza was deserted and the visitors were resting comfortably in their hosts' hammocks. Even in the ham-mocks, the Yạnomamö visitors are able to put on a silent display of their finery as they lie with their legs crossed, one arm behind their head, staring at the ceiling, waiting for their hosts to feed them ripe plantain soup from the bark troughs. It is almost as if they are strutting from a reclining position.

After the guests had been given their first round of soup, the men of Kạobawä's village assembled outside the entrance and came in to dance around the village for their guests. They, too, had an opportunity to put on a display of their own decorations, after which they retired to entertain their guests.

There were three bark troughs full of soup in the village. The first one was emptied in the process of bringing numerous gourdfuls to the some 100 visitors. After they had consumed this, the guests then assembled at the second trough and began eating there (Figure 5.5). Before this trough was finished, they moved as a

---

8. The film *The Feast* documents an alliance between the villages of Patanowä-teri and Mahekodo-teri and coincidentally has Ạsiawä performing the very same role there as he did in this feast.

**FIGURE 5.4** Visitors displaying themselves at the village center after they have each danced individually. They will now be invited to recline in particular hosts' houses.

group to the third trough and repeated their ceremonial consumption, before returning to their hammocks to rest and regain their appetites. Approximately two hours had passed from the time the first dancers entered the village until the guests retired from the third trough of soup. They had not yet eaten all of the contents—all in all, some 95 gallons of it—but managed to do so by morning.[9]

Shortly after dark the marathon chanting *(waiyamou)* began—and continued until dawn. Then, the visitors conducted their trade and were given the baskets of going-home food, boiled green plantains with smoked meat. The visitors would make requests through their headman, and Kąobawä would produce the item by enjoining one of the local men to give it. The item would be thrown at the feet of the man who wanted it. He would ignore it for a while and then give it a cursory examination, throwing it back on the ground. His peers would then examine it in greater detail and extol its virtues, while the giver would apologize for its defects. If it were a particularly poor item, just the opposite would occur; the giver would cite its not-so-obvious merits, while the recipient would draw attention to the conspicuous shortcomings. In every trade the hosts always feel as though they have been over generous, and the guests, after they depart, complain they have

---

9. During some feasts, the ashes of the dead are mixed with the boiled, ripe plantain soup and eaten by friends and relatives of the deceased. The feast also serves as a preliminary to a raid that involves two or more villages. The sponsor of the raid will entertain his allies in a feast the day before the raiding party departs. See Chapter 6 for a discussion of the raid.

**FIGURE 5.5** After a polite period of reclining in their hosts' hammocks, the visitors go to the large troughs of plantain soup and begin drinking it The soup trough can be used also as a crude canoe for crossing larger streams (see Chapter 1).

not received enough. The trade was conducted in an atmosphere of efficiency, but with considerable argumentation. The hosts had concealed their choicest items and vigorously denied having some goods, and the guests had done likewise—sinking their prize bows in a river before arriving at the feast, for example, and bringing an inferior one along in case one of the hosts asked for it during the trading. As this was the first time in some years that the two groups feasted together, there was nothing for either one to repay. Instead, the visitors asked for items *no mraiha* (to be repaid later) and the guests did the same.

By 8:00 A.M. the going-home food had been presented to the visitors, and the trade had been conducted very early by feast standards. Had the visitors been polite, they would have left for home at that time. Instead, they were decidedly impolite and decided to stay and witness the second, smaller feast that Kąobawä was going to conduct for the Karohi-teri. They had not arrived in time for the major event. This capped the series of insults the visitors had heaped upon Kąobawä's group. The visitors were warned that if they should stay, the hosts would consider this intimidation and challenge them to a chest-pounding duel.

It was obvious now that the visitors were looking for trouble, and Kạobawä's group was obliged to react or be subject to even further intimidation; hence, the challenge to pound chests: Kạobawä decided that enough was enough and he could no longer afford to overlook the brazen and continuing insults. At this point, the visitors broke camp and departed, much to the relief and joy of Kạobawä's group. In fact, they were pleased that they had been successful at intimidating their guests into leaving, and the men gloated over this accomplishment the rest of the day. They were convinced that their threats were credible enough to force their potential adversaries to withdraw, presumably because the Mahekodo-teri felt they were inferior in strength.

Kạobawä and his group held another feast for the Karohi-teri that same day, but without the assistance of the Lower Bisaasi-teri, who left shortly after the previous feast terminated.

## THE CHEST-POUNDING DUEL

The feast for the Karohi-teri was essentially the same as the one for the Mahekodo-teri and Boreta-teri. When the dancing was over and darkness fell, the men began to chant again. The first pair of chanters had not even completed their rhythmic presentation when the jungle around the village erupted with hoots and screams, causing all of the men in the village to jump from their hammocks and arm themselves. When the men had found their arrows and were prepared, they began yelling back at the unseen intimidators, rattling the shafts of their arrows together or against their bows and/or pounding the heads of axes against pieces of firewood or on the ground to make noise. The Boreta-teri and Mahekodo-teri men had returned to accept the chest-pounding challenge and entered the village, each man brandishing his ax, club, or bow and arrows. They circled the village once, feigning attack on particular men among the hosts, then grouped at the center of the village clearing. The hosts surrounded them excitedly, dancing with their weapons poised to strike, then entering into the mass of bodies to grab the particular opponent he wanted to settle his grudge with. Heated arguments about food theft and gluttony developed, and the hosts and guests threateningly waved their weapons in each other's faces. Within minutes the large group had bifurcated and the chest pounding began. The Karohi-teri aided Kạobawä and his followers, whose joint numbers were even further swelled when the Lower Bisaasi-teri rushed to the village after hearing the commotion. There were about 60 adult men on each side in the fight, divided into two arenas, each comprised of hosts and guests. Two men, one from each side, would step into the center of the milling, belligerent crowd of weapon-wielding partisans, urged on by their comrades. One would step up, spread his legs apart, bare his chest, and hold his arms behind his back, daring the other to hit him (Figure 5.6). The opponent would size him up, adjust the man's chest or arms so as to give himself the greatest advantage when he struck, and then step back to deliver his close-fisted blow. He would painstakingly adjust his distance from his victim by measuring his arm length to the man's chest, taking several dry runs before delivering his blow. He would then

**F I G U R E 5.6**   Chest-pounding duel at the feast.

wind up like a baseball pitcher, but keeping both feet on the ground, and deliver a tremendous wallop with his fist to the man's left pectoral muscle, putting all of his weight into the blow. The victim's knees would often buckle and he would stagger around for a few moments, shaking his head to clear the stars, but remain silent. The blow invariably raised a "frog"—a painful lump—on the recipient's pectoral muscle where the striker's knuckles bit into his flesh. After each blow, the comrades of the deliverer would cheer and bounce up and down from the knees, waving and clacking their weapons over their heads. The victim's supporters, meanwhile, would urge their champion on frantically, insisting that he take another blow. If the delivery were made with sufficient force to knock the recipient to the ground the man who delivered it would throw his arms above his head, roll his eyes back, and prance victoriously in a circle around his victim, growling and screaming, his feet almost a blur from his excited dance—like a ruffed-grouse doing a mating dance. The recipient would stand poised and take as many as four blows before demanding to hit his adversary. He would be permitted to strike his opponent as many times as the latter struck him, provided that the opponent could take it. If not, he would be forced to retire, much to the dismay of his comrades and the delirious joy of their opponents. No fighter could retire after delivering a blow without letting his opponent return it. If he attempts to do so, his adversary would plunge into the crowd and roughly haul him back out, sometimes being aided by the man's own supporters. Only after having received his just dues could he retire. If he had delivered three blows, he had to receive three or else be proven a poor fighter. He could retire with less than three only if he were injured. Then, one of his comrades would replace him and demand to hit the victorious opponent. The injured man's two remaining blows would be canceled, and the man who delivered the victorious blow would have to receive more blows than he delivered. Thus, good fighters are at a disadvantage, since they receive disproportionately more punishment than they deliver. Their only reward is status. They earn the reputation of being *waiteri*: fierce.

Some of the younger men in Kạobawä's group were reluctant to participate in the fighting because they were afraid of being injured, remaining on the periphery so as to not be easily seen. This put more strain on the others, who were forced to take extra turns in order to preserve the group's reputation. At one point Kạobawä's men, sore from the punishment they had taken and worried that they would ultimately lose the fight, wanted to escalate the contest to an ax duel (Figure 5.7; see the film *The Ax Fight* for a documentary of

**FIGURE 5.7** The fight nearly escalates to clubs and axes. Kạobawä prevented this by compelling the reluctant men to take turns at chest pounding.

this impressive form of fighting). Kąobawä was adamantly opposed to this, as he knew it would lead to bloodshed. He therefore recruited the younger men into the fighting, as well as a few of the older ones who had done nothing but demand that the *others* step into the arena, thereby reducing the strain on those who wanted to escalate the level of violence. A few of the younger men retired after a single blow, privately admitting to me later that they pretended to be injured to avoid being forced to fight more. The fighting continued in this fashion for nearly three hours, tempers growing hotter and hotter. Kąobawä and the headman from the other group stood by with their weapons, attempting to keep the fighting under control but not participating in it. Some of the fighters went through several turns of three or four blows each, their pectoral muscles swollen and red from the number of blows each had received. The fight had still not been decided, although Kąobawä's group seemed to be getting the worst of it. They then insisted on escalating the fighting to side slapping, partly because their chests were too sore to continue in that fashion, and partly because their opponents seemed to have an edge on them.

The side-slapping duel is nearly identical in form to chest pounding, except that the blow is delivered with an open hand across the flanks of the opponent, between his rib-cage and pelvis bone (Figure 5.8). It is a little more severe than chest pounding because casualties are more frequent and tempers grow hotter more rapidly when a group's champion falls to the ground, gasping for wind, and faints.[10] The side slapping only lasted 15 minutes or so before one of the more influential men of Kąobawä's group was knocked unconscious, enraging the others. The fighting continued for just a few minutes after this, but during these few minutes the men were rapidly changing the points of their arrows to war tips: curare and lanceolate bamboo. The women and children began to cry, knowing that the situation was getting serious, and they grouped into the farthest corners of their houses near the exits. One by one the men withdrew, returned to their houses, nocked their war arrows and drew their bows, aiming them right at their visiting opponents. The visitors pulled back and formed a protective circle around the few women and children who had come back with them, also fitting arrows into their bows and drawing them. The air was brittle with suspense. The village grew almost silent as the lines were drawn up and the two groups nervously aimed their arrows at each other. Kąobawä, Ąsiawä, and other brave men of the respective groups stepped into the no man's land separating the two groups of armed men and began arguing violently, waving axes and clubs at each other. Suddenly, several of the spokesmen from the visiting group surged toward Kąobawä and his supporters, swinging their axes and clubs wildly at them, forcing them back to the line of men whose bowstrings were now drawn taut. Kąobawä and his followers regained their footing, and

---

10. Shortly after this event, an argument developed between the Karohi-teri and some of their neighbors that precipitated a chest-pounding duel. The fight escalated to side slapping, then to side slapping with stones held in the fist. Two young men died from their injuries, presumably with ruptured kidneys.

**FIGURE 5.8** Chest pounding can be modified to a form in which men strike each other from squatting positions.

charged and repelled their adversaries at this point, driving them back with their own clubs and bowstaves, while the women and children from both groups began fleeing from the village, screaming and crying. It looked as if the Bisaasi-teri warriors were about to release their arrows almost point-blank at Kąobawä's attackers, but when he and his aides turned them back, the crisis was over. The leaders of the visiting group rejoined the other men, some of whom had now picked up glowing brands of firewood, and backed out of the village, weapons still drawn, their way illuminated by those who were waving the brands.[11]

Ķaobawä's group took no further action in this affair and was not invited to a reciprocal feast at Mahekodo-teri. Later in the year, their relationships worsened because of a club fight in yet another village, and for a while both groups threatened to shoot each other on sight. A temporary rapprochement developed after the club fight, when a group of raiders from Ķaobawä's group met a group of hunters from the Mahekodo-teri while en route to attack the village of one of their enemies (described in Chapter 4). The men from both villages traded with each other and departed on non-hostile terms, the raiders abandoning their raid and returning to their village lest they be later ambushed on the way home by the Mahekodo-teri. They remained on trading terms with each other, but their relationship was somewhat strained and potentially hostile.

In general, feasts are exciting for both the hosts and the guests and contribute to their mutual solidarity. Under normal circumstances, allies who customarily feast with each other do not fight. Nevertheless, even the best allies occasionally agree beforehand to terminate their feast with a chest-pounding duel, thereby demonstrating to each other that they are friends, but capable of maintaining their sovereignty and willing to fight if necessary. Ķaobawä's group had a chest-pounding duel with one of its staunchest allies in 1966, as each had heard that the other was spreading rumors that it was cowardly. Of the six feasts I witnessed during the first 18 months I spent with the Y̧anomamö, two of them ended in fighting.

Any Y̧anomamö feast can potentially end in violence because of the nature of the attitudes the participants hold regarding canons of behavior and obligations to display ferocity and because of the long-remembered incidents of the past. Still, the feast and its antecedent trade serve to reduce the possibility of neighbors fighting with each other at a more serious level of violence, and they do contribute to intervillage amity and mutual interdependence. Imagine what their politics might be like without the feasts and trading.

---

11. At this time, I was crouched in the house behind the line of bowmen, very anxious not only about Ķaobawä's safety, but for my own as well.

# 6

✳

# Yąnomamö Warfare

## LEVELS OF VIOLENCE

Up to this point we have only touched on the relatively mild forms of violence that occur among the Yąnomamö. The feast and alliance can and often do fail to establish stable, amicable relationships between sovereign villages. When this happens, the groups may coexist for a period of time without any overt expressions of hostility. This, however, is an unstable situation, and no two villages that are within comfortable walking distance from each other can maintain such a relationship indefinitely: They must become allies, or hostility is likely to develop between them. Indifference leads to ignorance or suspicion, and this soon gives way to accusations of sorcery. Once the relationship is of this sort, a death in one of the villages will be attributed to the malevolent *hekura* sent by shamans in the other village, and raids will eventually take place between them.

Yąnomamö warfare proper is to go on a raid (*wayu huu*). Most definitions of war emphasize that it is a "military contest between two independent groups" with the intent of "inflicting lethal harm." Raiding between villages fits this definition, but unless the developmental sequence behind each "war" is understood, much that is relevant to understanding Yąnomamö warfare would be missed (Chagnon, 1988a). The villages—the groups that, in this definition, wage wars—change in composition so rapidly that it is sometimes more meaningful to look at their wars as contests between groups of kinsmen who collectively may live in several different villages over short periods of time, sometimes inflicting lethal harm on the very "villages" whence they recently separated by fissioning. I will return to this issue below.

Not all of their lethal fighting can be considered as war, although the values associated with war—bellicosity, ferocity, and violence—undoubtedly increase the amount of all kinds of fighting.

War is only one form of violence in a graded series of aggressive encounters (Chagnon, 1967, 1988a). Indeed, some of the other forms of fighting, such as the formal chest-pounding duel, may even be considered as the antithesis of war, for they provide an alternative to killing. Duels are formal and are regulated by stringent rules about proper ways to deliver and receive blows. Much of Yąnomamö fighting is kept innocuous by these rules so that the parties concerned do not have to resort to drastic means to resolve their grievances. The three most innocuous forms of violence, chest pounding, side slapping, and club fights, permit the contestants to express their hostilities in such a way that they can continue to remain on relatively peaceful terms with each other after the contest is settled. Thus, Yąnomamö culture calls forth aggressive behavior, but at the same time provides a somewhat regulated system in which the expressions of violence can be controlled.

The most innocuous form of fighting is the chest-pounding duel described in the last chapter (Figure 5.6). These duels usually take place between the members of different villages and are precipitated by such minor affronts as malicious gossip, accusations of cowardice, stinginess with food, or niggardliness in trading.

If such a duel is escalated, it usually develops into a side-slapping contest (Figure 5.8). Occasionally, the combatants will "sue" for the use of machetes and axes, but this is rare. If machetes are used, the object of the contest still remains the same: Injure your opponent seriously enough so that he will withdraw from the contest, but try not to draw blood or kill him. Hence, opponents strike each other with only the flat of the blade when they resort to machetes. As you can imagine, this hurts.

In some areas the Yąnomamö modify the chest-pounding duel in another way. The opponents hold rocks in their clenched fists and strike their adversaries on the chest with an even more devastating blow, often concealing the rocks so that their opponents do not know they are "cheating." They try not to let the stone itself touch the flesh of the man they are fighting. Even without the use of stones, however, they are able to deliver their blows with such force that some of the participants cough up blood for days after having been in a duel, and occasional fatalities result.

Club fights represent the next level of violence (Figure 6.1). These can take place both within and between villages. Most of the club fights result from arguments over women, but a few of them develop out of disputes associated with food theft. Dikawä, a young man about 20 years old, came home one day and discovered a bunch of eating bananas his father, about 55 years old, had hung up to ripen in his house, above his hearth. Dikawä, however, ate a number of them without his father's permission. When his father discovered the theft, he ripped a pole out of his house and began clubbing Dikawä. This was one of those uncomfortable situations where the son was a little too big to punish by physical means by a father a little too old to handle it. Dikawä armed himself with a similar club and attacked his father, precipitating a general melee that soon involved most of the men in the village, each taking the side of the father or son. In some fights, individuals seem to join in the fighting just to keep the sides even. But kinship relationships play an important part in most fights (Chagnon and Bugos, 1979). If a group is badly outnumbered, they will be joined by remoter kin and friends whose sense of fairness stimulates them to take sides, no matter what the issue is. The net result of the above fight was a number of lacerated skulls, bashed fingers, and sore shoulders. The contestants try to hit each other on the top of the head, but when the fight gets out of hand, the participants swing wildly and rarely hit their opponents on the skull. More frequently, the blow lands on the shoulder or arm. Dikawä probably learned not to eat his father's bananas and start planting his own, and his father probably learned not to try to spank 20-year-old sons.

**FIGURE 6.1** A nocturnal club fight over infidelity. The men at center (obscured) and center left have just been struck on their heads, and blood is streaming down their hair, necks, and backs.

The clubs used in these fights are, generally, 8 to 10 feet long. They are very flexible, quite heavy, and deliver a tremendous wallop. In general shape and dimensions, they resemble pool cues, but are nearly twice as long. The club is held at the thin end, which is frequently sharpened to a long point in case the fighting escalates to spear thrusting, in which case the club is inverted and used as a pike. Most duels start between two men, usually after one of them has been accused of or observed *en flagrante* trysting with the other's wife. The enraged husband challenges his opponent to strike him on the head with a club. He holds his own club vertically, leans against it, and exposes his head for his opponent to strike. After he has sustained a blow on the head, he can then deliver one on the culprit's skull. But as soon as blood starts to flow, almost everybody rips a pole out of the house frame and joins in the fighting, supporting one or the other of the contestants (Figure 6.1).

Needless to say, the tops of most men's heads are covered with deep, ugly scars of which their bearers are immensely proud. Some men, in fact, keep their heads cleanly shaved on top to display these scars, rubbing red pigment on their bare scalps to define them more precisely. Viewed from the top, the skull of an accomplished man of 40 years looks like a topographical road map, for it is criss-crossed by as many as 20 large scars (Figure 6.2). Others keep their heads shaved for decorative reasons only, irrespective of the number of scars they bear. Some do not shave their heads at all.

Club fighting is more frequent in large villages, primarily because there are more opportunities for men to establish clandestine sexual liaisons without getting caught at it. Most affairs are, however, eventually discovered. The larger the village, the more frequent the club fighting; and as fighting increases, so too does the probability that the village will fission and result in two separate groups. Most village fissioning I investigated resulted from a specific club fight over a woman, a fight that was merely one such incident in a whole series of similar squabbles. In addition to size, the lineage structure and kinship composition of villages affects the frequency of conflicts (Chapter 4).

The village of Patanowä-teri split during the last month of my first field trip. One of the young men took the wife of another because she was allegedly being mistreated by the husband. This resulted in a brutal club fight that involved almost every man in the village. The fight escalated to jabbing with the

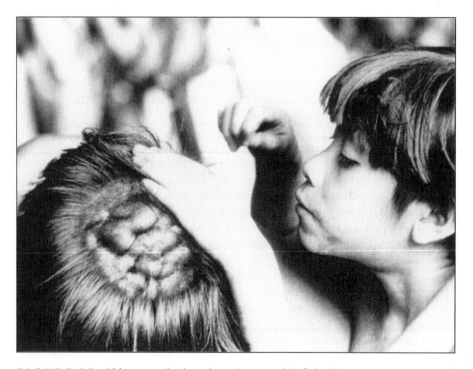

**F I G U R E  6.2**  Older men who have been in many club fights have enormous scars—of which they are very proud.

sharpened ends of the clubs when the husband of the woman in question was speared by his rival and badly wounded. The headman of the village, a "brother" (parallel cousin) of Kąobawä, had been attempting to keep the fighting restricted to clubs. When the husband's rival speared his opponent, the headman went into a rage and speared him in turn, running his own sharpened club completely through the young man's body. He died when they tried to remove the weapon. The wife was then given back to her legitimate husband, who punished her by cutting both her ears off with his machete.

The kinsmen of the dead man were then ordered to leave the village before there was further bloodshed. The aggrieved faction joined the Monou-teri and the Bisaasi-teri because these two groups were at war with their natal village, and they knew that they would have an opportunity to raid their own village to get revenge. The Monou-teri and the two Bisaasi-teri groups accepted these new arrivals; they were kinsmen and would actively prosecute the war against the Patanowä-teri. The hosts, of course, took several women from the refugees, the price a vulnerable group must pay for protection.

Spears are not commonly used by the Yąnomamö. A rare form of fighting, however, does involve the use of these weapons. It is a formal contest in the sense that the fight is prearranged and the participants agree beforehand to refrain from using their bows and arrows. Fights such as these take place when the members of two villages are not angry enough with each other to shoot to kill but are too furious to be able to satisfy their grudges with chest pounding or club fighting.

## THE RAID AND NOMOHORI

The raid is the next level in the scale of violence; this is warfare proper. The objective of the raid is to kill one or more of the enemy and flee without being discovered. If, however, the victims of the raid discover their assailants and manage to kill one of them, the campaign is not considered to be a success, no matter how many people the raiders may have killed before sustaining their single loss. Rerebawä told me of a raid he went on several years before I arrived. They managed to kill the headman of the village they raided, abduct his small son, and kill one more man as he fled to the village to recruit help. They were chased, but kept ahead of their pursuers for almost two days. Their pursuers caught up with them after dark on the second day and attacked them while they slept. They killed one man in his hammock, but in so doing, alarmed the others. A skirmish between the two groups developed, and the raiders managed to kill two more of their enemy in this struggle. Still, according to Rerebawä, the raid was not a good one because one of their own men was killed. The 10-year-old son of the slain headman was later shot by a man who now lives in Monou-teri. The little boy was persecuted and tormented by the other children. Finally, the man got sick of seeing this, so he shot the little boy as he was bathing in the stream. The boy also reminded him of his enemies.

Although few raids are initiated solely with the intention of capturing women, this is always a desired side benefit. A few wars, however, are started with the intention of abducting women. I visited a village in Brazil in 1967 that had a critical shortage of women. A group of missionaries had moved into this village a few years earlier and later learned of the treachery by which the group managed to obtain a number of their women. One of the missionaries gave me this account. The headman of the group organized a raiding party to abduct women from a distant group. They went there and told these people that they had machetes and cooking pots from the foreigners, who prayed to a spirit that gave such items in answer to the prayers. They then volunteered to teach these people how to pray. When the men knelt down and bowed their heads, the raiders attacked them with their machetes and killed them. They captured their women and fled.

Treachery of this kind, called *nomohori* (dastardly trick), is the ultimate form of violence. Kạobawä's group suffered a massacre in 1950, as I have mentioned earlier (see Prologue), but the treachery in this case was in revenge for an earlier killing. Still, their assailants attempted to abduct women after the objectives of their treachery were accomplished. Had it not been for their greed to capture women, the massacre would have been even more complete.

Generally, however, the desire to abduct women does not lead to the initiation of hostilities between groups that have had no history of mutual raiding in the past.[1] New wars usually develop when charges of sorcery are leveled against the members of a different group. Once raiding has begun between two villages, however, the raiders all hope to acquire women if the circumstances are such that they can flee without being discovered. If they catch a man and his wife at some distance from the village, they will more than likely take the woman after they kill her husband. If, however, the raiders are near the village, they may flee without dragging a captured woman along, as the body of their victim will be discovered quickly and pursuit will be immediate. Hence, they do not take a chance on hindering their flight by dragging a reluctant captive with them. A captured woman is raped by all the men in the raiding party and, later, by the men in the village who wish to do so but did not participate in the raid. She is then given to one of the men as a wife.

Most wars are merely a prolongation of earlier hostilities, stimulated by revenge motives. The first causes of hostilities are usually sorcery, killings, or club fights over women in which someone is badly injured or killed. Occasionally, food theft involving related villages also precipitates fighting that, if it leads to a death, precipitates raiding. This was the cause of the first raids between Kạobawä's group and the Patanowä-teri; they split from each other after a series of club fights over women. Each group made a new garden and returned periodically to the old one to collect peach-palm fruit, a crop that continues to produce long after the garden itself has gone to weeds. Someone stole the peach-palm fruit belonging to a man in the other group, resulting in another

---

1. This is changing as shotguns are becoming more common in villages where the Salesian missions operate along the Upper Orinoco. In 1990, a party of mission Yạnomamö from Mavaca, armed with shotguns, joined forces with a splinter of the Patanowä-teri and treacherously attacked a remote village that was becoming friendly with the Patanowä-teri. They killed two men with shotguns and abducted seven women. The fact that they had shotguns probably best explains why they would travel so far and arbitrarily attack a group with whom they had no previous quarrel.

food theft for revenge, a club fight, and then raiding, but it should be pointed out that the raiding came about only after a long history of disputes between the groups; food theft was merely the catalyst that finally initiated the hostilities. Food theft is often provoked by the intention of intimidating, not by hunger.

The Yąnomamö themselves regard fights over women as the primary causes of the killings that lead to their wars. I was in one of the more remote villages in 1967, visiting with people I had met on my first field trip. The headman of the village, Säsäwä, coveted my British commando knife and kept begging me to give it to him. He wanted me to tell him all about the knife, its origin, history, and how often it had been exchanged in trades. When I told him that it was used by people of my 'group' when they went on raids against their enemies, his interest shifted to our military exploits.

"Whom did you raid?" he asked.

"Germany-teri."

"Did you go on the raid?"

"No, but my father did."

"How many of the enemy did he kill?"

"None."

"Did any of your kinsmen get killed by the enemy?"

"No."

"You probably raided because of women theft, didn't you?"

"No."

At this answer he was puzzled. He chatted for a moment with the others, seeming to doubt my answer.

"Was it because of witchcraft?" he then asked.

"No," I replied again.

"Ah! Someone stole cultivated food from the other!" he exclaimed, citing confidently the only other incident that is deemed serious enough to provoke man to wage war.

Säsäwä was killed by raiders from the Salesian Mission of Platanal the following year. The son of the headman in that village blew his head off with a shotgun he obtained from the missionaries, one of the first shotguns obtained by the Yąnomamö of this area.

Perhaps the best way to illustrate Yąnomamö warfare, its causes, and the techniques of a raid is to give a history of the recent military activities of Monou-teri, a small village that split away from Kąobawä's group in the mid-1950s.

## A SPECIFIC WAR

The headman of the village, Matowä, was a particularly aggressive man. According to Rerebawä and Kąobawä, Matowä was the only fierce man in the entire village, the true *waiteri* (fierce one) of the group. I met him briefly in 1964.

Matowä frequently seduced the wives of other men, a factor that led to regular feuding in the village and resulted in a number of club fights. Of the numerous affairs he had, two in particular illustrate the nature of possible consequences. His youngest brother was married to an abducted Shamatari girl. Matowä seduced her, thereby enraging his brother. The young man was afraid to vent his anger on the real culprit, his brother, so, instead, he shot the wife with an arrow. He intended only to wound her, but the arrow struck her in a vital spot and she died.

Manasinawä, a man of some 55 years at the time I learned of this incident, joined Matowä's group with his wife and young daughter. He had fled from his own village in order to take refuge in a group that was raiding his own village, as he wanted to get revenge against them for a wrong they had committed. Matowä, who already had several wives, decided to take Manasinawä's wife from him and add her to his own household. This resulted in the final club fight that led to the separation of Kąobawä's group from the Monou-teri. Manasinawä's wife took her daughter and fled to yet another village. Kąobawä then organized a raid to recover the woman and child when their protectors refused to give them back. The two were taken by force from this group by Kąobawä's warriors. Nobody was killed in the incident. Manasinawä, his wife, and his daughter remained with Kąobawä's group, and he ultimately gave the daughter to Kąobawä for a second wife. Kąobawä still has her (Figure 1.8).

At this time, the groups of Matowä and Kąobawä, respectively, were still at war with the Patanowä-teri, from whom they had separated some 15 years earlier. Matowä's group, after separating from Kąobawä's, attempted to make peace with the Patanowä-teri, as they were now vulnerable and could ill afford to remain on hostile terms with them. Matowä's group also made an alliance with the two Shamatari villages, which had given them aid when they staged the revenging treacherous feast discussed in the last chapter. For about five years relationships between Matowä's group and the Patanowä-teri were relatively amicable, but as the former's alliances with the Shamatari grew in strength, their relationship to the Patanowä-teri grew cool once again.

The Patanowä-teri then became embroiled in new wars with several villages on the Orinoco River and turned to Kąobawä's group for aid, hoping to patch up their old grievances and remain at peace. The first day I began my fieldwork marked the initiation of complete peace between Kąobawä's group and the Patanowä-teri. They were having a feast together in Bisaasi-teri. Matowä's group, the Monou-teri, were not participating in the feast, but a number of men came anyway. They discovered seven Patanowä-teri women outside the main village and could not resist the temptation; they forcefully took them back to Monou-teri. Later that day the Patanowä-teri men discovered that the women were missing, so they searched the neighborhood and found the tracks of the Monou-teri men at the site of the abduction, where signs of struggling abounded. The next morning they went to Monou-teri armed with clubs; they were bound to get their women back, but did not care to start another shooting war with the Monou-teri. They took five of the women away from the Monou-teri in a heated struggle but had to pull back without the remaining two, unless they were willing to shoot to kill, because the Monou-teri were determined to keep the two women at all costs.

The significance of this incident is that the headman of Monou-teri realized that the Patanowä-teri would not risk getting into a shooting war with them since they already had more enemies than they could comfortably handle. Hence, this provided an excellent opportunity for the Monou-teri to abduct women with relatively little chance of getting shot in retaliation.

Matowä, the headman of Monou-teri, was furious because the Patanowä-teri had recovered so many of their women. He then threatened to ambush the Patanowä-teri when they left for home after the feast at Bisaasi-teri was over. The Patanowä-teri, in view of this, cut their stay short and left for home before the feast was over, hoping to avoid trouble with the Monou-teri.

However, Matowä was not satisfied that he had forced the Patanowä-teri to capitulate—to leave for home. He decided to raid them. In January of 1966 he and a party of men from Monou-teri raided the Patanowä-teri at the latter's village. They caught Bosibrei climbing a *rasha* tree, a prickly cultivated palm that must be climbed slowly and with the aid of a pair of moveable stick frames in order to avoid getting pierced by the needle-sharp thorns that protrude from the tree's trunk (Figure 2.11). Bosibrei was almost at the top of the tree when the raiders caught him; he made an excellent target silhouetted against the sky. They shot him and killed him with one volley of arrows as he reached for the fruits of the palm. Ironically, one of Matowä's "brothers," who also participated in this raid, was married to one of the Bosibrei's daughters.

The Monou-teri had anticipated their raid by clearing a new garden site across the Mavaca River, where they hoped to take refuge after the inevitable revenge raids from Patanowä-teri began. They had hoped to complete their garden before the raids became intense, as the Mavaca River would have provided a natural obstacle to Patanowä-teri raiders. The Patanowä-teri, however, were infuriated by this killing and raided the Monou-teri immediately. Two of the raiders were Matowä's parallel cousins, men he would call "brother." The raiders caught Matowä outside the new garden searching for honey. This was in the first week of February 1965. He had two of his wives with him and one child. He was looking up a tree when the raiders shot a volley of arrows into his body, at least five of which struck him in the abdomen. He managed to nock one of his own arrows and shoot at the raiders, cursing them defiantly, although he was probably mortally wounded. Then Bishewä, one of the raiders, shot a final arrow into Matowä, piercing his neck below his ear. He fell to the ground and died after being struck by this arrow.

The raiders did not attempt to abduct the women, as they were close to the Monou-teri campsite and they had to cross the Mavaca River to escape. The women ran back to the village to tell the others what happened. Instead of giving chase, as they ought to have done, according to Kąobawä and the others in Bisaasi-teri, the Monou-teri themselves fled into the jungle and hid until darkness, afraid that the raiders might return. Their awesome leader, Matowä, was dead and they were now demoralized.

The man who fired the fatal arrow into Matowä's neck was a son of the man the Monou-teri shot in their raid. Two of the men who shot Matowä were his classificatory brothers (members of the same lineage), three were brothers-in-law (including the man who shot the fatal arrow), and one was a man who had been adopted into the Patanowä-teri village as a child, after he and his mother were abducted from a distant Shamatari village.

The Monou-teri burned Matowä's corpse the next day. They held a mortuary ceremony that week and invited their allies, members of the two Shamatari villages and the two groups of Bisaasi-teri, to participate. Gourds of his ashes were given to specific men (who themselves could not drink them but would be responsible for vengeance) in several of the allied villages, an act calculated to reaffirm solidarity and friendship. Matowä's widows were given to his two eldest surviving brothers.

Kąobawä, a classificatory brother to Matowä, then assumed the responsibility of organizing a revenge raid. Matowä's own brothers failed to step forward to assume this responsibility, and for a while there was no leadership whatsoever in Monou-teri. Finally, Orusiwä, the oldest and most competent member of the village, emerged as the de facto village leader; somebody had to take the leadership responsibility. He was related to the slain headman as brother-in-law, and their respective descent groups dominated village politics. Hence, leadership in Monou-teri shifted from one lineage to the other, equally large, lineage.

Kąobawä delayed the revenge raid until April, giving the Monou-teri time to expand their new garden. This date also coincided with the beginning of the rains, thus reducing the possibility of a retaliation until the next dry season and providing the Monou-teri even more time to expand their new garden and abandon the old one.

The Monou-teri were afraid to return to their producing garden, so they divided their time between their newly cleared site, where they worked at cutting timber and burning it, and Kąobawä's village, where they took occasional rests to regain their energy. (See macro movements, Figure 2.12, where these moves are graphically shown.) They returned to their old site only to collect plantains, which they carried to the new site. Kąobawä's group then built a new *shabono* and fortified it, anticipating the war they knew would be inevitable. Up to this point, Kąobawä's group, Upper Bisaasi-teri, maintained two small *shabonos* a few yards apart from each other: *he borarawä*. In anticipation of the war, they coalesced into a single larger group and moved into the new *shabono* when it was completed. The visiting Monou-teri also helped them work on the new structure.

Meanwhile, the Patanowä-teri, knowing that they would be raided by the Monou-teri and their allies, also began clearing a new garden (Figure 2.12). They selected a site near one that was abandoned by Kąobawä's group many years ago, knowing that the peach-palm trees were still producing there. By this time the Patanowä-teri were in rather desperate straits. Their old enemies, the several groups on the Orinoco River, began raiding them with even greater frequency, after learning that the Monou-teri and Bisaasi-teri were again at war with them. A few additional villages began raiding the Patanowä-teri to settle old grudges, realizing that the Patanowä-teri had so many enemies that they could not possibly retaliate against all of them. This 'ganging up' on a weak adversary is very characteristic of Yąnomamö politics and warfare and is a solemn reminder to members of large villages to think twice about fissioning into two smaller, more vulnerable ones.

The Patanowä-teri then began moving from one location to another, hoping to avoid and confuse their enemies. They spent the dry season in turns at their main producing garden, with the Ashidowä-teri, their only ally, and at their new garden. Each group that raided them passed the word to other villages concerning the location of the Patanowä-teri. If they were not at one place, then they had to be at one of the other two. The raids were frequent and took a heavy toll. At least eight people were killed by raiders that year, and a number of others were wounded. Some of the dead were women and children, a consequence of the fact that the Patanowä-teri themselves sent a heavy volley of arrows into the village of one of their enemies and killed a woman. Females are normally not the target of raiders' arrows. Thus, the Patanowä-teri were raided at least 25 times while I conducted my initial fieldwork. They themselves retaliated as frequently as possible but could not return tit-for-tat. They managed to drive one of their main enemies, the Hasuböwä-teri, away from their garden, forcing them to flee across the Orinoco. They concentrated on raiding this group until they had killed most of the *waiteris* (fierce ones). They were so successful at doing this that the Hasuböwä-teri ultimately withdrew from the war, about as demoralized as the Monou-teri were. Several of my informants claimed that they did so because their fierce ones were all dead, and nobody was capable of prosecuting the war any further against a village as ferocious as Patanowä-teri.

When the Hasuböwä-teri withdrew from the raiding, the Patanowä-teri then concentrated on raiding the Monou-teri. Every time the Monou-teri returned to their main site they found the tracks of numerous men who had visited the village, tracks that always came from the direction of Patanowä-teri. Consequently, the Monou-teri moved into Kąobawä's group for protection, fearing to return to their old site until the jungle was inundated by the rains. Kąobawä's group resented this somewhat and made no bones about reminding the Monou-teri that they were eating large quantities of food from their gardens. When complaining became intense, the Monou-teri moved into the village of the Lower Bisaasi-teri and lived off their produce until the latter also began to complain. Then they traveled to the Mömariböwei-teri and lived with them for a while, returning to Kąobawä's village when these allies wearied of the visitors. When the hosts, the Lower Bisaasi-teri, for example, wanted to get rid of the Monou-teri, they would hold a feast in their honor. When the going-home food was presented to them, they had no alternative but to leave. It would have been insulting to remain after the food was presented. In between their moves they returned to their own producing site to collect plantains and carry them to their new garden. They subsisted there off the food they carried with them.

The Monou-teri soon resented being treated like pariahs by their allies and began to regain their courage. Much of this treatment was due to the fact that they failed to chase the raiders when Matowä was slain, displaying cowardice instead of ferocity. Many of the men in the Bisaasi-teri groups resented the Monou-teri for this and were not timid about displaying their disgust. The Monou-teri were a burden, as they rarely helped at expanding Bisaasi-teri's gardens and ate a good deal of food.

The raid Kąobawä organized to avenge Matowä's death took place late in April. His Shamatari allies, the Mömariböwei-teri and Reyaboböwei-teri, were invited to participate, but they failed to send a contingency. As allies never really trust each other, the raid was delayed because some of the Bisaasi-teri suspected that their allies were waiting for the raiders to leave so that they could descend on the poorly protected women and make off with captives. Finally, a few of them did arrive and the *wayu itou* (warrior line-up) got under way. Still, the Bisaasi-teri feared treachery on the part of their Shamatari friends, so the men of Lower Bisaasi-teri decided to stay home and protect the women left behind by the Monou-teri and Upper Bisaasi-teri raiders.

On the afternoon of the feast a *no owä*—an effigy of the enemy—was set up in the village, and some of the men who were to participate in the raid conducted a mock attack on the grass dummy, which was supposed to represent a specific Patanowä-teri man. They painted themselves black, crept slowly around the village with bows and arrows ready, searching for the tracks of the enemy. They converged at one point, spread out, crept toward the dummy, and, at Kąobawä's signal, let fly with a volley of arrows. The Yąnomamö are good archers. None of the arrows missed its mark, and the dummy, looking like a pincushion, toppled ominously to the ground, a dozen or more bamboo-tipped arrows protruding from it. Then the raiders screamed and ran out of the village, simulating their retreat from the enemy. They drifted back into the village, one at a time or in small groups, and retired to their hammocks to wait for darkness.

The village became unusually quiet shortly after dark. Suddenly, the stillness was pierced by an animal-like noise, half-scream and half-growl, as the first raider marched slowly out to the center of the village, clacking his arrows against his bow, growling his individualized fierce noise, usually a mimic of a carnivore: a wasp, or a buzzard. At this signal, not knowing fully what to expect and a little nervous, I crept from my own hammock and went to the center of the village with my tape recorder. The other raiders joined the first man, coming one at a time after short intervals, each clacking his arrows and growling some hideous noise. I turned my flashlight on for a few seconds but ultimately decided that this was possibly a bad idea—or even dangerous. I saw Kąobawä standing by and making sure the line was straight and faced the direction of the enemy; he would push or pull the individual warriors until they formed a perfectly straight line, joining them after the last one took his place.

The procession to the line-up took about 20 minutes, as about 50 or so men participated (Figure 6.3). When the last one was in line, the murmurs among the children and women died down and all was quiet in the village once again. I squatted there, unable to see much of what was going on, growing more nervous by the moment, half-suspecting that the warriors were sneaking up on me to murder me for tape recording a sacred rite. Then the silence was broken when a single man began singing in a deep baritone voice: "I am meat hungry! I am meat hungry! Like the carrion-eating buzzard I hunger for flesh!" It was Torokoiwä, one of Matowä's brothers. When he completed the last line, the rest of the raiders repeated his song, ending in an ear-piercing, high-pitched scream that raised goose bumps all over my arms and scalp. A second chorus, again led by Torokoiwä, followed the scream. This one referred to meat hunger of the kind characteristic of a particular species of carnivorous wasp. They

**FIGURE 6.3** Raiders lining up at dawn prior to departing for the attack on their enemy. They paint their faces black with masticated charcoal, as well as their legs and chests.

screamed again, becoming distinctly more enraged. On the third chorus, they referred again to the buzzard's meat hunger, and a few men simultaneously interjected such descriptions of their ferocity as, "I'm so fierce that when I shoot the enemy my arrow will strike with such force that blood will splash all over the material possessions in his household!" Then the line of warriors broke, and the men gathered into a tight formation, weapons held above their heads. They shouted three times, beginning modestly and increasing their volume until they reached a climax at the end of the third shout: "Whaaaa! Whaaaa! WHAAAA!" They listened as the jungle echoed back their last shout, identified by them as the spirit of the enemy. They noted the direction from which the echo came. On hearing it, they pranced about frantically, hissing and groaning, waving their weapons, until Kąobawä calmed them down, and the shouting was repeated two more times. At the end of the third shout of the third repetition, the formation broke, and the men ran back to the respective houses, each making a noise—"Bubububububububu"—as he ran. When they reached their hammocks, they all simulated vomiting, passing out of their mouths and bodies the "rotten flesh" of the enemy they had symbolically devoured in the line-up.

They retired for the night. Many of them wept and sang melancholy songs, mourning the loss of their friend and kinsman, Matowä, tenderly referring to him by endearing kinship terms. At dawn the women went to the gardens and gathered large quantities of plantains. These were carried to the raiders, wrapped with their vine hammocks, and deposited outside the village for the men to collect as they marched in single file to war.

The men painted themselves black again (Figure 6.3). Some even put on bright red loincloths which I had traded to them, as the warrior line-up is a spectacle in which the younger men can show off to the girls. The loincloths were left behind when the men departed. They tinkered with their bows and checked to see if the bowstrings were weak at any spot, sharpened their best arrow points, and waited nervously and impatiently for Kạobawä to signal for the line-up to begin again. The *wayu itou* was repeated, each man marching to the center of the village and taking his place in line. This time, however, they did not sing the war song. They merely shouted, as they had done the previous night, waited for the echo to return, and marched dramatically out of the village, filled with rage and determination. Their mothers and sisters shouted last minute bits of advice as they left the village: "Don't get yourself shot up!" "You be careful now!" And then the women wept, fearing for the safety of the raiders. The men picked up their supplies of food where the women had stacked them and left for Patanowä-teri.

Kạobawä had been complaining all year of severe pains in his lower back, abdomen, and urinal tract, and was in considerable pain when he walked. Still, he insisted on going on the raid, suspecting that the others would turn back if he did not lead it. The raiders had not been gone five hours when the first one came back, a boastful young man, complaining that he had a sore foot and could not keep up with the others. The next day a few more young men returned, complaining that they had malaria and pains in the stomach. They enjoyed participating in the drama of the *wayu itou*, for this impressed the women; but they were, at heart, afraid.

The raiders travel slowly their first day away from the village. They have heavy burdens of food and try to pace themselves so as to arrive in the enemy's territory just as their food runs out. They also attempt to reach a point in the enemy's neighborhood that will permit them to reach his village at dawn—far enough away so that enemy hunters will not discover their presence but close enough to the village that they can reach it in an hour or so from their last camp. The men use fire only when they camp at a considerable distance from the enemy's territory. As they approach their destination, they exercise greater caution. Their final evening is spent shivering in the darkness since they dare not make a fire to warm themselves. Most of the raiders emphasized this, as sleeping without fire is considered to be both dangerous and uncomfortable. The danger lies in the possibility of jaguar attacks, and in the fear that spirits will molest the unprotected raiders. On the last evening the raiding party's fierce ones have difficulties with the younger men; most of them are afraid, cold, and worried about every sort of hazard, and all of them complain of sore feet and belly aches, trying to find a justification for fleeing before contacting their intended victims.

The raiders always develop a strategy for attacking the unwary enemy. They usually split into two or more groups and agree to meet later at a predetermined location at some point between their own village and the enemy's. These smaller groups should contain at least four men—six, if possible—because the raiders retreat in a pattern. While the others flee, two men will lie in ambush, shooting any pursuers that might follow. They, in turn, flee, while their comrades lie in ambush to shoot at their pursuers. If there are any novices in the raiding party, the older men will conduct mock raids, showing them how they are to participate. A grass dummy or soft log is frequently employed in this, as was the case in the *wayu itou* held in the village the day before the raiders left. Particularly young men will be positioned in the marching party somewhere in the middle of the single file of raiders so they will not be the first ones to be exposed to danger should the raiders themselves be ambushed. These young men will also be permitted to retreat first. Matowä had a 12-year-old son when he was killed. This boy, Matarawä, was recruited into the raiding party to give him an opportunity to avenge his father's death. The older men made sure he would be exposed to minimum danger, as this was his first raid.[2]

The separated groups of raiders approach the village at dawn and conceal themselves near the commonly used paths to the source of drinking water. They wait for the enemy to come to them. A good many of the victims of raids are shot while fetching water or urinating outside the *shabono*.

Frequently, the enemy is wary and acts defensively at all times when there is an active war going on. Only large groups of people can leave the village, and these are well armed. Raiders will not attack a large group such as this. When the enemy is found to be this cautious, the raiders have no choice but to retreat or to shoot volleys of arrows blindly into the village, hoping to strike someone at a distance. They retreat after they release their arrows, depending on the gossip of other villages to learn if their arrows found their marks. Rarely, one of the raiders will attempt to enter the village during the night and kill someone while he sleeps. Matowä's younger brother allegedly accomplished this on one raid, but few men are brave enough to try it. Most of the time the raiders manage to ambush a single individual, kill him, and retreat before they are discovered. This is considered to be the most desirable outcome of the raid.

The women were nervous, frightened, and irritable while the men were away, and they were constantly on the lookout for raiders from other villages. This is always a time to suspect raiders, since allies occasionally turn on their friends when the women are poorly guarded, abducting as many as possible while their husbands are away.

---

2. Several years later, in about 1979, Matarawä was killed with arrows by a group of Daiyari-teri men who were avenging the deaths of two of their co-villagers killed in a chest-pounding duel with Kaobawä's people a few weeks earlier. This led to another war, one of the last that Kaobawä supervised. He and his allies drove the Daiyari-teri out of their area, forcing them to retreat far to the east, where they joined larger villages whence they had fissioned (Chagnon, 1990b).

After several days the women were so frustrated and anxious that fights began to break out among them. One woman got angry because another one, her sister and cowife, left her to tend a small baby. When the mother returned, the angry one picked up a piece of firewood and bashed her on the side of the head with it, knocking her unconscious and causing her ear to bleed profusely.

The raiders had been gone almost a week when Kąobawä and Shararaiwä, his youngest brother, staggered into the village, nearly dead from exhaustion. Kąobawä's pains had gotten so bad that he decided to turn back just before they reached the Patanowä-teri village. He could barely walk by that time and would not have been able to elude pursuers should the enemy have given chase. Shararaiwä decided to accompany him back lest he run into a group of Patanowä-teri hunters, or his condition grow even more severe. Shortly after they had dropped out of the raiding party, Shararaiwä stepped on a snake and was bitten. The rains had started, and the snakes were beginning to concentrate on the higher grounds, making walking a hazard. His leg began to swell immediately, and he could not walk. Hence, Kąobawä had to carry him on his back, despite the fact that he could barely walk himself. Carrying him for nearly two days, he managed to reach the Orinoco River. Here, he intended to make a bark canoe and float the rest of the way back down, but they located a dugout canoe someone had concealed, so they borrowed this and reached home about dark, three days after Shararaiwä had been bitten.[3] He survived the snake bite, but Kąobawä was very exhausted from the trip.

That night an advance party of the raiders returned, chanted briefly with Kąobawä, explaining that they had reached Patanowä-teri, shot and killed one man, and fled. The Patanowä-teri pursued them, got ahead of them at one point, and ambushed them when they passed. They wounded Konoreiwä of Monou-teri, shooting a bamboo-tipped arrow completely through his chest just above his heart.

The next morning the main body of raiders returned to the village, carrying Konoreiwä with them in a pole-and-vine litter. They had removed the arrow, but he was very weak and continuously coughed up mouthfuls of blood. They put him in a hammock and tended his fire for him. They asked me to treat his wound.

He lay in his hammock for a week, not eating or drinking all that time—the Yąnomamö have a taboo against taking water when wounded with a bamboo-tipped arrow, and Konoreiwä was slowly wasting away and becoming dangerously dehydrated. Finally, I could stand it no longer and made a batch of lemonade. I called for them to gather around, ceremoniously crushed an aspirin into the lemonade, and explained that this was very powerful medicine, so powerful that it had to be diluted with a large amount of water. I then demanded that he take some, which he gladly did, the others not interfering. By then he was so weak that he could not sit up, so I spoon-fed the liquid to him. A knowing glance passed between us as he gulped down the first spoonful of sweet liquid. He ultimately recovered.

---

3. The canoe was hidden in the brush by Kąobawä's nephew, who lives in a village up the Orinoco. He had come to Bisaasi-teri that day to visit and hid his canoe so that the Bisaasi-teri would not borrow it.

The two men who shot the fatal arrows into the Patanowä-teri were both brothers of the slain Matowä. They were killers of men and had to purify themselves by going through the *unokaimou* ceremony.

They were given spaces in Kạobawä's *shabono* for their hammocks. The area each man occupied was sealed off from the adjoining houses by palm leaves, and the men had their food brought to them for the week they were confined to this small area. They each used a pair of sticks to scratch their bodies and did not touch the food with their fingers when they ate, again using sticks to transfer the food from the container to their mouths. I was struck with the similarity between the *unokaimou* ritual purification and the first menses ceremony for pubescent girls.

At the end of their confinement, the vine hammocks they used while they were on the raid, along with the scratching sticks, were taken out of the village and tied to a particular kind of tree. The hammocks were placed about 6 feet above the ground and separated from each other by about 1 foot. After this was done, the men resumed their normal activities but began letting their hair grow.

Kạobawä felt that he had satisfied his obligation to avenge Matowä's death. The Monou-teri, however, wanted to prosecute the war further and continue raiding. It was at this point that Hontonawä of Kạobawä's group began to emerge as one of the more prominent men in the village. He stepped forward and actively prosecuted the war against the Patanowä-teri, encouraged by the esteem in which the Monou-teri held him. Still, he was not enthusiastic enough for the Monou-teri. On one raid he subsequently led, he elected to turn back and go home when the Patanowä-teri were not found at their main garden. The Monou-teri insisted that the party should continue on until they located the enemy, but Hontonawä refused to go any further. When he turned back, so did the entire party.

The Monou-teri and Bisaasi-teri raided against the Patanowä-teri six times while I lived with them, and each time the preparations for the raid closely followed the description given above. The Monou-teri returned to their producing site only when the jungle was inundated; only at that time could they exist without the support of their allies. The remainder of the year they had to take refuge with members of allied villages or expose themselves to the risk of being attacked by superior forces by remaining in their own producing garden.

The Monou-teri also raided the Patanowä-teri without aid from their allies. One of the raids was conducted near the end of the rainy season, and I was staying in their village at the time the raid was held.

A special ceremony took place the day before the raid. The gourds containing the ashes of the slain Matowä were put on the ground in front of his brother's house. Everyone in the village gathered around the ashes and wept aloud, violently. His bamboo quiver was brought to the gourds, smashed, the points taken out, and the quiver itself burned. While this was going on, the mourners were in a state of frenzy, pulling at their hair and striking themselves, screaming and wailing. One of his brothers took a snuff tube and blew some of the drug into the gourds containing the ashes (Figure 6.4). The tube was then cut in half, one of the dead man's arrow points being used to measure the point at which the snuff tube was cut. I was never able to determine whether the arrow points taken from the quiver were Matowä's possessions or were, in fact, the points removed from his body.

**FIGURE 6.4** Matowä's brothers assemble around his remains, blowing *ebene* into the gourd containing his ashes.

There were 10 of them, and my informants were too touchy about the matter for me to be able to ask too many questions; I received affirmative nods to both questions. In any event, the 10 bamboo points were distributed to the raiders, who fondled them and examined them carefully. Each man brought one with him on the raid that followed this ceremony. The severed snuff tube and the gourds of ashes were tenderly wrapped in leaves and put back in the thatch of the brother's house.

That night I think I became emotionally close to the Yąnomamö in a new way. I remained in my hammock and gave up collecting genealogies. As darkness fell Matowä's brothers began weeping in their hammocks. I lay there and listened, not bothering to tape record it or photograph it or write notes. One of the others asked me why I was not making a nuisance of myself as usual, and I told him that my innermost being (*buhii*) was cold—that is, I was sad. This was whispered around the village, and as each person heard it, he or she looked over at me. The children who inevitably gathered around my hammock were told by their elders to go home and not bother me anymore. I was *hushuo*, in a state of emotional disequilibrium, and had finally begun to act like a human being as far as they were concerned. Those whose hammocks were close to mine reached over and touched me tenderly, which moved me deeply.

The next day the raiders lined up, shouted in the direction of the Patanowä-teri, heard the echo come back, and left the village to collect their provisions and hammocks. I allowed them to talk me into taking the entire raiding party up the Mavaca River in my canoe. There, they could find high ground and reach the Patanowä-teri without having to cross the numerous swamps that lay between the two villages. There were only 10 men in the raiding party, the smallest the war party can get and still have maximum effectiveness. As we traveled up the river, the younger men began complaining. One had sore feet, and two or three others claimed to have malaria. They wanted to turn back because I had forgotten to bring my malaria pills with me as I had promised. Hukoshikuwä (Figure 6.5), one of Matowä's brothers, silenced their complaints with angry reprimands about their cowardice. I let them all out at the mouth of a stream they intended to follow. They unloaded their seemingly enormous supply of plantains and politely waited for me to leave. I sat among them and chatted, thinking that they were doing essential tasks as they fiddled with arrows and retied their provisions. Finally, one of them hinted that I should be leaving because I had a long

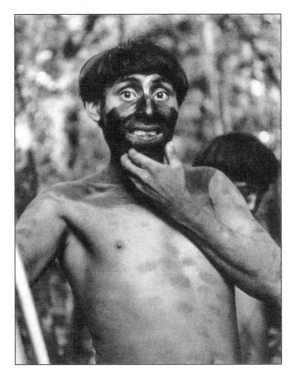

**FIGURE 6.5** Hukoshikuwä waiting for me to leave so he can lead his warriors into the jungle and to their enemies, the Patanowä-teri.

trip and might not get home before dark. It was then that I discovered they were dallying, trying to be polite to me. They all thanked me for taking them upstream in my canoe, one of the few times the Yąnomamö ever expressed gratitude to me, and I got in my canoe to leave. Hukoshikuwä came down to untie my rope for me and shove me off the bank. He watched, silently, as my canoe got caught up in the current and drifted away. He looked frightened, reluctant, anxious, but determined. After I had gotten my motor started and was under way, I looked back to see him turn, pick up his plantains and weapons, and disappear into the jungle. Even he was not enthusiastic about going on the raid, despite the fact that he lectured the younger members of the raiding party about their overt reluctance and cowardice. He was older, however, and had to display the courage that adult men are supposed to show. In short, although Hukoshikuwä probably had very little desire as an individual to participate in the raiding, he was obliged to do so by the pressures of the entire system. He could ill afford to remain neutral, as his very own kinsmen—even Kąobawä—implied by word and action that it was disgusting for him not to avenge the death of his brother; and some of his kinsmen in other villages openly accused him of cowardice for not chasing the raiders when they shot Matowä. Again, his erstwhile allies, when they complained about having to feed him and his relatives, were blunt and discourteous. The Shamatari allies even managed to demand a number of women from Hukoshikuwä's group in payment for girls they had given them earlier, when the Monou-teri were superordinate in the alliance pecking order. In short, if Hukoshikuwä failed to put on a show of military determination and vindictiveness, it would not be long before his friends in allied villages would be taking even greater liberties and demanding more women. Thus, the system worked against him and demanded that he be fierce, whether or not he wanted to be. Since his own group was small, it had to protect its sovereignty even more rigorously or be absorbed by a greedy ally whose protection would be tendered at the price of women.

Hukoshikuwä and his raiders did not locate the Patanowä-teri on this raid, although they searched for over a week. They knew it would be difficult to find them in the rainy season, largely because they would have to make many detours around impassable swamps. It was with this in mind that they brought their larger than usual supply of plantains.

The war was still being conducted, but on a less ambitious scale, when I returned to the Monou-teri a year later. They had managed to kill two Patanowä-teri and abduct two women. The Patanowä-teri only killed one Monou-teri, the headman. The Bisaasi-teri were still trying to avenge Matowä's death 10 years later and were actively raiding the Patanowä-teri but had by then acquired shotguns and were using them in the raids. At least two Patanowä-teri were killed with shotguns, including Kumaiewä, the headman, the prominent leader shown in the film *The Feast*.[4]

---

4. Kumaiewä had his head blown apart with a blast of a shotgun wielded by a man who then lived at the Salesian Mission of Mavaca. This was one of the first shotguns introduced to the Yąnomamö at this mission.

The Patanowä-teri group fissioned and subsequently lost a significant fraction of their size advantage. The Monou-teri completed their move to the new garden and lived there for several years but eventually coalesced with the Bisaasi-teri, terminating their career as a separate sovereign entity. They 'fused' with the people whence they had originally fissioned (Figure 2.15).

## GENERAL COMMENTS ON YĄNOMAMÖ VIOLENCE

In Chapter 2, I discussed what is now beginning to look like a major difference in the degree to which violence, warfare, and abductions characterize different areas of Yąnomamöland. My field research after 1990 has indicated there is still much to learn about these differences in the larger Yąnomamö area covered by this recent field research.

Most of my fieldwork up to 1990 was conducted in Kąobawä's area, and there warfare, violence, and abduction of women have been extremely important factors in their history as far back as I can trace it with informants who were very old—perhaps in their 70s or 80s—in 1964 when I began my work. They have long since died, for I have been studying the Yąnomamö now for nearly 50 years.

In 1988 I was invited by the editor of the prestigious journal *Science* to contribute the lead article for one of their monthly issues. I summarized what I then knew about warfare and violence among the Yąnomamö, a period of time that covered about 25 years of my field observations (Chagnon, 1988b).

I focused only on men who were alive at that time, men who lived in the many villages I had studied between 1964 and 1987. I discussed about a dozen villages, whose total population was nearly 1,400 people in 1987. I knew, for each of the living men, who they had killed during their careers to that date, where these deaths took place, what weapons were used, and the genealogies of all of these men and their victims for four or five generations—among other things.

Many extremely prominent men who had killed many enemies—like Matowä—were not even considered in this analysis. One Shamatari man I knew intimately, Möawä, was also not considered because he was dead in 1987. He alone had killed or participated in the killing of 22 other people, the record number of victims I have thus far recorded for a single man. (I discuss this particularly unpleasant man at length, and how difficult it was for me and his own co-villagers to live with him, in Chagnon, 1974, Chapter 5.)

Among the more significant results of my analysis were the following facts, which put the nature and extent of violence among Kąobawä's people into regional perspective:

1. Approximately 40% of the adult males participated in the killing of another Yąnomamö. The majority of them (60%) killed only one person, but some men were repetitively successful warriors and participated in the killing of up to 16 other people.
2. Approximately 25% of all deaths among adult males were due to violence.

3.  Approximately two-thirds of all people aged 40 or older had lost, through violence, at least *one* of the following kinds of very close *biological* relatives: a parent, a sibling, or a child. Most of them (57%) have lost two or more such close relatives. This helps explain why large numbers of individuals are motivated by revenge.

The most unusual and impressive finding, one that has been subsequently discussed and debated in the press and in academic journals, is the correlation between military success and reproductive success among the Yạnomamö. *Unokais* (men who have killed) are more successful at obtaining wives and, as a consequence, have more offspring than men their own age who are not *unokais*.

The most plausible explanation for this correlation seems to be that *unokais* are socially rewarded and have greater prestige than other men and, for these reasons, are more often able to obtain extra wives by whom they have larger than average numbers of children. Thus, "cultural success" leads, in this cultural/historical circumstance, to biological success (Irons, 1979a; Borgerhoff Mulder, 1987).

*Unokais* had, on average, more than two-and-a-half times as many wives as non-*unokais* and over three times as many children. Many people find this disturbing if and to the extent that the Yạnomamö represent more than just an isolated example, especially when it is known that, by comparative ethnographic standards (Knauft, 1987), their mortality rate due to violence is much *lower* than that reported for other tribal groups, where at least this statistic is known but where the associated reproductive facts are not. Some seem to be very concerned that this might have been a more general pattern in our history as a species, a concern that, to me, resembles the Yạnomamö fear that if we do not cook our food well we might all become feral, like the jaguar, or cannibals. If cultural success leads to biological success, then one would predict that if being a pacific religious leader consistently leads to greater male reproductive success, then more men would be priests and shamans.

The more appropriate question has to do with the likelihood that people, throughout history, have based their political relationships with other groups on predatory versus religious or altruistic strategies and the cost-benefit dimensions of what the response should be if they do one or the other. We have the evolved capacity to adopt either strategy. Turning the other cheek on neighbors who are led by men like Matowä might not be the best strategy if your own—and your group's—survival is of any concern, and it usually is. Men who do these things are generally called warriors or soldiers and, historically, those among them who survive seem to have been generously rewarded for their deeds: status, wealth, power, or other things that their societies deem valuable. We elect such men to Congress or the Presidency and give them medals. Among the Yạnomamö, where the 'government' does not include legislative and executive structures or metallurgy, they just get more wives and have more children. Important aspects of our biologies are similar, but our cultures are different ... but we all seem to reward such men with the tokens that are appropriate in the circumstances.

# 7

✴

# Alliance With the Mishimishimaböwei-teri

This chapter returns us to where the monograph began—the treacherous killing of Ruwähiwä in 1950 and how this incident dominated the next 20 or
so years of the political relationships between Ką̧obawä's people and the descendants of Ruwähiwä's village, many of whom eventually became known as
Mishimishimaböwei-teri.

Mishimishimaböwei-teri and Bisaasi-teri have a number of things in common but are also distinctive in some features. Many of the differences appear to
be the result of the sizes of the two villages—Mishimishimaböwei-teri is much
larger. Other differences appear to have more to do with the specific histories of
individuals and, in particular, the amount of polygyny that took place in immediately ascending generations. Polygyny rates, as explained in Chapter 4, are
important because they result in a few men leaving a large number of offspring
and grand-offspring. This, in turn, affects the composition of later villages and
the social relationships that occur in them—including both antagonisms and
friendly alliances between families linked by reciprocal marriages over time. In
some respects Mishimishimaböwei-teri is more like the village of Patanowä-
teri, the group from which Ką̧obawä's people separated in the 1950s. Both
were very large when I began studying them, and both were dominated by
members of relatively few but large patrilineal lineages (see Chagnon, 1974 and
1979a for data on lineage sizes).

In Chapter 1, I gave a brief account of my successful attempt in 1968 to
reach Mishimishimaböwei-teri with Karina, my young guide, and make first
contact with them. That was the trip when Bäkotawä abandoned me and I had
to chop a tree down and make a canoe from it to return back downstream. In
Chapters 1–6, I made frequent reference to the Shamatari in general and
Mishimishimaböwei-teri in particular.

In this chapter, I want to expand my discussion of Mishimishimaböwei-teri
and make a few comments about the importance of getting to know members of

several different villages of the same "tribe" in order to gain a more comprehensive view of a different culture. In Margaret Mead's generation the injunction given to new fieldworkers was to go to some small community chosen to be typical of an exotic culture, immerse yourself in the daily life of the people (become a "participant observer"), and spend a year there to observe and document the annual cycle of events. Then the fieldworker would return home, write up his or her notes, describing and explaining the exotic culture on the basis of limited experience in a single village at a single point in time in the history of that village. Most anthropologists rarely returned to "their people" for a second visit. Indeed, Margaret Mead's return to Manus made headlines when she revisited it 30 years after her initial field study. It was, even by anthropological standards, considered to be something quite unusual. My own experience has been that if I had not returned to the Yąnomamö, my "view" of their culture based on 15 months in just one village would have been rather lopsided.

There were some 250 or 300 Yąnomamö villages when I began my field studies. Each village is different in some ways from all the other villages, but all villages share many things in common, like peas in a pod but each with a different set of wrinkles. These wrinkles and variations give additional texture and complexion to the comparative aspect of anthropological field studies and help put sometimes differing ethnographic reports by different fieldworkers into perspective. In earlier chapters I have drawn attention to some of these differences—relative village sizes, patterns of marriage, rates of death due to violence, and frequencies of abducted women. While I am here being more explicitly comparative, it is important to keep in mind that the Mishimishimaböwei-teri and the Bisaasi-teri both come from populations that are quite similar to each other and tend to be characterized by large villages and relatively intense patterns of warfare (Chagnon, 1974; 1990a; 1990b) compared to other Yąnomamö populations and to villages that have been studied by other anthropologists (Lizot, 1976; Early & Peters, 1990; Ramos, 1995) or about whom well-advised nonanthropologists have written (Biocca, 1970; Cocco, 1972; Jank, 1977; Valero, 1984; Ritchie, 1995), although some of the Yąnomamö subgroups discussed by others also engage in relatively high levels of warfare.[1] Nevertheless, the villages and populations I have studied include approximately 25 percent of all living Yąnomamö in both Brazil and Venezuela and are therefore representative of a significant fraction of the Yąnomamö overall (Chagnon, 1991; 1995b; 1996a).

## CONCEPTIONS OF THE
## MISHIMISHIMABÖWEI-TERI

The Bisaasi-teri conceived of Mishimishimaböwei-teri as being "Sibarariwä's village." Sibarariwä was one of the most prominent men who lived there, a renowned headman. He indeed did live there when I arrived in 1968, but his prominence and political domination of the village had been eclipsed by one of

---

1. R.B. Ferguson (1995) attempts to claim that warfare is only "intense" in the areas I have worked in. cf. Chagnon, 1989c and 1996b.

his brother's sons, Möawä. The assassinated Ruwähiwä was one of Sibarariwä's many brothers, and Möawä was Ruwähiwä's oldest son.

While the Bisaasi-teri regarded their village as "Sibarariwä's village," other Yąnomamö groups to the east and south referred to them by a derogatory and insulting name—Bosikomima's village ("Plugged Asshole's village"). Bosikomima had also been a legendary headman. His true name was Matakuwä, "Shinbone." He had sired 43 children by 11 wives (see Figure 4.13) and his descendants comprised the dominant political faction in most of the Shamatari villages (Chagnon, 1974; 1979a). Sibarariwä and Ruwähiwä were two of Shinbone's sons. Indeed, some 75 percent of the nearly 1,000 inhabitants of a large sample of the Shamatari villages were descended from him or his father (ibid.).

I am still discovering Matakuwä's descendants and collateral agnatic kin (people descended from his brothers) in some of the new villages I began to study after 1990, but I can predict by now the villages they will be found in because I know the history of the fissions and village dispersals of the larger population. For example, I knew I would find some of them in Abruwä-teri, a very large Shamatari village in Brazil I had known about for many years, but was able to visit and work there only recently (1995).

It is not surprising that Mishimishimaböwei-teri was generally thought of as being "the village of Matakuwä" or "the village of Sibarariwä." One of the points that this underscores is that concepts of patrilineal descent are more highly developed in this area of Yąnomamöland and the Yąnomamö here tend to view whole villages in terms of the single most prominent patrilineal descent group, which, in this case, is Matakuwä's patrilineage. A case could be made that in the Shamatari region, villages are thought of as "single lineage villages," a characteristic of Amazon Basin tribesmen commonly mentioned in more comparative studies (Steward, 1948, Vol. 3; Steward & Faron, 1959).

Mishimishimaböwei-teri was the largest of the Shamatari villages and numbered some 270 people when I first met them in 1968. I returned to their village many times after that—it became my second "home" village.

After 1968, outside contacts and mission presence began to affect Kąobawä's village. Although the study of acculturation is an important and valuable element in contemporary field anthropology, there were many uncontacted Yąnomamö villages and I personally felt it was more important to learn as much about aboriginal patterns—especially patterns of demography and warfare—in these more remote and isolated villages. There would always be many opportunities to study acculturation later. I therefore stopped working in Kąobawä's village and would simply stop in and visit with him and his people before proceeding to the headwaters of the Mavaca River. This became something of a touchy point in my relations with the Bisaasi-teri, who wanted me to stay with them.

Mishimishimaböwei-teri was in the headwaters of the Mavaca River, relatively isolated from contact and difficult to reach by a three-day canoe trip and then a half-day or more of walking (See Figure 5.2). It would remain relatively pristine, longer than the more easily accessible villages like Bisaasi-teri. In addition, there were several other large Shamatari villages near Mishimishimaböwei-teri, some of them yet uncontacted—and whose members I also wanted to study. In 1971, I made first contact with the main group, the Iwahikoroba-teri, which nearly cost me my life.[2] In 1987 I contacted the remaining faction of them, who were by then living south of the Patanowä-teri in the Shanishani drainage. After 1990, I contacted several more Shamatari villages south and east of Mishimishimaböwei-teri and my current field studies focus on these groups.

Thus, while Kạobawä's village became dramatically influenced by the increased and increasingly intense contact with the outside world by the 1970s as the next chapter will discuss, many Shamatari villages remained pristine and isolated. While there are still a number of them that have not even yet been visited by outsiders, there are probably none left where nobody in the village has ever seen an outsider. There are always a few adventuresome young men in them who have walked out of the interior to visit distant mission or government posts in either Brazil or Venezuela.

## Comparisons of the Two Villages

The two villages have slightly different but parallel histories.[3] They both originated in or immediately adjacent to the Shanishani River drainage some 75 to 100 years ago, as shown in Figure 5.2, and have a similar set of socio-economic adaptations to this generally low-lying ecological niche (Chapter 2). During their migrations and resettlements they seem to have preferred this niche and have consistently chosen to live in this kind of ecological setting when alternatives were more readily available at lower risk. Successfully doing so has forced them to keep their village sizes large and be constantly prepared to deal harshly and often violently with neighbors who try to push them around and displace them. They seem historically to claim and defend areas that are much larger than would be required by simple subsistence needs alone, most likely because they themselves have to retreat periodically from enemies into other corners of their territory, something that would be difficult if these safe havens and refuge areas were colonized by others. This underscores the importance of the "social" component in the environments of human history and adaptation (Chagnon, 1968b; Alexander, 1979; 1987).

Both groups followed the same general migration path and direction for the most recent 50 to 70 years. They came from the east and gradually moved toward the west, avoiding each other but remaining in regular but usually hostile contact during their migrations. Kạobawä's people moved slightly toward the north in the most recent times, the Mishimishimaböwei-teri veered toward the south into the headwaters of the Mavaca River. It is as though they were simultaneously linked to each other as they moved, but because they were mutually hostile, they repelled each other and remained a comfortable military distance apart as their migration paths

---

2. I described this in detail in Chagnon, 1974.

3. A brief review of some of the figures in earlier chapters, especially Figures 2.14, 2.16, 2.17, and 5.2, would be a useful exercise here. They provide a graphic overview of the migration patterns of the two groups over time and the ecological zones within which members of the two groups have consistently chosen to live. Note that in Figure 5.2 the village of Mishimishimaböwei-teri is shown by one of its earlier names—Möwaraoba-teri.

followed a parallel course. (See map in Figure 5.2. Note that Mishimishimaböwei-teri on that map is called "Möwaraoba-teri," one of several earlier names.)

Both groups have frequently taken advantage of their relatively large sizes to coerce smaller groups around them, getting more women from them than they return in marriage alliances. There are, as a consequence, many women in both groups who have either been forcibly abducted from weaker neighbors or coerced from them by hard bargaining in putatively friendly alliances. Both groups have large numbers of unokais—men who have killed other men—and the rates of violent death among adult males are high in the ancestries of both groups (Chapter 2; Chagnon, 1974; 1988a; Melancon, 1982).

Because both groups are large, there generally has been more than one headman in the recent histories of both groups. And, also because headmen are often competitors for esteem and political power, villages fission into smaller groups because of rivalries among/between them. Kạobawä's group split several times between about 1960 and 1966, in part caused by rivals who budded away to become the single leaders of smaller villages. Nevertheless, for much of the time I lived in his village or returned to it during the late 1960s, Kạobawä was the single most influential man in his group. When I arrived in 1964 his village numbered about 225 people, but Hontonawä (Paruriwä) was making a bid for power and fissioned away in 1966, taking about half of the group with him.

Similarly, Mishimishimaböwei-teri had multiple political leaders, but most of them were members of the same patrilineal descent group, not surprising given the fact that Matakuwä had so many sons and grandsons. Sibarariwä fissioned away from Möawä just about the time of my first contact with the village in 1968 and, with the political support of other agnates, founded a new village, Ironasi-teri. It was located about a day's walk south of Mishimishimaböwei-teri and, over time, moved further to the northwest, ultimately becoming known as Kedebaböwei-teri. It numbered approximately 150 people in 1968, so Mishimishimaböwei-teri must have had a population of over 400 people just before I contacted it. This would have been the largest Yạnomamö village on record—at least under aboriginal, pre-contact circumstances. In 1968 and during all my visits until 1975, Möawä was the only headman of Mishimishimaböwei-teri. There were, of course, other prominent men, but everyone knew who the real headman was.

Large village size creates organizational problems: The more people there are in the village, the more likely it is that old antagonisms will be numerous and always near the surface, provoking frequent fighting within the village. Many Yạnomamö have given me, as a common reason for a village fission, an explanation like "… we were too many people in one village and were fighting with clubs all the time. We split into two villages just to stop the fighting." Sometimes the two new villages remain within sight of each other—to live, *he borara*—because it would be danger-ous to move far apart if they have active enemies.

Mishimishimaböwei-teri (and other large Yạnomamö villages) illustrates a widespread problem in the tribal world, and in my view, probably one that has repeatedly occurred in recent human history. That problem is how to effectively integrate and organize large, permanent human groups into amicable communi-ties, that is, into cohesive, well-integrated villages where solidarity is high and antagonisms or conflicts are efficiently resolved. By definition, primitive societies are those whose social and political lives are organized primarily or exclusively by principles of kinship, descent, and marriage ties. There appears to be an upper limit to the size that communities can grow if these principles alone are the founts of solidarity (Chagnon, 1975b; 1982). Beyond sizes of 300 or so people, something else appears to be needed to "glue" the village together—something new must be added to principles of organization. The development of clans and lineages is probably one organizational improvement over the local group amity based entirely on bilateral kinship. Another is the development of more formal conflict resolution mechanisms—adjudicators, go-betweens, peace-makers, or even "Leopard Skin Chiefs" as among the Nuer (Evans-Pritchard, 1940). Yet another is the development of increased authority of the political leaders, and this appears to be the direction that the Yąnomamö are following. Headmanship among the Shamatari in general and the Mishimishimaböwei-teri in particular appears to have taken a few halting steps in the direction of greater authority and autocracy than is true in other Yąnomamö areas where villages rarely get larger than 100 or so people (Chagnon, 1968b).

An effective way of exploring the strategic importance that conflict resolution plays in the evolution of social complexity and group size among humans is to consider how it is handled among the Bushmen of the Kalahari, the Yąnomamö, and the Kpelle of Liberia. This can be effectively and graphically accomplished by considering three well-known documentary films: *An Argument about a Marriage* (Marshall, 1966), *The Ax Fight* (Asch and Chagnon, 1974), and *The Cows of Dolo Ken Peye* (Silverman and Gibbs, 1970). Bushman groups rarely get larger than a few-score people, and often break up seasonally into smaller groups as water and food resources require. Conflicts among them are generally resolved by appeals to kinship and custom. Yąnomamö groups can get as large as 300 to 400 people, but conflicts cannot be resolved simply by appeals to kinship and custom. Lineage membership comes into play and people align with close agnates: Villages have more "structure" and more social complexity based on descent groups. There are also more customary ways to resolve conflicts—each increasingly more violent and dangerous than the previous way. Verbal arguments give way to pushing and shoving, which in turn gives way to chest-pounding duels or clubfights, which can, in turn, escalate to more dangerous contests where sharpened palmwood clubs, machetes, and even steel axes are used and the blows from them often prove to be lethal. But both the Bushmen and the Yąnomamö have one thing in common: Each has a societally acknowledged right ultimately to use lethal force to resolve disputes between them. Anyone can literally "take the law into his own hands" because that is where justice and judgment ultimately reside in such societies. There is no "government" to keep men in awe, no impersonal authority to decide who is right and who is wrong. As one of the Kung men in *An Argument about a Marriage* put it to his adversary, their dispute could be quickly settled with an arrow. Just one little arrow.

By contrast, the Kpelle dispute in *The Cows of Dolo Ken Peye* involved very different principles of conflict resolution. And, Kpelle communities were much larger—numbering many hundreds and even thousands of people. Not only were there lineages on top of kinship, but some lineages were of higher rank than others—there were chiefs and commoners. Moreover, there were not only "local" chiefs, there were also district chiefs with authority over several communities, and a Paramount chief with authority over everyone. There was also a "legal apparatus"—a system of specialists who would, with various mysterious techniques and skills, decide by "ordeal" who was guilty and who was innocent. The ordeal experts served the chiefs, not the commoners, so it should not be assumed that justice had its origins as a "blind," disinterested process designed to protect all members of society in an equal way (Daly & Wilson, 1988).[4]

There is a stark difference in the "style" of leadership as represented by Kąobawä and Möawä. It is possible that these differences in leadership style are as much a result of major differences in the sizes of their villages as an expression of their respective personalities. Möawä might have had to be more autocratic and dictatorial because he had larger and more constant organizational problems than Kąobawä did. Whatever the cause, there was a stark contrast between these two men and how they presided over their respective villages and represented their villages to others in the larger political arena.

Kąobawä was mild-mannered, diplomatic, quiet, pensive, unpretentious, and calm. Möawä was brutal, unpleasant, loud, openly aggressive, nasty to almost everyone around (including children), and constantly intimidated and threatened village residents. He was the nastiest and most unpleasant person I've met anywhere (Chagnon, 1974) and his reputation for nastiness was widely known in all the neighboring villages. For example, one of the first questions I would get from Yąnomamö men in other villages who learned that I had been regularly visiting and living in Mishimishimaböwei-teri was something like the following, always in low whispers and with great curiosity: "How do you get along with the headman? Has he been unpleasant to live with? How does he treat you?" Möawä's propensity for violence was legendary and his reputation in neighboring villages as a notorious killer was deserved. I published an article summarizing some 25 years of my field data pertaining to Yąnomamö warfare and lethal violence (Chagnon, 1988). In it I plotted the distribution of then-living Yąnomamö *unokais* (killers) by the total number of victims they were known to have either dispatched by themselves or helped kill.[5] The record number in that publication

---

4. An extraordinarily detailed analysis of the principles of conflict resolution among the Yąnomamö with specific focus on The Ax Fight can also be made by both students and instructors by using the revised *Ax Fight Interactive* available through Penn State Media Sales available with this book or from the publisher (Biella, Chagnon & Seaman, 1997). The user can explore subtle details of kinship, lineage relationships, marriage ties, personalities of the actors, and many other socially relevant dimensions of conflict among the Yąnomamö.

5. In many raids a victim is shot and killed by several of the raiders. All of them must *unokainou*—ritually purify themselves—and become *unokai*: killers of men. Thus, some men were members of a raiding party in which two or more of them shot arrows into a victim that proved to be fatal. It becomes widely known who the several men were who "killed" a particular victim. See Chagnon 1990b for a discussion of the "meaning" of the word "*unokai*."

was 16 victims for one man—who had help from other men in a number of his killings. By that date Möawä was dead, so his *unokai* record was not included in my published summary. However, according to multiple informants from different villages, Möawä had killed 22 people. They named all his victims and identified where they had lived. The vast majority of his victims were killed single-handedly by him. Informants emphasized that he had an unusual and devastating style, one he invented. They all seemed amazed at this. He would make very long *rahaka* arrow points—lanceolate-shaped bamboo points close to a foot long—that he would use as daggers. They were long, rigid, as sharp as knives, and pointed at both ends. He would lie in wait along a secluded part of a trail near the enemy's village and wait for a passerby. Then he would pounce on the victim from behind and thrust his arrow point down into the victim's lungs through the throat and silently flee.

Even people in his own village despised him but were mortally afraid of him. In about 1972 when I left his village after having spent an extremely unpleasant month there that season, I let it be known that I did not intend to go back to Mishimishimaböwei-teri so long as he lived there. I told several Yạnomamö men that I considered him to be an enemy and no longer wanted to be friendly with him. I was tired of his intimidation and constant threats against me.

## Contact between Bisaasi-teri and Mishimishimaböwei-teri

Kạobawä and his people told me many things about Mishimishimaböwei-teri during my first year of field studies. They were generally viewed as inveterate enemies, but from time to time there were touches of respect and occasional references that implied gratitude and friendship. The friendly references were usually in discussions of the tragic "treacherous feast" of 1950, the *nomohori* that always figured prominently in the Bisaasi-teri accounts of their recent history and why they hated the Shamatari except for a few individuals among them. One man in particular, a famous shaman named Dedeheiwä, was always mentioned. I will speak more about him below.

The *nomohori* happened at a place called Amiana-täka, and it was in revenge for the killing of Ruwähiwä described in the prologue of this book. Amiana was a garden next to a mountain bearing the same name, a garden cleared by the Iwahikoroba-teri. The very mention of Amiana would both anger Kạobawä's people and make them intensely sad. Many Bisaasi-teri died violently at Amiana—clubbed and hacked to death or shot with arrows as they frantically tried to escape the slaughter.

The revenge of Ruwähiwä was collaboratively orchestrated by the Iwahikoroba-teri and the Mishimishimaböwei-teri. Both had earlier been members of the same village but had fissioned from each other before Ruwähiwä was killed. The Iwahikoroba-teri invited Kạobawä's people to a feast. They were neutral allies at that time, so the Iwahikoroba-teri correctly predicted the Bisaasi-teri would come. But they also secretly invited the Mishimishimaböwei-teri, Ruwähiwä's "closest" people. These unknown guests hid in wait and attacked them by surprise as they lay defenseless in their hosts' hammocks.

A few of the Mishimishimaböwei-teri were opposed to the treachery and, during the incident, actually helped some of Kạobawä's people to escape the massacre. They broke holes in the palisade that surrounded the village and pushed many of the hapless Bisaasi-teri outside to safety. Dedeheiwä and some of his brothers were among them. For their help Kạobawä's people were grateful, even though they had not seen them since the massacre at Amiana.

But prior to the Amiana massacre, Kạobawä's people had abducted a woman named Yanayanarima, one of Dedeheiwä's sisters. She became the wife of one of Kạobawä's father's brothers and, by the logic of their kinship system, Yanayanarima was a "mother" to Kạobawä. Dedeheiwä would therefore be his classificatory mother's brother. Yanayanarima had a son, who was Kạobawä's "brother" because their respective fathers had been brothers (Figure 7.1). This man, Hukoshadadama, temporarily became a key player in the establishment of peace and alliance that later followed, as I will explain.

Rerebawä came with me on my early visits to the Mishimishimaböwei-teri and would spend many weeks there with me on each trip. He became the initial social instrument through which peace was established between the Mishimishimaböwei-teri and the Bisaasi-teri.

He was at first worried that they would be able to learn more details about him than he wanted them to know, rather than regard him as simply an "inmarried Karohi-teri" in Bisaasi-teri, a neutral party from a distant village. What worried him was that after the 1950 killing of Ruwähiwä and the subsequent *nomohori* at

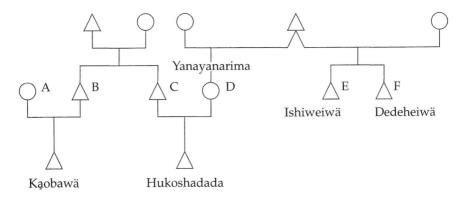

**F I G U R E  7.1**  Geneabgical relationships between Kạobawä, Hukoshadadama, and Dedeheiwä. In terms of tynomamö kinship classification rules, If Kạobawä and his "brother" (first parallel cousin) Hukoshadadama are related to Dedeheiwä in the same way: both must call him by the term "shoabe," meaning in this case "mother's brother." The rules are as follows. Ifyobawä's father ("B") was a full sibling to Hukoshadadama's father ("C"). Thus, both men called "B" and "C" by the term "father," and also called the wives of these men by the term for mother ("A" and "D"). Since Kạbawä classified and addressed Yanayanarima by the term meaning "mother," he would also have to use the term "shoabe" (mother's brother in this case) for her half-brothers—just as Hukoshadadama did. However, Hukoshadadama is related to Dedeheiwä ("F") genetically but Kạobawä is not. This is the principal reason that Hukoshadadama's role in the alliance was important ... blood is thicker than "fictive kinship." After the alliance devebped, Ishiweiwä moved to Kạobawä's village, as did two of his sons and one of Dedeheiwä's sons.

Amiana, his village, Karohi-teri, helped Bisaasi-teri raid the Shamatari[6] on several occasions. He was a very young man at the time, but went on some of the raids—raids in which the Bisaasi-teri killed Shamatari. On one raid the Shamatari managed to catch up to them and a deadly encounter followed, far away from any village. The Bisaasi-teri raiders and allies were camped in the forest, retreating home. The Shamatari pursuers waited until they were in their hammocks and asleep, and then attacked them. They killed one of the allied raiders, a man who was not a close relative of Rerebawä. Rerebawä quietly recalled with enormous detail how the man died in his hammock, blood gushing from his nose and mouth from the arrow that had been shot into his lungs.

Rerebawä was worried the Mishimishimaböwei-teri might already know or subsequently learn that he had participated in the raids against them as an ally of the Bisaasi-teri. They never learned this or, if they did, overlooked it diplomatically for reasons to be spelled out.

They treated Rerebawä with courtesy when the two of us would make our annual trip to their village and live with them. On our visit in 1970 the Mishimishimaböwei-teri decided to make a somewhat elaborate demonstration of their keen interest in establishing an alliance with Bisaasi-teri and also with his natal village, Karohi-teri.

Dedeheiwä and the other political leaders in Mishimishimaböwei-teri knew, through the grapevine, that the Karohi-teri were at war with the Mahekodo-teri, the group whence they had fissioned many years earlier. The son of the Mahekodo-teri headman had recently blown the head off of one of Rerebawä's close kinsmen with a shotgun he obtained from the Salesian Missionaries. This man, Säsäwä, was the head of the village of Makorima-teri. The Mishimishimaböwei-teri wanted to indicate to Rerebawä that they were on Karohi-teri's side and wanted to direct their supernatural violence against his enemies. They consulted with him to verify this, getting some information about people who lived in Mahekodo-teri. He provided it.

Dedeheiwä organized the Mishimishimaböwei-teri shamans and began an elaborate two-day shamanistic attack on the souls of children in Mahekodo-teri. Rerebawä watched the event carefully and with keen interest, because they were doing it on his behalf. They were making friends with him by killing the babies of his enemies by stealing and eating their souls.

I filmed the event with a small hand-held 16-mm Bolex camera, and tape recorded the sounds with my Uher recorder. In 1973, I published the film *Magical Death* that documented this incident, using some rather unorthodox methods to produce it. For example, the sound was not synchronized with the film. The tape recorder was on all the time, but the camera was being used only

---

6. The Iwahikoroba-teri and Mishimishimaböwei-teri at this time were still considered to be the same hated people, even though they had become two different but allied villages. The nomohori that they jointly sponsored made them, in the eyes of the Bisaasi-teri, just common and much hated enemy. I am using the more general term, Shamatari, to emphasize this even though the Bisaasi-teri raided each of them in their respective, separate locations.

a small fraction of the time. I had several hours of sound, but only some 60 minutes of film. I had to match the appropriate sound with the correct segment of film guided by what Rerebawä later told me when we returned to Bisaasi-teri, long before the film was even developed and I could see it. This basically amounted to something like: "When they were shouting at the spirit Ferereriwä, the man named Yoinakuwä was licking the body fat off his fingers in front of Möawä's house and Keböwä was running around waving his machete in the plaza…." However, it worked well enough to make a comprehensible documentary film. I provide a longer discussion of making this film in my essay in the revised Ax Fight Interactive DVD available through Penn State Media Sales (Biella, Chagnon and Seaman, 1997).

Rerebawä passed on to Kạobawä the political message that the Mishimishimaböwei-teri wanted peace with him and wanted to make an alliance. They wanted Kạobawä to visit them as a gesture of friendship.

The creation of this alliance was a fascinating process. It laid bare a number of important principles of Yạnomamö politics, the public manipulation of historical and genealogical facts to change them to fit immediate political needs, and how personalities, specific kinship ties, and sometimes even trivial incidents were called upon to make possible a detante between historically mortal enemies. It is easy to make war, but hard to make peace.

## The Social and Heroic Ingredients of Neolithic Peace

Kạobawä weighed everything carefully. He decided to show good faith and asked me if I would take him and several of the politically important men in his village with me to Mishimishimaböwei-teri. His decision dumbfounded me, knowing as well as I did the tragic 20-year background to his remarkable decision. Many people in his village had been orphaned by the treacherous acts of these same Shamatari. Some of their sisters and daughters had been captured and had spent their lifetimes with his enemies. His own father had died from wounds they inflicted at Amiana. In turn, his group had brutally killed Ruwähiwä, whose eldest son was now the headman of the village he was daring to visit, the most violent Yạnomamö I had met—going there with just a handful of his brothers. He had raided them ceaselessly since 1950 and his group had killed many of them. He had also successfully engineered a revenge nomohori on them, with the help of the Mọmariböwei-teri and Reyaboböwei-teri, two groups that had fissioned away from the Mishimishimaböwei-teri and allied themselves with Kạobawä (see Figure 5.2). On that nomohori they killed one of Sibarariwä's most prominent brothers, and one of his older sons. There were, understandably, hot-heads in both villages whose sense of vengeance and keen desire for it were palpable, and it was by no means clear what they would do if Kạobawä went to their village or they came to his.

This was risk-taking in spades. But it was also consummately intelligent, calculating, and weighing of social outcomes where mistakes could be fatal. It wasn't run-of-the-mill alliance building, like trading a dog for a basket and promising a hammock the next time. It involved political decisions that, if translated to scales we know in a nuclear age, gambled with the survival of whole nations. Ironically, it also involved an extraordinary degree of optimism about and faith in accurately predicting human nature.

Ķobawä himself had been one of my main informants on the bloody details of his group's relationships with the Shamatari, and Dedeheiwä had confirmed everything he said from the Shamatari viewpoint—and had added a lot more because he was considerably older than Ķobawä and could push the details of their respective histories further back. The further back it got, the grimmer it sounded to me. By their independent accounts of what each had done to the other, I thought it was foolish to even consider trying to make peace. I recalled how Ķobawä himself had earnestly and sincerely attempted to dissuade me from going there in 1966, 1967, and 1968, citing their deceit, treachery, and unpredictability as the main reasons for staying away from them. He told me they would at first pretend to be my friends to make me feel at ease, then when I was off guard and not expecting it, they would attack me with clubs and kill me, probably while I was sleeping.[7]

I was also worried I might be a contributor to an enormous disaster, but Ķobawä privately and repeatedly assured me that he knew what he was doing. He had given it serious thought and knew that the outcome would be peace—at least on this first visit. He assured me that if I refused to take him there in my canoe, he would eventually go by himself. But he told me he wanted me to be with him on his first peaceful contact because he knew that the Shamatari had accepted me and my role would be useful as a neutral intermediary and probably would contribute to the possibility of his success at making peace.

I observed in fascination how he chose the people he would bring. Torokoiwä, one of his brothers, would come because he was a well-known warrior, fearless, had impressive social presence, and was a skilled orator. Torokoiwä's mother had been a Shamatari. Rerebawä would come, because the Mishimishimaböwei-teri had already gotten to know him and had asked him to return with me whenever he wanted to. There were several others, each chosen for some specific and brilliant reason. But the choice that fascinated me most was Hukoshadadama, one of Ķobawä's parallel cousins whose mother was Yanayanarima, whom they had abducted many years ago from the Mishimishimaböwei-teri. She was Dedeheiwä's full sister.

Hukoshadadama was only a moderately prominent man in Ķobawä's village, primarily because he was a "brother" to Ķobawä. But he wasn't prominent in most intervillage political dealings and almost of no moment in the internal politics of Bisaasi-teri. He was, in fact, a bit dull and politically even a little incompetent. On the other hand, Dedeheiwä was indeed a prominent man in Mishimishimaböwei-teri—and a very competent and widely respected political leader and shaman. Dedeheiwä was Hukoshadadama mother's brother, a relationship that is extremely important and intimate in Y̧anomamö culture—in biological fact and in symbolic meaning.

---

7. The Mishimishimaböwei-teri treated me well on my first contact. Ķobawä's grim prediction was, however, accurate regarding my first contact with the Iwahikoroba-teri in 1971 (Chagnon, 1974).

Note that Kạobawä was also related to Dedeheiwä the same way, but not by blood. "Fictive kinship" wouldn't do here. Because blood was at stake, this alliance depended on blood. Hukoshadadama was related by blood to Dedeheiwä—but had never met him. Nevertheless, still he loved him because he was his real mother's real brother. I was fascinated at the increasing public repetitions by Hukoshadadama that he was desperate to visit his true *shoabe*, his mother's real brother. He longed for him. He wanted to know him better, to share his possessions with him, eat with him, hunt for him. He was very sad that he was not able to know his *shoabe a yai,* his true mother's brother.

In a sense, Hukoshadadama had the right "genes" and "genealogy," but Kạobawä had the power that could turn this into a political alliance. Hukoshadadama was simply a culturally useful neutral vehicle, because of his "right" genealogical relationship to Dedeheiwä, which could be used to initiate more important and enduring political relationships between the two groups that, as we shall see, ultimately came to pass.

For the brief period of time this new alliance was developing, Hukoshadadama was in the political limelight because he had the fundamentally necessary blood relationships on which the next step could more easily be built. That is most likely why he publicly and frequently lamented that he had never seen his *shoabe*, but wanted desperately to do so. It was a way of reminding all around him that he was important, perhaps the single most crucial element in the most important political step the whole village would be taking in the immediate future. Once that step was made, he faded into the political background. They just needed some of his genes and part of his genealogy for the initial, short, but crucial period when they were maximally useful, those parts that only he had because they came from his mother, Dedeheiwä's sister. They seemed to just "borrow" them and turn them into something more politically and socially useful. His biology was a social weapon.

We ascended the Mavaca as far as we could in my canoe and started inland.[8] About an hour later we unexpectedly heard humans far ahead of us. It was a party of hunters, but we weren't sure from which village. If they were Iwahikoroba-teri, we were in mortal danger. We were on the trail that linked their village to Mishimishimaböwei-teri. We signaled our presence by whistling, alerting them that they had visitors. Silence followed, and then we heard their short return whistle, acknowledging ours. We then each knew approximately where the other was located, and began moving toward each other cautiously, nervously, and silently. We had our weapons ready, and we knew they did also.

I recall how difficult it is to be ready to shoot, but yet try to look friendly and nonchalant, pretending that your weapons were not really ready to shoot *them*. As we got closer, we began shouting brief messages back and forth, becoming increasingly nervous as we inexorably approached each other, drawn by intense curiosity, moving carefully with great caution. Kạobawä shouted that I was with him and we were friendly. He was extraordinarily alert, like an animal who had detected either prey or a predator, his eyes dodging rapidly back and

---

8. I also discussed Kạobawä's initial visit to Mishimishimaböwei-teri in Chagnon, 1974.

forth scanning the dim, gray jungle ahead, turning his head this way and that to listen for sounds that would pinpoint those still hidden from our view but silently closing in on us, determining if we were being flanked by others. Deft silent motions with his arms fanned us out into an arc around him, separating us by several yards each. We knew without asking that we should conceal ourselves. He was *baröwo*, the first on the path, ahead of and leading us. We were the visitors: Those still hidden from our view were hopefully the hosts and it was now their responsibility to locate us. We waited silently, nervously. They grew nearer, and we knew they, too, had fanned out on the flanks of the one among them who came *baröwo*, first on his trail. He appeared cautiously. He was *moyawe*, alert, his weapons held low, his eyes rapidly scanning the jungle in front of him, looking for us. He asked me to confirm if I were among the visitors. He knew we were close, within arrow range. He crouched silently, showing no fear but communicating his cautiousness by remaining partially concealed in the foliage. He was waiting for us to reveal ourselves and for me to reply. It was Yoroshianawä, youngest of three politically important brothers in Mishimishimaböwei-teri. The oldest was the leader of one of the main political factions there. Yoroshianawä was about 25 years old, politically a middle-weight—a *browähäwä*—but astute for his youth and in this situation.

Kạobawä, still crouched and hidden, listened intently for a few seconds, his eyes slowly and carefully scanning the jungle ahead. He slowly stood up and revealed himself, fearlessly and with a gracefulness and dignity that is difficult to describe. The two naked men stood quietly and gazed intently at each other for a few seconds, sizing each other up. They were now separated by only 30 yards of jungle, but aware of the 20 years of war that had kept them at greater distances. They smiled at each other and verbally greeted each other, a signal for the rest of us on both sides to come forward. We did. The forest erupted with wild, excited shouts as Yoroshianawä's hunting party greeted us.

Nervously at first, the men from both groups eagerly and courteously mingled and chatted with each other, figuring out by vague and careful kinship allusions and tecknonymy who was whom, exploding into sincere expressions of joy at "discovering" precisely who the others were, hampered in this process by the excruciating difficulties of avoiding references to the dead men on each side that the others had killed. The person whose identity was "discovered" by someone in the other group would blush conspicuously, but would be elated that he was known as a person to them. The men in each group had done their genealogical homework prior to this anticipated meeting and had carefully determined who was still alive in the others' group and who would be the most appropriate, most neutral connecting relative to use in establishing each others' identities. As in daily social relationships, the medium of political alliance is also kinship and who is related to whom in what ways. They are offended if the name of a deceased close kinsman is inadvertently mentioned to establish someone's identity, but are immensely pleased when others are able to determine who they are genealogically, without having to allude specifically to the deceased relative that established that connection.

I watched and listened intently, curious about how Kạobawä would identify Yoroshianawä, the senior man in this hunting party. Kạobawä had shot

Yoroshianawä's oldest brother, Wadoshewä, on one of the revenge raids. His arrow struck him in the pelvis. A part of the arrow point remained buried deep in his hip. He recovered, but the wound crippled him forever. Wadoshewä walked with a severe limp.

A simple but yet magnificent event then took place that I will remember as long as I live. It may have been the most gracious and most meaningful social exchange I've ever seen in all the years I've lived among the Yąnomamö. Etiquette requires that hosts offer food to visitors as soon as they arrive. Yet the hosts were naked, hunting for game, and had nothing with them but their weapons and flimsy, small vine hammocks. Kąobawä and the men in his group knew and understood this and simply expected that they would be fed when we reached the village, still some two hours' walk away.

But Yoroshianawä was extraordinarily resourceful and politically astute. Once everyone in both parties knew who everyone else was, he turned to some of the younger men in his hunting party and hissed a few short orders. They scattered immediately, and ran off into the jungle in several directions. He himself unstrung his bowstave and immediately began digging a hole in the ground with it, working quickly and energetically. When it was about 18 inches in diameter and about 12 inches deep, he stopped, perspiring heavily from his intense effort, chatting happily and courteously with his guests, who watched him work. He whispered a command to one of the young hunters, who sprang to his feet and disappeared quickly into the jungle, returning in about 5 minutes with a bundle of broad leaves. Yoroshianawä lined the hole with the leaves, and before he was finished, the first group he had sent into the jungle was returning with quantities of palm fruits. Yoroshianawä began crushing them rapidly and deftly with his teeth, tossing the leathery hulls aside and spitting the large, slimy seeds into his leaf-lined pit, while young hunters ran back and forth to a nearby stream carrying little cuplets of clear, cool water in containers fashioned on the spot from leaves. As he filled the small, leaf-lined pit with palmfruits, they filled it with water. Within a few minutes the pit was full of palm fruits and water. He plunged both of his hands into the pit and began squeezing and kneading the slimy flesh from the seeds. After a few minutes he stood up, looked quickly around, spotted what he was looking for, and then bit off a twig from a nearby shrub, peeled it with his teeth, bit the tips of it off to fashion a "mixer," and then began twirling it vigorously between his powerful hands in the leaf-lined earthen pit, further agitating the sweet palm fruit flesh off the seeds, blending it with the water. It bubbled and frothed as he vigorously spun the mixing stick. He chatted happily, but worked intensely, kneeling on the soft, moist earth. After a few minutes he stopped and leaned back on his feet. He deftly flicked the debris off his arms, hands, and fingers, licked the sticky good stuff off, and then plucked a broad, small leaf from a nearby plant. He folded it into a cup, and gracefully dipped it into the pit to scoop up a cupful of the beverage. With admirable delicacy and charm, he paused for a moment until all eyes were on him, and walked over to Kąobawä. He squatted before him on his haunches, made a few brief, dignified and friendly comments, and then ceremoniously offered him this simple but special drink. "Bei. Please accept this tiny morsel of food from me as a gesture of my friendship and a welcome to my village." With comparable formality and poise, Kąobawä raised to a squatting position, accepted his sincere offering, drank it slowly and conspicuously, savoring it before his own group and his hosts, transforming this rather ordinary nectar into a political toast, and not just a sip of palm juice served in a folded leaf that it appeared to be.

Yoroshianawä then did the same for all the visitors, and with uncanny perception, served them in the rank order they deserved and expected. I can't remember what rank he accorded me, but it was not last. In the brief minutes since their meeting, he knew who was whom and what protocol was required. No books. No records. No names. No silverware. It was just the basic social awareness required by our species to deal with the social things that have most dramatically affected our survival over hundreds of thousands of years.

This was the most exquisite, sophisticated, and compelling display of honor, status, ceremony, and dignity I have ever seen. The palm juice drink was even served at just the right temperature.

It was still reasonably early in the afternoon, but the village was still two hours away. We decided to spend the night where we were.

The next morning we proceeded to the village, now confident that we would be warmly received and were probably in no danger. One of the Mishimishimaböwei-teri men had gone on ahead the previous afternoon to announce our coming.

Excitement was high when we marched into the village and struck our obligatory visitors' pose. A deafening roar of greetings erupted, armed men ran up to and danced around us, clacking their weapons above their heads, shouting excited greetings, welcoming us. We were then led to Möawä's section of the *shabono*, fed, and given the appropriate amount of time to eat and relax before the political monologues began.

Many of the most important men in the village had silently assembled around us, speaking softly to each other as we ate, not disturbing us. A number of people were conspicuous by their absence—men like Wadoshewä who still limped from the pelvic wound Kąobawä inflicted many years earlier. There were also some important Ironasi-teri men there, but Sibarariwä was either not with them or chose to absent himself from the village. Whatever peace might be worked out, he would not be part of it. His brother and his son were the two most recent fatalities in the war with Kąobawä—just a few years earlier.

Möawä barked a few orders that caused the curious children to scatter and the younger *huyas* to reluctantly skulk back to a comfortable distance and not crowd the area where the big men were assembled.

Kąobawä stood up and began the exchange (Figure 7.2). He recited the many good times and events of years past, before they became enemies. Grunts of approval and sincere supportive comments by the Mishimishimaböwei-teri punctuated his statements, interjected with perfect timing so as to not interrupt his monologue. He periodically paused, allowing Möawä and others to give brief comments, to which he and his men also grunted approvingly and offered their own brief supportive additions.

**FIGURE 7.2** Kạobawä addressing the Mishimishimaböwei-teri on the occasion of his first friendly contact with them in over 20 years.

I heard some of the biggest distortions of truth and history I've ever heard Yạnomamö political leaders unashamedly recite to each other. I had difficulty controlling my urge to laugh. I knew that the leaders of both groups knew they were each reciting bald-faced lies and agreeing with each other. However, they were politically necessary and useful distortions at this delicate moment. We probably would never have made it to the Fourth Glacial period if our ancestors had refused to lie. Strategically deployed, deception and self-deception are survival enhancing social tools.

The subject of the killing of Ruwähiwä—Möawä's father—came up in a highly stylistic, non-specific, and mutually acceptable way. Everyone agreed that the Bisaasi-teri were not the culprits—indeed, the Bisaasi-teri were praised for opposing it and trying to prevent it. Husiwä, they said, was the instigator. They fissioned away from him and then later killed him. It didn't matter here if the reasons for this had nothing to do with the immediate discussions. Other culprits included the Monou-teri, and the fact that Kạobawä's group eventually fissioned from them was publicly taken by all as hard evidence that Kạobawä's people were innocent in this treacherous act and even found it repugnant. Torokoiwä agreed with this amazing twist of truth—even though he was himself a Monou-teri! Then, the treacherous feast of 1950 at Amiana came up, and again history was rewritten and whitewashed on the spot. The Mishimishimaböwei-teri allowed as how they were opposed to that treacherous act, and many of them helped the victims escape. The actual instigators of this were the dastardly "Shamatari," from whom Möawä and his group had long since fissioned. Arms all pointed to the south, where some of the unidentifiable "Shamatari" now live, and to the northeast, where the Iwahikoroba-teri live. On hearing this fantastic distortion of fact I found it particularly difficult to keep a straight face. These very same men had, separately but on many different occasions, given me the detailed facts about both incidents and named the primary actors in them, many of whom were squatting on the ground in front of me … and in front of each other.

Because they did know and understand their own history they were not condemned to relive it. They simply changed it. It could be straightened out later as political expediency at that new time might require (cf Robertson 1973).

Kąobawä and his companions left the same day and returned to Bisaasi-teri. A peace had been forged and a new era of visiting and potential alliances had opened up. The Mishimishimaböwei-teri were invited to his village to feast and dance, and they agreed to come.

Some weeks later a group of men from Mishimishimaböwei-teri arrived in Bisaasi-teri to join Kąobawä and his warriors on a raid against the Patanowä-teri. They had left their women and children hidden in the forest, far from Bisaasi-teri. Long distances, like strong fences, make good neighbors and useful allies.

I watched the warriors conduct their *wayu itou*—the line up. It was the largest single raiding party I ever saw, some 60 men. They failed to find and kill any Patanowä-teri on that raid, but the Mishimishimaböwei-teri had demonstrated their good will and commitment to the new alliance (Figure 7.3).

Thereafter, regular visiting between the groups began, but mostly involving Mishimishimaböwei-teri men coming to Bisaasi-teri, an extremely long trip by

**F I G U R E  7.3**  Warriors from Mishimishimaböwei-teri and Bisaasi-teri preparing to leave on a raid against the Patanowä-teri to bolster their new alliance.

**F I G U R E  7.4**  Dedeheiwä instructing one of his adult sons in the skills of shamanism.

foot. Occasionally, a few young Bisaasi-teri men would paddle their tiny canoes up the Mavaca to visit the Mishimishimaböwei-teri, a long and strenuous trip.

One of Dedeheiwä's brothers, by then an old man, decided to move to Bisaasi-teri to be with Yanayanarima, his aging sister. Two of his sons and one of Dedeheiwä's sons married into and became permanent residents in Kąobawä's village and were warmly received and treated well. They became my good friends, guides, informants, and regular traveling companions for years after. Rerebawä, now a more mature man, had other responsibilities and was less free to travel with me.

Dedeheiwä also became a dear friend and extraordinary informant and would visit Kąobawä's village regularly (Figure 7.4). He and Kąobawä also became intimate friends. We all spent many happy hours discussing the past and the history of their respective villages.

Not all the visitors from Mishimishimaböwei-teri were warmly received. The Koro-teri group of the Bisaasi-teri who had fissioned away from Kąobawä was not part of the new alliance and their hostility to the Mishimishimaböwei-teri constantly threatened Kąobawä's alliance with them. They were usually unpleasant to Mishimishimaböwei-teri visitors and tried to provoke trouble. Some serious fights occurred, and one visitor was accused of trying to seduce a local woman and severely beaten with an ax. He died of his injuries after returning home. The Koro-teri had by then also begun to intimidate and threaten Kąobawä and members of his village. They had gotten shotguns from the Salesian Priest, to whose side of the river they had moved, and immediately began bullying everyone, threatening to kill them with their new shotguns. Kąobawä and his group remained aloof from the Salesian Missionaries and never got any guns—or much of anything—from them as a result.

**FIGURE 7.5** Möawä chanting to his *hekura* spirits in Mishimishimaböwei-teri.

One man who did come to visit, very much to my surprise, was Möawä (Figure 7.5). It was shortly after Kạobawä's trip to Möawä's village. I recall being astonished by a request he made of me—he wanted to see the "hesu kristu" that he had heard about from some of the Bisaasi-teri visitors, who told him that the people from "Diosi urihi-teri" (missionaries, people from "God-teri") had a *no owä* (effigy) of him. He wanted to see the *no owä* of Jesus Christ. In one sense this didn't surprise me—Möawä was an accomplished shaman and it seemed natural to me that he should be interested in the spirits and deities of other people, *their hekura*. By this date the Protestant Missionaries had abandoned their settlement at Bisaasi-teri, but the Salesian Mission was still there and growing larger. I took him across the river in my canoe and introduced him to the Salesian Priest, Padre José Berno, and explained that he wanted to see the Crucifix in the Mission's chapel. Padre Berno was thrilled and overwhelmed with gratitude. His spiritual message had reached even the remote heathen of Mishimishimaböwei-teri.

Möawä was stark naked except for his penis string. He was freshly painted in red and black with decorative plumes and beads hanging from his pierced ears. He had his bow and arrows with him. Padre Berno solemnly led us to the chapel, knelt, made the sign of the cross, and invited us in. He approached the large Crucifix reverently, a benevolent smile on his face, and swept his opened arms gently upward to present the Crucifix to Möawä, explaining in Spanish that this was the Son of God, the most important figure in his religion. Möawä, of course, couldn't understand a word of what he was saying. He was grinning from ear to ear, fascinated and amused by what he saw, and after looking at the Crucifix a few seconds, chuckled cynically and said to me in Yạnomamö: "Your *hekura* looks dead and is tied to some poles. He has thorns stuck into his head. He doesn't look powerful to me. How can he attack and kill your enemies if he is tied to poles like that?" Religious experts in all cultures tend to look invidiously at the deities and beliefs of others with open disdain and even contempt. Padre Berno's view of Möawä's religion and beliefs was even less charitable, but no less ethnocentric.

I didn't translate Möawä's comments and simply told the priest that he said that he "liked the Crucifix" and was grateful that the priest showed it to him. The priest was pleased with this. We left.

In the following years the Salesian Mission tried to persuade the Mishimishimaböwei-teri to move out of the Mavaca headwaters and downstream, where they would be easier to visit. In 1973 a large faction of the village did move downstream, but they did not remain there long. They returned to their original and safer location in the headwaters. They never really trusted the Bisaasi-teri and did not want to move to within easy striking range. Many Bisaasi-teri now had canoes and shotguns, and Kąobawä could not control those who had fissioned away from his village.

The main group of the Mishimishimaböwei-teri is still living in the Mavaca headwaters, and continues to be relatively isolated, although visiting between them and the Bisaasi-teri continues. They were fissioning into two groups in 1985 when I returned to work among them. One group was moving further up the Mavaca into extremely rugged foothills. I flew over one of their villages in late May 1996. It was approximately where I had last visited them in 1987 and where they were located in 1992 when I also flew over the village…on the banks of the high Mavaca. I didn't locate the second group on my 1996 trip. In September 1995 while I was working in Abruwä-teri, a large village in Brazil just across the Venezuelan border, I learned that many Mishimishimaböwei-teri were regularly visiting Yąnomamö villages in the Cauaburi river drainage in Brazil. This would be at least a 6- or 7-day walk from the Mavaca headwaters. They were visiting there, according to the Abruwä-teri, to get shotguns and ammunition and were allegedly at war with the Yąnomamö further down the Mavaca—who have had shotguns for many years now.

*The Deaths of Möawä and Dedeheiwä.*     Möawä died, probably of some respiratory infection, in about 1977–1978. When I reached Kąobawä's village in 1985, one of Dedeheiwä's sons was there. He called me aside and eagerly told me in very low whispers that "… the big one who used to live there is no longer alive. We are all happy now, and Yąnomamö from other villages visit us again because he is no longer there. They were our enemies when he was alive, but are now our friends." He urged me to return to the village, assuring me that life was much more tranquil than it was during all my previous stays, and that the Mishimishimaböwei-teri wanted me to come "home." He said that Dedeheiwä had also given me a new name: Mishimishimaböwei-teri. I was their village. Their village was me. That is about as high an honor as a Yąnomamö can achieve.

Dedeheiwä died in Mishimishimaböwei-teri in 1986, a very old man by that time. He was still active daily, curing his sick kinsmen and wreaking supernatural havoc among his enemies … dancing, prancing, and chanting melodic incantations to his *hekura* to the very end.

# 8

✳

# The Acceleration of Change
# in Yąnomamöland

The main purpose of this chapter is to focus on those forces of change that have most affected Kąobawä's village and the nearby villages to which he and the Bisassi-teri have been traditionally linked. I will, however, draw attention to broader patterns and trends.

The changes taking place in the Yąnomamö area are accelerating rapidly. Probably, more major change-provoking events have occurred there in the past 10 years than in the previous 100 years of Yąnomamö history. The previous edition of this monograph published in 1992 touched on only some of the new vectors of change, such as the 1987 gold rush in Brazil and its aftermath. Since then Venezuela's Federal Territory of Amazonas has become a new state, which has set into motion forces of change that might prove to be even more enduring and far-reaching than the gold rush. A major struggle between the Church and the State is currently being waged in Venezuela as the former privileges and political dominion of the Salesian Missions are being curtailed and replaced with secular counterparts. Numbers of villages of Venezuelan Yąnomamö are now caught up in this, especially those located at or within the sphere of influence of the Salesian Missions. Needless to say, individual Yąnomamö are learning about the politics of the outside world and are also being caught up in the Church/State conflict.

Before turning to these issues, let us first trace the gradual development of outside contact and how the forces of change began and then accelerated.

## GRADUAL VERSUS CATASTROPHIC CHANGE

Anthropologists have traditionally discussed the process of change that occurs when one culture impinges on another as "acculturation."

Earlier editions of this monograph discussed some of the kinds of changes that were taking place as members of a few Yąnomamö villages were beginning

233

to develop sustained contact with outsiders, and for these kinds of changes the word "acculturation" was probably appropriate. The experiences that a few individuals had as these gradual changes began taking place were even humorous and anthropologically instructive, such as the time I took Rerebawä to Caracas in the late 1960s in a military airplane. At that time he, and most of his covillagers, knew only about the neighboring Ye'kwana Indians and just the name "Caraca-teri," then thought by most to be the only non-Yąnomamö and non-Ye'kwana people in the cosmos. When we landed at the Venezuelan Air Force base in Maracay and I told him to get into the car, a vehicle he had never heard about or seen, he walked up to it, scratched his head, and at my insistent demands for him to get into it, he dived through the open window closest to him. It was not obvious that it had doors that opened. We drove to Caracas by night, and the pairs of bright auto headlights streaming at fantastic speeds toward us, and whizzing past by inches, terrified him, for he thought they were the *bore* spirits, supernatural beings that prowl the jungle by night with glowing eyes.

Some of these early signs of change were more portentous, as the time I asked why a particular Yąnomamö in a Salesian mission village had raided so far away and killed a man with a shotgun—in a village that his own had never had any contact with. Rerebawä said "If you give a fierce Yąnomamö man a shotgun, he will want to use it to kill with—simply because he has it." These became commonplace incidents as more and more Venezuelan Yąnomamö acquired shotguns from various missionaries and they continue, at an accelerating pace, to obtain more of them from yet other sources. It is far worse in Brazil, where shotguns are much cheaper and traded to the Yąnomamö there almost with the same abandon with which I traded machetes to them in Venezuela.


## VARIATION IN DEGREE AND KIND
## OF CONTACT

It is important to realize that the degree to which Yąnomamö groups have changed since the first edition of this book appeared in 1968 varies radically from one place to another, and, increasingly, from one country to another. There are growing numbers of Yąnomamö villages in Venezuela, like Kąobawä's, that are in direct contact with missionaries. Some villages, like Kąobawä's, have been in direct mission contact for up to 40 years now. Their cultural circumstances have changed markedly as a consequence. But there are yet some villages that have not been contacted, at least directly, and exist in circumstances very similar to those described in this book.

Many of the changes that are occurring among the Venezuelan Yąnomamö are the result of increasing Salesian (Catholic) mission activities at Ocamo, Mavaca and Platanal, where these missionaries have several main posts, and the extension of their influence to more and more neighboring villages.[1] These posts can be conceived as center points away from which mission influence and contact extends, usually following navigable rivers, but extending inland in some areas as well. Those Yąnomamö villages away from but relatively close to these centers are now becoming inexorably tied to and dependent on the mission posts. The missionaries have started schools and economic "cooperatives" in some of these outlying villages, sending Yąnomamö teachers that they have trained as their agents of acculturation.

As the distance from the mission posts increases, contact diminishes and becomes more irregular, especially if the villages are not on or near navigable rivers via which the missionaries and the Yąnomamö agents they train normally travel. To include these more remote villages into their expanding efforts, they must either walk into them or send groups of Yąnomamö men they have trained into them. This is inconvenient and inefficient. Consequently, they urge the inland groups either to move out to a navigable river or to move to the mission post itself. The policy of the Salesians has been to "reduce" as many of the widely separated, isolated Yąnomamö villages as they can to living at as few, large, and easily reachable villages as possible (see below for more discussion of "attraction and reduction"). Many of the recent village moves in the area of Kąobawä's village resulted from this policy: More and more villages are moving closer to the missions, or factions of larger villages are splitting away from the main group to do this. As this trend continues, mission villages are becoming larger and larger. There are nearly 500 Yąnomamö living at or near the Salesian Mission of Mavaca where Kąobawä's village is located. There are over 600 Yąnomamö living at or near the New Tribes Mission of Parima B in the highlands north of Kąobawä's village, and close to 400 living at the Dawson Evangelical Mission on the Padamo River. A similar trend is occurring on the Brazilian side of the border where there are six or seven Mission posts with populations of Yąnomamö in excess of 500 people. Needless to say, subsistence problems are developing as the local resources become depleted and the economic life of the Yąnomamö is becoming increasingly dependent on outside food and construction items. Coupled with this trend toward larger, more concentrated villages is the gradual decrease in the total number of Yąnomamö villages.

The spheres of Salesian mission influence have expanded dramatically in the past 20 years and now overlap extensively at places such as Ocamo, Mavaca, and Platanal in southern Venezuela. No Yąnomamö village on or near a navigable river or stream between these three mission posts can be considered to be living under relatively unacculturated circumstances at this point.

The pattern is similar in areas where Protestant missions operate among Venezuelan Yąnomamö, but the distances between their missions are so great

---

1. Two of these are located on the map labeled Figure 5-2. The Salesian mission of Mavaca is at the confluence of the Mavaca River with the Orinoco where Upper and Lower Bisaasi-teri are shown. The Salesian Mission of Platanal is located at the Yąnomamö village shown as Mahekodo-teri. The third, Ocamo, is immediately north of the area shown in Figure 5-2, where the Ocamo river hits the Orinoco. Finally, the satellite Mavaca mission, Mavakita, is located on the Mavaca River just downstream from where the mouth of the Shamata River is shown on Figure 5-2.

that their "spheres" of influence are unlikely to overlap. However, as mentioned above, one of the Protestant missions on the Padamo River at the village of Koshirowä-teri has grown in size and prominence in the past 10 years and is becoming an increasingly important point of contact with Venezuelan national culture, especially Venezuelan authorities. The people here are related to the Yąnomamö at the Salesian mission at Ocamo.

Similar patterns have developed in Brazil, and the "spheres of influence" emanating from mission posts in both countries are coming very close to each other. As I indicated in the previous chapter, members of Mishimishimaböwei-teri have recently begun to visit Salesian missions in Brazil.

There are now only a few significantly large areas where Venezuelan Yąnomamö groups continue to remain isolated enough that outsiders— missionaries and others—have not reached them or, if they have, the contacts have usually been very recent, very brief, and, often, once-only incidents. One such area is the eastern half of the Siapa River basin and the region immediately to the north of it in the Orinoco basin. After 1990, as a result of helicopter support from the Venezuelan government, I initiated work in this large area and visited a number of villages that had never been visited by outsiders before. But even as I work in this area, the sphere of mission influence expands inexorably into it. In 1995, while working in Abruwä-teri, a large village in Brazil near the Venezuelan border, I ran into young men who were from extremely remote villages in the Siapa and whom I had met in their own villages in 1990. I also know that other young men from their village were beginning to visit Mavakita, a satellite of the Salesian Mission at Mavaca.

Working in these "uncontacted" villages is not as romantic or exotic as it might sound at first glance. The Yąnomamö in these areas were already aware of a larger world and the sub-human foreigners, *nabäs*, unlike the first-contact experiences I had in the 1960s and 1970s, one of which is described in Chapter 1. I had known about some of these groups for many years because they figure prominently in the history of most of the groups I have been studying (Chagnon, 1966; 1974). Many of their current and former residents were already in my genealogies, and I had discussed their migration patterns and, occasionally, even the specific men who were their important political leaders (Figure 2.18). Not surprisingly, most of the individuals in these villages also knew about me through their contacts with other Yąnomamö I had visited regularly. I also flew over this area on two occasions in the late 1960s and located several of these villages by air. In addition, I had met individuals from some of these villages, many of them women who had been abducted and were living in villages I was regularly studying. There were, for example, a number of older women in Kąobawä's village from places like Konabuma-teri, Akawaiyoba-teri, Rahakaböwei-teri, or Bohorowabihiwei-teri—whose sites and current villages I am visiting only now. Many of the older people in the several Shamatari villages I had studied were born in this remote Siapa basin area, in ancient gardens I have recently been in or flew over and located with GPS instruments. I occasionally also met men from these groups who had married into the villages I was studying or visited these villages while I was there. In addition, many of the men in these remote villages had already seen a number of outsiders before my visits in 1990 and 1991, usually Brazilian missionaries they occasionally visited to obtain steel tools. In some villages they have to walk five or six days to get there. In 1972, a Venezuelan Border Commission team landed on an island in the Siapa River and made a trip down that river, briefly visiting several of the villages that were located immediately on or very near the Siapa River (Lizot, 1973b). In 1974, I brought one of my former graduate students to the upper Orinoco on the northern part of this area, and they briefly visited some of the isolated groups immediately to the south (Good, 1989).

Regardless of these sporadic and ephemeral contacts, this area is one of the last major redoubts of traditional Yanomamö culture and relatively unacculturated villages. It is possible that a similar area in that portion of the Parima Mountains drained by the Ocamo River to the northeast contains clusters of Yanomamö villages that are comparable in degree of isolation from outside contacts.

Thus, in Venezuela, there are Yanomamö villages that fall into at least four distinct grades or degrees of "contact:" There are three levels of contact associated with missionary activities, and a fourth that characterizes the few remote villages that are left—almost no direct contact. This makes it difficult to generalize about culture change, except to say that accelerating contacts with the outside world have created serious health problems for all of them. These problems differ in large measure as a function of the degree of contact they have with outsiders, which, in turn, is a function of their degree of isolation and inaccessibility.

That many groups are extremely changed since the first edition of this book appeared in 1968 should surprise no one in the late 1990s; that some still exist in isolation and relative independence from the outside world is nothing short of astonishing. They are the last of their kind, the last of the relatively unacculturated tribal world and, at this point in human history, the last relatively unacculturated tribal peoples *anywhere on earth.*

A similar pattern existed in Brazil up until very recently. All that was changed in 1987 and, tragically, there are probably no Yanomamö groups left anywhere in Brazil that are comparable in degree of isolation and absence of contact to those just described for the eastern portion of the Venezuelan Siapa basin and the Parima highlands on the Venezuelan side of the border. My 1995 field trip to Brazil confirmed this impression.

## THE 1987 BRAZILIAN GOLD RUSH

What began in 1987 developed into a cataclysm of enormous proportions. The catastrophic changes were the consequences of a gold rush on the Brazilian side of the border that simmered for several years and then exploded in 1987. Diseases brought by Brazilian gold miners—*garimpeiros*—then spread from one village to another, even to remote Venezuelan villages near the border, either because the Yanomamö there began visiting the mining area and brought home the sicknesses or because some Brazilian miners illegally crossed into Venezuela and brought diseases with them. I was in one of these very remote Venezuelan Yanomamö villages in 1991 when five Brazilian *garimpeiros*, lost, hungry, and very sick, staggered into it. My Venezuelan coresearcher, Dr. Charles Brewer, and I had them transported out by helicopter and handed over to Venezuelan authorities, who jailed them for a few days and returned them to Brazil. The Yąnomamö in this village had never been visited by *garimpeiros* before, but told us of similar recent visits by *garimpeiros* to the remote villages just to their east, close to the Brazilian border.

The 1987 Brazilian gold rush has been the most dramatic and devastating single event in recent Yąnomamö history. All previous forces that caused change pale in importance. It began near a place called Mucajai, a remote region I briefly visited in 1967, a Protestant mission site on the Mucajai River in Brazil's Roraima state.

I first learned about the gold rush in my backyard, in Santa Barbara, California, a few weeks after it began. My house guest was a Consolata priest named John Saffirio, who had been living among the Brazilian Yąnomamö for many years.[2] John was visiting me in Santa Barbara in September 1987 and was about to return to his mission in Brazil. He called his Bishop from my house. He was trembling when he finished the call. His Bishop told him that his mission at Catrimani had been closed by the Brazilian government and he couldn't go back to Yąnomamöland. The reason was that John and others in his mission were dutifully reporting the presence of illegal gold miners in Yąnomamö territory, filing official reports that obliged the authorities to remove them according to Brazilian law. As the gold fever intensified, the miners demanded that if they couldn't be there, then the missionaries and other "foreigners" shouldn't be there either. The government buckled under this pressure and ordered the missionaries, anthropologists, and others sympathetic to the Yąnomamö to leave the area. The miners then invaded the area in force—soon reaching approximately 40,000 in number.

It didn't take very long for the first ugly incident to occur: A group of miners clashed with a group of Yąnomamö near Mucajai, killing four of them with guns and desecrating their bodies. One miner was also killed by the Yąnomamö.

In a short time, over 100 airstrips were cleared deep in Yąnomamöland to support the mining operations. Scores of mining camps popped up almost overnight. The miners used destructive hydraulic pumps that sucked the river bottoms of their gold-bearing ore, passed it through troughs into which toxic mercury compounds were added to extract the gold from the mud, and let the poisoned residue flow freely back into the rivers. They occasionally raped Yąnomamö women and shot their men and children. The diary of a Brazilian gold miner, parts of which appeared in Venezuelan newspapers in 1990, recites

---

2. I met John in 1975 when I was on the faculty of the Pennsylvania State University. He had just entered the graduate program in anthropology at the University of Pittsburgh. Saffirio was familiar with my published work and wanted my advice and recommendations for his doctoral thesis. I suggested a topic and agreed to help him design the field research needed for his thesis. After he finished his fieldwork, I helped him code and analyze his data with computer programs I had developed for similar aspects of my own work. He completed his Ph.D. (Saffirio, 1985) and we have been good friends and regular correspondents ever since. On my 1995 field trip to Brazil, John was my gracious host during my stay in Boa Vista, Brazil.

one hideous incident after another that his group of "socios" (partners) partici-pated in or witnessed as they moved from camp to camp over a large area of Yąnomamöland.[3] Many of the officials of the then President José Sarney's gov-ernment turned a blind eye to this tragedy and accommodated even the slightest demands of the mining interests.

Eventually President Sarney, and many other Brazilian officials, began to real-ize that their public declarations, assuring their own citizens and the world that they were taking measures to protect and guarantee the rights of the Yąnomamö, were being received with considerable skepticism and were being viewed against past similar Brazilian promises when native Amazonian peoples who were "in the way" of progress had simply been exterminated.[4] International outcry and con-demnation of the Brazilian government followed almost immediately. Too many people knew about, were enchanted by, and were seriously interested in the future of the Yąnomamö. For example, by 1987 hundreds of thousands of people had read earlier editions of this book and many began writing letters of complaint to Brazilian officials. Dozens of other publications by knowledgeable anthropologists contributed to their international visibility.

A new Brazilian president, Ferdinand Collor de Mello took office in early 1990. He visited the Yąnomamö region within weeks of inauguration and, while a large press corps photographed him and made sure his intentions were publicized, he dramatically assured the world that he was going to correct this tragedy and ordered the destruction of some of the 100 illegal airstrips cleared by the miners.

The number of miners in Yąnomamöland was reduced significantly shortly after Collor de Mello took office. Cautious international optimism about the future of the Brazilian Yąnomamö followed, but Collor's government then began delaying imple-mentation of crucial programs already set into law and was seemingly backing away from his highly publicized intentions to stop the destruction and legally assure the Yąnomamö of a continuous tract of land. His predecessors had set into motion a pro-gram to demarcate some 21 small, discontinuous "islands" in this area for the Yąnomamö, leaving the rest open for development. This kind of division of the region would have assured the cultural demise of the Brazilian Yąnomamö.

Only 14 of the airstrips were subsequently dynamited, and many of these were put back in operation shortly afterward. As 1990 wore on, miners again began to enter the region. By early 1991 thousands of illegal miners were again reported to have entered Brazilian Yąnomamöland. High-ranking members of Collor's government, especially military officers, were effective in their opposi-tion to removing the miners and delaying the demarcation of their lands by refusing to establish effective policies to prohibit mining in this area. Rules or programs announced in the capital Brasilia were often ignored or defiantly resisted by local politicians and police, numbers of whom were receiving

---

3. "Diario de un Garimpeiro," Temas, El Diario, 1 April 1990, pp. 25-31. Caracas.

4. In 1967, a Brazilian Air Force pilot casually told me of dropping bombs on uncon-tacted native villages in the Amazon basin whose residents were suspected of being hostile to Brazilian pioneers. Other researchers in the Brazilian Amazon basin have mentioned to me similar conversations with Brazilian Air Force pilots.

monetary compensation from mining interests. Eventually almost all of the miners were removed by the Brazilian government, but from time to time clandestine small groups would sneak in.

## Massacre at Hashimo-teri

A major and tragic incident took place in 1993. A group of Brazilian *garimpeiros* attacked and massacred 17 members of Hashimo-teri, a Yąnomamö village near the headwaters of the Orinoco River. International outrage and protest followed immediately. But there was something new and different about this incident: The Hashimo-teri were Venezuelan Yąnomamö, and for the first time in the gold rush, the Venezuelan authorities became involved, outraged at this flagrant violation of their national border by illegal Brazilian miners and the genocide of Venezuelan Yąnomamö.

The Brazilian authorities quickly initiated a formal investigation, but soon discovered, to their embarrassment, that the massacred village was in Venezuela. Acting Venezuelan President, Ramon Velasquez, immediately appointed a Permanent Presidential Commission to investigate the massacre. I was included in this commission and went to Venezuela in September 1993 to participate in the investigation at the request of the Venezuelan president. Some of the most depressing and shameful political machinations I have witnessed during my career soon followed as various groups, organizations, anthropologists, and government agencies in both Brazil and Venezuela began fighting with each other about who had the right and legitimate authority to conduct this highly visible investigation. By this time, the Salesian Missions in Venezuela were alarmed at the increasing secularization of authority in this region, a region over which they had traditionally enjoyed near-autocratic political control. They were outraged that they had not been commissioned by the president to take charge of the investigation and responded with extraordinary aggressiveness to neutralize and discredit the officially appointed commission with every means available to them—newspapers, magazines, television, radio, and hastily organized "public" protest demonstrations by groups of missionized Venezuelan Indians dependent on and loyal to them. I have discussed these remarkable incidents elsewhere (Chagnon, 1993a; 1993b; 1993c) and will not go into the political issues here. It would suffice to say that despite the fact that a large number of the some 25 Brazilian miners involved in this massacre were identified, to this date not one of them has been tried and convicted and none of them are in jail. Probably none of them ever will be brought to trial.[5]

As many as 1,100 Brazilian Yąnomamö may have died from new sicknesses introduced by the miners or from traditional maladies that became epidemic

---

5. Ironically, some anthropologists, NGOs, and Salesian missionaries seem to believe that my attempt to investigate this massacre at the invitation of the President of Venezuela was as reprehensible as the act of genocide by the *garimpeiros* (Turner, 1994; Cappelletti, 1994. cf. Fox, 1994 and Wolf, 1994). This reaction underscores the importance of the political stakes involved in who speaks for and represents the Yąnomamö and, putatively in this case, their human rights.

following the influx of so many miners. For most Brazilian Yąnomamö groups, major aspects of their traditional culture and social organization have been forever changed, particularly those sensitive to the traumatic alterations in the demographic underpinnings of their marriage, kinship, and descent systems. The largely uncontacted Yąnomamö villages in the adjacent areas of Venezuela where I am currently working are in jeopardy because of their proximity to the Brazilian border. In a few villages that I visited in 1990 and 1991, I found suspicious shortages of children in some age categories, most likely the result of epidemic sicknesses in the immediate past. Most of the contacts these Venezuelan Yąnomamö groups have are with mission posts in Venezuela, but they are close enough to more remote villages known to have occasional indirect contacts with Brazilian miners to raise the possibility that they may now be exposed to sicknesses coming from the mining areas in Brazil. To my immense relief, the recent demographic data I collected in the more remote villages indicate that they are yet demographically intact and have not recently been hit by major epidemics (see Figure 8.3).

In contrast to the Brazilian policies, the Venezuelan government, under the leadership of then-President Carlos Andres Pérez, began developing exemplary policies toward the Yąnomamö and their neighbors and the tropical forests within which they dwell. President Pérez took steps in June 1991 to protect the territory that most of the Venezuelan Yąnomamö occupy by introducing legislation defining a very large area of T. F. Amazonas—32,000 mi$^2$— as either a "special biosphere reserve" or as a "national park" that will presumably be closed to mining and other development programs. Signing of this legislation was officially announced on August 1, 1991, by the Venezuelan government.

In late 1991, the constant stream of depressing news about what was happening to the Brazilian Yąnomamö took a dramatic turn for the better. President Collor de Mello signed legislation requiring the demarcation of a continuous tract of land embracing some 36,000 mi$^2$ (94,000 km$^2$), an area containing virtually all of the Brazilian Yąnomamö (James Brooke, *New York Times*, 18 November 1991), guaranteeing them exclusive rights to their traditional lands. He did so against powerful opposition from high-ranking Brazilian military officials, governors of the States of Roraima and Amazonas, and mining and economic development groups. A disaster of staggering proportions was averted: The Brazilian military, in a last-ditch attempt, wanted to exclude a strip of land approximately 12 miles wide along the entire border with Venezuela and turn it into a "security zone." Their reason was to prevent what they felt was a near-certain possibility that the Venezuelan and Brazilian Yąnomamö, if they were permitted to hold contiguous lands on both sides of the border, would rise up and declare themselves a separate "state," motivated to do so by communist-inspired agitators who want to "internationalize" the Brazilian Amazon.

In 1995, officials of the National Brazilian Indian Foundation (FUNAI) assured me, in Boa Vista, that no more than a few hundred illegal miners were still in the Yąnomamö area and they were systematically attempting to find them and expel them. Since then reports that larger numbers of illegal Brazilian miners have begun to enter the area have been reported in newspapers in Brazil and Venezuela.

# KĄOBAWÄ'S VILLAGE

It should be clear that broad generalizations about culture change among the many Yąnomamö groups are not possible. I will therefore comment on some of the changes that have occurred in the area where Kąobawä's village is found to illustrate more general issues by focusing on a single instance.

I was unable to return to the Yąnomamö between 1976 and 1984 when many important changes took place. When I resumed my field studies in 1985 I was stunned by what I saw. But it was like trying to make sense of a motion picture film when you could look at only the first few frames and the last few—and have to reconstruct what took place in between. Kąobawä, by then an aging but very dignified man, continued to be the respected leader in what remained of his once much larger and powerful village, Bisaasi-teri. The Protestant missionaries had long-since withdrawn from Kąobawä's area because of pressure from the Salesians. Since this part of Venezuela was still a federal territory and not a state, different laws are obtained here. The Venezuelan government enacted legislation in 1915—*The Law of the Missions*—that gave the Salesian Missions a large measure of secular authority in this area. They would be responsible for the normal social services (health, welfare, education, etc.) the state usually provides to citizens in more populated areas, but in Amazonas there were only Indians and it was cheaper to allow the Missions to deal with these matters there. Thus, the Salesian Bishop in Puerto Ayacucho, the capital of the territory, had as much civil authority as the appointed territorial governor in many things.

Despite the fact that Venezuelan law guarantees freedom of religion, the Protestant missionaries in T. F. Amazonas have always had to cope with the fact that the Salesian Bishop had far-reaching civil authority and that Salesian Bishops have consistently regarded Protestant missions as an obstacle to their efforts to convert the Yąnomamö to Catholicism. Press stories alleging fantastic conspiracies involving the *Evangélicos* (Protestants, many from the United States) routinely appeared all during the years of my research to discredit them and turn popular opinion against them. This is relatively easy to do in a predominantly Catholic country that has also periodically been strongly anti-American, especially in intellectual and academic circles. The *Evangélicos* were allegedly teaching the Yąnomamö how to speak English, not Spanish, and presumably trying to make them a "colony" of Yankee Imperialism. They were accused of clearing secret airstrips and flying unimaginable quantities of precious, rare minerals out of the country in the tiny Cessna planes that carried their personnel into and out of their mission posts. On one occasion, the National Guards arrested one of them because he was wearing an old pair of khaki fatigues—accusing him of planning a military revolution among the Indians. While some Brazilians feared the Yąnomamö would revolt and create a communist state, some Venezuelans feared they might become a capitalistic one, perhaps taking orders from Washington.

The Salesian missionaries viewed Kąobawä with a kind of paternalism, largely as just a former leader who was too fixed in his ways and too old to change, incapable of dealing with the new world they were helping to create. Younger men were emerging as leaders, their prominence being determined by new, non-traditional factors, such as ability to speak Spanish, doing personal favors for the local missionary, willingness to give up freedoms and traditions, willingness to enter a market economy, and exchange labor or products for material items from the outside world. These young men were, as a consequence, given exciting opportunities to travel to the territorial capital, to Caracas, and occasionally, to other countries. There, they would meet our kinds of political leaders, local anthropologists, directors of various government programs, and so forth, and become known to them, thereby increasing their familiarity with and control over the exotic skills needed to deal with the outside world. In Kąobawä's area, these emerging young leaders invariably come from one of the three Salesian mission posts and have been carefully groomed for these roles. The exotic experiences and privileges these young leaders have been afforded by the Salesians who selected them enable them to take a commanding lead in the process of the developing native leadership directions. Traditional leaders, even men like Kąobawä, are now almost totally disregarded in the process of encouraging the emergence of local leaders because they do not understand the rapidly changing situation or they consider it to be unimportant by the standards with which they have been traditionally familiar. Older leaders did not anticipate what would happen to leadership patterns when the younger men began learning Spanish and spending large amounts of time with the missionaries. The young men, when these changes first began, were viewed by the older men merely as youngsters who were able to coerce or persuade the foreigners into giving everyone more fishhooks or machetes. To a large extent, that is how these young men initially behaved: They had a kind of Robin Hood role—take from the "rich" missionaries and give to the "poor" members of the community.

Now, the stakes are much higher; acquiring near-exclusive political power in a political arena unfamiliar to leaders like Kąobawä. Unfortunately, the motives and actions of some of these young political contenders no longer appear to be community well-being. For example, a particularly ambitious man named "César" Dimanauwä was appointed as "commisario" of the Mavaca area in 1985, an official government position entailing a salary and considerable political authority by Venezuelan law: He was a kind of justice of the peace and policeman. Dimanauwä was not reluctant to use the police power his position guaranteed him to punish and harass those around him he disliked. I had to dissuade him from calling the Venezuelan National Guards from Puerto Ayacucho to arrest Kąobawä and others in his village and put them in jail. The provocation was that a group of visitors to Kąobawä's village from a distant, highly acculturated village on the Padamo River claimed that someone in Kąobawä's village stole some money from him while he was visiting there. César Dimanauwä's rather Draconian intent in this was probably motivated by the fact that Kąobawä's group was bent on punishing him for leading a gang rape on a young girl married to Kąobawä's brother's son a year earlier.

One of the most dramatic changes I noted when I resumed my fieldwork in Kąobawä's area in 1985 was the acceleration of village fissioning to the point that some Yąnomamö families were living in separate, square nuclear family houses. Apart from these scattered houses, there were 12 "villages" at Mavaca where there had initially been just two traditional *shabonos* as described in this monograph. These 12 villages were spread out along the banks of the Orinoco, mostly downstream from the Salesian Mission where the Mavaca enters the Orinoco. In 1985, Ķobawä's group, with 111 people, was still the largest Mavaca community and the most conservative. For example, nobody in his group owned an outboard motor and dugout canoe because they apparently resisted being caught up in and becoming dependent on S.U.Y.A.O.,[6] the name for the Y̧nomamö "cooperatives" the Salesians helped establish. To do so would have meant communal efforts to manufacture goods such as baskets, bows, arrows, and commercial production of manioc flour, and putting these products in the cooperative for community credit. Eventually the community would "earn" a motor that would be owned by the whole village, regardless of who did the productive work. Members of Ķobawä's group preferred to remain individuals, which seemed to be interpreted by the missionaries as collective "laziness."

I wanted to buy Ķobawä's group a boat and motor in 1987, but the missionaries urged me not to—they felt it would interfere in their attempts to get the Y̧nomamö to recognize the value and necessity of engaging in productive work to obtain a desired material object. We compromised: The missionaries allowed me to deposit $500 into the "village account," the members of the village then had to work to provide items until their account was large enough to enable them to purchase a communal motor—approximately another $500. Much to the chagrin of the missionaries, Ķobawä's group whittled the $500 credit away by purchasing communal gasoline so they could take long hunting trips or visit distant allies in boats and motors they managed to borrow from others.

Raymond Hames, my coresearcher, and I later gave a small outboard motor to one of the men in Ķobawä's village as payment for the several months he worked for us in 1985, 1986, and 1987. This motor became, in effect, the village motor.

There appear to be two reasons why the larger villages are chronically fissioning into increasingly smaller subgroups—at mission locations and in adjacent regions where the missionaries now visit.

One of the reasons is that warfare is diminishing and is less and less a worry to those who live at the mission posts. The Y̧nomamö at the missions now have increasing access to shotguns and ammunition, which reduces the probability that they will be raided by enemies who have only bows and arrows.

In this area, shotguns were originally obtained from the Salesian Missionaries or employees of the mission, but in recent years many have entered the area from Brazil via a long trading network involving several isolated, intermediate villages in the headwaters of the Mavaca and in the Siapa River basin. Even more recently some shotguns have come via the S.U.Y.A.O. cooperatives, which began stocking them in about 1989 but soon withdrew them after it was learned they were being used in killings. Finally, two Venezuelan National Guard forts were established in the area after the Brazilian gold rush began for purposes of border security. One of them, at the Salesian Mission at Platanal, became a source of some shotguns for the Y̧nomamö in that area.

---

6. *Shabonos Unidos del los Y̧nomamö del Alto Orinoco* (United Y̧nomamö Villages of the Upper Orinoco). The Salesians helped the Y̧nomamö develop this cooperative and, for the first several years of its existence, it was operated out of mission facilities. At Mavaca, it was still being run out of the Salesian Mission in 1987, but it was only a few years old at that time. In 1988, it was moved into a separate building near the mission.

Construction of a third military base was initiated in 1991 at Ocamo, but it was ultimately abandoned before it was completed. In an indirect sense, the Brazilian gold rush has had the effect of provoking the Venezuelan government to locate military personnel among the Yąnomamö that will increase health—and other—problems. The military post at Platanal was subsequently shut down. As of 1996, the only military installation in the heartland of the Venezuelan Yąnomamö is at a place called Parima B, adjacent to the Brazilian border where there is also a New Tribes Mission post and some 600 Yąnomamö ... the largest single concentration of Yąnomamö in Venezuela. As mentioned above, Kąobawä's area—the Salesian Mission at Boca Mavaca—is a close second with approximately 500 Yąnomamö inhabitants.

Shotguns now give those at the missions a tremendous advantage in fights with their distant neighbors, who have only bows and arrows. Thus, they live with a greater degree of security at mission locations and their neighbors do not raid them for fear of being shot with guns and, equally important, fear of being outflanked in their retreat by pursuers who can get ahead of them because they have outboard motors and canoes. Thus, the need to live in larger, nucleated *shabonos* for security is disappearing and mission Yąnomamö are abandoning their larger, more communal *shabonos* in favor of smaller, individual dwellings.

Unfortunately, the shotguns are not used only for passive deterrence or for hunting. Significant numbers of Yąnomamö in the remote villages are being shot and killed by raiders from mission villages who, now that they have an arms advantage, invent reasons to get "revenge" on distant groups, some of which have had no historical relationships with them.

It should not be assumed that the missionaries have provided shotguns or ammunition to the Yąnomamö to provoke or encourage their use in warfare—to which the Salesians and all missionaries are adamantly opposed. Indeed, the Yąnomamö assiduously conceal this information from the missionaries and insist that they only use the guns for hunting. On the other hand, some missionaries refuse to believe that guns or ammunition originating at their missions are used to kill other Yąnomamö and often dismiss such information as "rumors." In the late 1960s, I began collecting genealogical data on a group of villages immediately east of the Salesian mission at Ocamo, then directed by Padre Luis Cocco (see film *Ocamo is My Town*, Asch & Chagnon, 1974). He had provided a number of shotguns to the Yąnomamö at his mission. As my genealogical work progressed, I discovered that a number of men in the remote villages had been recently killed with shotguns by raiders from the Ocamo mission. I immediately paid a visit to Padre Cocco and drew his attention to this. At first he denied that people from his village were using shotguns to kill others. He was disturbed and upset that I should suggest such a thing. I asked him to call a young Yąnomamö man over and to ask that man if it were true. He replied: "Si, Padre." To his credit, Padre Cocco immediately confiscated all the shotguns at his mission.[7]

---

7. He later returned them when the Yąnomamö promised they wouldn't use them to kill other Yąnomamö.

In 1967, while working in Brazil near the Mucajai mission, I discovered that Yąnomamö men from the Protestant mission there had recently attacked and killed a group of men from a remote village with shotguns. When I brought this to the attention of the missionaries, who continued to supply them with ammunition, they conceded that they, too, knew about this incident. They defensively added that of the seven or so shotguns used, at least one or two had been provided by a Brazilian trader who had visited there. They weren't sure which guns were used in the killings and were not going to ask. One said: "If we ask and find out that *our* guns were used, we would have to confiscate them from the Yąnomamö. They told us that if we did that, they would move away from the mission. You don't know how hard we worked to establish our mission here. My husband carried our kerosene refrigerator on his back from the top of that mountain over there where the cargo plane dropped it off!"

In 1990, one of the remote villages, Hiomöta-teri, was treacherously attacked by "friendly" neighbors who had just formed an alliance with Salesian Mission Yąnomamö who had shotguns: They shot and killed two men and abducted seven women on the justification that members of the isolated village "failed to deliver dogs they had promised." Several of these women are living in Mavaca now. Later that year two more Hiomöta-teri youths were shot and killed in broad daylight while visiting a village near the Salesian satellite mission at Mavakita.

I was further angered and depressed to discover a number of recent shotgun killings in other extremely remote villages I have recently started working in, villages that are many days' walk from the mission groups that are now raiding them. The traveling distance has been greatly reduced by the use of motorized canoes for at least some portions of the trip. The circumstances surrounding most shotgun killings are well outside the traditional patterns of Yąnomamö warfare.

There is a second reason for fissioning into smaller communities or single-family households, in addition to the military security provided by the shotguns provide. This has to do with material possessions such as machetes, cooking pots, axes, clothing, and flashlights, and what it now takes to obtain them: hard work, selling labor. The first step is when large, traditional *shabonos* start to divide into "long houses," arranged in a circle like a subdivided *shabono*. These smaller residential units are walled on all sides to insure the occupants a large degree of privacy, totally different from the open, traditional *shabonos* where everything is visible and highly public. The Yąnomamö can more easily conceal their possessions in these walled structures so they do not have to give them to people from other villages who come to visit—and to beg for these items. Their willingness to forgo their cultural tradition of obligatory generosity with visitors is the result of the subtle process that is making them economic consumers at mission posts.

Initially, the missionaries generously gave these exotic items away, usually freely or, at least, with trivial reciprocity required. Then the missionaries began preferentially giving them to just the more important men or members of their families to encourage their cooperation. For example, as described in Chapters 4 and 5, Kąobawä's rival, Hontonawä (Paruriwä), was persuaded to fission from Kąobawä's group in 1968 and move across the river to the "Catholic" side, bringing some 100 people with him. A Catholic priest arrived there in 1965 and, to lure Hontonawä's group away from the Protestants, offered him and some of his prominent male followers shotguns and outboard motors if they would move. Over the next few years the children in Hontonawä's group learned Spanish at this mission and, now as young men, are emerging as the leaders there, and old Hontonawä, like Kąobawä, is no longer in charge and no longer enjoys the favor or material privileges that got him to move in the first place. Similarly, the initial favor and prominence enjoyed by Hĳoduwä,[8] the headman at the Ocamo mission, followed the same pattern. He is the Yąnomamö leader discussed by Padre Luis Cocco as "Capitan" in the film *Ocamo is My Town* listed at the end of this book. Padre Cocco was replaced at Ocamo in about 1974 by younger Salesians with a different policy, who focused on cultivating new leaders among the younger men there who had learned some Spanish. In 1985, when I saw Hĳoduä for the first time in 10 years, he almost wept. My presence reminded him of the good old days when Padre Cocco was in charge and he was the undisputed leader of the village. He told me, in the most peculiar mixture of Spanish and Yąnomamö I have heard, that he was now very sad and "*pobrecito*" because the new missionary did not respect him or freely give him the expensive material things he had previously enjoyed under Padre Cocco's regime.

Gradually, individuals had to do work to get desirable items—usually days of labor, such as hauling sand from the river during the dry season for making cement blocks used in construction of mission facilities. Today, as in "free lunches," there is no such thing as a free machete and everyone must invest a considerable amount of work to produce items that are equal in value, or engage in labor to that value. In addition, the number of items the Mavaca (and other missionized) Yąnomamö now perceive as "needs" has increased and includes some very expensive things, like shotguns, ammunition, boats, motors, gasoline, spare parts, tools, radios, tape players, watches, kerosene lanterns, and powerful head lamps with rechargeable lead-acid batteries. Quite understandably, individuals who have worked hard to obtain these things are becoming more and more reluctant to give their hard-earned possessions away to casual visitors. They can no longer replace them by simply asking the missionary for more.

Another far-reaching and related change is taking place at some of the mission posts, especially at Mavaca and Ocamo. Large numbers of Yąnomamö, sometimes whole communities, are moving to the mission in order to be closer to the source of material goods. When I published the first edition of this monograph in 1968, there were approximately 225 Yąnomamö at Mavaca, all related to each other and all from the same original village (save for the abducted women their group included). My 1987 census of the Mavaca group put the population at 485 individuals distributed in 12 separate, small "villages" and a few individual or extended family houses. Much of the increase in size was due to the immigration of several whole groups that formerly lived elsewhere, and also to the immigration of numbers of individuals from other distant villages.

---

8. This man is also known as "Sixto" or "Sisto" locally and in occasional publications about the Yąnomamö of the Ocamo region.

The process of "peasantization" is starting here. The community is becoming less and less self-sufficient in an economic sense, and is increasingly comprised of non-related or distantly related people. As this happens, new social problems are appearing, especially the widespread occurrence of theft—both among the Yąnomamö themselves and especially from foreigners who visit these places. The local original inhabitants at some mission villages complain openly about this as well, resenting the fact that so many strange Yąnomamö appear there (often at the invitation of the missionaries), camp for several days, beg food from them, and just before leaving, steal anything they can. In 1990 and 1991, despite the efforts of some of my Yąnomamö friends at the Ocamo mission to protect my possessions, two very expensive solar panels, one very expensive tape recorder, and a variety of other personal possessions of mine were stolen when I spent a few nights there. On one of my recent trips I woke at 3:00 a.m. in time to catch a young visiting Yąnomamö sneaking out of my hut with my $3,000 Toshiba computer! He probably thought it was a radio or tape recorder and when he discovered it wasn't, probably would have thrown it—and all the data in the hard drive—in the river.

## Reduction and Concentration of Yąnomamö Villages

The 1915 Venezuelan *Law of the Missions* authorized Catholic Missions to "attract and reduce" Indians to mission posts. Similar policies have historically characterized Spanish colonization of the New World—*de jure* or *de facto*. "Reduced" Indians lived at *Reducciones*.

The Salesian missionaries in Venezuela's Amazon area have been, for many years, encouraging the more remote Yąnomamö villages to move to more accessible areas on navigable rivers, or to a handful of large settlements where they can educate, transform, evangelize, and "civilize" them more efficiently. They had only limited success in these efforts until about 1975. Sometimes they succeeded in persuading a whole village to move to a more accessible area, but sometimes they managed to persuade only a fraction of the group to do so. In the early 1970s, the Salesians at Mavaca began visiting some of the remote villages in the upper Mavaca. As mentioned in Chapter 7, they persuaded a small fraction of the much larger Mishimishimaböwei-teri to fission and move far down the Mavaca River where they could be easily reached by motorized boat in a few hours. That group became known as the Haoyaböwei-teri. The Salesian missionaries then established a "satellite" post there, Mavakita, which subsequently became the operation point from which the effort to attract and reduce other remote villages continues to this day. Thus began the process by which the very isolated villages of the Mavaca headwaters began to have sustained contact with the Salesian missions, villages whose only contact with the outside world was my nearly annual trips into their communities where I would spend a month or two on each visit.

When I returned to the Mavaca area after this 10-year absence in 1985 with my coworker, Raymond Hames, we planned to go immediately into the headwaters of the Mavaca River to resume work I had begun with the Mishimishimaböwei-teri and their relatives, the Kedebaböwei-teri, still very large and very isolated groups. The Salesian missionaries at Mavaca informed us, with considerable confidence, that such a trip would not be necessary. They said they had persuaded both groups to make very long moves out to the lower Mavaca and settle at their satellite mission post, Mavakita, reachable in three to five hours, depending on the kind of motorized boat used. I was unaware of the Mavakita mission post until then. They assured us that both of these large groups were already en route to Mavakita to join the Haoyaböwei-teri, the small faction of the Mishimishimaböwei-teri they had persuaded to move there earlier.

Hames and I went to Mavakita and began the 1985 work there. He had never worked in this area before and was looking forward to documenting the contrast with Yąnomamö groups in the Padamo he had worked among in 1974–1975. A few of the Kedebaböwei-teri did visit Haoyaböwei-teri and were excited to see me again after a 10-year absence. They spent a day or two and then returned to their distant village, several days' walk inland. No Mishimishimaböwei-teri showed up. I suspect that both groups intended to move closer to the Salesian Mission, but my unanticipated return after a 10-year absence might have tipped the balance and caused them to change their minds about moving. The military risks were high if they moved closer to the Salesian Mission at Bisaasi-teri, but that was now the only place for them to get a regular supply of steel tools. It is possible that my return unintentionally threw a monkey wrench into Salesian plans to attract and reduce these groups to one of their accessible mission posts.

We left Mavakita shortly afterwards and went into the headwaters of the Mavaca, where we found the Mishimishimaböwei-teri—near the same site I had last seen them 10 years earlier. They had numbered about 270 people during the period from 1968, when I first contacted them, to 1974, the last time I visited them. Now they numbered only 188 people, a reduction mainly due to the fission that took some of them to Haoyaböwei-teri where the Mavakita mission post was established. The Kedebaböwei-teri (164 people in 1987) told me that they had given up waiting for my annual returns and getting the medicines I always brought, along with the basic trade goods they desired. They said that is why they were considering a move to Mavakita or to a site on the lower Mavaca so they could get these items from the Salesian missionaries. Neither group moved to Mavakita as the Salesian missionaries said they would in 1985, although the Kedebaböwei-teri were later persuaded to move out to a navigable portion of the Mavaca River in 1987. Hames and I worked among them in their new location in 1987 just as they were beginning to occupy it. I visited them again in 1990 at this site. They were complaining about increasing sickness and their disappointment that the missionaries were not bringing the medicines they promised, one of the advantages that was supposed to have accrued from their move to a navigable portion of the Mavaca River.

**Increased Contact and Sickness.**   The mortality statistics in Kedebaböwei-teri between 1987 and 1992 are tragically instructive. In 1985 when I learned that the Salesians were urging them to move out to a navigable stretch of the Mavaca River, I was annoyed and concerned. This would unnecessarily subject the Kedebaböwei-teri to the acculturation policies of the Salesian Missions. The Salesians could not possibly "serve" another village this large, this remote, and this unacculturated, given how many other villages they were simultaneously trying to acculturate with the few personnel at their disposal. By now the Salesians had trained a number of young men to work for them as motor operators, cooks, and sometime school teachers. When these young men, usually wielding shotguns, arrived in motorized canoes in more remote villages while I was there, they usually lorded over their more "primitive" peers and were quite arrogant with them. Moving to a navigable stretch of the Mavaca exposed the Kedebaböwei-teri to chronic contact with the outside world, enough to cause health problems, but not enough contact to provide reliable and effective health services—or other alleged benefits promised to them by the missionaries.

In 1987 I found the Kedebaböwei-teri camped along the Mavaca River, living in a temporary village of three-cornered *yanos*—temporary huts normally used while camping. They had cleared and planted a huge garden prior to moving out, but it was almost entirely yuca (manioc), a crop that normally accounts for only about 10 percent of their cultivated plots. The Salesian brother had urged them to plant yuca so they could sell it to the mission after they processed it into manioc flour with machines he would provide them. Thus, before they had even cleared and planted gardens for their subsistence needs they were contracted by the Salesian Mission to produce refined food to exchange for Mission-provided goods.

I was also angered to see that the brother had commissioned them to construct a "school" at their new location, even before the Kedebaböwei-teri had built their *shabono*. The "school" was a large, open hut with a double-gabled roof and equipped with tables and chairs. Attached to the back of it was a makeshift storage area for the food the brother planned to use to entice the children to attend classes: oatmeal, rice, milk, sugar, and salt, things that cause Yąnomamö teeth to rot and fall out. It didn't take long for fighting over these essentially unguarded foods to occur. In early 1988, a violent club fight occurred in which a young man named Maroko was beaten to death with a club over accusations of theft of the "school food."

There were 164 people in Kedebaböwei-teri when they moved out to the Mavaca in 1987. Between 1987 and 1990 five adult deaths occurred at this site, not extraordinary by "aboriginal" standards. Between 1990 and 1992, another 10 deaths occurred, a higher mortality rate than normal. Increased contact with the outside was affecting their health and mortality rates. In January 1992, when I returned for a brief visit to this area, the alarming news reached me that a major epidemic had struck the Kedebaböwei-teri: 21 people died within the span of a week or so just before I arrived, all of them mature to old adults, most of them males, and most of these the most prominent leaders in the village. Sibarariwä, the fabled headman discussed earlier, was among them, along with the headman of the village, Örasiyaborewä. The rest of the Kedebaböwei-teri fled into the jungle to escape the epidemic, but it was probably too late. About a year later a Venezuelan medical doctor who was with me in 1992 told me that almost the entire population died. I have been unable to return there to verify his claim.

Minimally, in the span of approximately one week, nearly 14 percent of a "largely unacculturated Yanomamö village" perished from sicknesses that they were exposed to simply because they were persuaded to move out to a navigable stretch of a large river where they could be more easily acculturated by missionaries.

These are not simply mortality statistics to me. These are men and women I had known for 20 years, friends I had visited and revisited repeatedly, deaths that probably would not have happened if the Kedebaböwei-teri had remained inland and outside the range of mission contact. Ironically, Sibarariwä, who had been extremely aloof with me for nearly 20 years, had suddenly become warm and friendly with me the year before. He was then quite old. He called me aside and told me in great earnest that he would like to "tell me the truth" about the entire history of the Aramamisi-teri. He knew I had been asking other older informants about them, and he insisted that he knew more about them than any living person—and he was probably right. I was looking forward to working with him, and touched by his sincerity after watching him watch me skeptically for 20 years. What the world might eventually know about the history of the Aramamisi-teri population will be much less because of his senseless death. He assured me that he and all other "Shamatari" are ultimately "Aramamisi-teri" and he intended to explain why by providing the genealogical and historical informa-tion that would demonstrate this.[9]

The most depressing aspect of this tragic epidemic is that the Salesian mis-sionaries at Mavaca, just a few hours by boat from Kedebaböwei-teri, learned about the epidemic shortly after it began but did not send someone there to investigate it. Yet they were the ones who urged the Kedebaböwei-teri to move out to a site on the navigable Mavaca River ... where they could more easily obtain medicines if they got sick.

The Salesians also persuaded the Washäwä-teri, a large faction of the tradition-ally elusive Iwahikoroba-teri, to move close to Mavakita, to a navigable stretch of the Washäwä kä u, a tributary of the Mavaca River. This put them into semi-regular contact with the outside world for the first time in their history.

They moved to this new location just prior to my 1985 visit. I made a cen-sus of their village in 1985 and repeated it in 1987 and 1991. Between 1987 and 1991 they sustained a mortality rate of 15 percent, one of the highest mortality rates for the 16 villages to which I compared them.

Figure 8.1 summarizes the mortality data for the 17 villages I censused in 1987 and then, in 1991, determined who in these villages had died during the four-year period. The rates range from 0 to approximately 25 percent.

---

9. By late 1990, I had enough genealogical data from both Shamatari informants like Dedeheiwä and older men and women in the new villages I was then studying in the Siapa headwaters to independently conclude that the Shamatari were indeed part of a larger population that included many groups currently known as Aramamisi-teri and had separated from them (Chagnon, 1991).

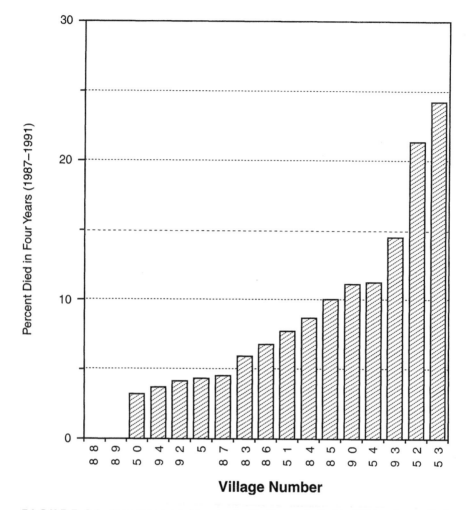

**FIGURE 8.1** Four-year mortality rates in 17 villages studied in 1987 and restudied in 1991. An exhaustive census of 17 Yąnomamö villages was made in 1987. There were 1,047 residents at that time. In 1991, each village was reinvestigated to determine who had died during the intervening four-year period. The numbers of deaths in each village are expressed in percentages of each village's total population. Village numbers are shown on the X-axis and four-year mortality on the Y-axis.

If the villages are grouped into three categories that reflect their degree of contact with the missions, a disturbing pattern emerges (Figure 8.2). Those living at the missions have a low four-year mortality rate (about 5 percent), as do those living in remote areas (about 6.5 percent). But those with just intermediate contact, such as the Kedebaböwei-teri and Washäwä-teri just mentioned, suffered nearly a 20 percent mortality rate over the same period of time. The reason for this unusually high mortality rate appears to be that they had enough irregular contact to be exposed to new sicknesses, but were sufficiently remote from mission medical services that they died before word of their sickness spread and help

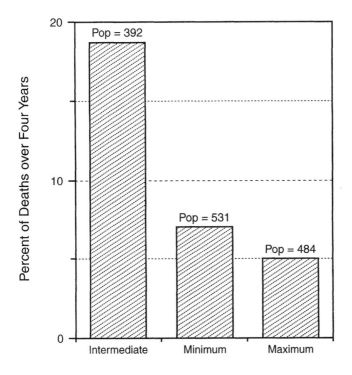

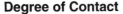

**Degree of Contact**

**FIGURE 8.2** Four-year mortality rates by degree of contact with Salesion mission posts in 17 villages. The data from Figure 8.1 were arranged into three categories characterizing the relative degree of contact each village had with mission posts. "Maximum" contact describes villages whose members live at a Salesian mission post (Boca Mavaca only). "Minimum" contact describes villages in remote areas that are sporadically visited by residents of the Salesian missions (Platanal and Boca Mavaca). "Intermediate" contact describes villages that are easily reachable by motorized boats, sometimes followed by relatively short walks, from Salesian missions (Platanal and Boca Mavaca). Numbers of 1987 residents in each category are shown above each of the bars. The villages with intermediate contact suffered the highest mortality rates during the four-year period.

arrived—if, indeed, any help was sent. No help was sent to the Kedebaböwei-teri in the 1992 epidemic just described, although the Salesians were aware of "rumors" that they were sick. In fact, it was the Salesian Missionaries who initially told me and my medical companions about these "rumors."

The low mortality rates for mission villages is probably due to the fact that they have been in chronic contact with outsiders for 30 years and have lived through most of the health shock that initial contact produces. Perhaps more important is the fact that they have immediate access to medical attention at the mission. However, some of the mission groups, especially those living immediately downstream from the

Mavaca Mission, had somewhat higher death rates for the same period, possibly due to water-borne contamination. A great deal of pollution has been dumped directly into the Orinoco in front of the mission settlement at Mavaca, much of it by employees of the Venezuelan Malaria control station that was located there for over 25 years but was abandoned in about 1988. I bathed at this site several times in 1986 and had to wear shoes to avoid getting injured by the large quantity of broken glass, tin cans, discarded outboard motor parts, sheet metal roofing, and other civilized debris that littered the once clean, sandy bottom of this stretch of the Orinoco River.

**Age/Sex Distributions and Mortality Patterns.**   Much of my previous and current demographic fieldwork has important epidemiological dimensions and can be used to develop informed and effective health delivery programs by those responsible for the future health conditions among the Yąnomamö…if they choose to do so.

There are two ways that the field researcher can reach some reasonable conclusions about the effects of diseases on populations such as the Yąnomamö. The data summarized in Figures 8.1 and 8.2 is just one way to do this. It entails taking a census at two different points in time and determining on a name-by-name basis who died between the two censuses.

The second way to reach conclusions about unusually high mortality rates is to examine age and sex distributions, i.e., how many people of each sex there are in, for example, 10-year age categories. This is probably the most reliable method for detecting high mortality rates in villages for which you do not have a previous census and therefore cannot accurately identify who has died in the recent past. There are several reasons why getting this kind of "historical" data is difficult in the case of the Yąnomamö. First, the Yąnomamö are most reluctant to tell you about recently deceased individuals, so, unless they have been married or have produced offspring, you often do not even know they existed. For example, if an 18-year-old unmarried girl dies, her existence will not be uncovered as "wife" of someone or "mother" of someone and your informants are unlikely to volunteer information about her, that is, "so-and-so" had a "young sister" who died three years ago. Therefore, in a new census of a group you have not visited before, you always miss some individuals, including people who may have died just a few weeks or months before your initial visit. Second, epidemics usually kill very young children and very old adults. You will probably be able to detect the dead adults, since they will have had children and therefore appear as "father" or "mother" of other people who survived. You might even be able to get a reasonable estimate of that adult's year of death—if he or she has a young child. A male parent could not have died much before the birth of the child, and the mother certainly would have died after the child's birth. But, in general, you are unlikely to be able to accurately determine when the adults died—the Yąnomamö are not able to keep accurate track of time, at least not accurately enough for some kinds of demographic and epidemiological studies. You will probably never be able to get reliable data on deceased children, since the Yąnomamö try to push these tragic memories out of their consciousness and, after a few years, forget about deaths of many young children. While the specific mothers may remember their deceased children, it is imprudent and offensive to ask a woman directly about them and you must rely on other informants and work very cautiously and discreetly, but these informants always forget some of the dead children.

In the absence of a previous census, the most reasonable way to get a feeling for unusually high recent mortality rates is to use age and sex distribution data. The Yąnomamö population is typical of the primitive world in that there are large numbers of children and relatively few adults. Thus, a very large fraction of the members of a typical village or group of villages would be children under the age of 11 years—usually between 30 percent and 40 percent of the entire population. When you find a village or group of villages where this is not true, there is reason to believe that something drastic and recent has happened to remove these children. This assumes, of course, that your sample size is modestly large, for there are wide fluctuations in numbers of individuals in various age categories in villages that are very small.

Figures 8.3 and 8.4 show age and sex distributions in two different clusters of Yąnomamö villages that I recently visited and in which I made complete censuses.

The first cluster includes eight villages with a total (pooled) population of 797 people. This is a "normal" looking age/sex distribution for the Yąnomamö in that a very large fraction of the individuals are children between birth and 10 years—nearly 40 percent of the current population falls into this age category. Since under "normal" mortality conditions there is always a relatively high infant mortality rate in tribal populations, even in the absence of epidemics, the next age category is usually much smaller, as it is in this case: About 21 percent of the population falls between the ages of 11 and 20 years. Continued high mortality rates, even in the absence of epidemics, makes the successive age category smaller, and so on, giving the age/sex distribution diagram the shape of a "pyramid," very wide at the bottom and very small at the top. By comparison, the shape of the age/sex distribution in our own population looks more like the Washington

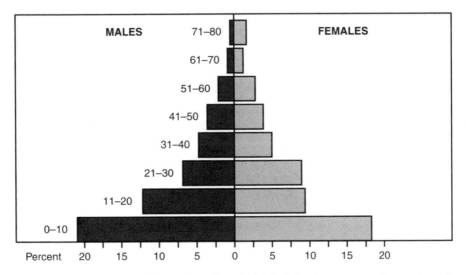

**FIGURE 8.3** Age/sex distribution of 797 individuals in eight remote villages studied in 1991. The villages show a "normal" population structure not affected by recent major epidemics.

Monument—but slightly wider at the bottom than at the top. This is because with advances in medical knowledge and technology we have radically reduced mortality among infants and young children compared to the primitive world: Almost all children born in our population have a very high chance of surviving to a reasonably old age. This is not true in the primitive world.

Figure 8.3 is very similar in overall characteristics to the Yąnomamö population characteristics I have repeatedly documented under nonepidemic circumstances for the past 32 years. The villages on which Figure 8.3 is based are all in the remote Siapa basin and have had no direct contact with either missionaries or gold miners, although some individuals from most of these villages have walked to Brazil and have visited missions there—and probably gold miners in some cases. While they were, in 1992, still "demographically intact," in that they do not exhibit characteristics that suggest recent and severe epidemics, they are nevertheless in considerable danger, since they are at some risk of being exposed to new diseases at the mission posts they visit, which they might then bring back to their remote villages where a disease can spread and lead to high mortality rates. However, their isolation makes it unlikely that "missionized" Yąnomamö, especially in Brazil, will visit them very regularly and bring diseases with them, since the Yąnomamö visiting patterns usually entail "trade good-poor" villages visiting "trade good–rich" villages rather than vice versa, and Brazilian missionaries are unlikely to try to evangelize across the international border and illegally visit these remote villages. They are too remote for Venezuelan missions to reach at this moment…unless airstrips are cleared or helicopter transportation is used.

Figure 8.4 tells a very different and probably much unhappier story. It is also based on eight villages I censused in 1991, four of which I had censused in 1987 as well. The total population of these eight smaller villages is 474. The general shape of

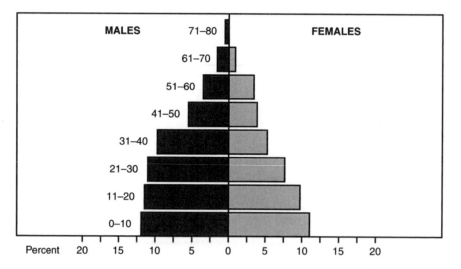

**FIGURE 8.4**  Age/sex distribution of 474 individuals in eight villages with "intermediate" contacts with the outside—studied in 1991. These villages show evidence of a major recent epidemic that caused many children to die.

the population pyramid is very different from that given in Figure 8.3: There are comparatively few children, especially in the age category birth to 10 years. This very strongly suggests that large numbers of children have died recently, that is, an epidemic (perhaps more than one) has hit them recently. In this case I have a previous complete census on four of the villages and know exactly who died in at least those four villages; these data confirm that higher-than-normal mortality rates have occurred in these villages in the past four years, especially among children. In fact, the four villages I censused in this group are also among those with high mortality rates due to "intermediate" contact discussed above (Figure 8.2). If we wanted to "guess" at how many children are missing (i.e., might have died) in Figure 8.4, we could do the following kind of calculation, which assumes that all the mortality caused by a hypothetical epidemic fell on children between birth and 10 years of age. We would want to know how many children there should be in those villages whose current age/sex distribution is given in Figure 8.4. In order for the population distribution shown in Figure 8.4 to look like the one shown in Figure 8.3, we would have to have 38.6 percent of the population be between birth and 10 years of age, but in fact only 23.0 percent of the population falls in that age category: Figure 8.4 seems to be missing about 15.6 percent of its children. We would have to add another 10.4 percent male children and 5.2 percent female children for Figure 8.4 to look like Figure 8.3 for the youngest age category. If we did that and recalculated the age/ sex distribution for Figure 8.4, the resulting figure would look much like the one shown in Figure 8.3—38.6 percent of the population would be below the age of 11 years and the proportions of the other ages and sexes would be reduced accordingly.

None of the eight villages whose age/sex characteristics are summarized in Figure 8.4 are in contact with Brazilian miners. They are all in the Shanishani drainage or in the Washäwä drainage and their only outside contact, which is sporadic, is with personnel (natives as well as non-natives) at the Salesian Missions at Mavaca and Platanal, the latter location also including a Venezuelan National Guard military contingent. Contact with foreigners at the Salesian Missions in Venezuela is the most likely explanation of the high mortality patterns in these groups.

These mortality patterns are probably characteristic of what happens when isolated tribesmen are exposed to contact with the outside world. There is usually a very high initial mortality pattern shortly after regular contact begins. This happened in the Upper Mavaca River in 1973 when regular visiting from the Mavaca Mission began (Chagnon & Melancon, 1984, describes and analyzes such an epidemic in the Upper Mavaca area). Mortality rates probably remain fairly high if the continued contact is sporadic and not accompanied by effective medical attention. Chronic contact, and the more reliable medical services this usually brings, gradually leads to the decline and then stabilization of mortality rates. While this pattern has probably been widespread and predictable where native peoples have come into initial contact with the outside world, it is not inevitable. For the Yąnomamö groups discussed here I am convinced that much of the high mortality in the villages with "intermediate" contact can be controlled or eliminated if effective health programs are put in place. If representatives of our culture, such as missionaries, are going to engage in sporadic contact with remote villages, they should be obliged to provide these groups with effective and reliable medical attention.

There is an irony in what the Venezuelan state and the Catholic Church are bringing about in the Yąnomamö area. Venezuela gave the Salesian Missions free reign to tend to the needs of their Amazon Indians, to attract and reduce them to their posts, and educate them to become citizens of their country. This process has exposed all Yąnomamö to new diseases that will continue to plague them. It has also caused them to become aware of and hungry for many exotic things in our culture, a culture that is unlikely to provide them with the same access to positions of dignity, prestige, and opportunity non-Indians have, and therefore they are unlikely to be able to purchase what it is that we caused them to want. The solution to these new "needs" and aspirations will cost money. Western civilization, motivated by the lofty but questionable goal of converting the "heathen" to make them God-fearing and more like us has given the missionaries the charge to go forth to do these noble deeds. They have succeeded, but these new souls have become not only marginal Christians, but marginal citizens with expensive social needs and expectations. The sword may follow the Bible, but the bursar follows both. Now almost everyone in on the original decisions wants someone else to pay for the costs that all of this entails, including the Salesian Missionaries who have helped accomplish all of these marvelous deeds. They have imposed Western culture on them without their advised consent and now want them to pay their own way into it, ideally with cash. The well-intended attempts by the Salesians to help the Yąnomamö establish "cooperatives" is, essentially, a program to make the Yąnomamö pay their own way into civilization (Chagnon, 1997). But "cooperatives" are too little, too late, and can never "pay" for the costs that this transition will entail. It won't take long for the increasingly civilized Yąnomamö to figure out that they can take a great leap forward by selling access to the gold beneath their feet to obtain what the missionaries, acting on behalf of the state, taught them to want but won't let them have…unless they pay in cash. Nor will it take long for greedy Westerners to realize that it is important to win the loyalty of the handful of emerging Yąnomamö leaders and speak for them. That is already going on.

**Education and Growing Awareness of the Outside World.**   The children at Bisaasi-teri, including those in Kąobawä's village, now regularly attend school at the Mission and follow an academic year like that found all over Venezuela. They even have the equivalent of a "school bus" system—a very large dugout canoe that goes to each of the 12 "villages" every morning to pick the school children up and returns them the same way in the afternoon.

The school calendar has now affected fundamental aspects of traditional Yąnomamö subsistence economy in this area. I recall being dumbfounded by the answer to a question I asked one of the Bisaasi-teri men in 1986:

"When are you going on your next *waiyumö* (week or more hunting and gathering trip)?"

"Vacación dähä yamakö waiyumö huu." (We will go gathering during the school vacation break.)

In discussions of other activities, like hunting trips or visits to neighboring villages, I also heard conversations in which the planning was around "the weekend, when school is out."

Fluency in Spanish is developing at a rapid pace at Mission locations, as well as the ability to read and write both Spanish and Yąnomamö.

Even some individuals in more remote villages have been to the mission school at Mavaca and are remarkably literate, causing me some embarrassment in 1985 when I returned after a 10-year absence. I was updating my census and demographic data in Haoyaböwei-teri, the small group that had fissioned from the Mishimishimaböwei-teri after 1976 and was living near the satellite Salesian mission post, Mavakita. My informant, a young man named Ushubiriwä, some 22 years old, was at my side. He wasn't even pubescent the last time I saw him, but now he had two wives. He worked for Brother Juan. I had a portable computer with me and opened a file that contained my earlier data on his group. He watched in fascination as I scanned through the file, looking for my demographic and genealogical summary of vital events in his life. I stopped the scanning when I came to his record. He stared at the LCD screen: His face lit up as he hissed an explicative in disbelief. He grabbed me by the arm with one hand and mischievously jabbed me in the ribs with the elbow of his other, and, grinning from ear to ear, whispered excitedly, faking anger, "You have my [dead] father's name in your machine!"

He then pointed to the screen, traced out each entry with his finger and read for me, in whispers, the entire line under his name...father's name, mother's name, garden of birth, village of residence, and so on. Thankfully his "entrance" into the world of reading and writing was, at least for that moment, balanced by a corresponding reduction in his sensitivity to the cultural prohibition on using the names of deceased people publicly. In fact, he seemed gleefully pleased that he and I shared a mysterious skill. He then mischievously asked me to show him the "records" of several other people whose dead parents' names we both knew, and, as I cautiously produced the records he requested, he excitedly, but very quietly, assured me in gleeful whispers: "You've got it right!"

On that same field trip Ushubiriwä and another young man accompanied me on a brief trip to a more remote village. We camped along a small stream the first night. As we settled into our hammocks to sleep, he and our companion began conversing. I wasn't paying much attention to what they were saying, but they got louder and more excited as they continued, and I began hearing things that seemed familiar, but strangely out of context. It gradually began to dawn on me why their conversation seemed so out of place: They were talking about the movie *Jaws!* They both had seen it at the Salesian mission and were fascinated by it. I felt somewhat insulted when they asked me if I had seen *Jaws,* as if I were some country bumpkin from the remote outback. I tried to restore my dignity by dishonestly saying: "No, but I read the book."

Awareness of the larger world and global issues is also emerging at the Mission locations. A particularly cosmopolitan Yąnomamö man, whom I had first known as an infant in a very remote village in 1968, asked me rhetorically one day, in Spanish: "I understand your people have the atomic bomb. Is that true?"

Their growing awareness of the larger world includes, of course, increasing knowledge of the events that affect them more directly, such as the gold rush in Brazil. A few of them from the Salesian missions have gone to Brazil to meet the Yąnomamö there and discuss some of these issues. They now know what "gold" is and how *nabäs* (foreigners) go crazy when they believe they can find it...and are vaguely aware of the devastation these *nabäs* can inflict on the Yąnomamö in pursuit of it.

A few of the mission Yąnomamö in Venezuela are also intrigued by the excitement of visiting Caracas and places beyond and know that, in Brazil, one of their tribesmen, Davi Kobenawä Yąnomamö, has taken many exciting trips to far away places and has been invited to talk to important leaders in these places. Davi Kobenawä Yąnomamö was educated by New Tribes missionaries in a village on the Demini River in Brazil, where he learned Portuguese. He is being promoted as a spokesman for the Yąnomamö by his non-Yąnomamö supporters in Brazil, intelligent and well-intended advocates of the Yąnomamö cause, largely because *our* culture must deal with other cultures through "leaders" or we do not know how to deal with problems in other cultures at all.

But this entails risks and the danger that if Yąnomamö "leaders" can be that easily created by interested outside parties, every interested group will create and promote their own leader in order to advance their own special interests. For example, in 1990 the Brazilian mining interests produced their own Yąnomamö leader, a young man called Marcelo Yąnomami who advocated *their* rights just as strongly as Davi Kobenawä advocates the policies of his mentors, which, fortunately, are more consistent with Yąnomamö future well-being. In an article published in the Brazilian journal *Veja* in January 1990, Marcelo Yąnomami argued, obviously reflecting the interests of his mining mentors, that "the Indian has the right to explore the material riches in his territory in any manner he wishes," that is, turn it over to powerful Brazilian mining interests for a modest fee.

The problems could become very complex when various religious groups begin advocating particular leaders at their respective missions, a process that is now under way at Salesian missions in Venezuela. Yąnomamö political self-awareness is just beginning at a few of the points of contact and will be fraught with many future difficulties. This is the first time I have witnessed the birth of such a phenomenon and I am astonished at how manipulative and self-serving the various "outsiders" are in establishing and grooming the candidates whose political positions seem to reflect those of their mentors as much as anything else (Chagnon, 1997).

The problems the Yąnomamö will face as political self-awareness emerges and "leaders" come forth will be complicated also by the fact that not all of the outside advisors are simply local missionaries, anthropologists, or others who live nearby. International concern for the future of the Yąnomamö has grown rapidly because of the highly publicized tragic impact of the 1987 gold rush on the Yąnomamö who live in Brazil. This has set into motion some extraordinary activities in the past seven or eight years, many of which must be absolutely baffling to the Yąnomamö ... and many of them are baffling to me as well. There is now developing a kind of competition among many interest groups, including missionaries, "survival" groups, conservation activists, individuals, anthropologists, government agencies, and others.

The goal or prize appears to be winning the exclusive or preeminent privilege of speaking for and representing the Yąnomamö to the world at large—advising them on how to deal with it—and possibly taking credit for "saving" them from the horrors of civilization. Potential Yąnomamö "leaders" are becoming pawns in this contest and the Yąnomamö themselves just a "commodity."

A major stimulus for this competition is the high visibility of the Yąnomamö and their corresponding significance or utility as symbols of the plight of all indigenous peoples, especially in the Amazon, and the conservation of the world's tropical forests and biodiversity, especially the Amazon forests. Not unexpectedly, many groups are attempting to associate the highly publicized issues of Yąnomamö survival with their own programs, apparently aware that the very name "Yąnomamö" will bring attention to their programs. For example, in 1989 the English branch of the World Wildlife Fund sponsored a fund-raising tour in the United States, featuring the popular rockstar, Sting, and a children's chorus. They sang charming songs about wild birds, insects, and animals of the tropical forest. The program was, astonishingly, entitled "Yąnomamö." So far as I have been able to determine, nothing about this tour had anything to do with the Yąnomamö except that its promoters knew that their name would attract public attention and, presumably, donations—earmarked for worthy conservation causes elsewhere, but not for the Yąnomamö themselves. It is possible to entertain seriously the notion that most of the members of the tour then thought that a Yąnomamö was an endangered owl or a rare hummingbird. While it is immensely to the benefit of the Yąnomamö that so many groups are aware of their plight and identify strongly with efforts to help them, it is to be hoped that contributions made on behalf of the Yąnomamö cause actually get to the Yąnomamö.[10]

## CONTENDING INFLUENCES AND CONFLICTING INFORMATION

Perhaps the simplest way to illustrate the nature of the kinds of political problems that are beginning to emerge in Kąobawä's area is to give a concrete example that illustrates the kinds of difficulties that Yąnomamö leaders—newly emerging ones and traditional ones—face as they are being made more and more aware of the larger world and have to make important decisions now about who, from the outside world, is a friend and who is not, and the conflicting information that is being put into circulation among them.

A major factor in this confusion has to do with the extremes that currently exist among Venezuelan Yąnomamö villages regarding awareness of the outside world and how information about that world enters their culture (Chagnon, 1997). Complex information about the outside world usually enters at mission posts where some individuals are quite sophisticated and know how to interpret it, but in passing

---

10. Sting ultimately went on, to his credit, to advocate successfully land and human rights of other Brazilian native groups, especially the Kayapo Indians.

it on to groups that are more remote and less familiar with that world, the information gets garbled, distorted, and seriously misinterpreted. For example, many Yąnomamö at the missions, because they have some education, know that *garimpeiros* utilize a substance called mercury to extract gold from the soil and mud; they also have been told that the mercury residue that runs into the rivers is toxic and can cause fish, animals, and humans to die over time. It is poisonous. They've never actually seen this happen but can understand the process without any difficulty. However, when this information gets passed on to other, more remote villages it becomes transformed and translated into concepts and cultural meanings that are very different because the Yąnomamö there have no similar technical basis for their interpretations. But they do understand "harmful magic" and "charms," and believe that enemies can and do "poison" them with substances like *oka* and cause them to sicken and die. By the time the complex information reaches them, mercury has become something like *oka,* a magical substance that enemies blow at you to kill you, or put into your water for the same reason: It is the *oka* of a foreign people or village called Garibero *(garimpeiro).*

In May 1991, I was asked to escort a Venezuelan television team into the remote Yąnomamö area and assist them in making a documentary about the Yąnomamö to publicize sympathetically their health and cultural survival problems to the Venezuelan populace. My coworker was Charles Brewer-Carias, a Venezuelan colleague I have known for 30 years: We had previously collaborated in biomedical studies of the Yąnomamö in the 1960s and 1970s.

We spent the first three days in Hiomöta-teri filming what a "remote" village was like. We then tried to move to one of two other, less-known groups but found their *shabonos* empty. We therefore decided to spend the next few days in Dorita-teri to document an example of a Yąnomamö village that had "intermediate" contact but was still in a remote area. Brewer and I had briefly visited there several months earlier and had received a euphoric reception from them—they begged me to return and live with them as I had done many times in the past.[11] The Venezuelan Air Force helicopter dropped us off, with no equipment, in an abandoned garden near the *shabono* and immediately left to refuel. The pilot was instructed to return in two or three hours with our equipment and the rest of our party. There were seven of us: four Venezuelan TV crew members, me, Charles Brewer and his research assistant, Javier Mesa.

As soon as the drone of the helicopter faded, I heard angry, violent shouts from some dozen Dorita-teri men, all armed with bows and arrows, who had come out to intercept us.[12] I immediately knew we were in serious trouble. They had no idea who was with me. They insulted and berated me, saying

---

11 The film *Yąnomamö: A Multidisciplinary Study* includes footage of both me and Brewer during our collaboration with our biomedical coresearchers in 1968. Ironically, that film was shot among the Patanowä-teri, who subsequently fissioned, and the largest group is known today as the Dorita-teri, the village in which the following incident occurred.

12. We later learned that they had been sent out to shoot me with arrows and kill me. They apparently desisted when they discovered that there were six other men with me.

that I was their enemy and they did not want me to come back. They said they wanted to kill me. I asked them why they were so violently angry. They kept their distance, shouting abusive insults and accusations at me. I asked them if I could come into their *shabono* and talk with them. They disappeared into the *shabono* and consulted with the others. Finally, an angry shout came out: "Come into the *shabono*; be quick about it! We will talk here!"

I entered first, squeezing through the very low and narrow entry. My Venezuelan companions followed. I was the only one they appeared to recognize and the only one who spoke Yąnomamö. Their violent anger was directed at me. There were no women or children visible—they had fled into the nearby garden because they feared that a violent confrontation would occur. Most of the adult men present, some 20 or so, all clutching their bows and arrows, were assembled in a semicircle around a man of approximately 50 years, clearly the *pata* (big one). His name was Harokoiwä and I had known him since he was a young man.

Harokoiwä was wearing a dirty baseball cap and an even dirtier T-shirt. He glared at me and angrily demanded that I come over to him. My companions remained some 10 yards or so behind me, except Brewer, who stayed close to me, slightly behind and to my right. I reminded them that Brewer had been with me in 1968 when we did biomedical work in their village and they acknowledged that they remembered him once I pointed that out. Harokoiwä began rocking rhythmically sideways, violently denouncing me for killing their babies and causing epidemics among them, slapping his thighs as he rocked from side to side to emphasize his hostile declarations. When he got through reciting his denunciations, he reached down and picked up his ax, thrust it menacingly into my face and drew it back over his head, poised to crush my skull with it. He began rocking to and fro, toward and away from me, repeating his denunciations but, this time, telling me he was now going to kill me with his ax. He was measuring the distance and swing needed to do just that with a single blow.

I kept moving closer to him, making it difficult for him to make an effective swing, and he kept trying to maintain an optimal striking distance. At this point some of them, inflamed by Harokoiwä's violence and vitriolic accusations, surged toward me and Charles, but we held our ground; one of them grabbed at Charles' arm, but on noting its strength and our apparent fearless resolve, backed away.[13] I managed to calm Harokoiwä down, reciting all the good things I had done for his group during the past 27 years—all the medicines I had brought when I heard they were sick and the time I and my medical companions walked into their remote village and vaccinated them for measles, which saved them from a devastating epidemic that was then decimating all the groups around them (Neel, et al., 1970; see below). I asked them who told them these lies. He said "many people" had told him this when he visited the Salesian Mission at Platanal, some three-day walk away, including "Alfredo," a man

---

13. Kąobawä made an especially poignant comment to me about two years earlier, about showing fear before your enemies: "Never show fear to your enemy! Be strong and calm. The moment you reveal that you are afraid, you are in mortal danger! That is when your enemy will kill you."

from that mission who is emerging as one of the new Yąnomamö leaders there. Alfredo was a *policía,* a policeman (probably meaning he was now the Yąnomamö *commisario,* replacing César Dimanauwä discussed above). He said that Alfredo told them to keep me out of their village because I took photographs of them that caused their babies to die (ID photos used for census purposes). All the mysterious deaths in their village since I began visiting them were due to my ID photographs. They wanted to kill me to avenge all these deaths. Alfredo also told them that I sold these photographs to foreigners in my country for vast amounts of *madohe* (trade goods) and also cheated them that way. He told them I put strange substances in their water that poisoned the fish and the people who drank it. He told them that I would also the cause the game to disappear in their area—the noise of the helicopter I had arrived in would frighten the game away forever and cause them to become hungry.

Brewer and I assured them we would investigate these accusations with the "big" police in Caraca-teri, perhaps even inviting them and Alfredo to participate in that discussion.

The accusation that the noise of our plane would cause the game to flee made it clear to me that Alfredo was being "coached" by someone familiar with the standard jargon used to describe one of the harmful things that Brazilian *garimpeiros* do. This is an effect commonly alleged by Brazilian and French anthropologists regarding the presence of gold miners among the Brazilian Yąnomamö: Their frequent aircraft landings at the illegal mining camps causes the game animals in those areas to flee and become scarce. A more likely explanation of game scarity would be increased hunting pressure by shotgun-wielding miners, or shotgun-wielding Yąnomamö whose hunting efficiency increases dramatically with shotguns (Hames, 1979). It was clear to me that someone who knew what the *garimpeiros* did was informing the Yąnomamö that I was a *garimpeiro.*[14]

We left the *shabono* after talking with them for some time. I was angry they threatened to kill me—which they might have done had I been alone. During the hour or so we sat outside in the hot sun waiting for the helicopter, groups of men came out periodically to talk, continuing to express their anger and hostility at my rumored malevolent deeds, but softening their position each time. Eventually a group of older women came out, allegedly to fetch water. They stopped and talked with me. I was touched by the sympathy that they expressed toward me—they called me affectionate kinship terms and assured me that they did not believe the lies. After several groups came and went, the headman, Harokoiwä finally came out. His violent anger had abated, but he was still very aloof and reserved. He asked me to come back into the *shabono*—explaining that

14. Just a few months earlier the Kedebaböwei-teri, anxious to have me return to their village and live with them, told me that they were angry with Salesian Brother Juan Finkers at the Mavaca mission because he told them that they should drive me out of their village if I showed up because both Brewer and I were prospecting for gold in their area, that is, we were garimpeiros. Finkers has more recently (1994) claimed that I am directly or indirectly responsible for the murder of two of my close friends and informants, whose alleged deaths I have not yet been able to verify, but intend to do at the earliest opportunity.

the women were criticizing him for how he treated me, arguing that I was the "nephew" of one of them, the "brother" of another, and the "father" of his own wife. I told him I would think about it for a while, adding that I never return to villages where people threatened to kill me because of lies and rumors spread by my enemies. It is important to understand that lethal incidents can be and are provoked because of false rumors and accusations that one is sending charms to kill the others—as described in the prologue of this book. The helicopter eventually returned and we departed.

I have nearly been killed by the Yąnomamö several times during the 32 years spanned by my field research. Those were totally distinct situations from the above, and understandable in their own terms. I knew, in those cases, that it was risky to go to some of the places where this was a possibility, but I was willing to take those known risks. Most of the yet-living Yąnomamö men who threatened to or tried to kill me in the past are now friends of mine—and we even joke, albeit gingerly, about those long-ago situations. I had come to believe that this was now, in the 1990s, all but an extremely remote possibility, for the Yąnomamö have come to know, accept, respect, and consider me as a welcome friend because I have treated them fairly, have not taken sides in their quarrels or wars, provided them with medicines, treated their sick, and regularly brought them the material things I knew they desired and needed ... mostly at a time when they had no other access to them.

My personal safety will probably be increasingly at risk if I return to Yąnomamö villages—even Kąobawä's—located at or near Salesian missions. In 1993 one of the Salesian Missionaries was quoted in a Venezuelan newspaper as saying in effect that the Salesians "can not guarantee Chagnon's safety if he should appear in one of their missions." I never needed the "protection" of Salesians any time during my research career and, indeed, they probably needed my interventions with the Yąnomamö on their behalf more than vice versa. With this paper trail now announced, a possible unfortunate fatal incident at one of their missions no doubt exonerates them from any complicity in it...and they have dutifully warned me and the world about their deep concerns for my safety. The Salesian spokesman failed to mention that the Yąnomamö henchmen at their missions are now potentially hostile toward me because of the provocative misinformation they deliberately provided to them to incite this hostility.

In August 1991 I flew over Dorita-teri in a helicopter en route to Ashidowä-teri, a village just south of them, where I landed and did my research (described in the *New York Times*, 11 September 1991). Two days later Harokoiwä and a large delegation of men from Dorita-teri arrived at Ashidowä-teri, marched straight across the *shabono,* and assembled in front of the section of the village I was living in, next to Itąoböwä, the Ashidowä-teri headman. They had seen and heard the helicopter and guessed that I might be on it. I was apprehensive that a new and even more serious incident was about to unfold and was dumbfounded at the absolute, flagrant lack of courtesy and diplomacy he and his companions exhibited toward the Ashidowä-teri and their headman—almost as if they weren't even there. Harokoiwä was from a bellicose village; the Ashidowä-teri were clearly subordinate politically and were now peripheralized refugees.

He announced loudly as he marched across the plaza that he wanted to talk to me. I came out of my hut and met him in front of it, as is politically appropriate. He stood before me, surrounded by the contingent of armed men with him, and immediately went into a dramatic, impassioned speech, explaining how he and his people had thought things over, reflected on my long-term friendship with them, and decided they had been lied to by Alfredo and "foreigners" at the Salesian Mission, naming one priest and one nun, and two young Yąnomamö leaders at the Salesian Mission of Ocamo who had assured them I was bad, put mysterious poison in their water, chased their game animals away with my helicopter, and caused their babies to die by taking photographs of them. He assured me that he had acted only on these lies when he threatened to kill me and now, after deciding they were lies, wanted me to come and live in his village and become friends with me again. I responded formally, agreeing with everything he said, adding my own twists and nuances, assured him of my friendship, and then offered him and his men gifts. This defused our crisis. They left.

A week later my research companions and I moved by helicopter to his village and spent a very pleasant week with him and his people, as I had done many times in the past. I learned several new things during that week. One was that "people" at Platanal did not like me because I brought trade goods—machetes, axes, fishhooks, and so on—directly to them without going through the Yąnomamö (and Priests) at the mission and gave these things away freely to them. So long as I could visit the Dorita-teri they did not have to go to the mission to get these things and become caught up in the economic process of having to produce goods to obtain machetes, pots, fishhooks, and so on. The other, and saddest thing, was that the Dorita-teri had suffered 25 percent mortality since my last census of them four years earlier, from an epidemic that killed mostly children and old people. This is the highest mortality rate I documented for the 17 villages I censused in 1987 and again in 1991. Their only contact with outsiders was with people from Platanal, not *garimpeiros,* a mission community that then included increasing numbers of non-Yąnomamö residents, including a National Guard contingent.

## Political, Moral, and Philosophical Dilemmas

Very complex political, moral, and philosophical issues are involved regarding whether agents of our kind of culture should encourage the Yąnomamö to change or try to prevent that from happening. There is an ethical issue involved in the question of interfering with what could legitimately be viewed as an increasing need for the Yąnomamö to become more dependent on at least some aspects of Western culture. One of these is medical help. It is now not possible to halt or reverse the processes of contact already under way, and since we initiated the contacts that brought new sicknesses, we are obligated to correct this and provide the medical programs that will do it.

Politically, the question is: who should be involved in or responsible for guiding the changes if change it will be? What policies should guide those who advise the Yąnomamö?

The two most important factors in the cultural survival and future welfare of native peoples like the Yąnomamö have to do with land and health. Venezuelan President Carlos Andres Pérez, by his 1991 decrees, set into motion laws that will presumably guarantee the cultural survival of the Venezuelan Yąnomamö insofar as this depends on their unobstructed, exclusive rights to their habitat and the prohibition of economic development of these habitats. The Brazilian government, under former President Ferdinand Collor de Melo, also acted to safeguard Yąnomamö lands on that side of the border the same year that Venezuela established a biosphere reserve intended to protect the Yąnomamö there. Brazil also declared Yąnomamö territory off limits to miners and established it formally as a native reserve.

The newest factor in this complex situation is the designation of the Venezuelan Amazonas as a new state in 1992. It is no longer a federal territory. Coupled with this important political change is the parallel process in Venezuela of "decentralizing" the national government, which means giving state governments more control over what happens locally. Increasing secularization of this area also means increasing interest in development of this area. The resources logically available to the State government of Venezuela's Amazon area fall into just a few logical categories: Mineral wealth, eco-tourism, and federal subsidies. Whichever route is followed, the Yąnomamö will become increasingly exposed to our kind of world and will be incorporated into it (Chagnon, 1997).

My anthropological interests now include a new component. I started out as just another anthropologist, a scientist, attempting to document and explain a different culture as best I could. By repetitively returning and becoming more and more intimately associated with people like Kąobawä and Rerebawä, I became "involved"" in their culture and want to do what I can to help them, to insure that they and their children are given a fair shake as the inevitable changes occur in their villages (Figure 8.5). I do so by becoming an advocate of their rights and their chances to have a decent future, one that does not condemn them to becoming inferior members of the lowest possible rung of the socioeconomic ladder, bums and beggars in Puerto Ayacucho, alcoholics and prostitutes in the ghettos of Caracas.

The future of the Yąnomamö is now hanging in a delicate balance. They are the most highly visible native people in the world, in large part due to the wide use of this monograph in anthropology courses in its several editions. If the Yąnomamö can not survive with dignity given this kind of visibility and international admiration, what chance does some other, largely unknown, native group have—*anywhere?* If the Yąnomamö go down, so also might many other native peoples—and the biospheres they have kept intact until the present. The Yąnomamö are now a symbol for all tribesmen and their habitats, everywhere.

Kąobawä's most beloved child, Ariwari, died just before I returned to his village in 1985. He was by then a young man, had a new wife, and an infant child. He had much to live for, but died of a disease brought there by outsiders.

**FIGURE 8.5** Let us hope the future for the Yąnomamö will have room for the happiness expressed on this boy's face, a boy who died of an introduced respiratory infection in the late 1960s.

Rerebawä died in Kąobawä's village in 1994. News of his death saddened me and I thought about the many months and many years we spent together, living dangerously, taking risks, joking with and teasing each other about my balding head and his lengthening beard, daring to go where others were afraid to go, being hungry or being full as luck or chance would have it, and the great hunting trips we took together. *Ya buhii mraraiyo maikätä.*

# 9

# REFLECTIONS ON THE Y̧NOMAMÖ

## ~ Fieldwork & Anthropology ~

*An Interview with Napoleon A. Chagnon, With*
*Questions Posed by William G. Irons*

**CSCA Editor's Introduction:** The first edition of *Yąnomamö* was published in 1968. It was revised in 1977, 1983, 1992, and 1997, and is now in its sixth edition. In the more than 40 years since its publication, this case study has enjoyed broad and increasing popularity—perhaps unprecedented for a single work of ethnography (now approaching one million new copies sold).

The *Yąnomamö* continues to be used extensively today within university classrooms, as well as read widely by members of a broad scientific community in both the United States and internationally. Many of its readers regard it as an authoritative work for their research purposes because of the unusually large amounts of data it contains. It is unusual for a monograph written largely for use in undergraduate courses to achieve this standard.

The following is an interview of the author by Professor William G. Irons (Northwestern University), described by the author as "one of my best friends and colleagues who knows my research and publications as well as anybody." "We entered Graduate School at Michigan in anthropology in 1961 and have been in continuous contact ever since, some 50 years, sometimes as members of the same department and other times as co-editors of publications."

# I.

IRONS: How do you explain the continuing success of your case study *Yąnomamö*? What is it about your ethnography that contributes to its continuing appeal across the decades?

CHAGNON: I think it reaches out and grabs the reader's attention at the outset. When we were both graduate students at Michigan and studying for the Ph.D., I recall reading a number of ethnographies that made me feel that "...I was there, with the natives the author was discussing...." One of the ethnographers was Bronislaw Malinowski, whose prose was both riveting and enchanting, as in his *Coral Gardens and Their Magic*, or *Argonauts of the Western Pacific*. Another great ethnographer and writer was Douglas Oliver. Some portions of his description of the "big-man" system in the New Guinea Highlands in his *A Solomon Island Society: Kinship and Leadership Among the Siuai of Bouganville* was like reading an exciting novel.

So, I decided, even before I began my field work among the Yąnomamö, that they and their culture could be presented and described in a way that invited the reader, indeed, enticed the reader to be a part of the world that I had experienced and that the Yąnomamö lived in, to meet real people like Rerebawä, Kąobawä, Bahimi, Ariwari, and Dedeheiwä. I also learned in graduate school that the "philosophy of art" was a way to illustrate the whole by providing a clear and compelling description of a specific case. For example, the overall plight of the Jews in rural Russia at the turn of the century can be captured in the delightful things that Tevye—the "fiddler on the roof"—did. In that sense, then, *Fiddler on the Roof* was an artistic way of illustrating a larger whole by focusing on a specific instance.

But the plight of the same people can also be rendered intelligible by meticulous statistical data on violence, pogroms, persecution, and deaths. I wanted my monograph—my description of Yąnomamö culture and society—to capture both the spirit of art and of science and to portray a sense of universal humanness of the Yąnomamö and try to make the reader understand how the forces in their culture led them to make decisions they sometimes did not want to make ... just as the forces in our culture lead us to make similar decisions. For example, almost all Yąnomamö would prefer to live in peace and amity with their neighbors but must deal with threats from neighbors that jeopardize their security. When this happens they must make decisions that are sometimes costly to themselves and their close kin, but failing to do so could be even more costly. We, for example, do similar things and endure very large costs to protect our own security, like submitting to noisome screenings at airports or paying huge sums of money to equip and maintain permanent military forces to assure our national security.

In this approach I think I have succeeded. For example, over the past 40 years I have gotten hundreds of letters from undergraduate students expressing their delight with my *Yąnomamö* monograph and their fascination with and admiration of them as a people. Many of them ask, for example, if I could give

Kąobawä or Bahimi a little gift on their behalf, or ask me if Rerebawä ever made a garden in Bisaasi-teri—and most of them ask me to urge him not to! I do not recall that any of their letters expressed dislike for or disgust with the Yąnomamö or their culture. I find this particularly heartening and refreshing because a small group of academically jealous detractors assume that the way I have described the Yąnomamö here is "demeaning" to them and have criticized me openly in the press. But the way that undergraduates have responded to the Yąnomamö after reading my monograph gives me a sense of satisfaction that the choice I made to combine the philosophy of art and science in an ethnographic monograph was an effective one.

Finally, this monograph through its six editions has also exemplified my advocacy of Yąnomamö rights, especially for their health and well-being through, particularly, the data it contains in the later editions on mortality patterns caused by introduced diseases where they have increasing contact with the outside world and by my participation in and advocacy of medical research efforts that included both a practical and humanitarian component.

## II.

IRONS:    Do you think there is something about the Yąnomamö as a people that continues to engage and fascinate readers?

CHAGNON:  Yes, I do think there are a number of things about the Yąnomamö that grab the attention of anyone who reads my monograph. Some of these are the same ones that caused me, on the occasion of seeing my first Yąnomamö, to realize that they were a very special people and led me to decide that I had to keep coming back to learn more about them before they were radically changed by outside contact. Let me list just a few of these that seem to attract and hold the attention of readers.

First, there were many villages and many people—unknown to the world in the mid-1960s, and large numbers of them—that had never been contacted by outsiders. My first estimate was "about 10,000" Yąnomamö. Several editions of my monograph relate my accounts of contacting some of these groups. This, I think, nursed the hope we all have that the tribal world continues in the remaining but rapidly vanishing unexplored corners of the world. My last estimate of the numbers of Yąnomamö was 25,000. By that time, many of them had been counted in some kind of "official" censuses taken in Venezuela and Brazil by various organizations.

Second, the Yąnomamö had differing and fascinating "personality" types. Some people were witty and mischievous, like Rerebawä, but had many other characteristics that changed as they aged. Different leaders had different "styles" of leadership. Kąobawä's style was more sedate than, for example, Paruriwä's (Hontonawä's) who lived in a faction of the same group just downstream: He was brash, boisterous, and pretentious. And, both of these leaders differed from

Möawä from Mishimishimaböwei-teri. He was an exceptionally violent man—he killed more people than any Yąnomamö I knew of among the some 5,000 Yąnomamö my records include. He was also contemptuous of many people in his own village and treated them badly. He was selfish and refused to share scarce items with others, such as medicines I brought for the whole group but that he commandeered for his own selfish use. There were yet other "styles" of leadership that seemed to vary by village size: The larger the village, the more severe and draconic leadership seemed to be because kinship and marriage ties were not able to provide the kind of cohesion that held large groups together—and large groups were able to survive longer in a milieu of chronic warfare. Möawä's style of leadership hints at what tribesmen had to do to take the next step toward political complexity: Kinship organization had to be replaced by political institutions such as formal chiefs who wielded authority that was not based on kinship alone. And there were renowned shamans like Dedeheiwä. His spiritual influence and knowledge spilled over into other social arenas: Dedeheiwä also enjoyed considerable political influence in his village and in the larger geographical region. Interestingly, many Yąnomamö headmen are also adept shamans and I can easily imagine situations where the political authority of headmen would be bolstered by "spiritual" authority, a pattern that is frequently found in early "chiefdoms" and "pristine states."

Third, as my field studies continued and previous editions were replaced by new editions, I was able to show how the social complexity of villages seemed to correlate with geography and ecological factors such as elevation, drainage characteristics, species abundance, and whole "zones" that resembled what I called the "fertile crescents" of Yąnomamöland where rapid population spurts occurred and led to major diasporas into adjacent, unpopulated areas and how new groups developed and overcame what I described as "social circumscription"—the reluctance of groups to "leapfrog" over or go around neighbors who were impeding their expansion (Chagnon, 1968b; Carneiro 1987). Thus, students were able to appreciate the ways in which differences in cultural/ecological variables affected village size, and how this in turn affected the political influence of that village.

Fourth, each new edition exposed emerging new problems facing the Yąnomamö and in this sense, the monograph and my continuing study of the Yąnomamö projected a "dynamic" aspect to what ethnography as a branch of science entailed. The monograph was not simply a single slice in time, a "snapshot" of a society "frozen" at a single point in time and in its history, nor in the life of the people discussed. It was a kind of continuing narrative of a people being changed over time and an account of the forces of that change—contact with the outside world, the transition in the larger political world around them from a federal territory to statehood, their incorporation at mission posts into political entities with which they were unfamiliar—*alcaldes*, the power of identity and the importance of names that outsiders assigned to them, names that sometimes separated five brothers into different families like Gonzalez, Lopez, Villegas, and so forth. The people who gave them these new and foreign names were completely ignorant of their individual identities as members of lineages and thereby undermined traditional Yąnomamö sources of kinship, amity, and solidarity: membership in their *mashi*...their patrilineal lineage.

I could list more items that endeared the Yąnomamö to a large international audience. Suffice it to say that the Yąnomamö became, over time, one of the most famous indigenous peoples in the world, and much of their visibility was due to the success of this monograph and to the some 20 ethnographic films I have made about them with the late Timothy Asch (listed at the end of this edition). The international community that holds the Yąnomamö in such high repute accepts them for what they are as described in this case study, including the features of their culture they share with us, such as the importance of defending the integrity and survival of one's own group with force when necessary, of protecting one's family from harm and violence directed at them from other groups of Yąnomamö and, increasingly, from non-Yąnomamö outsiders.

## III.

IRONS: What can you tell me about how your involvement with evolutionary theory led to your addition of material to later editions of *Yąnomamö*?

CHAGNON: One of the first "controversies" that my Yąnomamö study provoked was the protein debate between me and Marvin Harris. Harris was trying to establish a "scientific" theory of culture that was evolutionary but dominated by "materialist" assumptions, one of which can be summarized as follows: If conflict and warfare existed in "band and tribal societies" then it had to be because of a shortage of "scarce strategic material resources." My Yąnomamö work constituted a conspicuous exception to his theory because my demographic data showed that the Yąnomamö had exceptionally low population densities but that conflict and warfare were common among them, a pattern that was also very common in the Amazon basin. Moreover, they did not appear to be fighting over some scarce strategic material resource.

As my monograph was becoming more and more popular, Harris seemed increasingly compelled to "explain" the Yąnomamö away by arguing that what they were really fighting over was scarce animal protein. Although he had absolutely no evidence for his claim, he continued to insist, for example, that I had not shown that the Yąnomamö were getting adequate amounts of high-quality animal protein in the form of lean, red meat. Thus, in 1972 I organized a major field project that included three of my graduate students and met in New York with Harris and several of the prominent students he trained at Columbia. We discussed the issues that might solve this disagreement with data and asked them what kinds of data they wanted us to collect. We then left for the field where my three students were scheduled to spend a year or so in various areas of Venezuelan Yąnomamöland collecting data on this issue as well as data they would use for their respective doctoral dissertations. One indelible statement that Harris made at that time was something to the effect that if we could show that the Yąnomamö consumed the equivalent of "...one Big Mac per day..." he would eat his hat.

Table 2.2 of this edition (and in both the fourth and fifth editions) summarizes data on this issue, showing, among other things, a correlation almost the opposite of what Harris' theory predicts: It could be argued that an abundance of protein rather than a scarcity "causes" people to make war. Harris' response was something to the effect that he didn't really mean that they had an actual shortage of protein. He modified his position: He said what he really meant was that they perceived that they had a shortage of protein. In other words, no amount of empirical data would solve this issue because Harris' position was based on an unassailable axiom: Whenever humans fought, you can be sure the cause is some scarcity of a strategic material resource ... or the perception that a scarcity existed. He refused to accept the Darwinian view, accepted in all of the other sciences, that reproduction is a central principle in Darwinian theory and evolution by natural selection. It was clear to the Yąnomamö that most of their fighting was over women, that is, a resource that was not "material" in the Marxist sense. But to say that was to imply that biology had to be taken into consideration in the explanation of their behavior.

This, I believe, was what really lay behind my disagreement with Harris: He believed that human conflict had nothing to do with biology. However, "women" were quintessentially biological. Darwinian theory was undergoing breathtaking changes in the 1960s, 70s, and 80s with the work of William Hamilton, George Williams, Robert Trivers, Richard Alexander, and many others. Both your work and mine got caught up in this exciting period, one that had important implications for understanding the behavior of all animals, including humans. The turning point was an explosive one in particular for cultural anthropology: the 1975 publication *Sociobiology: The New Synthesis* by Harvard biologist Edward O. Wilson. One particularly unsettling argument for cultural anthropologists was that humans had an evolved biological nature as well as a cultural nature and both "natures" had to be incorporated into theories of human behavior, an idea that had been systematically opposed in both sociology and cultural anthropology ever since Durkheim's 1895 *The Rules of the Sociological Method*.

The publication of Edward O. Wilson's *Sociobiology* set off a firestorm of politically motivated attacks from people with left-wing orientations (Segerstrale, 2000). Conspicuous among these attacks was a book by Lewontin, Rose, and Kamin (1984), *Not in Our Genes*, which declared at its outset that the authors' goal as members of the "radical science movement" was the creation of "a more just—a socialist—society" and that sciences like sociobiology have the purpose of "hindering the creation of that society by acting to preserve the interests of the dominant class, gender, and race" (pages ix–x). My research and yours became caught up in what was known as the "sociobiology debate" (Segerstrale, 2000). The underlying assumption of those attacking sociobiology (the evolutionary theories of Hamilton, Trivers, Williams, Alexander, and Wilson) was, as stated above, the belief that sociobiology would discourage movements for greater social justice.

This basic assumption of the "radical science movement" was never tested empirically until 2007 when a survey of political opinions among evolutionary psychology graduate students was published (Tybur, Miller, and Gangestad, 2007). Evolutionary psychology is an outgrowth of sociobiology. If it were true that sociobiology and evolutionary psychology encourage right-wing politics, these students should have predominantly right-wing political views. It turned out that their political views were far to the left of the majority of the U.S. population. If one puts the U.S. population on a continuum from the farthest to the right to the farthest to the left, these graduate students' opinions fell among the 5% of the population that are farthest to the left. There was absolutely no support for this basic assumption of the radical science movement. The Tybur et al. study is the only published test of this basic belief of the radical science movement. It suggests that sociobiology's threat to the struggle for social justice existed only in the imaginations of certain scientists. Despite this, many of our publications were vilified as right-wing sociobiology. See for example Philip Kitcher's *Vaulting Ambitions* (1985), which systematically trashes much of the research published in our 1979 book *Evolutionary Biology and Human Social Behavior* and ends by saying that "the mistakes [contained in publications like our 1979 edited volume] ... threatened to stifle the aspirations of millions." My 1988 study of the reproductive success of *unokais* was also caught up in the "sociobiology debate."

The data I presented in the fifth edition and again here on Yąnomamö *unokais* is directly related to evolutionary theory in both a "cultural" sense and a "biological" sense. An *unokai* in Yąnomamö society is a man who has gone through the ritual, described in Chapter 6, intended to purify him for participating in the killing of some other human. Since most lethal conflicts among the Yąnomamö involve disputes over women at some point in the development of the dispute, the status of *unokai* by definition is intimately related to reproductive striving. While writing my 1988 *Science* paper I decided to check for a correlation between *unokai* status and reproductive success, that is, to check on whether men who were successful in war were also successful reproductively. This, of course, was a theory that you proposed in one of your chapters in our co-edited 1979 volume, a chapter entitled "Cultural and Biological Success" (Irons, 1979). The gist of this idea, known now as the "cultural-and-reproductive-success" hypothesis is that in every society there are standards of success, standards by which people can be ranked as having higher or lower status and prestige. In natural fertility populations—populations in which contraception is not extensively practiced—people with higher status have higher reproductive success. Most human populations until a few generations ago were natural fertility populations. People of higher status are better at acquiring mates and at acquiring the resources for rearing children. Thus status striving, a universal human trait, is an evolved adaptation which during most of human evolution led to a higher reproductive success.

The standards of success vary from one society to another. Among the Yąnomamö it is *waiteri* and being an *unokai* is a reliable sign that one is *waiteri*.

In some societies it is status in a religious hierarchy, or political rank, or knowledge, or wealth. The accomplishments or qualities that confer status tend to be those that are the most useful assets to bring to a social alliance in that society. Among the Yąnomamö, where coping with the threat of violence is a constant concern, they want allies, friends, brothers-in-law, who are *waiteri*. The cultural-and-reproductive-success hypothesis has been tested in many natural fertility populations and the data have consistently confirmed the hypothesis (Irons, 1998). As it turns out one of the studies confirming the cultural-and-reproductive-success hypothesis was my 1988 *unokai* study. The correlation was very clear: *Unokais* had approximately 2.6 times the average number of wives and approximately 3.1 times the average number of offspring than men of their own age who had not killed, that is, non-*unokais* (Chagnon, 1988a).

My 1988 paper in *Science* was published just after some of 40,000 Brazilian gold miners (*garimpeiros*) invaded Yąnomamö territory in Brazil. My persistent detractors were outraged because what it reported for the Venezuelan Yąnomamö, among other things, might be taken by those who wanted to oppress the Brazilian Yąnomamö, take their lands away from them, and otherwise harm them as justification for their "reprehensible" acts of violence. Henceforth almost everything I published on the Yąnomamö was distorted by the small handful of my critics as evidence that I was the cause of much of the suffering inflicted on the [Brazilian] Yąnomamö by Brazilian citizens.

## IV.

IRONS: At the end of the fifth edition (1997) you write with concern and passion about "Political, Moral, and Ethical Dilemmas" that were affecting the lives, communities, and dignity of the Yąnomamö. Which dilemmas today continue as immediate threats? Which are of most concern to you?

CHAGNON: All of the dilemmas I ended the fifth edition with continue and have worsened in some cases. While the Yąnomamö on both the Venezuelan and Brazilian sides of the border currently have their territories [land] protected by the actions of both governments, health problems have generally worsened. Diseases that I never saw in my early work—like hepatitis—are now common and lead to great suffering and death. Statehood for the Venezuelan Amazonia territory has led to increased control over the area by the Salesian missions and the expulsion of Evangelical missions (*infra*)—and thereby terminated the health services they provided in the extremely remote villages in which they operated. The Salesians have also recently banned all anthropological research among the Venezuelan Yąnomamö. As a result, reliable demographic information about mortality patterns is now almost impossible to obtain because these patterns might implicate their political policies, such as the Catholic Church's legally sanctioned 500-year-old practice of "attract and reduce" isolated groups from the deep forest to settle at their missions on major rivers.

One of my new concerns is what the long-term effects will be of the increasing awareness the Yąnomamö now have of their international image as a "famous" people, a symbol of the plight of all native peoples and of the threatened ecosystems they live in. Increasing numbers of young Yąnomamö men in both Brazil and Venezuela are now being wooed by people with political agendas, including some anthropologists. They are being asked to make statements about events that affect them, and can be easily manipulated to say what they think their interrogators want them to say. This has important implications for the future of cultural anthropology and to what extent it should sacrifice scientific objectivity for political advocacy and whether some balance between the two can emerge. My position is that an effective advocacy program should stick with facts that others can verify, that is, should not sacrifice the scientific method and not simply "invent" false claims.

With their increasing visibility and fame, the Yąnomamö have become a prized goal in the sense that many NGO groups and organizations now want to be associated with their name. The Yąnomamö have become a kind of commodity. Some advocacy groups, it would appear, want to be their exclusive representatives and, in effect, own them and shape or direct their social, economic, and political future. In this new arena the competition is not only "fierce" but sometimes draconic. Not many years ago, for example, it was an open question whether or not Roman Catholicism or Evangelical Protestantism would prevail in some Venezuelan Yąnomamö areas. That question has now been settled: the Salesian missions—the Catholic Church—prevailed by exerting an enormous amount of political pressure on the State (Venezuela). The State then solved the issue by simply expelling the Evangelical missionaries (the New Tribes Missions) from the Yąnomamö area and from Venezuela in 2005. The Evangelicals were given 90 days to leave the country (*Gaceta Oficial de Venezuela*, No. 427). Yet Venezuela professes to defend "freedom of religion."

My long-term study of the Yąnomamö, including the first five editions of this monograph, have been caught up in this war and now play a central role in it. But this monograph is not the place to discuss the complex issues that are involved because many of them are about reprehensible academic politics, not about professionalism and teaching anthropology. I think it suffices to refer the reader to three articles that have respect for facts and provide a reasonable summary of the issues to date. One is an early article by John Tooby (2000), an anthropologist who subsequently also directed an investigation of the accusations against me and my medical colleagues (see the UCSB Report). Another appeared as the issues were reaching a peak midway in the scandal, an article by two concerned anthropologists, Thomas Gregor and Daniel Gross (2004) and the criticism of this article in the *Anthropology News* with a response by Gregor and Gross. The third and most recent article is by Alice Dreger, an historian of science (Dreger, 2011). Thus far the discussion by my critics has been dominated by unfounded and sometimes astonishing accusations and acts of sabotage of my recent field trips. I will address some of these in the last few chapters of my forthcoming book, *Noble Savages*, to be published in the fall of 2012 by Simon & Schuster; for example, in the last chapter I introduce new material about the 1968 measles epidemic that struck many villages of Venezuelan Yąnomamö, and in particular, a tragic new flare-up of the epidemic among the Mahekodo-teri as a direct consequence of the irresponsible actions of a Salesian priest by the name of Padre Sanchez. He repeatedly refused to evacuate a recently arrived Brazilian man at Platanal who had an active case of measles. I informed him that the Mahekodo-teri, who lived at Platanal, were en route home after participating in a feast in Patanowä-teri and had not been vaccinated by our medical team because we had run out of vaccine. When the Mahekodo-teri returned to Platanal many of them got measles from the Brazilian man and many of them died. When they started dying, Padre Sanchez abandoned them and fled downstream to the Salesian mission at Mavaca, where our team had vaccinated the Yąnomamö several weeks earlier. He told the medical team there that "he could not bear to see so many Yąnomamö dying."

Finally, I want to thank the instructors who assign this case study to their students. They play an invaluable role in didactic anthropology by guiding students to monographs that raise significant social issues that capture both traditional anthropological concerns and yet are instructive at the current moment in our own society—recurrent problems faced by members of tribal societies and ethnic minorities. I consider it an honor that your instructor has assigned this case study to you. If you read it with care, you will probably absorb more ethnographic data than is commanded by the majority of my critics in what has now become The Yąnomamö Wars. And, you will have an advantage in the debate should you choose to get involved in these issues regardless of the side you take.

The famous French anthropologist, Claude Lévi-Strauss, published a thoughtful book in 1961—50 years ago—entitled *Tristes Tropiques*, just as my anthropological career began. It was translated into English as *A World on the Wane*. It was about an historical era that was rapidly disappearing, the world of tribesmen like the Yąnomamö. I hope that this monograph on the Yąnomamö has given you glimpses of that fleeting and irreplaceable moment in human history as it was when I first went there and what it has changed into in many parts of the globe. But there still remain exciting and new challenges for anthropologists and, hopefully, this monograph inspires some of you to learn more about anthropology.

# Glossary

**affines:** Relatives by marriage. These can also include blood relatives when, for example, a man marries his mother's brother's daughter. The word "cognate" is used to describe those blood relatives who are related by marriage. Cognates also include kinsmen who have a common ancestor.

**agnates:** Persons who trace their relationships to each other through males. This is distinct from cognatic kinship, where the relationship may be traced through either males or females.

**banana, wild:** A distant relative to the common banana, but producing a fruit pod that is very different from the banana. The pod contains seeds that taste like maize. It is the only American member of the Musaceae family. Plantains and bananas now cultivated by the Yąnomamö were probably introduced to the Americas after Columbus.

**bifurcating merging:** A term used to describe the widespread type of kinship system in which an individual's paternal relatives are distinguished (bifurcated) from maternal relatives in the terminology. Furthermore, a single term is used in reference to, for example, father and father's brother; that is, they are merged

terminologically into the same kinship category. The Yąnomamö have the most commonly found variant of this type, the Iroquois system. See *Iroquois kinship terms*.

**bilateral cross-cousins:** In practical terms, an individual's mother's brother's children together with his father's sister's children. Unilateral cross-cousins are mother's brother's children or father's sister's children, but not both. These two terms are frequently used in discussions of types of marriage rules found in primitive societies. Mother's brother's daughter is a *uni* lateral cross-cousin; properly speaking, she is a matrilateral cross-cousin. In Yąnomamö (Iroquois) kinship this person is simultaneously father's sister's daughter. Some societies have rules forbidding marriage with the latter type of cousin, that is, they have a unilateral cross-cousin marriage rule. See *cross-cousins*.

**cognates:** Individuals who are related to each other through either males or females. See *affines, agnates*.

**corporation:** A group of people sharing some estate, having definite rights with respect to each other and to the estate, and able to demonstrate their membership to that group by citing a recognized rule concerning recruitment,

**cross-cousins:** The children of a man and his sister are cross-cousins to each other. The children of a man and his brother are parallel cousins to each other. Similarly, the children of a woman and her sister are parallel cousins.

**demography:** The study of populations with the intention of gathering certain kinds of vital statistics, such as birth rate, death rate, and family size.

**demonstrated kinship:** Tracing relationships to kinsmen by citing the putative biological links. See *lineage*.

*garimpeiro:* A Portuguese word meaning gold miner or gold prospector, or one who works in a gold mine.

*he /he borara/:* A Yąnomamö term to describe a settlement pattern in which two communities (*shabonos*) are located close to each other. This could be as close as a few meters or as far as a mile or so.

**Iroquois kinship terms:** Classifying both kinds of cross-cousins (matrilateral and patrilateral) into the same kinship category and distinguishing them from brothers and sisters and parallel cousins. In most Iroquois systems the parallel cousins are called by the same terms that are used for brothers and sisters.

**levirate:** A rule enjoining a man to marry the widow of his dead brother.

**lineage:** A kinship group comprising people who trace relationships to each other through either males or females, but not both. If the relationship is traced through males, as among the Yąnomamö, the group so defined is a patrilineage. The distinctive feature of the lineage is that the relationships are demonstrated by citing genealogical links. In a clan, relationships are merely stipulated by citing the fact that the two individuals in question belong to the same named kinship group. In short, a clan is a named lineage, the members of which do not remember or do not care how they are related to each other biologically. See *demonstrated kinship*.

**local descent group:** Among the Yąnomamö, a group of people who are related to each other patrilineally, who live in the same village, and one of whose major functions is to arrange marriages for the younger members of the group. It is usually the older males of the group who arrange the marriages.

**machete:** A broad-bladed, long knife commonly used throughout South America for cutting brush. The closest English or North American equivalent is the cutlass.

**matrilateral:** Tracing relationships on the mother's side.

**parallel cousins:** Cousins who are descended from two brothers or from two sisters.

**patrilateral:** Tracing relationships on the father's side.

**plantain:** A member of the banana family. The fruit looks like the common banana, but is considerably larger. When ripe, the fruit resembles the common banana in taste, but differs in that its texture is crude and stringy. Plantains are usually eaten cooked. Green plantains resemble raw potatoes in taste, even after cooking. Plantains appear to have been introduced to the Americas after the arrival of Europeans, but they spread with such rapidity that many travelers described them as being native crops. (See Reynolds, 1927.)

*shuwahimou:* A Yąnomamö word describing the act of a woman who, on her own initiative, leaves her natal village to find a mate in a different village. Often the women who do this are fleeing from undesirable marriages arranged by others.

**siblings:** One's brothers and sisters.

**sororal polygyny:** A type of marriage in which a man marries two or more women who are related to each other as sisters.

**teknonymy:** The practice of addressing an individual by the name of one of his children rather than by his own personal name. A kinship term is used in combination with the child's name, such as "father of."

# References Cited

Albert, Bruce, 1989, "Yanomami 'Violence': Inclusive Fitness or Ethnographer's Representation?" *Current Anthropology* 30:637–640.

——, and Alcida Ramos, 1988, "O exterminio 'académico' do Yanomami," *Humanidades* 18:85–89. Brasilia.

——, and ——, 1989 "Yanomami Indians and Anthropological Ethics,"*Science* 244:632.

Alexander, Richard D., 1979, *Darwinism and Human Affairs*. London: Pittman Publishing Ltd. (Also published by the University of Washington Press.)

——, 1987, *The Biology of Moral Systems*. New York: Aldine de Gruyter.

Arvelo-Jimenez, Nelly, 1971, *Political Relations in a Tribal Society: A Study of the Ye 'cuana Indians of Venezuela*. Latin American Studies Program, Dissertation Series, No. 31. Ithaca, NY: Cornell University Press.

Asch, Timothy, and Napoleon A. Chagnon, 1970, *The Feast* (16mm film). Penn State Media Sales, 171 Outreach Building, University Park, PA 16802.

——, and ——, 1974, *New Tribes Mission* (16mm film). Penn State Media Sales, 171 Outreach Building, University Park, PA 16802.

——, and ——, 1975, *The Ax Fight* (16mm film). Penn State Media Sales, 171 Outreach Building, University Park, PA 16802.

Aspelin, L., 1975, *External Articulation and Domestic Production: The Artifact Trade of the Mamainde of Northwestern Mato Grosso, Brazil*. Latin American Studies Program, Dissertation Series, No. 58. Ithaca, NY: Cornell University Press.

Barandiaran, Daniel de, 1966, "La fiesta del Pijiguao entre los Indios Waikas," *El Farol* 219:8–15. Caracas.

Bates, Daniel, and Susan Lees, 1979, "The Myth of Population Regulation." In N. Chagnon and W. Irons, Eds., *Evolutionary Biology and Human Social Behavior: An Anthropological Perspective*. North Scituate, MA: Duxbury Press, pp. 273–289.

Becher, Hans, 1960, *Die Surára und Pakidái: Zwei Yanonämi-Stämme in Nordwest Brasilien*, vol. 26. Hamburg, Germany: Mitteilungen aus dem Museum fur Völkerkunde.

Beckerman, Stephen S., 1978, "Reply to Ross," *Current Anthropology* 19(1):17–19.

Berlin, Elois A., and Edward Markell, 1977, "An Assessment of the Nutritional and Health Status of an Aguaruna Jivaro Community, Amazonas, Peru," *Ecology of Food and Nutrition* 6:69–81.

Biella, Peter, N. Chagnon, and G. Seaman, 1997, *Yąnomamö Interactive: The Ax Fight.* (CD-ROM). Fort Worth, TX: Harcourt Brace & Co (to be revised in 2012 and distributed as a DVD by Penn State Media Sales, 171 Outreach Building, University Park, PA 16802).

Biocca, Ettore, 1970, *Yanoáma: The Narrative of a White Girl Kidnapped by Amazonian Indians.* New York: E. P. Dutton & Co.

Booth, William, 1989, "Warfare Over Yąnomamö Indians," *Science* 243:1138–1140.

Borgerhoff Mulder, Monique, 1987, "On Cultural and Reproductive Success: Kipsigis Evidence," *American Anthropologist* 89:617–634.

Briggs, Asa, 1983, "The Environment of the City." In Donald Ortner Ed., *How Humans Adapt: A Biocultural Odyssey.* Washington, DC: Symposia and Seminar Series, Smithsonian Institution, pp. 371–394.

Brooke, James, 1990, "An Almost Untouched Jungle, Gold Miners Threaten Indian Ways," *New York Times,* Sept. 18.

——, 1991, "Ashidowa-teri Journal," *New York Times,* Sept. 11.

Carneiro da Cunha, Maria, 1989, "To the Editor," *Anthropology Newsletter,* American Anthropological Association, Vol. 30, p. 3.

Carneiro, Robert L., 1960, "Slash and Burn Agriculture: A Closer Look at Its Implications for Settlement Patterns." In Anthony Wallace, Ed., *Men and Cultures. Selected Papers of the Fifth International Congress of Anthropological and Ethnological Sciences.*

Philadelphia, PA: University of Pennsylvania, pp. 229–234.

——, 1961, "Slash and Burn Cultivation Among the Kuikuru and Its Implications for Cultural Development in the Amazon Basin." In Johannes Wilbert, Ed., *The Evolution of Horticultural Systems in Native South America, Causes and Consequences: A Symposium.* Anthropologica, Supplement Publication No. 2, pp. 47–67, Caracas.

——, 1970, "A Theory of the Origin of the State." *Science* 169:733–738.

Chagnon, Napoleon A., 1966, Ph.D. Thesis, University of Michigan, Michigan.

——, 1967, "Yąnomamö—The Fierce People," *Natural History* 76:22–31.

——, 1968a, "The Culture-Ecology of Shifting (Pioneering) Cultivation Among the Yąnomamö Indians," *Proceedings VIII International Congress of Anthropological and Ethnological Sciences,* Tokyo 3:249–255.

——, 1968b, *Yąnomamö: The Fierce People,* 1st edition. Case Studies in Cultural, Anthropology. New York: Holt, Rinehart and Winston.

——, 1972, "Social Causes for Population Fissioning: Tribal Social Organization and Genetic Microdifferentiation." In G. A. Harrison and A. J. Boyce, Eds., *The Structure of Human Populations.* Oxford: Clarendon Press, pp. 252–282.

——, 1973, *Magical Death* (16mm film). Penn State Media Sales, 171 Outreach Building, University Park, PA 16802.

——, 1974a, *Studying the Yąnomamö.* Studies in Anthropological Method. New York: Holt, Rinehart and Winston.

——, 1974b, "Yąnomamö." In *Primitive Worlds,* National Geographic Society Special Publication Series. No. 127, pp. 141–183.

——, 1975a, "Genealogy, Solidarity and Relatedness: Limits to Local Group Size and Patterns of Fissioning in an Expanding Population." *Yearbook of Physical Anthropology* 19:95–110. American Anthropological Association, Washington, DC.

——, 1975b, Response to Marvin Harris' "Protein Theory of Warfare," *Psychology Today* 8(12):6–7.

——, 1979a, "Is Reproductive Success Equal in Egalitarian Societies?" In N. A. Chagnon and W. Irons, Eds., *Evolutionary Biology and Human Social Behavior: An Anthropological Perspective.* North Scituate, MA: Duxbury Press, pp. 374–401.

——, 1979b, "Mate Competition, Favoring Close Kin and Village Fissioning among the Yąnomamö Indians." In N. A. Chagnon and W. Irons, Eds., *Evolutionary Biology and Human Social Behavior: An Anthropological Perspective.* North Scituate, MA: Duxberry Press, pp. 86–131.

——, 1980, "Kin Selection Theory, Kinship, Marriage and Fitness Among the Yąnomamö Indians." In G. W. Barlow and J. Silverberg, Eds., *Sociobiology: Beyond Natural Nurture?* Special Symposium Publication No. 35, American Association for the Advancement of Science. Boulder, CA: Westview Press, pp. 545–571.

——, 1981, "Terminological Kinship, Genealogical Relatedness and Village Fissioning Among the Yąnomamö Indians." In R. D. Alexander and D. W. Tinkle, Eds., *Natural Selection and Social Behavior: Recent Research and New Theory.* New York: Chiron Press, pp. 490–508.

——, 1982, "Sociodemographic Attributes of Nepotism in Tribal Populations: Man the Rule Breaker." In King's College Sociobiology Group, Ed., *Current Problems in Sociobiology.*

Cambridge: Cambridge University Press, pp. 291–318.

——, 1988a, "Life Histories, Blood Revenge, and Warfare in a Tribal Population," *Science* 239:985–992.

——, 1988b, "Male Manipulations of Kinship Classifications of Female Kin for Reproductive Advantage." In L. Betzig, M. Borgerhoff Mulder and P. Turke, Eds., *Human Reproductive Behaviour: A Darwinian Perspective.* Cambridge, MA: Cambridge University Press, pp. 23–48.

——, 1989a, "To the Editor," *Anthropology Newsletter,* American Anthropological Association, Vol. 30, pp. 3, 24.

——, 1989b, "Response to Ferguson," *American Ethnologist* 16:565–569.

——, 1989c "Yąnomamö Survival," *Science* 244:11.

——, 1990a, "On Yąnomamö Violence: Reply to Albert," *Current Anthropology* 31:49–53.

——, 1990b, "Reproductive and Somatic Conflicts of Interest in the Genesis of Violence and Warfare Among Tribesmen." In J. Haas, Ed., *The Anthropology of War.* Cambridge, MA: Cambridge University Press, pp. 77–104.

——, in press, *Noble Savages,* New York: Simon and Schuster.

——, in press, "Filming the Ax Fight." In Biella, Peter, N. Chagnon & G. Seaman *Yąnomamö Interactive: The Ax Fight.* DVD. Penn State Media Sales, 171 Outreach Building, University Park, PA 16802.

——, and Timothy Asch, 1974a, *A Man Called Bee: Studying the Yąnomamö* (16mm film). Penn State Media Sales, 171 Outreach Building, University Park, PA 16802.

——, and ——, 1974b, *Ocamo Is My Town* (16mm film). Penn State Media Sales, 171 Outreach Building, University Park, PA 16802.

——, and ——, 1975, *Moonblood: A Yąnomamö Creation Myth as Told by Dedeheiwä* (16mm film). Penn State Media Sales, 171 Outreach Building, University Park, PA 16802.

——, and Paul Bugos, 1979, "Kin Selection and Conflict: An Analysis of a Yąnomamö Ax Fight." In N. A. Chagnon and W. Irons, Eds., *Evolutionary Biology and Human Social Behavior: An Anthropological Perspective.* North Scituate, MA: Duxberry Press, pp. 213–238.

——, and Raymond Hames, 1979, "Protein Deficiency and Tribal Warfare in Amazonia: New Data," *Science* 203:910–913.

——, and ——, 1980, "La 'hipótesis proteica' y la adaptación indígena a la cuenca del Amazonas: una revision critica de los datos y de la teoría," *Interciencia* 5(6):346–358. Caracas.

——, and William Irons, Eds. 1979, *Evolutionary Biology and Human Social Behavior: An Anthropological Perspective.* North Scituate, MA: Duxberry Press.

——, P. LeQuesne, and J. Cook, 1971, "Yąnomamö Hallucinogens: Anthropological, Botanical, and Chemical Findings," *Current Anthropology* 12:72–74.

——, and T. Melancon, 1984, "Reproduction, Numbers of Kin and Epidemics in Tribal Populations: A Case Study." In Nathan Keyfitz, Ed., *Population and Biology: Bridge Between Disciplines.* International Union for the Scientific Study of Populations. Liege, Belgium: Or-dina Editions, pp. 147–1671.

——, J. Bortoli, and M. Eguillor, 1988, "Una aplicación antropológica practica entre los Yanomami: Colaboracion entre Misioneros y Antropólogos," *La Iglesia en Amazonas,* Puerto Ayacucyho, Venezuela, pp. 75–83.

——, Chagnon, Napleon A, 1991, "GIS, GPS, Political History and Geodemography of the Aramisi Yąnomamö Expansion." In C. A. Behrens and T. Sever, Eds., *Applications of Space-Age Technology in Anthropology.* NASA, Science and Technology Laboratory. Mississippi: John C. Stennis Space Center, pp. 35–62.

——, Chagnon, Napleon A, 1995a, "L'ethnologie du déshonneur: Brief Response to Lizot," *American Ethnologist* 22(1):187–189.

——, Chagnon, Napleon A, 1995b, "GPS And Documenting Political and Military Aspects of a Contemporary Agricultural Revolution." In *Conference Proceedings,* Trimble Surveying & Mapping Users Conference, Aug. 9-11, 1995. Sunnyvale, CA, pp. 63–83.

——, Chagnon, Napleon A, 1995c, "indio também é gente." Interview in *Veja Magazine,* Dec. 6, 1995. Saõ Paulo.

——, Chagnon, Napleon A, 1996a, "Chronic Problems in Understanding Tribal Violence and Warfare." In *Proceedings of the CIBA Foundation Symposium No. 194,* London, pp. 202–236.

——, Chagnon, Napleon A, 1996b, Review of R.B. Ferguson's *Yanomami Warfare.* American Anthropologist, Vol. 98, No. 3, Washington, DC. pp. 670–672.

Cocco, Luis, 1972, *Iyéwei-teri: Quince años entre los Yąnomamös.* Caracas, Venezuela: Librcria Editorial Salesiana.

Cock, J. H., 1982, "Cassava: A Basic Energy Source in the Tropics," *Science* 218(4574):755–762.

Conklin, Harold C., 1961, "The Study of Shifting Cultivation," *Current Anthropology* 2(1):27–61.

Daly, Martin, and Margo Wilson, 1988, *Homicide.* Hawthorne, NY: Aldine de Gruyter.

Darwin, Charles, 1859, *On the Origin of Species by Means of Natural Selection, or the Preservation of Favored Races in the Struggle for Life.* London: John Murray.

—— , and —— , 1871, *The Descent of Man, and Selection in Relation to Sex*, 2 vols. London: John Murray.

Divale, William T., and M. Harris, 1976, "Population, Warfare, and the Male Supremacist Complex," *American Anthropologist* 78:521–538.

Dreger, Alice, 2011, "'Darkness' Descent on the American Anthropological Association: A Cautionary Tale," *Human Nature*, Vol. 22[3] pp. 225–246. Available electronically on SpringerLink: http://www.springer link.com/openurl.asp?genre=article& id=doi:10.1007/s12110-011-9103-y

Durkheim, Emile, 1933 [1893], *The Division of Labor in Society*. George Simpson, translator. Glencoe, 111.: The Free Press.

——, 1958 [1895], *The Rules of the Sociological Method*. George E. Catlin, Ed., John H. Mueller and Sarah A. Solovay, translators. Glencoe, 111.: The Free Press.

Early, John D., and John E. Peters, 1990, *The Population Dynamics of the Macajai Yanomama*. New York: Academic Press.

Evans-Pritchard, E. E., 1940, *The Nuer*. London: Oxford at the Clarendon Press.

Ferguson, R. Brian, 1995, *Yanomami Warfare*. Santa Fe, NM: School of American Research Press.

Fortes, Meyer, 1959, "Descent, Filiation and Affinity: A Rejoinder to Dr. Leach," *Man* 59(309):193–197 and (331):206–212.

—— , 1969, *Kinship and the Social Order: The Legacy of Lewis Henry Morgan*. Chicago, IL: Aldine.

Fredlund, Eric V., 1982, *Shitari Yąnomamö Incestuous Marriage: A Study of the Use of Structural, Lineal, and Biological Criteria When Classifying Marriages*. Ph.D. dissertation, anthropology department, The Pennsylvania State University, University Park.

*Gaceta Oficial de Venezuela*, No. 427, November 2005.

Garcilaso de la, Vega, 1966, *Royal Commentaries of the Inca, Part One*. Austin, TX: University of Texas Press. (Originally published in 1609 and 1616/7.)

Good, Kenneth, 1989, *Yanomami Hunting Patterns: Trekking and Garden Relocation as an Adaptation to Game Availability in Amazonia, Venezuela*. Ph.D. thesis, University of Florida, Gainesville.

Gregor, Thomas A., and Daniel R. Gross, 2004, "Guilt by Association: The Culture of Accusation and the American Anthropological Association's Investigation of *Darkenss in El Dorado*," *American Anthropologist* 106(4):687–698.

—— , and —— , 2005, "Gregor and Gross Reply," *Anthropology News*, pp. 28–29.

Gross, Daniel R., 1975, "Protein Capture and Cultural Development in the Amazon," *American Anthropologist* 77(3):526–549.

Hames, Raymond, 1978, *A Behavioral Account of the Division of Labor Among the Ye'kwana Indians of Southern Venezuela*. Ph.D. dissertation, University of California, Santa Barbara.

—— , 1979, "A Comparison of the Efficiencies of the Shotgun and the Bow in Neotropical Forest Hunting," *Human Ecology* 7(3):219–252.

—— , 1989, "Time, Efficiency, and Utility in the Amazonia Protein Quest," *Research in Economic Anthropology* 11:43–85.

—— , 1992 "Variation in Paternal Care Among the Yąnomamö." In B. Hewlett, Ed., *The Father's Role: Cultural and Evolutionary Perspectives*. Chicago, IL: Aldine de Gruyter.

—— , 1996, "Costs and Benefits of Monogamy and Polygyny for Yąnomamö Women," *Ethology and Sociobiology* 17(3):181-199.

Hames, Raymond and William Vickers, Eds., 1983, *Adaptive Responses of Native Amazonians*. New York: Academic Press.

Harner, Michael, 1977, "The Ecological Basis for Aztec Sacrifice," *American Ethnologist* 4:117–135.

Harris, Marvin, 1974, *Cows, Pigs, Wars, and Witches: The Riddles of Culture*. New York: Random House.

——, 1975, *Culture, People, Nature: An Introduction to General Anthropology*, 2nd edition. New York: Thomas Y. Crowell.

——, 1977, *Cannibals and Kings: The Origins of Cultures*. New York: Random House.

——, 1979, "The Yąnomamö and the Causes of War in Band and Village Societies." In M. Margolies and W. Carter, Eds., *Brazil: An Anthropological Perspective, Essays in Honor of Charles Wagley*. New York: Columbia University Press, pp. 121–132.

Howell, Nancy, 1990, *Surviving Fieldwork*. American Anthropological Association, Special Publication No. 26. Washington, DC.

Hume, Doug, n.d., *Website on Darkness in El Dorado*. URL: http://www.nku.edu/~humed1/

Hurault, J., 1972, *Français et Indiens en Guyane*. Paris: Union Generale d'Edition.

Irons, William, 1979a, "Cultural and Biological Success." In N. A. Chagnon and W. Irons, Eds., *Evolutionary Biology and Human Social Behavior: An Anthropological Perspective*. North Scituate, MA: Duxbury Press, pp. 257–272.

——, 1979b, "Investment and Primary Social Dyads." In N. A. Chagnon and W. Irons, Eds., *Evolutionary Biology and Human Social Behavior: An Anthropological Perspective*. North Scituate, MA: Duxbury Press, pp. 181–213.

——, 1980, "Is Yomut Social Behavior Adaptive?" In J. Silverberg and G. Barlow, Eds., *Sociobiology: Beyond Nature-Nurture?* Selected Symposium, American Association for the Advancement of Science, No. 35. Boulder, CO: Westview Press, pp. 417–463.

——, 1998, "Adaptively Relevant Environments Versus Environment of Evolutionary Adaptedness," *Evolutionary Anthropology* 6(6): 194–204.

Jank, Margaret, 1977, *Mission: Venezuela*. Stanford, FL: Brown Gold Publications Bookroom.

Keesing, Roger M., 1975, *Kin Groups and Social Structure*. New York: Holt, Rinehart and Winston.

Kitcher, Philip, 1985, *Vaulting Ambitions*. Cambridge, MA: MIT Press.

Layrisse, J. McCluer, E. Migliazza, W. Oliver, F. Salzano, R. Spielman, R. Ward and L. Weitkamp 1971, "Studies on the Yanomama Indians," *Proceedings of the Fourth International Congress of Human Genetics. Human Genetics*, Sept. 1971, pp. 96–111.

Leach, Edmund, 1957, "Aspects of Bridewealth and Marriage Stability Among the Kachin and Lakher," *Man* 57(59):5–55.

——, 1970, *Claude Levi-Strauss*. Modern Masters Series. New York: Viking Press.

Lee, Richard, 1968, "What Hunters Do for a Living, or How to Make Out on Scarce Resources." In R. B. Lee and I. DeVore, Eds., *Man the Hunter*. Chicago, IL: Aldine, pp. 30–43.

——, 1979, *The !Kung San: Men, Women, and Work in a Foraging Society*. Cambridge, MA: Cambridge University Press.

——, 1984, *The Dobe !Kung*. Case Studies in Cultural Anthropology. New York: Holt, Rinehart and Winston.

——, and Irven DeVore, Eds. 1968, *Man the Hunter*. Chicago, IL: Aldine.

——, and ——, 1993, The *Dobe Ju/'hoansi*, 2nd edition. New York. Harcourt Brace & Co.

Levi-Strauss, Claude, 1961, *Tristes Tropiques*. J. Russel, translator. New York: Criterion Books.

——, 1969 [1949], *The Elementary Structures of Kinship*. (1969 English translation.) Boston, MA: Beacon Press.

Lewontin, Richard C., Steven Rose, and Leon J. Kamin, 1984, *Not in Our Genes*. New York: Pantheon Books.

Lizot, Jacques, 1971a, "Aspects économiques et sociaux du changement culturel chez les Yanomami," *L 'Homme* 11(1):32–51.

——, 1971b, "Remarques sur le vocabulaire de párente Yanomami" *L'Homme* 11(2):2538.

——, 1971c, "Société ou économie? Quelques thémes á propos d'une communaute d'Amérindiens" *Journal de la Société des Américanistes* 60:136–175.

——, 1972, "Poisons Yanomami de chasse, de guerre et de peche," *Antropológica* 31:3–20.

——, 1973a, "El rio de los periquitos: Breve relato de un viaje entre los Yanomami del Alto Siapa" *Antropológica* 37:3–23.

——, 1973b, "Onomastique yanomami," *L'Homme* 13(3):60–71.

——, 1975, *El Hombre de la Pantorrilla Preñada*. Monografia No. 21, Fundación La Salle de Ciencias Naturales. Caracas.

——, 1976, *Le Cercle de Feux*. Paris: Editions du Seuil. (Published in English in 1985 as *Tales of the Yanomami*, Cambridge University Press, Cambridge Series in Social Anthropology, Cambridge.)

——, 1977, "Population, Resources, et Guerre chez les Yanomami." *Libre* 2:111–145.

——, 1978, "L'Economie Primitive." *Libre* 4:69–113.

——, 1988, "Sobre la guerra: Una respuesta a N. A. Chagnon (Science, 1988)" *La Iglesia en Amazonas* 44:23–34.

——, 1994, [1989] "On Warfare: An Answer to N.A. Chagnon," *American Ethnologist* 21:841–858. (Originally published in *La Iglesia en Amazonas* (the official journal of the Venezuelan Salesian Missions) in Spanish: "Sobre La Guerra: Una Respuesta a N.A. Chagnon.")

Malinowski, Bronislaw, 1922, *Argonauts of the Western Pacific*. London: Routledge and Kegan Paul, Ltd.

——, 1935, *Coral Gardens and Their Magic*, 2 vols. London: Allen & Unwin.

Marshall, John, 1966, *An Argument about a Marriage* (16mm film). Documentary Educational Resources, Watertown, MA.

Mauss, Marcel, 1954 [1925], *The Gift*. (1954 English translation.) New York: The Free Press.

Melancon, Thomas, 1982, *Marriage and Reproduction Among the Yąnomamö Indians of Venezuela*. Ph.D. Dissertation. PA: The Pennsylvania State University.

Miller, John J., 2000, "The Fierce People: The Wages of Anthropological Incorrectness," *National Review*, Nov. 20, 2000.

Murphy, Robert L., 1960, *Headhunter's Heritage*. Berkeley, CA: University of California Press.

National Academy of Sciences, 1980, *Firewood Crops*. Washington, DC: National Academy of Sciences.

Neel, James V., 1970, "Lessons from a 'Primitive' People," *Science* 170: 815–822.

——, Timothy Asch, and Napoleon A. Chagnon, 1968, *Yąnomamö: A Mutidisciplinary Study*. (Film: On DVD). Penn State Media Sales, 171

Outreach Building, University Park, PA 16802.

——, Centerwall, W. R., N. A. Chagnon, and H. L. Casey, 1970, "Notes on the Effect of Measles and Measles Vaccine in a Virgin-Soil Population of South American Indians," *American Journal of Epidemiology* 91:481–429.

——, T. Arends, C. Brewer, N. Chagnon, H. Gershowitz, M. Layrisse, Z. Neitschmann, Bernard, 1980, "The Limits to Protein." In R. Hames, Ed., *Studies in Hunting and Fishing in the Neotropics. Working Papers on South American Indians*, K. Kensinger, general editor. Bennington, VT: Bennington College, pp. 131–135.

Oliver, Douglas, 1955, *A Solomon Island Society, Kinship and Leadership Among the Siuai of Bougainville.* Cambridge, MA: Harvard University Press.

Ortiz de Montellano, Bernard R., 1978, "Aztec Cannibalism: An Ecological Necessity?" *Science* 200:611–617.

Ramos, Alcida Rita, 1995, *Sanuma Memories: Yanomami Ethnography in a Time of Crisis.* Madison, WI: University of Wisconsin Press.

Reynolds, Philip Keep, 1927, *The Banana: Its History, Cultivation and Place Among Staple Foods.* Boston, MA: Houghton Mifflin Company.

Rice, A. Hamilton, 1921, "The Rio Negro, the Casiquiare Canal, and the Upper Orinoco, September 1919-April 1920," *The Geographical Journal* 58:321–343.

Ritchie, Mark A., 1996, *Spirit of the Rainforest.* Chicago, IL: Island Lake Press.

Robertson, A. F., 1973, "Histories and Political Opposition in Ahafo, Ghana," *Africa* XLIII(1):41–58.

Ross, Eric B., 1978, "Food Taboos, Diet, and Hunting Strategy: The Adaptation to Animals in Amazon Cultural Ecology," *Current Anthropology* 19(1):1–36.

Saffirio, Giovanni, 1985, *Ideal and Actual Kinship Terminology Among the Yanomama Indians of the Catrimani River Basin (Brazil).* Ph.D. thesis, University of Pittsburgh, Pittsburgh.

Sahlins, Marshall D., 1968, "Notes on the Original Affluent Society." In R. Lee and I. DeVore, Eds., *Man The Hunter.* Chicago, IL: Aldine, pp. 85–89.

——, 1989, *Tribesmen.* Englewood Cliffs, NJ: Prentice-Hall.

Salamone, Frank, Ed., 1997, *The Yanomami and Their Interpreters: Fierce People or Fierce Interpreters?* Lanham, MD: University Press of America.

Secoy, Frank R., 1953, *Changing Military Patterns on the Great Plains. Monographs of the American Ethnological Society.* E. Goldfrank, editor, Locust Valley, NY: J. J. Augustin.

Segerstrale, Ullica, 2000, *Defenders of the Truth.* Oxford: Oxford University Press.

Service, Elman R., 1969, "Models for the Methodology of Mouthtalk," *Southwestern Journal of Anthropology* 25:68–80.

Silverman, Marvin, and James Gibbs, 1970, *The Cows of Dolo Ken Peye: Resolving Conflict Among the Kpelle.* New York: Holt, Rinehart and Winston.

Spindler, George, D., Ed., 1970, *Being an Anthropologist: Fieldwork in Eleven Cultures.* New York: Holt, Rinehart and Winston.

Steward, Julian, 1948, *The Tropical Forest Tribes*, vol. 3, Handbook of South American Indians. Bulletin 143, Bureau of American Ethnology, Smithsonian Institution. Washington, DC.

——, and Louis Faron, 1959, *Native Peoples of South America.* New York: McGraw-Hill.

Swedlund, Allan C., and George J. Armelagos, 1976, *Demographic Anthropology.* Dubuque, Iowa: Wm. C. Brown Co.

Taylor, Kenneth, 1974, *Sanuma Fauna: Prohibitions and Classification.* Monografía No. 18, Fundación La Salle de Ciencias Naturales. Caracas.

Tooby, John, 2000, "Jungle Fever: Did two U.S. scientists start a genocidal epidemic in the Amazon, or was the *New Yorker* duped?" *Slate Magazine*, http://www.slate.com/?id=91946

——, and UCSB Preliminary Report, n.d, "The major allegations against Napoleon Chagnon and James Neel presented in Darkness in El Dorado by Patrick Tierney appear to be deliberately fraudulent." http://www.anth.ucsb.edu/ucsbpreliminary report.pdf

Turnbull, Colin, 1965, *Wayward Servants: The Two Worlds of the African Pygmies.* Garden City, NY: Natural History Press.

——, 1972, *The Mountain People.* New York: Simon and Schuster.

——, 1983, *The Mbuti Pygmies: Change and Adaptation*, Case Studies in Cultural Anthropology. New York: Holt, Rinehart and Winston.

Turner, Terry, 1991, "Major Shift in Brazilian Yanomama Policy," *Anthropology Newsletter* 32:1 ff. American Anthropological Association.

Tybur, Joshua M., Geoffrey F. Miller, and Steven Gangestad, 2007, "Testing the Controversy: An Empirical Examination of Adaptationists' Attitudes toward Politics and Science," *Human Nature* 18(4):313–328.

Valero, Helena, 1984, *Yo Soy Napéyoma. Relato de Una Mujer Raptada por los Indígenas Yanomami.* Fundación La Salle de Cincieas Naturales. Monografía No. 35. Caracas.

Vickers, William T., 1978, "Reply to Ross," *Current Anthropology* 19(1):27.

Wilbert, Johannes, 1972, *Survivors of El Dorado.* New York: Praeger.

Williams, George C., 1966, *Adaptation and Natural Selection: A Critique of Some Current Evolutionary Thought.* Princeton, NJ: Princeton University Press.

——, Ed., 1971, *Group Selection.* New York: Aldine-Atherton.

Wright, Sewall, 1922, "Coefficients of Inbreeding and Relationship," *American Naturalist* 56:330–338.

Zerries, Otto, 1955, "Das Lashafest der Waika Indianer," *Die Umschau in Wissenschaft und Technik* 55:662–665.

——, 1964, *Waika: Die Kulturgeschichtliche Stellung der Waika-Indianer des Oberen Orinoco im Rahmen der Völkerkunde Südamerikas.* Munich, Germany: Klauss Renner Verlag.

# Ethnographic Films on the Yąnomamö

During the several years of my field research among the Yąnomamö, I filmed selected activities that, I felt, could not be adequately documented by the more traditional means of note-taking and written descriptions. It became apparent that a more thorough filming effort would be necessary to document Yąnomamö culture and behavior than what I could accomplish by myself. Thus, in 1968 James V. Neel and I invited an anthropological filmmaker, Timothy Asch, to join us in the field for several weeks. Our collaborative effort during the 1968 season resulted in two films funded by the Human Genetics Department through a grant from the U.S. Atomic Energy Commission: *The Feast* and *Yanomamö: A Multidisciplinary Study*, the latter film incorporating much of the footage that I had taken in previous years with a hand-held Bolex camera with no synchronous sound system.

In 1971, Asch and I applied for and received a grant from the National Science Foundation to extend our film collaboration. We hired a sound man, Craig Johnson, who joined us in the project. We shot approximately 80,000 feet of synchronous-sound film in 1971 during a one-month period (February 26 through March 29) in the village of Mishimishimaböwei-teri, a remote Shamatari village that had become the focus of my field investigations at that time (see Chagnon 1974) and whose residents I continued to study for many more years.

We produced 18 additional documentary films from footage we shot during our 1971 film collaboration. All of these were produced while I was on the faculty of the Pennsylvania State University from 1972 to 1981.

In 1973, independently of Asch, I made a film about Yąnomamö shamanism entitled *Magical Death* to make the point that an anthropologist, working alone with only a hand-crank Bolex camera using 100 foot rolls of film and no synchronous sound system, could make a commendable documentary film in difficult field conditions. *Magical Death* won the Blue Ribbon Award at the American Film Festival in 1974.

The films listed below can be rented or purchased from the following distributor. In a few cases distribution contracts are still pending.

Penn State Media Sales

Penn State Public Broadcasting

171 Outreach Building

University Park, PA 16802

web: mediasales.psu.edu **<http://mediasales.psu.edu>**

phone: 814-863-4011

fax: 814-770-2111

email: **mediasales@outreach.psu.edu**

## CURRENT LIST OF YĄNOMAMÖ FILMS

*The Feast*, 1970, 29 min. This film focuses on the alliance practices of the Yąnomamö and documents the emergence of a specific alliance during the context of a feast held in the village of Patanowä-teri in 1968.

*Yanomamö: A Multidisciplinary Study*, 1971, 43 min. This film describes the nature of multidisciplinary field research by a team of human biologists, geneticists, serologists, dentists, and anthropologists. It includes an ethnographic vignette of Yąnomamö culture and is very useful in showing how many scientific disciplines can collaborate in the study of human populations and culture.

*Magical Death*, 1973, 28 min. This film depicts the interrelationship of religion, politics, and the use of hallucinogenic snuff in shamanism. It focuses on a specific two-day incident in the village of Mishimishimaböwei-teri during which all the prominent shamans of the group collectively demonstrated their good will toward visitors from Bisaasi-teri by practicing harmful magic against enemies of the latter.

*A Man Called Bee: Studying the Ygnomamö*, 1974, 40 min. This film illustrates the methods of field research used by Chagnon during 42 months of fieldwork among the Yąnomamö, emphasizing investigations of genealogy, settlement patterns, politics, demography, and mythology.

*Ocamo Is My Town*, 1974, 23 min. This film describes the attitudes, accomplishments and objectives of a Salesian missionary who spent 14 years in a Yąnomamö village. Skeptical about the possibility of immediate success in Christianizing the Yąnomamö, the priest emphasizes the importance of his attempts to introduce practical measures that will help soften the impact of civilization when it eventually comes to this village.

*Arrow Game*, 1974, 7 min. This film depicts Yąnomamö boys learning to shoot accurately under duress and to dodge arrows shot in return. Man-sized arrows with the points removed are used in this somewhat hazardous game, which terminates when one of the boys is hit in the face with an arrow—damaging his ego more than his face.

*Weeding the Garden*, 1974, 14 min. Even the most prestigious members of the village must engage in all the economic activities. Dedeheiwä, the most respected shaman in the village, weeds his garden, interrupted periodically by his wife and children, who groom him while he rests.

*A Father Washes His Children*, 1974, 13 min. Dedeheiwä, respected shaman and political leader, takes his younger children to the river and bathes them. His wife remains in the village and recovers from a minor sickness.

*Firewood*, 1974, 10 min. Yanomamö women spend several hours each day collecting firewood and maintaining the family fire. The irksomeness of chopping and carrying firewood is shown as a woman strenuously brings home the daily kindling. Her older son quietly babysits for his infant brother while the mother works.

*A Man and His Wife Make a Hammock*, 1974, 9 min. Yanomamö hammocks are manufactured on a pole frame consisting of two upright poles between which the spun cotton threads are plaited. A strong headman, Möawä, quietly works on the hammock while one of his wives and infant daughter rest in their hammock and quietly chat with him.

*Children's Magical Death*, 1974, 8 min. A group of young boys between the ages of 4 and 10 years imitate the shamans as they blow wood ashes into each other's nostrils through hollow reeds. Their amusing pantomime clearly reveals how socialized they have become by observing the elders. This film should be used in conjunction with *Magical Death*.

*Climbing the Peach Palm*, 1974, 9 min. Fruits from the cultivated peach palm tree can only be harvested by climbing the spiny trunk. The Yanomamö have invented an ingenious device—a climbing frame—for this purpose. Young men carefully ascend the thorny tree with this vine-and-pole frame, lowering the bunches of fruit with long vines.

*New Tribes Mission*, 1974, 12 min. Dedicated members of the New Tribes Mission, an Evangelical Protestant missionary group, explain their reasons for attempting to bring Christianity to the Yanomamö.

*The Ax Fight*, 1975, 30 min. A fight erupts in Mishimishimaböwei-teri, involving clubs, machetes, and axes. The structure of kinship and marriage ties is revealed by the participants as they take particular sides in the fighting. Slow-motion replay and freeze-frame editing make this film useful as a methodological tool in both ethnographic and ethnocinematographic studies.

*Tapir Distribution*, 1975, 12 min. The distribution of meat, particularly large game animals, reveals within-group alliance patterns based on kinship and marriage ties. The village headman presents his kill to his brothers-in-law, who ceremoniously redistribute the meat and cooked vegetables to household heads within the village. After the ceremonial distribution the women move in to distribute the scant remains, followed by the village dogs.

*Tug of War*, 1975, 9 min. The more playful and amicable aspects of daily life are illustrated by this film, which portrays a group of women and children in a tug-of-war during a rainstorm.

*Bride Service*, 1975, 10 min. A young man returns from hunting and collecting with a large wild turkey and a heavy basket of wild fruits. Through his father, he presents the food to his father-in-law. A 10-year-old girl is sent to fetch the food. She is embarrassed and self-conscious, complicating her own situation by collapsing under the weight of the load amidst the laughter of village onlookers.

*The Yąnomamö Myth of Naro as Told by Kąobawä*, 1975, 22 min. The intimate relationships among Man, Spirit, and Animal are revealed in the amusing and complicated myth of Opossum *(Naro)*, who invents harmful magic to treacherously slay his brother and acquire the latter's two beautiful wives. Kąobawä's dramatic and intimate presentation of the story brings out his acting and narrative skills. English voice-over narration.

*The Yąnomamö Myth of Naro as Told by Dedeheiwä*, 1975, 22 min. The same myth that is described above is told by Dedeheiwä, an accomplished and renowned shaman who lives in a remote village far to the south of Kąobawä's village. This film provides an excellent contrast for students interested in comparative mythology. English voice-over narration.

*Moonblood: A Yąnomamö Creation Myth as told by Dedeheiwä*, 1975, 14 min. The origin of Man (Yąnomamö) is revealed in the myth of Peribo (Moon), who, in Ancestral times, descended to earth and ate the ashes of the deceased Ancestors. Moon is shot in the belly by one of the Ancestors, his blood spilling to earth and transforming into fierce people. English voice-over narration.

*Jaguar: A Yąnomamö Twin-Cycle Myth*, 1976, 22 min. The Ancestor, Jaguar, nearly devours all of humanity. All that remains is Curare-Woman, who is too "bitter" to eat, and her pregnant daughter, hidden in the roof. Jaguar discovers the daughter and eats her, but Curare-Woman saves the unborn twins, Omawä and Yoasiwä, who miraculously grow to adulthood and exact their revenge on Jaguar. English subtitles.

# Index

Note: Page numbers in italics refer to photographs or figures. Page numbers followed by "n" refer to footnotes